Choose Your Character

25 BIBLE PERSONALITIES WHO INSPIRE INTEGRITY

RON MEYERS

Soar with Eagles

A Publisher Driven
by Vision and Purpose
www.soarhigher.com

Choose Your Character:
25 Bible Personalities Who Inspire Integrity

Copyright © 2012 by Ron Meyers. All rights reserved.

ISBN-13: 978-0-9834528-0-5
Library of Congress Control Number: 2011945602

No part of this book may be reproduced, stored in a retrieval system, or transmitted in any form or by any means, electronic, mechanical, photocopy, recording, or any other — except for the inclusion of brief quotations in a review — without written permission from Soar with Eagles.

All Scripture quotations in this publication are taken from the Holy Bible, Today's New International Version®. Copyright © 2001, 2005 by International Bible Society®. Used by permission of International Bible Society®. All rights reserved worldwide.

First Edition

OTHER BOOKS BY RON MEYERS

- *Habits of Highly Effective Christians*
- *Habits of Highly Effective Christians Study Guide*
- *Rise to Seek Him: The Joy of Effective Prayer*

Published by
Soar with Eagles
2809 Laurel Crossing Circle, Rogers, AR 72758 USA
www.soarhigher.com

Design and editing by Carrie Perrien Smith

Printed in the United States of America

Contents

INTRODUCTION..xiii

CHAPTER 1: NOAH..1
  God Reacts to What People Do...1
  Why Does God Contend with Mankind?..3
  Judgment Is an Act of Love and Mercy...4
  Noah Had Thick Skin..5
  Believe the Unbelievable..7
  Grace Is Also Found in the Old Testament....................................8
  Noah Had Faith 9
  Noah Was Honored by God with an Everlasting Covenant......10
  Noah's Sin after the Flood Teaches Us
  to Be Careful after Great Victories 10
  The Immoral Level of Noah's Time
  Will Be Reached Again before Jesus' Return...............................12

CHAPTER 2: ABRAHAM..15
  The Bible Does Not Begin with Abraham 15
  Terah Moved from Ur toward Canaan, but Only Got to Haran.............16
  God Initiated the Call of Abraham..17
  Abraham Began a Journey without Knowing Where It Would Lead....18
  Abraham Built Altars Everywhere He Went...............................19
  Abraham Failed as a Cross-Cultural Missionary........................20
  God Remained Faithful to His Flawed Son Abraham 20
  Abraham's Wife Demonstrated Great Faith................................22
  Abraham Separated from Lot Honorably....................................23
  Abraham Informally, Yet Successfully, Trained His Staff.........25
  Abraham's Vision Gets a Revision..26
  Abraham Tried to Help God Fulfill His Promise........................28
  Abraham's Covenant with God was Confirmed by Circumcision 29
  Abraham Was an Intercessor 31
  Abraham Was Really Tested..33

CHAPTER 3: JACOB ... 37
- Signs from the Womb ... 37
- Valuing the Valuable ... 39
- The Inappropriateness of Deceit ... 40
- When Love Blinds ... 42
- Waiting for God's Time ... 45
- Persevering in Prayer — and Limping ... 46
- The Problems of Favoritism ... 48
- Needless Grief ... 50
- God Uses Even Flawed Vessels Who Pray ... 52
- The Long-Range Consequences of Looking Forward ... 52

CHAPTER 4: JOSEPH ... 57
- Joseph's Dreams Went to His Head ... 57
- Joseph's Brothers Sold Him into Slavery ... 59
- Joseph Succeeded in Management and Resisted Temptation ... 60
- God Protected Joseph and Gave Him More Success in Prison ... 62
- Joseph Developed Further and Even Served Others in Prison ... 62
- In God's Time, Joseph Received a Life-Changing Opportunity ... 64
- Joseph Was Not Vindictive but Recognized God's Providence ... 66
- A Lesson Regarding Being as Opposed to Position ... 67
- Joseph Forgave Those Who Had Treated Him Unfairly ... 69
- Joseph Looked Forward to God's Future for Israel ... 70

CHAPTER 5: MOSES ... 73
- Moses Models Transparency and Tells It Like It Is ... 73
- Human Beings Have Great Needs ... 75
- Humans Quarrel with and Oppose the Persons Best Able to Help Them ... 76
- The Success of God Pivots on Three Things ... 77
- God Gave Moses the Solution ... 79
- Moses Followed God's Instructions ... 79
- Moses Became Angry with God's People ... 79
- Though God's Tool Was Faulty, God Still Cared for His People's Needs ... 81
- God Pronounced an Irrevocable Punishment on Moses ... 82
- The People's Quarrel Was with the Lord, Not Moses ... 84

CHAPTER 6: ZIPPORAH 87
Three Verses Are Enough 87
Moses Fled from Egypt the First Time in Fear, Not Faith 89
Moses Resisted God's Plan for His Return to Egypt to Deliver Israel 92
What Really Happened on the Road to Egypt? 93
Zipporah's Role as Informant to Jethro 94
Was Zipporah Moses' Cushite Wife? 97

CHAPTER 7: BALAAM 101
The Spiritual Battle Is Real 101
Balaam's Outward Start Was Right — But What of His Heart? 103
Balaam Followed Through Correctly — At First 104
A Review of Balaam's Second through Seventh Prophecies 106
Moab Seduces Israel with Serious Consequences to Israel 108
Numerous Other Biblical References Fill in the Gaps 109
Conclusions 111

CHAPTER 8: JOSHUA 113
Joshua Patiently Served as God Carefully Prepared Him 113
Joshua Heard From and Obeyed God 115
Joshua Thought Ahead and Planned for the Next Steps 116
Joshua Celebrated Important Spiritual Events 116
Joshua Solved Problems 117
Joshua Experienced Recovery 117
Joshua Divided His Task into Small Parts 118
Joshua Experienced Miracles 119
Joshua Carried Out God's Judgment 119
Joshua Challenged Others to Assume Responsibility 120
Joshua Led by Example 121

CHAPTER 9: SAMUEL 123
The Advantages of Having Godly Parents 123
Samuel Learned Early How to Discern God's Voice 125
A Stern Warning about Disciplining Children 126
Prayer Was an Important Part of Samuel's Ministry 128
The Leader of the School of Prophets 130
Samuel Was Fruitful 131

CHAPTER 10: SAUL 133
- Saul Was God's Choice at the Beginning 133
- Saul's First Military Venture 135
- Saul Presumptuously Offered Sacrifices 137
- Saul Failed the Second Test 138
- Saul Became Jealous of David 141
- Saul Was Plagued by an Evil Spirit 142
- Saul's Self-destructive Behavior 144

CHAPTER 11: DAVID 147
- Obscurity Is No Problem for God 148
- The Basis for Confidence 149
- Submitting to God's Training Program 150
- David Was a Wise Leader of Soldiers 151
- David's Heart for God 152
- Beginning Well Is Not Enough 153

CHAPTER 12: ELIJAH 157
- Elijah Was a Human Being Like Us 157
- Elijah Was Not Enamored or Preoccupied with Earthly Finery 158
- Elijah Spent Much Time Alone with God 161
- Elijah Discerned God's Plan and Prayed Accordingly 162
- Elijah Publicly Challenged the Political and Religious Systems 163
- Elijah Addressed Important National Issues 164
- Elijah Received Encouragement from God in a Moment of Weakness 166
- Elijah Was Involved in International Developments 168
- Elijah Trained Future Ministers and Mentored a Successor 170
- Elijah Was Worth Chariots and Horsemen 170

CHAPTER 13: ELISHA 173
- Elisha Valued the Role of a Prophet 173
- Elisha Served 174
- Elisha Sought Spiritual Things 175
- Elisha Called Down a Curse on the Youth Who Jeered at Him 176
- Elisha Was Not Enamored by Strong, Influential Political Figures 179
- Elisha Understood Cross-Cultural Issues 180
- Elisha Presided Over a Flourishing School of Prophets ... 181
- Elisha Saw Clearly into the Spirit World 184
- Elisha Recognized the Ministry Value of Music 184

CHAPTER 14: ESTHER 189
- Esther Was Submissive 190
- Esther Showed Concern for Others 191
- Esther Resisted the Temptations of the Successful 192
- Esther Fought Her Battle by Praying 193
- Esther Planned Carefully and Did Not Hurry 194
- God Answered Esther's Prayers Even Before She Prayed 195
- Esther Exercised Patience 195
- Esther Remained Objective 196
- Esther Boldly Pressed Her Advantage 198
- The Bible Supports National Defense 199

CHAPTER 15: JOB 201
- The Four Pillars of Job's Righteous Life 202
- God Took Pleasure in Job's Righteousness 204
- God Had a Protective Hedge around Job 205
- God Knew Job's Ability 206
- The High Purpose in Human Suffering (Scriptures) 208
- Suffering's High Purposes (Theological Statements) 210
- Job Maintained His Righteousness 211
- Job's Personal Ethics Policy 212
- Job Repented When God Showed Him a Clearer Picture 214
- An Optimistic Application to Ourselves 215

CHAPTER 16: ISAIAH 219
- Isaiah Responded to a Need and God's Question 219
- Isaiah Understood the Rewards of Faith 221
- Isaiah Enjoyed a Picturesque Understanding of the Messiah 222
- Isaiah Understood the Paradox in the Divine and Human Partnership 224
- Isaiah Allowed His Readers to Interpret Conflicting Messages 226
- Isaiah Understood God's Willingness to Engage Humans Intellectually 229
- Isaiah Understood the Superiority of God's Thoughts and Ways 231
- Isaiah Understood Death Is Sometimes the Most Gracious Gift 232
- Isaiah Understood the Need for Constant Prayer 234

CHAPTER 17: JEREMIAH 237
- Jeremiah Understood His Call 238
- Jeremiah Understood Tearing Down as Preparation for Building 240
- Jeremiah Understood Idolatry as Spiritual Adultery 242
- Jeremiah Had a Strong Message from God
  and Could Not Help but Speak 243
- Jeremiah Appreciated the Difference
  between God's and Human's Value Systems 244
- Jeremiah Submitted to God's Plan and Wanted God's Correction 246
- Jeremiah Understood Development through Difficulties 247
- Jeremiah's Word for Pastors: Love and Care for Sheep 248
- Jeremiah Preached Timely and Specific Messages 249
- Jeremiah Knew the Faithfulness of God 250
- Jeremiah Learned through Suffering 251
- Jeremiah Knew the Value of Humbling Himself before God 252

CHAPTER 18: EZEKIEL 255
- Ezekiel Was a Prophetic Priest in Exile in Babylon 256
- Israel Is Favored among the Nations 258
- God's Plans for Israel Are Set Aside for a Time Because of Her Sin 259
- Ezekiel Predicted Israel Would Regather After Punishment 260
- Ezekiel Is Famous for This Prophecy Regarding Israel's Restoration 261
- After Israel's Restoration, Gog and
  Magog Wage a Great War on Israel 262
- That War Has Not Yet Occurred 265
- Amazing and Unprecedented Destruction
  Will Fall on the Attacking Army 266
- Does Oil Lie Buried beneath Israel's Surface? 268
- Ezekiel Describes the Return of Temple Worship 269
- Israel's Glorious State Surpasses Former Glories 270

CHAPTER 19: DANIEL 273
- Daniel Was Moved Involuntarily from the Familiar to the Foreign 274
- Daniel Valued Spiritual Things
  More Than the Food of the King's Court 275
- Daniel Was Methodical in Prayer 276
- Daniel Was Courageous 276
- Daniel Identified with Others When He Prayed 277
- Daniel's Experience Gives Us Insight
  into the Realities of Spiritual Warfare 278

Daniel Prophesied about the
Eventual Triumph of the Kingdom of God 279

CHAPTER 20: HOSEA 283
Understanding Metaphors 284
Hosea's Marriage Is a Metaphor 286
The Metaphor of God as Husband Elevates
the Role of Physical Intimacy in Marriage...288
The Metaphor of God as Husband Teaches
the Fruitfulness of Intimacy with God 292
The Metaphor of God as Husband Demonstrates God's Jealousy.......295
This Metaphor Is Fully Developed in Christ and His Church..............296

CHAPTER 21: MARY 299
Mary Willingly Subjected Herself to Potential Ridicule and Scorn 299
God Spoke Supernaturally to Joseph on Her Behalf 301
Mary Saw the Bigger Picture...302
Mary Was Warned of Personal Suffering 303
Mary, Joseph, and Jesus Received
Supernatural Provision and Protection 304
Mary and Joseph Observed God's Son in His Father's House 306
Mary Refused to be Insulted and Gave Good Advice at Cana 307
Mary Was Jesus' Mother Biologically and Spiritually 308
Mary Also Bore Some of Jesus' Stigma..309
Mary Is Visible Near the Cross 311
Mary Was Present on Resurrection Morning
and Later in the Upper Room 312
Epilogue 312

CHAPTER 22: PETER...315
Peter Was Called to Follow Jesus and Fish for Men..............................316
Peter Learned from Jesus about Support for Civil Governments.........316
Peter Learned the Need for Daily Cleansing
in the Process of Sanctification..318
Peter Learned the Need for Quiet Submission......................................319
Peter Denied Jesus Three Times
but Was Tactfully Restored by Jesus 321
Peter, the Missionary to Samaria (Peter's First Missionary Trip).........322
Peter, the Missionary to Caesarea (Peter's Second Missionary Trip) ...324
Peter, the Missionary to Antioch (Peter's Third Missionary Trip).......326
Peter, the Pro-Family Man..329

CHAPTER 23: PHILIP 333
God Uses a Wide Variety of Motives 333
Expect a Fight If You Are Successful in Ministry 335
Make Room for the Ministry of Others 336
Obedience Is Success 337
Wherever You Go, God Is at Work Before You Get There 338
Receptor-Oriented Communication Is Effective 338
Let God Open the Doors 341
Baptism and Post-Baptismal Care 341
Ministry in "Closed" Places 342
Don't Forget Your Family 343

CHAPTER 24: PAUL 345
Paul Teaches Us That What We Finish
Is More Important Than What We Begin 345
Paul Knew the Difference between Opposition and a Closed Door 346
Paul Connected the Great Themes of Faith and Righteousness 348
Paul Understood and Experienced Suffering 350
Paul Interpreted the Jewish Message to the Non-Jewish World 352
Paul Did Not Abandon His Jewish Roots 354
Paul Had a Radical Desire for His People to Know God 356
Paul's Church-Planting Mission Team
Was Mobile and Autonomous 357
Paul Knew Who He Was 358

CHAPTER 25: PHOEBE 363
Phoebe Was an Actual Person 364
Phoebe Represents Thousands of Women Like Her 366
Phoebe Was Instructed in Public Ministry 369
Paul Addressed the Issue of Order
and One Particular Disorderly Woman 371
Phoebe Was Not Like the Women
Paul Addressed in His Letter to Timothy 374
How Do We Regard "Phoebes" Today? 377
Are You a "Phoebe"? 378

AFTERWORD 381

ABOUT THE AUTHOR: Ron Meyers 383

ACKNOWLEDGEMENTS

God is creative and the Author of creativity. When an idea develops in our spirits, the Creator is at work in tandem with one of us creatures. I base this opinion on Isaiah 26:12. It says, "All that we have accomplished you have done for us."

Partnership with God is marvelous. He works through our personalities, vocabularies, and temperaments in an amazing blend of the divine with our human elements. I may be tempted to think it is I who wrote this book. However, I know that whatever I appear to accomplish happens only with God's enablement. For this reason, my first acknowledgment is to God for His partnership in this writing project. This is not to blame Him for the imperfections (those would be mine) but to acknowledge His involvement.

Not only has God helped conceptually; He has also providentially provided the time to write the chapters. I enjoy the challenges and demands of our conference work but consequently our schedule is quite rigorous. But God has changed that several times.

Due to local elections in the northern part of the Congo in June 2008, an Empower Africa Christian Leadership Conference was canceled. We had just finished one in Brazzaville and with the sudden schedule change, I offered to conduct a partial conference featuring character development using Bible characters. The teachings from Bible characters were very warmly received. That is how this book got started. Then a three-week ministry trip to Mozambique the following August was canceled, and I used those weeks to write more chapters. Finally in August 2010, another ministry trip cancelation afforded the time to put the finishing touches on the chapters.

Today, these character studies are available in book form. They can be used as an independent study by individuals or for mere reading pleasure. You may also use them as the basis to conduct your own teaching series to help other Christians grow in character.

In the early stages of the development of these ideas, I read the first manuscripts to my wife Char. I am grateful for her patience as we read the chapters through together. Our good friend Kay Watson in Ontario, Canada also read the manuscript and made thoughtful comments. I am thankful for these. My missionary friend Millard Parrish also helped edit these pages. His sharp eye, biblical insights, and theological understanding have benefited me greatly.

I recently re-connected with my missionary hero Cecil Murphy. He has become an author and a developer of authors. He offered me the gracious gift of a scholarship with a professional Christian writer to edit the manuscript of this book. That is how Kathy Ide and The Christian PEN became involved in this work. Her keen mind and literary skills have helped make this book what it is today. I will always be indebted to her.

This is the third book for me to publish with Soar with Eagles and Carrie Perrien Smith. She maintains friendly personal warmth while at the same time displaying a high degree of professional competency. She and her team are a joy to work with. Carrie did a great job with the cover design, and her artistic talents are obvious throughout the pages of the book.

In summary, through various circumstances and multiple persons, God has helped with this book. I hope it brings praise and glory to Him. That is my intention.

Ron Meyers

For more information about Ron Meyers and Leadership Empowerment Conferences, please visit www.leresources.com.

INTRODUCTION

In 1986, after thirteen years of a teaching, preaching, administrating, and church-planting ministry in Korea, our family of four prepared to return to the United States. We knew our work in Korea was completed. Many of our former students had become pastors. When they came to say good-bye, many told us things like, "We learned a lot from you in the classroom and from your sermons, but we learned more by watching your family in your home." From that observation, my wife Char and I learned that our actions at home speak more loudly than our public words.

I tell that story whenever I teach at Leadership Empowerment Conferences because I want my listeners to live family lives that validate, illustrate, and support the sermons they preach. I teach that family life is not an interruption to our public ministry; rather, it is an opportunity to demonstrate the credibility of our message.

So it is with the Bible's characters. The writers of the Bible speak to us with their words, and the Bible's characters speak to us with their lives. Some of their messages are so powerful, their actions need only a few observations to bring to light the spiritual inspiration and brilliant insight the human writers and the divine Writer intended.

What can we learn today from Noah's life? How could Esther's wise dealings with her husband help us to be more influential and effective for God? What traps would we avoid if we examined Balaam's behavior? Why might Paul's strong recommendation of Phoebe reverse much of what the Christian Church has believed for centuries about women ministers? Times, cultures, traditions, and societal values may change from century to century, but human nature does not change. Bible characters can teach us biblical character.

According to Romans 15:4, we are to learn life lessons from the Old Testament. "For everything that was written in the past was written to teach us, so that through the endurance taught in the Scriptures and the encouragement they provide we might have hope."

First Corinthians 10:11–12 says, "These things happened to them as examples and were written down as warnings for us, on whom the culmination of the ages has come. So, if you think you are standing firm, be careful that you don't fall!"

Following those principles, we can learn lessons from the narratives and characters in both Testaments. Their stories still speak to us today.

Many more Bible characters could have been added to this book. Here are three criteria I used for selecting the ones to include.

First, I tried to choose stories that contained valuable lessons for Christians who want to increase their influence. In my travels in Europe, Africa, Asia, South Pacific, and North America, I have met many intelligent, dedicated, sincere, zealous, and teachable brothers and sisters. It is my hope that the ideas in this book can help them, and others like them, become even more effective, successful, influential, and fruitful in the work God gives them.

Second, I wanted to deal with a broad range of subjects. I feel an obligation to avoid a rehash of themes already addressed in other books. Instead, I chose to point out new applications drawn from familiar stories.

Third, I looked for the human interest factor. Good lessons should be couched in literature written as interestingly as possible. Even though I don't expect you to read these chapters just for entertainment, I do harbor the hope that they will be interesting.

I used a few of Joel Rosenberg's ideas in the chapter on Ezekiel and Joel David Hamilton's ideas in the chapter about Phoebe. With those two exceptions, these lessons are my own observations made from years of studying the Bible. In 1963, when I was nineteen, I began to read the Bible through a couple of times each year. After about seven years, I cut back to reading it through just once each year, a habit I have maintained ever since.

After all these readings, I have come to feel like I know the Bible characters. I have a sense for what they thought, why they acted the way they did, and what they did right and wrong. In teaching and preaching, and now in this book, I have used their lives to teach people how to live biblical and principled lives.

Here I present to you twenty-five acquaintances of mine as I have come to know them. I have chosen to present them in the order in which they appear in the Scriptures. This does not in any way indicate the importance of any one character over another; each reader will find some chapters more applicable than others. There is something here for everyone.

We tend to become like persons we highly regard. Our behavior, vocabulary, and even facial expressions give testimony to this phenomenon. Whom do you admire? With whom do you like to converse? Which of the personalities in the Bible do you esteem? Whose story do you most enjoy reading? Your selection of whom to respect and whose company you keep reveals your personal character. Can you see ways in which you are becoming like them?

We normally appreciate the person who does what he says he will do — his actions match his words. Likewise, we value the person who says what he means and means what he says — his actions and words reflect his true thoughts and intentions. Both of these ideas are included in my personal definition of *integrity*, a word included in the subtitle of this book.

Integrity, as it relates to personal character, usually refers to a person's honesty and morality. It might be helpful though to take a closer look at this word *integrity*. It comes from the same root word from which the words *integrate* and *integrated* come.

Persons of integrity purposely *integrate* their own thoughts, words, and behaviors. Growing Christians work at making their own hearts and minds, thoughts and ideas consistent with the godly character portrayed in Scripture. With integrity, they will also work at making what they say and do completely consistent with these thoughts, ideas, and intentions. This ensures that their words and actions will accurately reflect who and what they are on the inside and what they are becoming. There will be no trace of guile, deception, or hypocrisy. Those of us who follow the Lord instead of the world will work together with God to transform ourselves internally and externally, developing and maintaining personal consistency and integrity.

As you review the personal character of the people in this book, I hope you will cultivate a desire to become a person of integrity. If you do, you will find that you are consistent with yourself, and therefore happier with yourself. You will also increase your opportunities to favorably influence others by your example. This is character worth choosing.

I hope that as you read this book and spend time with these people from the Bible, your character will more closely reflect the best of theirs. You are already making choices about who you will become. When you choose those people with whom you spend time, or about whom you read, you choose your character.

CHAPTER 1
NOAH

Noah's life has poignant messages for Christians today. For example, did you realize that when God contends with us, He is complimenting us? And did you know that God protects us from bigger punishments and more severe judgments by giving us smaller, merciful judgments? Did you know that Noah was one of the most thick-skinned persons in the Bible?

This story introduces us to some important concepts that help us understand how God works and why He does what He does. They enable us to appreciate His motives and goals and the limitations He places on Himself in pursuit of His eternal plan and purpose. Because Christians are God's representatives on earth, it is to our advantage to understand these lessons. The story of Noah also provides a foundation for principles we will learn from the other twenty-four characters presented in this book.

Two major players dominate this story: God and Noah. We will learn important lessons from each of them by looking at the way they relate to each other.

God Reacts to What People Do

God does not perform His works arbitrarily or unilaterally. He watches what people do and acts accordingly. He sent a flood in Noah's time because people were sinning grievously. He acted in a way that was appropriate in view of what people were doing. He still does that today.

Of course God loves everyone. Nevertheless, when people acknowledge, love, and worship Him, they please Him more. Consequently, they receive more of His favor. When people sin against Him, He is merciful to judge them so the human race learns there is a moral authority in the universe.

Observe what God is doing and question Him. We learn something if we stop and look at what mankind is doing that may have precipitated God's reaction.

In the case of the flood, it is easy to see that God was responding to man's condition. "When human beings began to increase in number on the earth, the sons of God saw that the daughters of man were beautiful, and they married any of them they chose. *Then* the Lord said, 'My Spirit will not contend with human beings forever, for they are mortal; their days will be a hundred and twenty years'" (Genesis 6:1-3 emphasis mine). God did what He did when humankind did what humankind did.

This principle is explained further in the following verses:

> *The Lord saw* how great the wickedness of the human race had become on the earth, and that every inclination of the thoughts of the human heart was only evil all the time. *The Lord regretted* that he had made human beings on the earth, and his heart was deeply troubled. *So* the Lord said, "I will wipe from the face of the earth the human race I have created — and with them the animals, the birds and the creatures that move along the ground — *for* I regret that I have made them." (Genesis 6:5-7, emphasis mine)

God's treatment of us is contingent upon our attitude and behavior toward Him. He watches us and responds accordingly. "Come near to God and he will come near to you" (James 4:8). "Trust in the Lord with all your heart and lean not on your own understanding; in all your ways submit to him and he will make your paths straight" (Proverbs 3:5-6). If we do not like the treatment God is giving us, perhaps we need to examine our attitude toward Him to discover why He is treating us the way He is.

The judgment of the flood was God's appropriate response to the behavior of the human race.

People are responsible for their actions. The curses and blessings in the Bible are contingent on our behavior.

God's responses are more dependable and predictable than ours. Man is capricious; God is principled. The best use of the human power of choice is to pursue God. When we do that, He responds in ways we like.

Why Does God Contend with Mankind?

"Then the Lord said, 'My Spirit will not contend with human beings forever, for they are mortal; their days will be a hundred and twenty years'" (Genesis 6:3).

Three alternatives in dealing with mankind were before God.

- He could ignore the progress of increasing sin and eventually destroy everyone or let them destroy themselves.
- He could violate the free will with which He created mankind and force them to repent and become godly.
- He could contend with them.

Let's examine these alternatives.

He could ignore the progress of increasing sin and eventually destroy everyone or let them destroy themselves.

God acts in ways consistent with His love and is, therefore, merciful. He loves the human race He created. His lofty desire is for us to develop into the something good He knows we can become. Because of that, He elected not to abandon the race, but instead to lead us toward righteousness.

He could violate the free will with which He created mankind and force them to repent and become godly.

God created mankind with a free will. He wanted to enjoy fellowship, love, and worship from thinking creatures who — as a result of their own volition — fellowshipped, loved, and worshipped Him. Overriding the free choices of the human race would have aborted God's plan for intentional and willing fellowship. God did not abandon His hope for such meaningful fellowship. Illustrating God's commitment to the free choice principle, He not only created mankind with volition but also created an environment in which humankind's power of choice could be exercised. God was unwilling to abandon His plan.

He could contend with them.

God was left with the third alternative: He could still reach out in wisdom and love in an attempt to win the hearts of people and yet give them a choice. So He sent His Spirit to contend with man. He continues to operate this way. In much the same manner as in Noah's day, so even now the Holy Spirit is holding back evil. The Scripture says, "For the secret power of lawlessness is already at work; but the one who now holds it back will continue to do so till he is taken out of the way" (2 Thessalonians 2:7).

God's children can cooperate with God and prove more useful to Him when we understand that He is not willing to either abandon the people He loves nor violate their freedom of choice. This is why we must reason with, cajole, coax, urge, and lovingly attempt to persuade people to receive Christ. In this way, we follow God's example, neither abandoning nor using force.

Furthermore, we have a deadline. The day will come when God's Spirit will no longer contend with the human race. But until He stops, we too should continue. We must be urgent but loving, giving others good reasons to turn to God.

Judgment Is an Act of Love and Mercy

God is powerful, loving, and perfectly wise. Everything He does is consistent with these qualities. Whatever powerful action He takes emanates from His love and perfect wisdom.

How can we find the most useful interpretation of this principle in the story of the flood? The flood displays God's amazing control and power over natural phenomena. Waters from multiple sources, wonderfully timed, converged on the surface of the earth just when the ark was complete. This illustrates God's power to initiate the plan He conceived in wisdom and love. His impeccable wisdom, operating in conjunction with His love, led Him to the best and most loving of plans.

Without the flood, millions more souls would have been born into a corrupted and ruined race. The flood was wisely designed and powerfully implemented in order to avoid the necessity of punishing and condemning millions more souls to suffering forever in a godless eternity. For that reason, the judgment of the flood is a flawless display of His love toward the human race. One could shudder to think what evils might have reigned and what wretched existences might have occurred had the pre-Noah race continued. The flood was an act of mercy. It would have been unloving for God to have allowed the human race to continue as it was.

> "The judgment of the flood is a flawless display of His love toward the human race."

God is slow to anger and quick to forgive. Yet because of His perfect holiness, He must punish sin. A distorted view of God's character leads some to imagine that God is vindictive. But God's judgments are not mere punishments. They are merciful warnings, corrections, and lessons from which we are expected to learn. He corrects once to avoid the necessity of punishing forever.

What lesson can we learn from God's gracious correction and judgment? Understanding mercy and judgment enables us to correctly help the people around us grow and become more responsible. In the long run, correction (appropriately administered) and discipline (given in love) are much more caring, merciful, and effective than permissiveness and leniency.

Noah Had Thick Skin

The Bible does not state that the unrighteous people of Noah's time ridiculed or mocked him. However, we can assume that people did so. History, psychology, and morality teach us that unrighteous people mock righteous people. They ridicule anyone who attempts to warn them of their error and unrighteousness. This is true even when the warnings are motivated by love and concern and based on a correct evaluation of their wickedness.

Noah was a righteous man in an ungodly world. Noah's generation was so corrupt God determined to destroy the entire human race. In the midst of this moral darkness, Noah's life was radiant with righteousness.

> But Noah found favor in the eyes of the Lord. This is the account of Noah and his family. Noah was a righteous man, blameless among the people of his time, and he walked faithfully with God.

Noah had three sons: Shem, Ham and Japheth. Now the earth was corrupt in God's sight and was full of violence. God saw how corrupt the earth had become, for all the people on earth had corrupted their ways. (Genesis 6:8–12)

Because of evil and violence, God divinely revealed to Noah that a great flood would destroy mankind from the face of the earth. God furthermore gave Noah an unusual and humanly impossible responsibility: to build a huge boat, forty-five feet (13.716 meters) high, 450 feet (137.16 meters) long, and 75 feet (22.86 meters) wide, capable of saving his own family and representatives of the animal kingdom.

So God said to Noah, "I am going to put an end to all people, for the earth is filled with violence because of them. I am surely going to destroy both them and the earth. So make yourself an ark of cypress wood; make rooms in it and coat it with pitch inside and out. This is how you are to build it: The ark is to be three hundred cubits long, fifty cubits wide and thirty cubits high. Make a roof for it, leaving below the roof an opening one cubit high all around. Put a door in the side of the ark and make lower, middle, and upper decks. I am going to bring floodwaters on the earth to destroy all life under the heavens, every creature that has the breath of life in it. Everything on earth will perish." (Genesis 6:13–17)

> **Noah endured the mocking, suffered as the laughingstock of his day, and year after year patiently continued to build his boat.**

This task, conducted in an atmosphere of unrighteousness and ridicule, required faith, physical labor, and tremendous persistence. Surrounded by curious, godless, and unbelieving neighbors, Noah endured the mocking and suffered as the laughingstock of his day. But year after year, he patiently continued to build his boat. The consistence of his faith, his dogged obedience, and his steadfast belief in his impossible task demand our respect and appreciation. Noah did not yield to peer pressure. His example challenges us to more staunchly pursue our assigned tasks.

We need Noah's thick skin. We too labor year after year. The wicked seem to escape punishment, and the righteous suffer. We would do well to remember faithful Noah. He eventually received his reward. So will we if we persist in the face of pressures.

Believe the Unbelievable

From a scientific standpoint, the universal flood is perhaps the most difficult story in the Bible to accept as true, second only to the creation of the universe. The unlikelihood of the events in this story requires the reader to believe what is impossible or consider the tale as only an allegory.

The lessons to be learned from Noah's experiences are not mere symbols. Noah's story is history, and history is God's allegory, written for our instruction. Just as individuals can learn from their own personal experiences, humanity can learn from our collective experience.

If we toss the story of Noah out as fiction, parable, or myth, we must toss out other portions of the Bible, because this story is referred to by many other Bible writers. Toss out Noah and the flood, and you might just as well toss out the whole Bible. Belief in a universal flood is therefore also a test of the credibility of the rest of the Bible.

In Ezekiel's writings, for example, Noah is placed along with Daniel and Job as an illustration of a righteous person who could only save himself.

> Even if these three men — Noah, Daniel, and Job — were in it [a country], they could save only themselves by their righteousness, declares the Sovereign Lord ... as surely as I live, declares the Sovereign Lord, even if Noah, Daniel, and Job were in it, they could save neither son nor daughter. They would save only themselves by their righteousness. (Ezekiel 14:14, 20)

The story of a universal flood has been ridiculed by many liberal theologians, unbelievers, and atheists. Yet both Jesus and Peter referred to Noah. Jesus said, "As it was in the days of Noah, so it will be at the coming of the Son of Man" (Matthew 24:37). Peter warned the people of his day as Noah had warned his neighbors of coming judgment. "... if he did not spare the ancient world when he brought the flood on its ungodly people, but protected Noah, a preacher of righteousness, and seven others ... By these waters also the world of that time was deluged and destroyed" (2 Peter 2:5; 3:6). Peter also referred to "those who were disobedient long ago when God waited patiently in the days of Noah while the ark was being built. In it only a few people, eight in all, were saved through water" (1 Peter 3:20).

If the story of Noah was fiction, Jesus and Peter would have been wrong to refer to it as fact.

Even the Chinese language reflects the reality of a worldwide flood. The Chinese character for *ship* is made up of three parts: *eight, people,* and *boat.* Noah, his wife, and his three sons and their wives would make eight people in a boat.

Years ago, I read of a mountain hiker who found a large wooden structure in the icy mountains of Ararat. I certainly do not base my belief in Noah's story on secular speculation. But what if God, for the benefit of a future skeptical generation, is saving evidence of the truth of the Bible by preserving Noah's ark in the mountains of Turkey?

Grace Is Also Found in the Old Testament

"But Noah found favor in the eyes of the Lord" (Genesis 6:8). This short sentence introduces the reader to the wonderful concept of God's grace.

Some preachers and Bible scholars contrast God's grace in the New Testament with His rigid requirements in the Old. But the Bible contains many references to God's firm justice in the New Testament. It also contains numerous illustrations of His compassion, loving kindness, and mercy in the Old Testament. Furthermore, the book of Hebrews states that God is unchanging and has fixed purposes. "Because God wanted to make the unchanging nature of his purpose very clear to the heirs of what was promised, he confirmed it with an oath" (Hebrews 6:17). God is firm and merciful. Both aspects are a part of who He is.

Today, we often hear an emphasis on the grace of God. We are indeed blessed to live in New Testament times. But some have an inaccurate concept of God as weak, unconditionally forgiving, always merciful and compassionate, and never judging. That image is inconsistent with who God is. Such teaching leads to what some call "cheap grace." Cheap grace stems from an inappropriate emphasis on forgiveness with no appreciation for justice and righteousness. Satan wants to lull us into unjustified ease and rest, sung to sleep by the lullabies of God's graciousness.

God gave people in Old Testament times the law, but His grace is also shown repeatedly. How many times did David say, "His love endures forever"? If He had judged harshly, no one would have had a chance of ever pleasing God. Noah found grace in God's eyes. As a result, he and his family were saved. That same grace extends to us today. You are I are given the same opportunity Noah had. We can obey God, live righteously, and enjoy abundant life. The alternative is to ignore God and eventually suffer serious consequences. God needs Christians today who appreciate and value grace.

> "But some have an inaccurate concept of God as weak, unconditionally forgiving, always merciful and compassionate, and never judging."

Noah Had Faith

Did Noah know about the law of buoyancy, by which the air within the shell of the ark would displace enough water to make the ark weigh less than the water it displaced so it could float? How could he know that principle would apply even with the ark's heavy beams, animals, and food supplies? How much understanding did he have that the ark would be safe when the rains came? Surely obeying God required Noah to exercise blind faith. "By faith Noah, when warned about things not yet seen, in holy fear built an ark to save his family. By his faith he condemned the world and became heir of the righteousness that is in keeping with faith" (Hebrews 11:7).

By his faith — clinging to and trusting in God's word to him — Noah became an heir to the righteousness of (right standing with) God. In doing so, he condemned his world. He showed it was possible to believe and obey, thereby removing any excuse from others in his generation.

Noah's kind of faith was later demonstrated by Abraham. By it, they both became perfect in God's sight. We can too. We are saved the same way Noah and Abraham were, by faith expressed and proven in obedience, in works. "Noah did everything just as God commanded him" (Genesis 6:22). "And Noah did all that the Lord commanded him" (Genesis 7:5).

God needs men and women today who will complete their hard tasks as Noah did in his day.

Noah Was Honored by God with an Everlasting Covenant

God promised Noah He would never again send a great flood to destroy the earth. "I now establish my covenant with you and with your descendants after you and with every living creature that was with you — the birds, the livestock, and all the wild animals, all those that came out of the ark with you — every living creature on earth. I establish my covenant with you: Never again will all life be destroyed by the waters of a flood; never again will there be a flood to destroy the earth" (Genesis 9:9-17).

God gave the human race the rainbow as a sign of this covenant. Every rainbow we see is a reminder of God's favor on Noah, who was blessed because he believed and was obedient. The treasured lessons of resilient faith in the face of obstacles — and obedience in the face of ridicule — can be for us "pots of gold" and the end of every rainbow.

Speaking through Isaiah, God referred to this covenant and compared Isaiah's day with Noah's. "To me this is like the days of Noah, when I swore that the waters of Noah would never again cover the earth. So now I have sworn not to be angry with you, never to rebuke you again" (Isaiah 54:9). Because Noah served God faithfully, we have God's promise that no worldwide flood will happen again.

Noah's Sin after the Flood Teaches Us to Be Careful after Great Victories

Just after the narrative about God's covenant with Noah, we read a story of failure. "The sons of Noah who came out of the ark were Shem, Ham, and Japheth. (Ham was the father of Canaan.) These were the three sons of Noah, and from them came the people who were scattered over the whole earth" (Genesis 9:18-19). After that, a problem developed.

Noah, a man of the soil, proceeded to plant a vineyard. When he drank some of its wine, he became drunk and lay uncovered inside his tent. Ham, the father of Canaan, saw his father's nakedness and told his two brothers outside. But Shem and Japheth took a garment and laid it across their shoulders; then they walked in backward and covered their father's nakedness. Their faces were turned the other way so that they would not see their father's nakedness (Genesis 9:20-23)

The vineyard was not the problem. Even drinking wine was not the problem, as indicated by these Scriptures:

- "… wine that gladdens human hearts, oil to make their faces shine, and bread that sustains their hearts" (Psalm 104:15).
- "Go, eat your food with gladness, and drink your wine with a joyful heart, for God has already approved what you do" (Ecclesiastes 9:7).
- "The Ephraimites will become like mighty warriors, and their hearts will be glad as with wine. Their children will see it and be joyful; their hearts will rejoice in the Lord" (Zechariah 10:7).
- "Stop drinking only water, and use a little wine because of your stomach and your frequent illnesses" (1 Timothy 5:23).

Noah got intoxicated. What can we learn from Noah's sin of drunkenness? He was right to plant a vineyard and all right to make wine "that gladdens human hearts," but he was wrong to get inebriated. Drunkenness causes one to lose control of one's mind. God says we are to be in charge of our thoughts.

> "God says we are to be in charge of our thoughts."

Drinking moderately, with the use of biblical self-control, is a debated subject in the international body of Christ. Each person should be persuaded in his own mind. For me, it is better to abstain from any drinking than to offend a brother with the use of liberty and possibly cause someone to stumble.

While controlled drinking may be debated, to be inebriated is clearly wrong according to the Bible. Here are some verses that address this issue:

- "Let us behave decently, as in the daytime, not in carousing and

> drunkenness, not in sexual immorality and debauchery, not in dissension and jealousy" (Romans 13:13).
> - "… and envy; drunkenness, orgies, and the like. I warn you, as I did before, that those who live like this will not inherit the kingdom of God" (Galatians 5:21).
> - "For you have spent enough time in the past doing what pagans choose to do — living in debauchery, lust, drunkenness, orgies, carousing and detestable idolatry" (1 Peter 4:3).

Noah is credited with building the first recorded altar, perhaps the first altar ever built (Genesis 8:20). But neither building an altar nor enjoying the distinction of having built the first recorded altar is of any value, because his behavior did not match his worship.

One sin led to another. Noah's inebriation led to the foolishness of unnecessary exposure of his nakedness. Sin contaminates, breeds evil, and produces an atmosphere for further sinning. One person's sin too often brings out the worst in others.

Sin develops momentum. It escalates. It increases. It is easily compounded. But in all instances, we have a choice. God's people must be men and women of self-control twenty-four hours of every day.

The Immoral Level of Noah's Time Will Be Reached Again before Jesus' Return

Jesus taught that we should be ready for His return just as Noah was ready for the flood.

> But about that day or hour no one knows, not even the angels in heaven, nor the Son, but only the Father. As it was in the days of Noah, so it will be at the coming of the Son of Man. For in the days before the flood, people were eating and drinking, marrying and giving in marriage, up to the day Noah entered the ark; and they knew nothing about what would happen until the flood came and took them all away. That is how it will be at the coming of the Son of Man. Two men will be in the field; one will be taken and the other left. Two women will be grinding with a hand mill; one will be taken and the other left.

> Therefore keep watch, because you do not know on what day your Lord will come. But understand this: If the owner of the house had known at what time of night the thief was coming, he would have kept watch and would not have let his house be broken into. So you also must be ready, because the Son of Man will come at an hour when you do not expect him. (Matthew 24:36-44)

Jesus taught that the morality of the end times would be comparable to Noah's time. We would do well to consider this lesson when interpreting events in our society. The slide of today's civilizations into immorality is so gradual that it would be easy to miss. But anyone who has lived sixty years or more on this earth will recall, for example, it was considered a shame when someone had to get married because of premarital sex. Today, however, an unmarried woman with the courage to marry the father of her child and allow the fetus to live is considered virtuous in comparison to the woman who kills her unborn baby. Have we forgotten that premarital sex is against the Word of God?

The current increase of immorality is just one of the signs that Jesus will soon return to earth. Our later study of Ezekiel will provide another kind of information about Bible prophesy and reading the signs of our times. His return need not take us by surprise. The flood may have surprised the wicked of Noah's day, but it did not surprise Noah and his family.

For Further Thought

- Do you think it would be easier to believe the rest of the Bible if we believed the story of Noah?
- What do you believe about the grace and severity of God? How does that belief impact the way you present the message of Jesus to others?
- How can faith enable you to be thick skinned, resilient, tough, and persevering in the assignments God gives you?
- What have you learned about the rewards God grants to the faithful and obedient?
- How can what you believe about drinking bring glory to God and a positive influence to others?
- In what way(s) is the morality of this generation an indication of how soon Jesus may return to earth?

CHAPTER 2
ABRAHAM

Did you know there's a lesson hidden in the first eleven chapters of Genesis that is significant for worldwide missions? The Bible says Abraham was "taken" from Ur, and when he left home, he didn't know he was headed to Canaan. Do you know what it's like to begin a journey without knowing your destination?

Abraham is one of the most outstanding persons in the Bible. He is the founding father of the Jewish people, the chosen of God. The lessons from his life are applicable and useful for us today. Here we will observe fifteen of those lessons.

The Bible Does Not Begin with Abraham

Most ancient books dealing with the founding of a nation, its civilization, and its religion begin with the story of its founder. The founder is usually a local hero, and the civilization and religion of the people is local in scope. The gods of Ur, Babylonia, and Egypt are all different from one another because the location and culture in each is different. But this is not true in Israel's case.

Abraham does not appear in the Bible narrative until Genesis 12. God was very active in the preceding eleven chapters of

> "The Bible does not begin with Abraham because Abraham's God is not just a family deity or a local god."

the Bible. He created the universe (Genesis 1), brought about a worldwide flood (Genesis 6), established nations and language (Genesis 11), and recorded all the nations (Genesis 10). The Bible does not begin with Abraham because Abraham's God is not just a family deity or a local god. He is the one universal God. He always has been and always will be.

If God is the true God, He must necessarily be the only God. One cannot say, "Isis is the real God," and, "Jehovah is the real God." These two opposing statements cannot both be true. Following that line of thought, Ur's god and Egypt's god cannot both be the real God. Abraham's God is the one true God. He alone offers historic proof in ancient literature — the Bible — that He is the universal God, and He is the only God to make that claim. The literature of Ur, Babylon, and Egypt make no such claim.

I do not want to worship a mere product of a poet's imagination. I want to worship, know, serve, obey, and give myself to the one true God.

The first lesson we can learn from Abraham is that the God he worshipped is the only universal God and therefore the only true God. He is the only One deserving of our worship, love, and obedience.

Terah Moved from Ur toward Canaan, but Only Got to Haran

Terah took his son Abraham, his daughter-in-law Sarah, and his grandson Lot, and "set out from Ur of the Chaldeans to go to Canaan" (Genesis 11:31), but he stopped along the way and settled in Haran. Terah did not arrive at his intended destination. He allowed something to interfere with his goal. He died at Haran at age 205 without ever reaching Canaan.

> *Terah was a quitter. Abraham was a finisher. Which will you be?*

Haran is the name of both Abram's brother who died in Ur (Genesis 11:28) and of the place they stopped at on the way from Ur to Canaan. This may be a coincidence or it is possible that the backward-looking Terah named the place Haran after his deceased son. At any rate, Terah was content to stay in Haran and did not complete his journey. He did not face the future; he faced the past. The devil wants to keep you in your past failures, losses, and disappointments. God wants to talk to you about your future and move you to new possibilities and opportunities.

The only reason we even know of Terah is because his persevering, faith-filled, forward-looking, obedient son, Abraham, did not quit. Abraham worshipped God, believed the promise, arrived in Canaan, acted on the promise, and experienced what God had for him. Terah was a quitter. Abraham was a finisher. Which will you be?

I want to follow Abraham's example. I want to be a finisher. We can rise above the failures of our forebears as Abraham did over his.

God Initiated the Call of Abraham

God is the initiator of everything good. Ideas may come to us, but they do not start with us. Ideas that begin in our imagination may lead to failure. If our ideas originate with God, and we cooperate with His plan, we can be sure they will come to pass.

"Here is a trustworthy saying: Whoever aspires to be an overseer desires a noble task" (1 Timothy 3:1). The desire to serve as a Christian leader, for example, is a positive thing. But how do you know if that idea came from God?

Jeremiah 17:9 says the heart of man is deceitful and wicked. We are capable of thinking selfish, egotistical thoughts and harboring vain ambitions. We cannot trust our own evaluations of our character. Paul the apostle said, "I care very little if I am judged by you or by any human court; indeed, I do not even judge myself" (1 Corinthians 4:3).

How then do we know if we are called of God in a particular situation or if we are just following our own imagination?

God uses a variety of means to call people to ministry. He also calls a broad spectrum of personality types. What criterion does God use when He selects those whom He wants to use in His ministry? I don't have a definitive answer, but every minister must remember that the call of God on his or her life constrains him or her to do the work of the ministry. If you are involved in ministry, you need to ask yourself, "How do I know it is God who called me?"

Abraham, Jeremiah, Isaiah, David, Amos, and Paul all knew the answer to that question.

Jeremiah and Paul couldn't *not* minister. Jeremiah said it this way: "But if I say, 'I will not mention him or speak any more in his name,' his word is in my heart like a fire, a fire shut up in my bones. I am weary of holding it in; indeed, I cannot" (Jeremiah 20:9). Paul said, "Yet when I preach the gospel, I cannot boast, for I am compelled to preach. Woe to me if I do not preach the gospel!" (1 Corinthians 9:16). When many of the disciples were defecting, Jesus asked the twelve if they would also leave. Peter answered, "Lord, to whom shall we go? You have the words of eternal life" (John 6:68). For one who is called, nothing else satisfies.

Abraham Began a Journey without Knowing Where It Would Lead

"Go from your country, your people, and your father's household to the land I will show you" (Genesis 12:1). Caution tells us to not release one job until we have secured our next one. I was taught in Bible college to not resign one church position unless I had another one to go to. Usually, this is a good posture. Yet God sometimes wants us to demonstrate our confidence, faith, and trust in Him by our willingness to leave something even before we know the next step. God required this of Abraham, and Abraham responded correctly.

Yet Abraham had some idea of where this might lead him; it was not a total leap into the dark unknown. His father, Terah, had set out for Canaan. Abraham knew that. So he had at least a hint about where God might take him.

> **The tension between faith and reason gives man the opportunity to play a kind of quest game with God.**

What about us? Do we use logic or reason when we make decisions? Do we exercise blind faith instead of making reasonable and rational choices? Every Christian leader wants to exercise faith, but no one wants to do something foolish in the name of faith. So what is the relationship between faith and reason in making career- or ministry-related decisions?

Faith should not be unreasonable, and reason should not automatically quench faith. God has given us both a measure of faith and rational decision-making powers. Faith and reason are each from God.

The tension between faith and reason gives man the opportunity to play a kind of quest game with God. We constantly search for Him and His will. We are discoverers, explorers, pioneers, and accomplishers. It is easier and safer to stay with the routine, the familiar, and the proven. However, God challenges us to a more interesting adventure with Him. We must learn to trust Him and move only when He tells us to.

Abraham Built Altars Everywhere He Went

When Abraham arrived at Shechem, and later in his journey when he arrived in the hills east of Bethel, he built altars to the Lord (Genesis 12:6-8). He did this because of who he was. His behavior was consistent with what he believed. He believed in family and household worship and leading those with him in worship of the true God. God reveals Himself to worshippers. Worshipping Him changes and enlarges us in many ways.

Worship precedes structural programs. Abram was not a church, a mission, an organization, or a public entity of any kind. He was only an individual with possessions and employees. Yet everywhere he went, he built an altar and worshipped.

Worship does not depend on location, form, or facilities. These factors may help create an atmosphere in which worship can more easily take place, but worship is not limited to or controlled by location. Jesus made this clear in His conversation with the woman by the well at Sychar, recorded in John 4:20-24.

> [The woman said,] "Our ancestors worshiped on this mountain, but you Jews claim that the place where we must worship is in Jerusalem."
>
> "Woman," Jesus replied, "believe me, a time is coming when you will worship the Father neither on this mountain nor in Jerusalem. You Samaritans worship what you do not know; we worship what we do know, for salvation is from the Jews. Yet a time is coming and has now come when the true worshipers will worship the Father in the Spirit and in truth, for they are the kind of worshipers the father seeks. God is spirit, and his worshipers must worship in the Spirit and in truth."

Being a worshipper is more important than being in a place where people worship. We are not to give up meeting together (Hebrews 10:25). In the assembly, however, the condition of the worshipper's heart is more important than merely being among worshippers in a place of worship, saying or singing what worshippers say and sing.

Abraham Failed as a Cross-Cultural Missionary

Genesis 12:10–20 tells us of Abraham's experience in Egypt, at which time he feared for his life because of his wife's beauty. Abraham put Sarah's moral purity at risk, and even chanced losing her, because of his narrow-minded, selfish concern for his own life.

Isaac did the same thing in Genesis 26:1–11. When he lived in Gerar among the Philistines, he also called his wife his sister in an effort to preserve his own life.

We can learn several lessons from Abraham's and Isaac's misjudgment:

- We should not assume there is no fear of God in others, even though they are different from us. The Pharaoh of Egypt and King Abimelek of the Philistines both had a conscience and responded favorably to God's dealings with them. We should strive to be sensitive to what God is doing among the people where we serve and work.
- The ethical level of the "heathen" was higher than Abraham's in this situation. Abraham was called of God to be a blessing to all nations, but because of his selfishness and failure, he almost became a curse to the nations. We must learn to live right for the sake of the One whom we represent and whose message we carry.
- Our children are watching us, and they tend to repeat our successes and failures. Isaac repeated Abraham's error in spite of the fact that Pharaoh behaved more morally than his father, Abraham, had. Isaac's lie, however, was worse because Rebekah was not his half-sister.

God Remained Faithful to His Flawed Son Abraham

Even though Abraham had the faith to leave his home and go to a strange country, he still had weaknesses. Abraham was a peace-loving man, even to the point of seeking peace at any price. He seems to have protected himself by distancing himself. Perhaps he originally chose to marry his sister rather than a non-family member in order to avoid being emotionally vulnerable outside the family unit. Did he compartmentalize his relationship with Sarah? Was she his wife in bed, but otherwise his sister, hence the easy half-truth?

On an emotional level, he seems to have connected more readily with his children and Lot than with his wife. He was more willing to lose her to other men — Pharaoh and later Abimelek — than he was to send Ishmael away. He refused to get involved when Sarah was incensed with Hagar. When she consulted him about it, Abraham avoided the situation, calling Hagar the slave of Sarah when she was more than that: She was a secondary wife to Abraham and was carrying his child.

> "Our children are watching us, and they tend to repeat our successes and failures."

Sarah may have been flattered to be chosen twice for a king's harem. But surely Abraham's willingness to give her up was not flattering. His apparent emotional indifference must have been painful for Sarah over the course of their marriage. Abraham may have manipulated Sarah, in effect repudiating his marriage.

Abraham, being childless at the time, may have taken on a fatherly role with his nephew Lot after Haran's death, thus leading Lot to travel with Abraham. This peace-lover showed his courage when he mustered 318 trained servants to rescue Lot. Where was Abraham's heart and courage when his wife was taken by other men? If he could later defeat four kings, could he not have shown a little more courage here with Pharaoh in Egypt and afterward with Abimelek in the Negev?

God doesn't directly address the issue of Abraham's emotional indifference. Perhaps the scathing rebukes he received from Pharaoh and Abimelek were exactly what Abraham needed. It appears that Pharaoh and Abimelek held Sarah equally responsible for this deception. But the important lesson is to learn how to glorify God in our family dealings. The best sermon is a life.

Later, when Sarah wanted to send Hagar and Ishmael away, Abraham was greatly distressed. But God told him he should listen to Sarah. This may have been the turning point in Abraham's attitude toward his wife.

For though he married again after her death, and had concubines and children by them, he sent these children away. Of all his wives, only Sarah was buried in the family plot.

Abraham was flawed, yet God called him and worked with him as he was, addressing problems as they occurred in His own unfailing wisdom. He never abandoned Abraham, even as He never abandons us. He works in the lives of those who have faults. He graciously makes us aware of our shortcomings as He perfects His own marvelous character into our lives. We can commit our all into His trustworthy hands.

Abraham's Wife Demonstrated Great Faith

Sarah exercised tremendous faith on her first foreign assignment as well as her later one in the Negev. Even though her husband made big mistakes, God protected obedient Sarah.

> When Abram came to Egypt, the Egyptians saw that Sarai was a very beautiful woman. And when Pharaoh's officials saw her, they praised her to Pharaoh, and she was taken into his palace. He treated Abram well for her sake, and Abram acquired sheep and cattle, male and female donkeys, male and female servants and camels.
>
> But the Lord inflicted serious diseases on Pharaoh and his household because of Abram's wife Sarai. So Pharaoh summoned Abram. "What have you done to me?" he said. "Why didn't you tell me she was your wife? Why did you say, 'She is my sister' so that I took her to be my wife? Now then, here is your wife. Take her and go!" Then Pharaoh gave orders about Abram to his men, and they sent him on his way, with his wife and everything he had. (Genesis 12:14–20)

Having known Abraham all her life, perhaps Sarah understood, loved, and forgave him. Abraham may have said to her, "If you love me, do this for me." When she was asked to prove her love by denying her marriage, she did it — twice. These incidents show the depth of Abraham's insecurity and fear while at the same time revealing Sarah's faith and character. She could have said to her husband, "If you love me, you will defend me." But she did not.

In this account, we notice three things:

- Though her husband was wrong, Sarah did not argue with him.
- She allowed herself to be placed in danger, trusting God for protection.
- God protected her.

We are to learn from Sarah's example.

So nobly did Sarah conduct herself that she received a high commendation in 1 Peter 3:1-6, in which Peter instructed Christian women how to have real inner beauty. Peter commends Sarah and tells New Testament women to duplicate her attitude and behavior. This tells us that Sarah was a good role model to follow. Otherwise, we might think Sarah was merely complicit, codependent, and easily manipulated. Cooperation is commendable, but codependency — going along with a partner's wrong behavior when it would be better to confront the partner — is counterproductive.

> "She could have said to her husband, 'If you love me, you will defend me.' But she did not."

In verses five and six, Peter addresses Sarah's beautiful behavior and cooperative attitude.

> For this is the way the holy women of the past who put their hope in God used to adorn themselves. They submitted themselves to their own husbands, like Sarah, who obeyed Abraham and called him her lord. You are her daughters if you do what is right and not give way to fear. (1 Peter 3:5-6)

Beautiful behavior and attitude is superior to physical beauty in God's eyes as well as in the eyes of godly people.

Abraham Separated from Lot Honorably

God told Abraham in Genesis 12:1, "Go from your country, your people and your father's household." But Genesis 12:4 and 13:1 tell us, "Lot went with him." Eventually the herdsmen of Lot and Abraham quarreled because they both had so many flocks, herds, and tents. Part of Abraham's problem with Lot may have been due to the fact that Abraham did not fully obey God. The command for him to go to Canaan included the instruction to leave his people and his father's household. Yet he allowed Lot to travel with him.

The positive aspect of Abraham's example is that he proposed a peaceful separation:

> So Abram said to Lot, "Let's not have any quarreling between you and me, or between your herders and mine, for we are close relatives. Is not the whole land before you? Let's part company. If you go to the left, I'll go to the right; if you go to the right, I'll go to the left." (Genesis 13:8-9)

Separations occur in the course of doing God's will. Sometimes separation is better than trying to harmonize or coordinate highly divergent ministry methods or visions.

In the New Testament, Paul and Barnabas separated over a disagreement about whether to take John Mark with them on the third missionary journey (as recorded in Acts 15:36-41).

Solomon said, "There is a time for everything, and a season for every activity under the heavens" (Ecclesiastes 3:1). Ecclesiastes 3 gives us fourteen illustrations. "A time to join together and a time to separate" is not on that list, but it is included in the "everything" of verse one. There are times in life and ministry when it is appropriate to separate from a group, just as there are times when it is appropriate to join.

When it is time to separate, we must do so honorably. Separations can be hurtful, bitter, and disappointing, and they can leave long-term emotional scars. Yet separations are part of growth.

In family studies and child psychology, we learn that a mentally healthy child goes though a developmental process called "individuation/separation." The child learns that he or she is an individual separate from his or her parents and gradually grows in the desire and ability to operate independently. Growth and maturity in the individuation process involves separation from those with whom we are joined. It is part of the same processes of life God used to develop us to the point where we are ready for individuation.

Our separations do not have to be contentious. We can and should maintain unity of the spirit even as we go our separate ways. God may use a difference of opinion or divergence of vision, focus, or priority to direct us to move or change. But as we move from place to place, phase to phase, stage to stage, and ministry to ministry, each change can be done honorably, decently, and in order.

We are not God's only children. The ones we leave behind or those we release are His too. "Do nothing out of selfish ambition or vain conceit, but in humility consider others better than yourselves" (Philippians 2:3). We must esteem others better than ourselves, wish them success, and celebrate growth and development even as we separate from them.

If someone's vision, calling, gifts, or ministry operation is different from the one God has given you, celebrate both diversity of gifts and unity of the Spirit. Either separate in an honorable way or remain together and allow your different gifts to complement each other.

> **Either separate in an honorable way or remain together and allow your different gifts to complement each other.**

Do you have hurtful memories of a separation you wish you could do over again in an honorable way? Correct mistakes made in the past if you can, but determine that from now on, separations will be peaceful and celebrative.

Abraham Informally, Yet Successfully, Trained His Staff

There is no explanation in Genesis 14 of how Abraham's team received its training. Based on the story's outcome, however, we know they must have been trained well and thoroughly. The Scripture says these "trained men" performed with great results against overwhelming odds.

> The four kings seized all the goods of Sodom and Gomorrah and all their food; then they went away. They also carried off Abram's nephew Lot and his possessions, since he was living in Sodom. A man who had escaped came and reported this to Abram the Hebrew.

Choose Your Character

> Now Abram was living near the great trees of Mamre the Amorite, a brother of Eshkol and Aner, all of whom were allied with Abram. When Abram heard that his relative had been taken captive, he called out the 318 trained men born in his household and went in pursuit as far as Dan.
>
> During the night Abram divided his men to attack them and he routed them, pursuing them as far as Hobah, north of Damascus. He recovered all the goods and brought back his relative Lot and his possessions, together with the women and the other people. (Genesis 14:11–16)

These warriors (318 men born in his household) and Abraham (their commander-in-chief) recovered from the armies of four kings what five kings and their armies had been unable to defend and protect. At night, Abraham and his men attacked in multiple groups, routed, then pursued the enemy, recovering Lot and his possessions, women, and other people. This was an amazing battle.

Psalm 91:7 says, "A thousand may fall at your side, ten thousand at your right hand, but it will not come near you." This appears to be the basis for Psalm 18:29, which says, "With your help I can advance against a troop; with my God I can scale a wall."

Often in our church work, we face overwhelming odds. Other organizations seem to have plentiful human and financial resources, connections, and favor, while we labor along with few resources other than God. We can take a lesson from Abraham and train our few. Prepare them. Conduct Bible studies in homes. Instruct people in the church who have leadership abilities.

Abraham and his 318 trained men claimed a victory over four kings and their armies. The time came when Israel had a standing army. God is the same today. You may eventually develop a team of workers, schools, recognition, and abundant human resources, but begin by training the few workers you have now.

Abraham's Vision Gets a Revision

> After this, the word of the Lord came to Abram in a vision: "Do not be afraid, Abram. I am your shield, your very great reward."
>
> But Abram said, "Sovereign Lord, what can you give me since I

remain childless and the one who will inherit my estate is Eliezer of Damascus?" And Abram said, "You have given me no children; so a servant in my household will be my heir."

Then the word of the Lord came to him: "This man will not be your heir, but a son coming from your own body will be your heir." He took him outside and said, "Look up at the heavens and count the stars — if indeed you can count them." Then he said to him, "So shall your offspring be."

Abram believed the Lord, and he credited it to him as righteousness.

He also said to him, "I am the Lord, who brought you out of Ur of the Chaldeans to give you this land to take possession of it." (Genesis 15:1–7)

This second vision adds four things to the original promises of Genesis 12:

- Protection (Genesis 15:1)
- Great reward (Genesis 15:1)
- Offspring (Genesis 15:4–5)
- Land (Genesis 15:7)

The earlier vision said nothing about offspring, just that God would make Abraham into "a great nation." The earlier vision said nothing about land. But this time, God said He was giving Abraham the land of Canaan.

We may relish the idea of God being our shield, our protector, our great reward, our close friend, helper, comforter, blessing, and our source of blessings. But God said this to Abraham after he obediently traveled into the unknown. God rewards faith.

How long has it been since your vision was revised? How long has it been since God spoke to you? Is your vision out of date? Has your passion cooled? Have you become discouraged? Has your vision lost its clarity? Or has your faith grown through the passing of time as you continue to wait on the Lord for the fulfillment of your vision? Open your heart to the fine-tuning, refocusing, or clarification God may want to make in your vision. Your plans should be flexible and your visions current.

God spoke a second time to Abraham, and He will speak again to you.

Abraham Tried to Help God Fulfill His Promise

Now Sarai, Abram's wife, had borne him no children. But she had an Egyptian servant named Hagar; so she said to Abram, "The Lord has kept me from having children. Go, sleep with my servant; perhaps I can build a family through her."

> Abram agreed to what Sarai said. So after Abram had been living in Canaan ten years, Sarai his wife took her Egyptian servant Hagar and gave her to her husband to be his wife. He slept with Hagar, and she conceived. When she knew she was pregnant, she began to despise her mistress. (Genesis 16:1-4)

With the passing of time, and with no apparent miracle child from God, Abraham and Sarah developed a human plan. God's plan and Abraham and Sarah's plan were so different from each other that centuries later, in the New Testament, the two are referred to in contrast. Galatians 4:21-31 tells of the two covenants and the children of the slave woman in contrast to the children of the free woman. Here is Paul's conclusion:

> Now you, brothers, like Isaac, are children of promise. At that time the son born in the ordinary way persecuted the son born by the power of the Spirit. It is the same now. But what does the Scripture say? "Get rid of the slave woman and her son, for the slave woman's son will never share in the inheritance with the free woman's son." Therefore, brothers, we are not children of the slave woman, but of the free woman. (Galatians 4:28-31)

Every time we take matters into our own hands, not waiting for God's miracle but trusting in the flesh and getting ahead of God, we are following Abraham and Sarah's "We'll do it our way" attitude. When we wait for God, experience His miracles, and do things in His timing, we have a "We'll do it God's way" attitude. Ishmael and Isaac — Hagar and Sarah — represent these two different principles.

This does not mean that all the physical descendants of Ishmael on earth today have an "I'll do it my way" attitude. I have some fine Palestinian and Arab friends who are wonderful Christian people.

Abraham's attempt to help God keep His promise teaches us an important lesson. Wait for God's miracles; don't attempt to "help" Him with your own human plan.

Abraham's Covenant with God was Confirmed by Circumcision

When Abram was ninety-nine years old, the Lord appeared to him and said, "I am God Almighty; walk before me faithfully and be blameless. Then I will make my covenant between me and you and will greatly increase your numbers."

Abram fell facedown, and God said to him, "As for me, this is my covenant with you: You will be the father of many nations. No longer will you be called Abram; your name will be Abraham, for I have made you a father of many nations. I will make you very fruitful; I will make nations of you, and kings will come from you. I will establish my covenant as an everlasting covenant between me and you and your descendants after you for the generations to come, to be your God and the God of your descendants after you. The whole land of Canaan, where you now reside as a foreigner, I will give as an everlasting possession to you and your descendants after you; and I will be their God. This is my covenant with you and your descendants after you, the covenant you are to keep: Every male among you shall be circumcised. You are to undergo circumcision, and it will be the sign of the covenant between me and you." (Genesis 17:1-11)

God told Abraham that circumcision was a sign of God's people's covenant with Him.

"Any uncircumcised male, who has not been circumcised in the flesh, will be cut off from his people; he has broken my covenant."

God also said to Abraham, "As for Sarai your wife, you are no longer to call her Sarai; her name will be Sarah. I will bless her and will surely give you a son by her. I will bless her so that she will be the mother of nations; kings of peoples will come from her."

Abraham fell facedown; he laughed and said to himself, "Will a son be born to a man a hundred years old? Will Sarah bear a child at the age of ninety?" And Abraham said to God, "If only Ishmael might live under your blessing!"

Then God said, "Yes, but your wife Sarah will bear you a son, and you will call him Isaac. I will establish my covenant with him as an everlasting covenant for his descendants after him. And as for Ishmael, I have heard you: I will surely bless him; I will make him fruitful and will greatly increase his numbers. He will be the father of twelve rulers, and I will make him into a great nation. But my covenant I will establish with Isaac, whom Sarah will bear to you by this time next year."

When he had finished speaking with Abraham, God went up from him. On that very day Abraham took his son Ishmael and all those born in his household or bought with his money, every male in his household, and circumcised them, as God told him. Abraham was ninety-nine years old when he was circumcised, and his son Ishmael was thirteen; Abraham and his son Ishmael were both circumcised on that same day. And every male in Abraham's household, including those born in his household or bought from a foreigner, was circumcised with him. (Genesis 17:14-27)

Abraham acted on the instructions of God and circumcised each of the males in his household.

The following seven observations help us understand the spiritual meaning of circumcision and how it deteriorated into a symbol of reliance on doing the works of the law.

- Circumcision was primarily a sign of a covenant between God and Abraham, along with his descendents.
- Circumcision signified a covenant with God emphasizing the blessing of God and separation from the world by Abraham's descendents.
- It originally had a wonderful meaning, but was replaced by an even better new covenant.
- Circumcision became a symbol of man's efforts to keep the law. Some Judaistic believers in the New Testament wanted to require that Gentile believers also be circumcised.
- Church leaders met and decided that circumcision was not required under the new covenant.
- Circumcision is not currently required of Christians.

These six observations enable us to appreciate and celebrate the original covenant meaning of circumcision — separation from the world, separation to God. Another observation, however, has a special meaning in the African context:

> Circumcision was for males only, not females.

Some African cultures practice infant female circumcision. This act destroys genitals, removing or hindering pleasure in love-making when the females become adults. Scripture opposes this practice. God provides many detailed instructions to Abraham, but there is no mention of female circumcision.

Scripture presents a high view of women. Sexual pleasures are a gift from God to be enjoyed by both males and females within the confines of marriage. The Song of Solomon, for example, portrays the desire for love of the Shulammite shepherdess as something that should and would be fulfilled. First Corinthians 7 clearly says that married partners should provide sexual gratification for each other. And Hebrews 13:4 says that the marriage bed is pure. These instructions prove that God wants women to enjoy making love too.

The Bible teaches specifically against mutilation of our bodies. "Do not cut your bodies for the dead or put tattoo marks on yourselves. I am the Lord" (Leviticus 19:28). Female circumcision debases women and robs them of pleasure with their husbands. When women are treated honorably they can be lovingly responsive to their husbands.

Abraham Was an Intercessor

> The men turned away and went toward Sodom, but Abraham remained standing before the Lord. Then Abraham approached him and said: "Will you sweep away the righteous with the wicked? What if there are fifty righteous people in the city? Will you really sweep it away and not spare the place for the sake of the fifty righteous people in it? Far be it from you to do such a thing — to kill the righteous with the wicked, treating the righteous and the wicked alike. Far be it from you! Will not the Judge of all the earth do right?"
>
> The Lord said, "If I find fifty righteous people in the city of Sodom, I will spare the whole place for their sake."
>
> Then Abraham spoke up again: "Now that I have been so bold as

to speak to the Lord, though I am nothing but dust and ashes, what if the number of the righteous is five less than fifty? Will you destroy the whole city for lack of five people?"

"If I find forty-five there," he said, "I will not destroy it."

Once again he spoke to him, "What if only forty are found there?"

He said, "For the sake of forty, I will not do it."

Then he said, "May the Lord not be angry, but let me speak. What if only thirty can be found there?"

He answered, "I will not do it if I find thirty there."

Abraham said, "Now that I have been so bold as to speak to the Lord, what if only twenty can be found there?"

He said, "For the sake of twenty, I will not destroy it."

Then he said, "May the Lord not be angry, but let me speak just once more. What if only ten can be found there?"

He answered, "For the sake of ten, I will not destroy it."

When the Lord had finished speaking with Abraham, he left, and Abraham returned home. (Genesis 18:22-33)

Abraham's insistence and persistence, his appeal to the mercy of God, and his concern for those for whom he prayed, all indicate that Abraham cared about people and was willing to intercede on their behalf. He is a model for prayer warriors to examine and duplicate.

> "Some of the things God is willing to do and wants to do He does not do because there is no one interceding."

History is changed by intercessors. History is made by prayerful people. Prayer warriors seek to know the plans of God and then cooperate with Him by interceding on behalf of what He wants to do.

We do not know why God waits for people to pray, but Scripture gives evidence that He does. Some of the things God is willing to do and wants to do He does not do because there is no one interceding. "I looked for a man among them who would build up the wall and stand before me in the gap on behalf of the land so I would not have to destroy it, but I found none" (Ezekiel 22:30).

> I urge, then, first of all, that requests, prayers, intercession and thanksgiving be made for everyone — for kings and all those in authority, that we may live peaceful and quiet lives in all godliness and holiness. This is good, and pleases God our Savior, who wants all men to be saved and to come to a knowledge of the truth. (1 Timothy 2:1-4)

Will you follow Abraham's example and stand in the gap before God on behalf of cities, people, God's purposes, His kingdom, and His church? Through intercession for others, you have an opportunity to move far beyond the geographic boundaries of provinces, states, and nations and bless people who may never know of your efforts on their behalf. God loves intercessors.

Abraham Was Really Tested

Abraham was a slow learner where his wife was concerned. Yet what an awesome act of devotion and obedience to God he rendered when he offered up his son Isaac. God knows what He's doing in all His dealings with us. This is beautifully demonstrated with Abraham, who loved and trusted his God.

> Some time later God tested Abraham. He said to him, "Abraham!"
>
> "Here I am," he replied.
>
> Then God said, "Take your son, your only son, whom you love — Isaac — and go to the region of Moriah. Sacrifice him there as a burnt offering on a mountain I will show you."
>
> Early the next morning, Abraham got up and loaded his donkey. He took with him two of his servants and his son Isaac. When he had cut enough wood for the burnt offering, he set out for the place God had told him about. On the third day Abraham looked up and saw the place in the distance. He said to his servants, "Stay here with the donkey while I and the boy go over there. We will worship and then we will come back to you."

Abraham took the wood for the burnt offering and placed it on his son Isaac, and he himself carried the fire and the knife. As the two of them went on together, Isaac spoke up and said to his father Abraham, "Father?"

"Yes, my son?" Abraham replied.

"The fire and wood are here," Isaac said, "but where is the lamb for the burnt offering?"

Abraham answered, "God himself will provide the lamb for the burnt offering, my son." And the two of them went on together.

When they reached the place God had told him about, Abraham built an altar there and arranged the wood on it. He bound his son Isaac and laid him on the altar, on top of the wood. Then he reached out his hand and took the knife to slay his son. But the angel of the Lord called out to him from heaven, "Abraham! Abraham!"

"Here I am," he replied.

"Do not lay a hand on the boy," he said. "Do not do anything to him. Now I know that you fear God, because you have not withheld from me your son, your only son."

Abraham looked up and there in a thicket he saw a ram caught by its horns. He went over and took the ram and sacrificed it as a burnt offering instead of his son. So Abraham called that place The Lord Will Provide. And to this day it is said, "On the mountain of the Lord, it will be provided."

The angel of the Lord called to Abraham from heaven a second time and said, "I swear by myself, declares the Lord, that because you have done this and have not withheld your son, your only son, I will surely bless you and make your descendants as numerous as the stars in the sky and as the sand on the seashore. Your descendants will take possession of the cities of their enemies, and through your offspring all nations on earth will be blessed, because you have obeyed me."

Then Abraham returned to his servants, and they set off together for Beersheba. And Abraham stayed in Beersheba. (Genesis 22:1–19)

Moriah, the mountain on which God told Abraham to sacrifice his son, is likely the hill near Jerusalem where Solomon built the temple. Or it may be Golgotha, where God the Father did to His Son what Abraham did symbolically.

Today, we fail to appreciate the full impact of this story because we already know the end. But Abraham did not know how things would work out. Also, we know God does not require human sacrifices. But Abraham lived in an age when people did not know that. And Isaac was Abraham's dearly beloved son, born to him in his old age as a result of God's promise to him years earlier. So this was a real and difficult test for Abraham.

Wouldn't it be nice if, after we passed numerous tests in our formative ministry years, we could coast along during our final, more productive years? This is not the case. We will face tests as long as we live and work in ministry because God is continually preparing us for important assignments and responsibilities here and in the next life. This is a lifelong process. If you stay focused on God's goals for you, you will pass every test triumphantly.

This test of Abraham's faith defies human logic. We cannot begin to comprehend the trauma of such a request, to slay one's own beloved son. But Abraham obediently did what God told him to do. As we move into the more influential years of mature ministry, may Abraham's example inspire and encourage us.

For Further Thought

- How do you know God has called you into Christian work?
- Are you a worshipper, building altars everywhere you go?
- In a cross-cultural situation, do you give others the benefit of the doubt on moral issues?
- What lesson can you learn by observing Sarah's faith and her willingness to cooperate with her husband even when he was making a mistake?
- What will you do differently next time you need to separate from a colleague?
- What do you feel the Lord would have you do to develop and train your staff?
- Do you revise your goals and objectives periodically? If so, what advantage do you find in doing this?
- What did you learn the last time you tried to "help" God with your own human strength or wisdom?
- What righteous act of obedience in your life has become a badge of success to you the way circumcision was to some in the early church?
- Did you learn anything new about intercession from Abraham's prayer for Sodom and Gomorrah?
- Have you experienced anything like what Abraham did when he was asked to sacrifice his son?

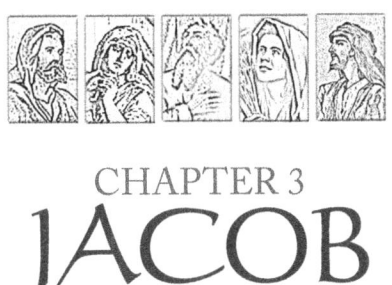

CHAPTER 3
JACOB

Jacob, grandson of Abraham, was a wrestler even before he was born. As an adult, he was a plotter, a trickster, and a schemer. Since I too can be like that when I try to control people and situations, I can identify with Jacob. Yet God blessed Jacob even though he was deceitful. Why? Schemer Jacob had two redeeming spiritual qualities. He valued the spiritual blessings in his heritage, and he knew the power of prayer. Jacob's prayer life was a powerful, life-changing element in his life. I want to follow his lead in both of those aspects.

As Christians, we influence others. We lead others to the degree that we influence them. The following ten lessons from the life of Jacob will help us increase our godly influence.

Signs from the Womb

Even before Jacob was born, indications of a brotherly struggle were apparent.

> This is the account of the family line of Abraham's son Isaac. Abraham became the father of Isaac, and Isaac was forty years old when he married Rebekah, daughter of Bethuel the Aramean from Paddan Aram and sister of Laban the Aramean.
>
> Isaac prayed to the Lord on behalf of his wife, because she was childless. The Lord answered his prayer, and his wife Rebekah became pregnant. The babies jostled each other within her, and she said, "Why is this happening to me?" So she went to inquire of

the Lord. The Lord said to her, "Two nations are in your womb, and two peoples from within you will be separated; one people will be stronger than the other, and the older will serve the younger."

When the time came for her to give birth, there were twin boys in her womb. The first to come out was red, and his whole body was like a hairy garment; so they named him Esau. After this, his brother came out, with his hand grasping Esau's heel; so he was named Jacob. Isaac was sixty years old when Rebekah gave birth to them. (Genesis 25:19–26)

The name Esau means "hairy," and Jacob means "he grasps the heel," which has become a Hebrew idiom for "he deceives."

Accurate interpretation of human situations and life circumstances is one of the ways God speaks to us. Job's friend Elihu said to Job, "For God does speak — now one way, now another — though no one perceives it" (Job 33:14). Elihu calls our attention to the need to listen.

We can miss God's messages if we fail to inquire of Him. But Jacob's mother, Rebekah, didn't. She wanted to understand the deeper and spiritual meaning of what was happening, so she asked God.

We do not know the intensity of the struggle that went on in Rebekah's womb or why she inquired of God concerning this. But when she asked God to help her understand the unusual wrestling match, God gave her the answer.

> "We can miss God's messages if we fail to inquire of Him."

God speaks to us through dreams, conversations, events of nature, counsel from friends, and supernatural signs. But these do us no good unless we are open to hearing from God by any means at any time. We should live our lives openly before Him, acknowledge His involvement, and try to humbly interpret the details of life so we catch everything He is saying to us.

But we should not be merely imaginative or dreamy or make something out of nothing. Be open to interpret circumstances, but be cautious lest your imagination deceive you. Learn to hear, discern, and listen to the voice of God by whatever circumstances He uses to communicate with you. Some of us ignore the signs God gives us. Others imagine any unusual phenomenon to be a sign from God. Somewhere between these two extremes is a wise and sensitive position. Let us strive for that balanced middle ground.

Valuing the Valuable

> Once when Jacob was cooking some stew, Esau came in from the open country, famished. He said to Jacob, "Quick, let me have some of that red stew! I'm famished!" That is why he was also called Edom.
>
> Jacob replied, "First sell me your birthright."
>
> "Look, I am about to die," Esau said. "What good is the birthright to me?"
>
> But Jacob said, "Swear to me first." So he swore an oath to him, selling his birthright to Jacob.
>
> Then Jacob gave Esau some bread and some lentil stew. He ate and drank, and then got up and left.
>
> So Esau despised his birthright. (Genesis 25:29–34)

It is fair to assume that Esau and Jacob both heard the same family stories and oral traditions from their parents. Terah, they would have been told, was the father of Abraham, Nahor, and Haran. Haran died, leaving the two brothers, Abraham and Nahor. Abraham became the paternal grandfather of Esau and Jacob; Nahor, father of Bethuel, became grandfather of Rebekah and great-grandfather of Esau and Jacob.

Stories of their grandfathers, Bethuel and Abraham, would have been told around the fire in the evenings. Among those stories would have been Abraham's call from God and his travels to Canaan, God's plan for him, his experiences in Egypt, and rescuing Lot.

What caused Esau to take this family heritage so lightly? And what stirred Jacob to seriously ponder, value, and prize that heritage? We don't know. But Jacob's behavior does indicate that he valued the birthright Esau despised.

The same thing happens today. People who live side by side, with almost all of life's circumstances appearing the same, often have highly divergent value systems. Some live for this life and others for the next one. Some see only the physical world, while others recognize the permanence and lasting value of presently invisible realities. The Christian who would influence people toward kingdom life will value the promises, heritage, and abundant spiritual life God offers. We will best lead by example if we follow Jacob's good pattern.

The Inappropriateness of Deceit

Coached by his mother, Jacob learned to obtain his goals by deceit. We cannot know how much blame to lay at Rebekah's feet and how much belongs to Jacob. Neither do we know if Rebekah was motivated by the revelation God had given her while the children were in her womb. Nevertheless, the influence he received from his mother may help us understand Jacob's deceitfulness, though it will not excuse it.

Isaac had grown old. Before he died, he prepared to bless his firstborn, Esau. But Rebekah, perhaps remembering what God had shown her while the two sons wrestled in her womb, wanted Jacob to receive the blessing instead. Notice what Genesis 27:8–29 says:

> "Now, my son, listen carefully and do what I tell you: Go out to the flock and bring me two choice young goats, so I can prepare some tasty food for your father, just the way he likes it. Then take it to your father to eat, so that he may give you his blessing before he dies."
>
> Jacob said to Rebekah his mother, "But my brother Esau is a hairy man while I have smooth skin. What if my father touches me? I would appear to be tricking him and would bring down a curse on myself rather than a blessing."
>
> His mother said to him, "My son, let the curse fall on me. Just do what I say; go and get them for me."
>
> So he went and got them and brought them to his mother, and she prepared some tasty food, just the way his father liked it. Then Rebekah took the best clothes of Esau her older son, which she had in the house, and put them on her younger son Jacob. She also covered his hands and the smooth part of his neck with the

goatskins. Then she handed to her son Jacob the tasty food and the bread she had made.

He went to his father and said, "My father."

"Yes, my son," he answered. "Who is it?"

Jacob said to his father, "I am Esau your firstborn. I have done as you told me. Please sit up and eat some of my game, so that you may give me your blessing."

Isaac asked his son, "How did you find it so quickly, my son?"

"The Lord your God gave me success," he replied.

Then Isaac said to Jacob, "Come near so I can touch you, my son, to know whether you really are my son Esau or not."

Jacob went close to his father Isaac, who touched him and said, "The voice is the voice of Jacob, but the hands are the hands of Esau." He did not recognize him, for his hands were hairy like those of his brother Esau; so he proceeded to bless him. "Are you really my son Esau?" he asked.

"I am," he replied.

Then he said, "My son, bring me some of your game to eat, so that I may give you my blessing."

Jacob brought it to him and he ate; and he brought some wine and he drank. Then his father Isaac said to him, "Come here, my son, and kiss me."

So he went to him and kissed him. When Isaac caught the smell of his clothes, he blessed him and said, "Ah, the smell of my son is like the smell of a field that the Lord has blessed. May God give you of heaven's dew and of earth's richness — an abundance of grain and new wine. May nations serve you and peoples bow down to you. Be lord over your brothers, and may the sons of your mother bow down to you. May those who curse you be cursed and those who bless you be blessed."

Jacob agreed to the deceitful plan his mother proposed. Years later, he deceived his father-in-law when planning to depart for Canaan after twenty years in Paddan Aram. "Moreover, Jacob deceived Laban the Aramean by not telling him he was running away" (Genesis 31:20).

The end does not justify the means. Lying is never appropriate. If you want to be an influential Christian, you must establish a reputation for always telling the truth.

The moral exception to this rule would be if an evil person were seeking to kill an innocent person. In that case, deceit to protect the innocent is appropriate. Human life has the greater value in such cases.

God could have worked supernaturally to bring the blessing to Jacob since Esau did not value it. He had already told Rebekah that the older would serve the younger. The Lord would take care of His word to Rebekah without Rebekah and Jacob resorting to deceit.

> **If you want to be an influential Christian, you must establish a reputation for always telling the truth.**

And God could have enabled Jacob to depart from Laban without personal loss. As it turned out, when Laban caught up with Jacob, God spoke to Laban in a dream and warned him not to injure his son-in-law, Jacob. God clearly proved His ability to protect His own. He does not need us to deceive others in order for us to advance our own agendas.

When Love Blinds

It is right to be in love with one's spouse. Proverbs says to be "intoxicated with her love" (Proverbs 5:19). But nowhere does the Bible suggest we are to put aside our rationale or the thinking part of ourselves. We are to keep every thought under control.

We are to love God with our minds. We are not to let our emotions cause us to behave irrationally.

Jacob loved Rachel. That was fine, but he should still have kept his wits about him in dealing with her. How many difficulties between suitors or married partners would be solved if we made sensible decisions, not just emotional ones?

> Now Laban had two daughters; the name of the older was Leah, and the name of the younger was Rachel. Leah had weak eyes, but Rachel had a lovely figure and was beautiful. Jacob was in love with Rachel and said, "I'll work for you seven years in return for your younger daughter Rachel."
>
> Laban said, "It's better that I give her to you than to some other man. Stay here with me." So Jacob served seven years to get Rachel, but they seemed like only a few days to him because of his love for her. (Genesis 29:16–20)

Jacob's love for Rachel is commendable to a degree. But if he could not see the wrong that needed to be confronted, he loved her too blindly.

Many years later, as Jacob was taking his family back to Canaan, "Rachel stole her father's household gods" (Genesis 31:19). Jacob was very much in love with Rachel, but perhaps he did not know her very well. He evidently had no idea that she had taken her father's household gods, nor that she even valued them. He should have been more in touch.

Why would she take the idols if they were meaningless to her? She evidently valued them in some way. Jacob should have been in closer contact with his wife's thinking. Further, he should have been strong enough to confront her if she was wrong.

Husbands and wives need to use their heads to prevent avoidable problems. I love my wife, but I occasionally confront her. She loves me, and she also confronts me. We both like it that way. We feel much safer.

Jacob and his family secretly gathered his herds and left Laban's home to return to his homeland of Canaan. Meanwhile, Rachel secretively took a fateful step. "When Laban had gone to shear his sheep, Rachel stole her father's household gods" (Genesis 31:19). Laban, discovering the theft, pursued Jacob and confronted him.

> "Now you have gone off because you longed to return to your father's household. But why did you steal my gods?"
>
> Jacob answered Laban, "I was afraid, because I thought you would take your daughters away from me by force. But if you find anyone who has your gods, that one shall not live. In the presence of our relatives, see for yourself whether there is

anything of yours here with me; and if so, take it." Now Jacob did not know that Rachel had stolen the gods.

So Laban went into Jacob's tent and into Leah's tent and into the tent of the two female servants, but he found nothing. After he came out of Leah's tent, he entered Rachel's tent. Now Rachel had taken the household gods and put them inside her camel's saddle and was sitting on them. Laban searched through everything in the tent but found nothing.

Rachel said to her father, "Don't be angry, my lord, that I cannot stand up in your presence; I'm having my period."

So he searched but could not find the household gods. (Genesis 31:30–35)

Sometime later Jacob and his family moved farther into Canaan.

Then they moved on from Bethel. While they were still some distance from Ephrath, Rachel began to give birth and had great difficulty. And as she was having great difficulty in childbirth, the midwife said to her, "Don't despair, for you have another son." As she breathed her last — for she was dying — she named her son Ben-Oni. But his father named him Benjamin.

So Rachel died and was buried on the way to Ephrath (that is, Bethlehem). Over her tomb Jacob set up a pillar, and to this day that pillar marks Rachel's tomb. (Genesis 35:16–20)

One can only imagine the grief Jacob felt as he buried his beloved wife. He had many disappointments in family and business during his twenty years in Paddan Aram. However, Rachel had been the thrilling and beautiful exception to his many sorrows. She had been his comfort and joy. And now she was gone.

We do not know how Jacob grieved, or if he remembered saying that whoever took Laban's idols should die. If so, he surely regretted not keeping his tongue in control. Jacob ignorantly and tragically pronounced his beloved Rachel's death sentence.

It takes strong moral fiber to confront someone dearly beloved. It is better to be strong, show tough love, and enjoy the advantages of character growth than overlook a loved one's fault in weakness.

Christians of influence today cannot afford to allow emotions to distract them from the serious task of leading God's people. They must model morally upright behavior, attitudes, policies, and service. Each of us must ask the Holy Spirit to help us know how to apply this lesson to our own situations.

We must keep our tongues in control, even when strong emotions press us in other directions. That is the character development that increases the Christian's authority. A person who leads by mere emotion will not be dependable, because emotions are not dependable. Emotions have a healthy role to fulfill. However, assisting others in rational decisions that require accountability, responsibility, and authenticity is not one of them.

> "It takes strong moral fiber to confront someone dearly beloved."

Don't let your love blind you. No matter how much you love your spouse, staff member, or child, keep your head about you. Confront wrong; you will both benefit.

Waiting for God's Time

We are not informed about how many times during his twenty years in Paddan Aram Jacob longed to return to Canaan. But we do know that he stayed, endured, and waited, until the day God gave him the direction he needed.

The following narrative tells the story of Jacob's rapid departure from Paddan Aram.

> Jacob heard that Laban's sons were saying, "Jacob has taken everything our father owned and has gained all this wealth from what belonged to our father."
>
> And Jacob noticed that Laban's attitude toward him was not what it had been.
>
> Then the Lord said to Jacob, "Go back to the land of your fathers and to your relatives, and I will be with you."
>
> So Jacob sent word to Rachel and Leah to come out to the fields

where his flocks were. He said to them, "I see that your father's attitude toward me is not what it was before, but the God of my father has been with me." (Genesis 31:1–5)

During the night, before Laban caught up with Jacob, God told Laban not to harm Jacob. Would God have protected Jacob if Jacob had fled prematurely? We are not told the answer to this question. But we do know that Jacob was moving in God's timing and that God supernaturally protected him, his wives, his children, and his livestock.

Scripture contains many illustrations of moving in God's timing. Jacob knew this. Later, he moved to Egypt only when God directed him to do so. His descendant, David, knew the value of waiting behind the balsam trees for the sound of marching in the branches. That let him know it was God's time to move into battle.

God's time is always worth waiting for.

Persevering in Prayer — and Limping

As Jacob neared Canaan, he knew he would soon be facing his brother. Had Esau forgiven him? Was Esau still seeking revenge? In an attempt to pacify his brother, Jacob sent liberal gifts ahead with his family while he stayed behind alone to pray.

Even though he had done everything he could think of to appease Esau, Jacob knew that bigger issues were involved than could be purchased with a mere gift of livestock. So Jacob prayed.

> Then Jacob prayed, "O God of my father Abraham, God of my father Isaac, Lord, you who said to me, 'Go back to your country and your relatives, and I will make you prosper,' I am unworthy of all the kindness and faithfulness you have shown your servant. I had only my staff when I crossed this Jordan, but now I have become two camps. Save me, I pray, from the hand of my brother Esau, for I am afraid he will come and attack me, and also the mothers with their children. But you have said, 'I will surely make you prosper and will make your descendants like the sand of the sea, which cannot be counted.'" (Genesis 32:9–12)

Jacob was in a desperate situation. But his strong desire and intense passion toward God is illustrated by the wrestling that took place by the brook Jabbok.

The Lord often uses hard times to cause us to pursue Him passionately.

> That night Jacob got up and took his two wives, his two female servants and his eleven sons and crossed the ford of the Jabbok. After he had sent them across the stream, he sent over all his possessions. So Jacob was left alone, and a man wrestled with him till daybreak. When the man saw that he could not overpower him, he touched the socket of Jacob's hip so that his hip was wrenched as he wrestled with the man. Then the man said, "Let me go, for it is daybreak."
>
> But Jacob replied, "I will not let you go unless you bless me."
>
> The man asked him, "What is your name?"
>
> "Jacob," he answered.
>
> Then the man said, "Your name will no longer be Jacob, but Israel, because you have struggled with God and with human beings and have overcome."
>
> Jacob said, "Please tell me your name."
>
> But he replied, "Why do you ask my name?" Then he blessed him there.
>
> So Jacob called the place Peniel, saying, "It is because I saw God face to face, and yet my life was spared."
>
> The sun rose above him as he passed Peniel, and he was limping because of his hip. Therefore to this day the Israelites do not eat the tendon attached to the socket of the hip, because the socket of Jacob's hip was touched near the tendon. (Genesis 32:22-32)

Jacob's desperate and impassioned words, "I will not let you go unless you bless me," are powerful. They express complete commitment to the process. And they challenge us to keep praying until we receive the answer. If we give up before we get our answer, we are not praying like Jacob.

The name change from Jacob (which means "supplanter" or "cheater") to Israel (which means "he struggles with God") has profound implications for Jacob, his descendants, and anyone in subsequent generations who wants to pursue God tenaciously. Jacob's insistence that God answer his prayer and his determination to pray until he got his answer challenge us to persevere as Jacob did.

Hosea presents us with an interesting insight into the Genesis account of Jacob at Jabbok. Genesis gives us the contents of the prayer, and Hosea tells us of the passion: "In the womb he grasped his brother's heel; as a man he struggled with God. He struggled with the angel and overcame him; he wept and begged for his favor. He found him at Bethel and talked with him there" (Hosea 12:3–4).

Jacob, now Israel, evidently exerted himself physically, for he walked with a shuffle for the rest of his life. If we allow Israel's limp to symbolize a brokenness or humility before God, an acknowledgment of human dependence on God, then we too must learn to walk with a shuffle, recognizing that we are nothing without God. Dependence on God actually makes more things possible. In our spirits, we can be stronger when we recognize our weakness. We are more victorious when we walk with a spiritual limp.

> "If we give up before we get our answer, we are not praying like Jacob."

The Problems of Favoritism

Impartiality in dealing with our children is not a small issue. God delights in kindness, justice, and righteousness (Jeremiah 9:24). Many family problems could be avoided, reduced, or even eliminated if parents would acknowledge their partiality toward one child or children over others and change their attitudes and behavior.

Children are a gift from God. He gives us these precious gifts, and it is right for us to appreciate each gift equally. "Children are a heritage from the Lord, offspring a reward from him" (Psalm 127:3).

Jacob and Esau experienced favoritism from their parents.

> The boys grew up, and Esau became a skillful hunter, a man of the open country, while Jacob was content to stay at home among

> the tents. Isaac, who had a taste for wild game, loved Esau, but Rebekah loved Jacob. (Genesis 25:27-28)

Each brother had a parental ally. We can imagine what kind of sibling rivalry was generated by this situation.

Having experienced favoritism growing up, and the problems and grief that resulted from it, Jacob should have learned the importance of loving each child equally. But in the next generation Jacob followed his father's example and repeated his father's error. Jacob loved Joseph more than he loved Joseph's brothers.

> Now Israel loved Joseph more than any of his other sons, because he had been born to him in his old age; and he made a richly ornamented robe for him. When his brothers saw that their father loved him more than any of them, they hated him and could not speak a kind word to him. (Genesis 37:3-4)

Jacob experienced grief with his sons' infighting and later suffered sorrow from the loss of his son Joseph. This sorrow was partially due to Jacob's creation of the tension and jealousy that existed between Joseph and his brothers as a result of Jacob's obvious favoritism.

Each child is unique, and each child should be trained to be successful with his or her gifts. Not all children are athletic, musical, academically inclined, or physically attractive. However, each child is uniquely created and is a precious gift from God. All children should be appreciated for his or her uniqueness and encouraged to develop in keeping with that child's own natural gifts, not criticized for not having the gifts God did not give him or her. This is the deeper meaning of "Start children off on the way they should go and even when they are old they will not turn from it" (Proverbs 22:6). Our children will be more successful if we raise them in keeping with their natural gifting.

> **Each child is unique, and each child should be trained to be successful with his or her gifts.**

Tradition may value one gender over another for cultural reasons, but this too is incorrect. God creates both little boys and little girls, and He has a plan for each. Parents have the awesome privilege of guiding their children along the paths that will lead them to be successful, fulfilling God's plans and dreams for them.

"One who is slack in his work is a close relative of one who destroys" (Proverbs 18:9). This instructive bit of wisdom indicates that not aggressively pushing forward in the right direction of an enterprise is not much different from actively destroying something. The difference is only in the degree of the error. The slacker does not push forward and his neglect damages the potential success; the destroyer actively tears down and thereby thwarts the development of potential. Both destroy because both do not push forward in the development of the project.

Let's apply this to raising children. Parents should help each child develop in a way consistent with his or her abilities. Otherwise, the parents are not contributing to the child becoming what he or she could become. In other words, a parent "destroys" a child by not helping him or her fulfill his or her potential.

If you want to be and raise an effective and influential Christian, you need to come to terms with the issue of fairness in your family. The family is the training ground for society's leaders; the skills we need to lead others are parental skills. The family is where you prove your qualifications for influencing others (see 1 Timothy 3:4–5).

What tensions exist in your family due to partiality? In what way are you overlooking the potential of one of your children? Do you love each one the same? Do you show that love equally? Are you affectionate with each of your children? Are you proactive about raising each of them to develop his or her full potential? Do you love one child more than the other? The Holy Spirit will show you what to do if you need to make any changes.

Needless Grief

Jacob had bemoaned the loss of Rachel and now wept over the loss of Rachel's son, Joseph. But his despair over the loss of Joseph was in vain. Joseph was not really dead, as Jacob had been led to believe. While nomadic life for Jacob's family continued in Canaan, Joseph was learning lessons in Egypt that would position him to be useful to Egypt and to all of Jacob's family.

Most of our own worries are not only unnecessary but counterproductive. Psychologists say that more than 95 percent of the things we worry about never come true. What percent of the things you have worried about in the past actually happened? Does that much energy expended in worrying about a problem that did not exist justify the amount of worry you invested?

When the opportunity presented itself, Jacob's other sons sold Joseph into slavery. They led their father to believe Joseph had been killed by a wild animal.

> Then they got Joseph's robe, slaughtered a goat and dipped the robe in the blood. They took the ornamented robe back to their father and said, "We found this. Examine it to see whether it is your son's robe."
>
> He recognized it and said, "It is my son's robe! Some ferocious animal has devoured him. Joseph has surely been torn to pieces."
>
> Then Jacob tore his clothes, put on sackcloth and mourned for his son many days. All his sons and daughters came to comfort him, but he refused to be comforted. "No," he said, "in mourning will I go down to the grave to my son." So his father wept for him.
>
> Meanwhile, the Midianites sold Joseph in Egypt to Potiphar, one of Pharaoh's officials, the captain of the guard. (Genesis 37:31-36)

We live at the level of our perceptions. We react emotionally to what we *think* is happening even when it differs from reality. Jacob was living at the level of his perception — a misperception of what was happening with Joseph. Jacob's needless anxiety illustrates the wisdom of praying about everything and not worrying about anything. To pray rather than worry is not irresponsibility; it is authentic responsibility — response ability — the ability to respond correctly.

> "Prayer is productive; worry is counter-productive."

Prayer is productive; worry is counterproductive. If the enemy can cause a man or woman of God to be preoccupied with apprehension, he can handicap us greatly. Christians of character refuse to be disabled by anxiety.

Choose Your Character

God Uses Even Flawed Vessels Who Pray

Pharaoh was the king of Egypt, and Jacob was a foreign commoner. Pharaoh was a ruler, Jacob was a refugee with a promise. Did royalty bless the foreign traveler? Did the powerful bless the powerless? Who blessed whom? Yes, the powerful blessed the less powerful. Jacob, not Pharaoh, was the powerful one. Jacob knew God and how to pray. Jacob blessed the monarch. Is there a lesson here?

If we wish to be people of spiritual power as Jacob was, we too can be positioned to bless others. The invisible world has power over the physical world. There isn't anything that cannot be solved by prayer.

> Then Joseph brought his father Jacob in and presented him before Pharaoh. After Jacob blessed Pharaoh, Pharaoh asked him, "How old are you?"
>
> And Jacob said to Pharaoh, "The years of my pilgrimage are a hundred and thirty. My years have been few and difficult, and they do not equal the years of the pilgrimage of my fathers." Then Jacob blessed Pharaoh and went out from his presence. (Genesis 47:7–10)

Those who spend time with God are equipped to bless others. We become like those with whom we spend time. The more time we spend with God, the more we take on His character, attitudes, optimism, confidence, and courage.

> **"Those who spend time with God are equipped to bless others."**

Can you imagine God afraid? Can you envision God wringing His hands and fretting? Let us learn to be close to God so that we are equipped to bless others at every possible juncture. I want to be a God-chaser. That will equip me to be a blessing to people around me.

The Long-Range Consequences of Looking Forward

Jacob lived like he had a future. He planted that faith in his sons. Today, the descendants of Jacob still have that hope and confidence. The accurate and dramatic fulfillment of Bible prophecy, especially regarding the rise of the nation of Israel, is a reminder that our sovereign God has history in His control.

Jacob looked forward and gave his children instructions regarding the return of his body to Canaan.

> Then Jacob called for his sons and said: "Gather around so I can tell you what will happen to you in days to come."
>
> All these are the twelve tribes of Israel, and this is what their father said to them when he blessed them, giving each the blessing appropriate to him.
>
> Then he gave them these instructions: "I am about to be gathered to my people. Bury me with my fathers in the cave in the field of Ephron the Hittite, the cave in the field of Machpelah, near Mamre in Canaan, which Abraham bought along with the field as a burial place from Ephron the Hittite. There Abraham and his wife Sarah were buried, there Isaac and his wife Rebekah were buried, and there I buried Leah. The field and the cave in it were bought from the Hittites."
>
> When Jacob had finished giving instructions to his sons, he drew his feet up into the bed, breathed his last and was gathered to his people. (Genesis 49:1, 28-33)

The history of the human race will have an appropriate conclusion. God has a massive, intricately developed plan that is unfolding even today. No other religious book contains details of human history, written in advance as prophecy, such as we find in the Bible.

Jacob looked forward. The ability to look forward to what God has in the future belongs to all who serve Jacob's God.

Daniel and Ezekiel recorded far more prophetic information than either Jacob or his son Joseph did. But Jacob and Joseph, by their actions, demonstrated their

> "Jacob's dying request to be carried back to Canaan was his way of expressing the value he placed on his spiritual heritage."

Choose Your Character

expectation of God's future for their descendants. Their instructions to take their remains back to the Promised Land reinforced their belief in the future of Israel as a nation. Jacob's dying request to be carried back to Canaan was his way of expressing the value he placed on his spiritual heritage.

I like to capture the messages of Bible personalities and communicate them in a way that speaks to our grandchildren's young minds. A song is one way to do this. My wife and I have a grandson named Jacob. In July of 2004, just months after Jacob was born, I wrote this song while I was flying from Mahajanga on the west coast of Madagascar to Antsiranana at the northern tip. We sing it often for our Jacob.

> Once a wise boy named Jacob
> Sought the blessings that his brother had scorned.
> Through a trick he obtained the promise,
> And Jacob got a blessing from God.
>
> Jacob knew the power, the power for every hour.
> Jacob knew the power of the promises of God.
>
> Today a wise boy named Jacob
> Seeks the blessings many others have scorned.
> Through prayer he obtains the promise,
> And Jacob gets a blessing from God.
>
> Jacob knows the power, the power for every hour.
> Jacob knows the power of the promises of God.

For Further Thought

- Can you think of a time when you did not confront your spouse (or someone else close to you) when you probably should have? What will you do differently next time something like this happens?
- What criteria would you suggest for determining God's timing in the decisions and moves you will make in life?
- What does it mean to you that Jacob limped after his wrestling match by the Jabbok? Is this something you would like to incorporate into your prayer life?
- When you were growing up, did you experience any negative results from favoritism? How will you guarantee that you will treat your children with equality?
- Have you ever grieved needlessly? What was the major lesson you learned from that experience?
- Have you ever had an opportunity to pray a blessing on another person that you can trace back to your private times of prayer?
- In what way are you living with an expectation for heaven and the arrival of God's kingdom on earth?

CHAPTER 4
JOSEPH

Did you know that Joseph emphasized his dreams of future grandeur beyond just relating it to his family? How hard-hearted would Joseph's brothers have to have been in order to sell their blood brother into slavery? Did you know that the same dreams that caused Joseph trouble as a youth served his best interest and stabilized his faith through the dark, difficult years of imprisonment? These are a few of the things we will examine in this chapter.

Joseph's name appeared in our previous chapter about his father, Jacob. In this chapter, Joseph's narrative carries forward another generation. When Moses recorded Israel's history in the book of Exodus, years after Jacob's and Joseph's lifetimes, Joseph's story received the most thorough treatment.

Joseph was a dreamer. Early in life, these dreams caused him trouble. Later, his dreams encouraged him to maintain his integrity and holiness, helping him through trouble. He eventually even interpreted dreams for others. Joseph knew the power of a dream.

Joseph's Dreams Went to His Head

Joseph became proud in his youth. He allowed his dreams to make him believe he was better than his brothers. Joseph's father questioned his favorite son, because Joseph seemed to believe he was superior even to his parents.

> Joseph had a dream, and when he told it to his brothers, they hated him all the more. He said to them, "Listen to this dream I

had: We were binding sheaves of grain out in the field when suddenly my sheaf rose and stood upright, while your sheaves gathered around mine and bowed down to it."

His brothers said to him, "Do you intend to reign over us? Will you actually rule us?" And they hated him all the more because of his dream and what he had said.

Then he had another dream, and he told it to his brothers. "Listen," he said, "I had another dream, and this time the sun and moon and eleven stars were bowing down to me."

When he told his father as well as his brothers, his father rebuked him and said, "What is this dream you had? Will your mother and I and your brothers actually come and bow down to the ground before you?' His brothers were jealous of him, but his father kept the matter in mind. (Genesis 37:5–11)

The Hebrew form of the word translated "told" in Genesis 37:5 is an accentuated form of the verb. In the Hebrew language, a grammatical addition to a verb changes the nuance to a stronger form with the same meaning. For example, that same grammatical addition makes the verb *kill* become "slaughter." In Joseph's case, *told* becomes "told with emphasis" or "bragged." In other words, young Joseph did not just tell his brothers about his dreams, he told them with apparent boasting. This paints a different picture than if Joseph had humbly related his dream in a neutral manner. Joseph had not yet learned God's purpose for dreams.

> "Dreams hold us on target, inspire us to action."

Dreams give hope, focus, and direction for our energies. Energy without a dream is frantic and meaningless activity. Dreams hold us on target, inspire us to action. Dreams give us healthy ambition and motivate us. Dreams are not given to us by God to inflate our egos, but to encourage us to accomplish things for Him. Dreams are often from God, as were these two of Joseph's.

But dreams are not always from God; sometimes they are the product of human imagination. It is far better to adopt a "wait and see" attitude toward dreams than to become puffed up and proud because of them. Let's learn from Joseph's error. Even if our dreams are from God, humility is the wiser attitude as we wait to see if the dream is from God or not.

Give God your dreams. If He gives them back to you, they are yours; if He does not, they never were.

When dreams get in our spirit, they can do us good and lead us forward. But when they go to our heads, they can become big problems for others and for ourselves.

Joseph's Brothers Sold Him into Slavery

While running an errand for his father, Joseph approached his brothers. As he did, they plotted against him.

"Here comes that dreamer!" they said to each other. "Come now, let's kill him and throw him into one of these cisterns and say that a ferocious animal devoured him. Then we'll see what comes of his dreams."

> When Reuben heard this, he tried to rescue him from their hands. "Let's not take his life," he said. "Don't shed any blood. Throw him into this cistern here in the wilderness, but don't lay a hand on him." Reuben said this to rescue him from them and take him back to his father.
>
> So when Joseph came to his brothers, they stripped him of his robe — the richly ornamented robe he was wearing — and they took him and threw him into the cistern. The cistern was empty; there was no water in it.
>
> As they sat down to eat their meal, they looked up and saw a caravan of Ishmaelites coming from Gilead. Their camels were loaded with spices, balm, and myrrh, and they were on their way to take them down to Egypt.
>
> Judah said to his brothers, "What will we gain if we kill our brother and cover up his blood? Come, let's sell him to the Ishmaelites and not lay our hands on him; after all, he is our brother, our own flesh and blood." His brothers agreed.
>
> So when the Midianite merchants came by, his brothers pulled

Joseph up out of the cistern and sold him for twenty shekels of silver to the Ishmaelites, who took him to Egypt. (Genesis 37:19–28)

The story of Joseph includes a vicious betrayal by blood brothers. Those who sold Joseph into slavery were not his enemies or even strangers; they were his family. Later in the narrative, the brothers reflected on their betrayal. They said to one another, "Surely we are being punished because of our brother. We saw how distressed he was when he pleaded with us for his life, but we would not listen; that's why this distress has come on us" (Genesis 32:21).

Joseph's character was about to be tested. He was seventeen when these developments occurred. Not until he was thirty years of age did he become prime minister of Egypt. With this incident, thirteen years of character development began for seventeen-year-old Joseph.

> "When reverses occur, do not assume all is lost."

When reverses occur, do not assume all is lost. God is at work — working on you, perhaps.

Joseph Succeeded in Management and Resisted Temptation

Satan will try to kill, steal, and destroy your dream. You will be tested as you wait on God to fulfill your dream. Joseph's trust in God, after his character was refined, made him a loving son, magnanimous brother, and powerful national leader. Joseph's God, coupled with faith, morality, and character on Joseph's part, led him to success and the fulfillment of his dreams.

When enduring the temptation of Potiphar's wife, Joseph gave her a wise response: "How then could I do such a wicked thing and sin against God?" (Genesis 39:9). Joseph would not compromise his morality.

> Now Joseph had been taken down to Egypt. Potiphar, an Egyptian who was one of Pharaoh's officials, the captain of the guard, bought him from the Ishmaelites who had taken him there.
>
> The Lord was with Joseph so that he prospered, and he lived in the house of his Egyptian master. When his master saw that the

Lord was with him and that the Lord gave him success in everything he did, Joseph found favor in his eyes and became his attendant. Potiphar put him in charge of his household, and he entrusted to his care everything he owned. From the time he put him in charge of his household and of all that he owned, the Lord blessed the household of the Egyptian because of Joseph. The blessing of the Lord was on everything Potiphar had, both in the house and in the field. So Potiphar left everything he had in Joseph's care; with Joseph in charge, he did not concern himself with anything except the food he ate.

Now Joseph was well-built and handsome, and after a while his master's wife took notice of Joseph and said, "Come to bed with me!"

But he refused. "With me in charge," he told her, "my master does not concern himself with anything in the house; everything he owns he has entrusted to my care. No one is greater in this house than I am. My master has withheld nothing from me except you, because you are his wife. How then could I do such a wicked thing and sin against God?" And though she spoke to Joseph day after day, he refused to go to bed with her or even be with her.

One day he went into the house to attend to his duties, and none of the household servants was inside. She caught him by his cloak and said, "Come to bed with me!" But he left his cloak in her hand and ran out of the house. When she saw that he had left his cloak in her hand and had run out of the house, she called her household servants. "Look," she said to them, "this Hebrew has been brought to us to make sport of us! He came in here to sleep with me, but I screamed. When he heard me scream for help, he left his cloak beside me and ran out of the house."

She kept his cloak beside her until his master came home. Then she told him this story: "That Hebrew slave you brought us came to me to make sport of me. But as soon as I screamed for help, he left his cloak beside me and ran out of the house." (Genesis 39:1-18)

If men and women of God will keep their faith focused on the fulfillment of their God-given dreams, it will help them through temptations. Satan can only kill, steal, and destroy when we yield to his temptations. Knowing that sin is against the God we love gives us power to resist.

God Protected Joseph and Gave Him More Success in Prison

The narrative does not say that Potiphar was angry *with Joseph*, just that he was angry. Potiphar would have known all too well the nature of his own intimate relationship with his wife. He knew his wife's moral level and was also aware of Joseph's high moral character. If Potiphar had believed Joseph were guilty of his wife's accusation, he would have had Joseph killed. Since Potiphar only put Joseph in prison, we may conjecture that Potiphar knew Joseph was innocent. Joseph's reputation was already at work for him. Maybe the prison bars were not so much intended to keep Joseph in, but to keep Potiphar's wife out.

> When his master heard the story his wife told him, saying, "This is how your slave treated me," he burned with anger. Joseph's master took him and put him in prison, the place where the king's prisoners were confined.
>
> But while Joseph was there in the prison, the Lord was with him; he showed him kindness and granted him favor in the eyes of the prison warden. So the warden put Joseph in charge of all those held in the prison, and he was made responsible for all that was done there. The warden paid no attention to anything under Joseph's care, because the Lord was with Joseph and gave him success in whatever he did. (Genesis 39:19–23)

Joseph's reputation for morality saved him. As a Christian of influence in the body of Christ, you too will experience accusations. The best defense is holiness, morality, ethical behavior, trustworthiness, and honesty. Arm yourself with these in advance, as Joseph did.

Joseph Developed Further and Even Served Others in Prison

We might think that Joseph had already endured enough, been tested sufficiently, and had proven himself true. But God was not finished developing him.

> Some time later, the cupbearer and the baker of the king of Egypt offended their master, the king of Egypt. Pharaoh was angry with his two officials, the chief cupbearer and the chief baker, and put them in custody in the house of the captain of the guard, in the same prison where Joseph was confined. The captain of the guard assigned them to Joseph, and he attended them.
>
> After they had been in custody for some time, each of the two men — the cupbearer and the baker of the king of Egypt, who were being held in prison — had a dream the same night, and each dream had a meaning of its own. (Genesis 40:1-5)

When his fellow prisoners asked for an interpretation of their dreams, Joseph could easily have responded by saying, "Ha! Dreams. They don't mean anything." But he did not. Joseph knew dreams could have meanings and interpreted their dreams for them. The king's cupbearer received a good interpretation for his dream.

> When the chief baker saw that Joseph had given a favorable interpretation, he said to Joseph, "I too had a dream: On my head were three baskets of bread. In the top basket were all kinds of baked goods for Pharaoh, but the birds were eating them out of the basket on my head."
>
> "This is what it means," Joseph said. "The three baskets are three days. Within three days Pharaoh will lift off your head and impale your body on a pole. And the birds will eat away your flesh."
>
> Now the third day was Pharaoh's birthday, and he gave a feast for all his officials. He lifted up the heads of the chief cupbearer and the chief baker in the presence of his officials: He restored the chief cupbearer to his position, so that he once again put the cup into Pharaoh's hand — but he impaled the chief baker, just as Joseph had said to them in his interpretation. The chief cupbearer, however, did not remember Joseph; he forgot him. (Genesis 40:16-23)

This further delay would have been a difficult test for Joseph. He was in Egypt because his brothers had sold him, in prison on false charges, and forgotten by a prison mate whom he had helped. Would it ever end? Yes, it would. Two years later, when Pharaoh had a dream that no one could interpret (or because the meaning was so bad that no one had the courage to interpret it), the stage was set. Joseph had been humbled, mellowed, tried, tested, and proven. He was ready. If Joseph had not endured until this juncture, he would not have been able to seize the opportunity that came his way in a timely manner.

What events surround you today? What is happening in your neighborhood, village, city, and nation? What opportunities might the Lord be preparing for you at the same time He is preparing you for them? Remember Joseph and stay faithful.

In God's Time, Joseph Received a Life-Changing Opportunity

Sovereign opportunities are providentially arranged. No human has the power to appear to another in a dream. No one could make Pharaoh have a certain kind of dream. No one can know the future or declare what will be and then make it happen the way God can. Christians who follow Joseph's model also follow the God Joseph trusted.

> Then Joseph said to Pharaoh, "The dreams of Pharaoh are one and the same. God has revealed to Pharaoh what he is about to do. The seven good cows are seven years, and the seven good heads of grain are seven years; it is one and the same dream. The seven lean, ugly cows that came up afterward are seven years, and so are the seven worthless heads of grain scorched by the east wind: They are seven years of famine.
>
> "It is just as I said to Pharaoh: God has shown Pharaoh what he is about to do. Seven years of great abundance are coming throughout the land of Egypt, but seven years of famine will follow them. Then all the abundance in Egypt will be forgotten, and the famine will ravage the land. The abundance in the land will not be remembered, because the famine that follows it will be so severe. The reason the dream was given to Pharaoh in two forms is that the matter has been firmly decided by God, and God will do it soon." (Genesis 41:25–32)

Joseph told the king the meaning of the dream. His assignment was fulfilled. But Joseph did not stop there. He went beyond the requested interpretation of the dream and counseled the king regarding what to do about the problem. Joseph had an answer for a question that had not yet occurred to Pharaoh.

Have you learned to anticipate questions and have an answer ready? This is a fine mark of a leader — whether in the military, academia, business, or church leadership. It is one thing to evaluate, analyze, or articulate the nature of a problem. It is quite another to be prepared to offer a concrete, practical, and workable solution.

> **Joseph had an answer for a question that had not yet occurred to Pharaoh.**

Joseph did not have much time to develop a plan, but he seized the moment and rose to the occasion. He suggested the administrative strategy that would guide the Egyptian commodities policy for the next fourteen years, including the food crisis that loomed ahead. He was ready. Joseph suggested to the king:

> "And now let Pharaoh look for a discerning and wise man and put him in charge of the land of Egypt. Let Pharaoh appoint commissioners over the land to take a fifth of the harvest of Egypt during the seven years of abundance. They should collect all the food of these good years that are coming and store up the grain under the authority of Pharaoh, to be kept in the cities for food. This food should be held in reserve for the country, to be used during the seven years of famine that will come upon Egypt, so that the country may not be ruined by the famine."
>
> The plan seemed good to Pharaoh and to all his officials. So Pharaoh asked them, "Can we find anyone like this man, one in whom is the spirit of God?"
>
> Then Pharaoh said to Joseph, "Since God has made all this known to you, there is no one so discerning and wise as you." (Genesis 41:33-39)

Joseph's hour had arrived. He had been humbled and stretched as he waited on God through discouraging trials. Now he had the wisdom needed for that hour. He was ready. Will you be ready when your hour arrives?

Joseph Was Not Vindictive but Recognized God's Providence

Forgiveness is a mark of greatness. The foolish always try to prove they are right, seek to be vindicated, and desire to be recognized or honored.

The mellowed and humbled Joseph was no longer bragging about his dreams and proudly proclaiming his superiority. He was kind, loving, and understanding. Those are the marks of great character.

When famine overtook the land of Canaan, Jacob sent his sons to Egypt to buy food on two different occasions. Joseph recognized them both times, but did not immediately reveal that he was their brother. Only after some time passed did he reveal his identity.

> Then Joseph could no longer control himself before all his attendants, and he cried out, "Have everyone leave my presence!" So there was no one with Joseph when he made himself known to his brothers. And he wept so loudly that the Egyptians heard him, and Pharaoh's household heard about it.
>
> Joseph said to his brothers, "I am Joseph! Is my father still living?" But his brothers were not able to answer him, because they were terrified at his presence.
>
> Then Joseph said to his brothers, "Come close to me." When they had done so, he said, "I am your brother Joseph, the one you sold into Egypt! And now, do not be distressed and do not be angry with yourselves for selling me here, because it was to save lives that God sent me ahead of you. For two years now there has been famine in the land, and for the next five years there will be no plowing and reaping. But God sent me ahead of you to preserve for you a remnant on earth and to save your lives by a great deliverance.
>
> "So then, it was not you who sent me here, but God. He made me father to Pharaoh, lord of his entire household and ruler of all Egypt. Now hurry back to my father and say to him, 'This is what your son Joseph says: God has made me lord of all Egypt. Come down to me; don't delay. You shall live in the region of Goshen and be near me — you, your children, and grandchildren, your

flocks and herds, and all you have. I will provide for you there, because five years of famine are still to come. Otherwise you and your household and all who belong to you will become destitute.'" (Genesis 45:1–11)

Joseph recognized that God had worked providentially through the betrayal of his brothers, the temptation by his boss' seductive wife, the unjust prison years, and his successful administrative years as Egypt's prime minister. God can use those who recognize His handiwork. Those who blame others and carry grudges are not good tools in God's hands. Those whose character is a reflection of His compassionate, forgiving, and gracious heart — those who are easy to get along with and are easily entreated — are those who best represent Him. Those are the tools He uses the most. Strive to be that kind of tool in God's hands.

> God can use those who recognize His handiwork.

A Lesson Regarding Being as Opposed to Position

I wonder if Jesus had Abraham's descendants in mind when He said, "The last shall be first, and the first last" (Matthew 19:30). Abraham's son Isaac was elevated above Ishmael, the older. Although Jacob was Isaac's second-born, he became greater than his brother Esau. In the next generation, Jacob's eleventh son became ruler of the family. And Joseph's second-born, Ephraim, was elevated above his older brother, Manasseh.

> Now Israel's eyes were failing because of old age, and he could hardly see. So Joseph brought his sons close to him, and his father kissed them and embraced them.
>
> Israel said to Joseph, "I never expected to see your face again, and now God has allowed me to see your children too."
>
> Then Joseph removed them from Israel's knees and bowed down with his face to the ground. And Joseph took both of them, Ephraim on his right toward Israel's left hand and Manasseh on his left toward Israel's right hand, and brought them close to him. But Israel reached out his right hand and put it on Ephraim's head, though he was the younger, and crossing his arms, he put

his left hand on Manasseh's head, even though Manasseh was the firstborn.

Then he blessed Joseph and said, "May the God before whom my fathers Abraham and Isaac walked faithfully, the God who has been my shepherd all my life to this day, the Angel who has delivered me from all harm — may he bless these boys. May they be called by my name and the names of my fathers Abraham and Isaac, and may they increase greatly on the earth."

When Joseph saw his father placing his right hand on Ephraim's head he was displeased; so he took hold of his father's hand to move it from Ephraim's head to Manasseh's head. Joseph said to him, "No, my father, this one is the firstborn; put your right hand on his head."

But his father refused and said, "I know, my son, I know. He too will become a people, and he too will become great. Nevertheless, his younger brother will be greater than he, and his descendants will become a group of nations." He blessed them that day and said, "In your name will Israel pronounce this blessing: 'May God make you like Ephraim and Manasseh.'" So he put Ephraim ahead of Manasseh. (Genesis 48:10–20)

Let no man or woman called and chosen by God regret, fret, or in any way concern him or herself with sequence among siblings within his or her family or position in an organization. God looks at the character of a person, not the position. Character is superior to position any day. Be what God wants you to be, and He will place you where and use you how He wants to use you.

> "God looks at the character of a person, not the position."

"Who are you?" is a more important question than "Where are you?" "What is your character?" is a greater issue than "What is your rank?" The answer to "What are you?" is far more important than the answer to "What is your title?"

Joseph Forgave Those Who Had Treated Him Unfairly

After their father, Jacob, was no longer present to keep the peace among the family, the older brothers felt it necessary to guarantee their safety. After all, they had unjustly treated and offended Joseph. Joseph's brothers had witnessed their father's deep, ongoing, excessive grief over the "death" of Joseph. Perhaps they had not forgiven themselves. That could be part of the reason they fabricated a story to protect themselves.

> When Joseph's brothers saw that their father was dead, they said, "What if Joseph holds a grudge against us and pays us back for all the wrongs we did to him?"
>
> So they sent word to Joseph, saying, "Your father left these instructions before he died: 'This is what you are to say to Joseph: I ask you to forgive your brothers the sins and the wrongs they committed in treating you so badly.' Now please forgive the sins of the servants of the God of your father." When their message came to him, Joseph wept.
>
> His brothers then came and threw themselves down before him. "We are your slaves," they said.
>
> But Joseph said to them, "Don't be afraid. Am I in the place of God? You intended to harm me, but God intended it for good to accomplish what is now being done, the saving of many lives. So then, don't be afraid. I will provide for you and your children." And he reassured them and spoke kindly to them. (Genesis 50:15-21)

Joseph had already put any idea of revenge so far out of his mind that he was grieved that his brothers even thought he might still carry a grudge. In character, he was head and shoulders above his brothers. Someone who carries grudges is small in character. People who are big in character release those who have injured them.

How you treat those who treat you well does not reveal much about your character. How you treat those who cause you damage is a true test of your character.

Joseph Looked Forward to God's Future for Israel

By faith, Joseph anticipated God's eternal purpose for the nation of Israel just as his father, Jacob, had. We may deduce this through the instructions Joseph gave his family regarding what to do with his body. His last wish was forward-looking.

> Joseph stayed in Egypt, along with all his father's family. He lived a hundred and ten years and saw the third generation of Ephraim's children. Also the children of Makir son of Manasseh were placed at birth on Joseph's knees.
>
> Then Joseph said to his brother Israelites, "I am about to die. But God will surely come to your aid and take you up out of this land to the land he promised on oath to Abraham, Isaac and Jacob." And Joseph made the Israelites swear an oath and said, "God will surely come to your aid, and then you must carry my bones up from this place." (Genesis 50:22-25)

The sovereignty, greatness, wisdom, and excellence of our God is shown in many ways, and human history is one of them. The unfolding of the transgenerational plan of God for the nation of Israel is impossible to explain any other way than by the direct work of God among people. How else could prophets predict millenniums ago that the nation of Israel would once again gather to its own land after centuries of dispersion?

The events in the Holy Land since 1948 are a fulfillment of God's plan for His people. Jacob and Joseph wanted to be buried in the Holy Land. They instructed their families to take their remains back there. The only rationale available is that they saw into the future and knew God had a plan for their family to become a nation.

As you read the Hebrew prophets, notice how often they refer to the restoration and re-gathering of God's people Israel to their Promised Land. Watch the unfolding history of Israel today. It indicates what time it is in God's plan for the nations. We are indeed living in the last days.

Jesus will soon return to earth and set up His kingdom. Those who treasure this hope and look to the future with expectation share in the spirit and blessing of Jacob and Joseph. The prophets Ezekiel and Daniel also saw clearly into the distant future and recorded for us the fulfillment of God's glorious plan for the human race.

A strong eschatology (the doctrine of future things) is a good basis for the Christian's hope. It is also a firm foundation for character development. The Christian with a clear sense of what God is doing in the world has kingdom-related motivation that favorably impacts his or her life, behavior, ministry, and leadership.

For Further Thought

- What unfair frame-ups similar to Joseph's have you experienced, and how is God using them to develop you?
- Can you identify any way(s) in which you can serve others while you are in "prison" developing yourself for God?
- Does Joseph's steadfastness during his prison years have any lesson(s) for you as you seek God and wait for Him to use you more influentially?
- Can you see the greatness in Joseph's character in the noble way in which he forgave his brothers? How will you forgive those who have hurt you?
- Have you ever been distressed over your position when you should have been concerned about what kind of character you were developing and who you were becoming?
- What are you doing to make certain that you are forward-looking and expectant rather than backward-looking and despondent?

CHAPTER 5
MOSES

Did you know that our source of information about Moses is Moses himself? And he tells us the bad as well as the good. Did you know that Moses made a serious error that cost him his opportunity to lead the Israelites into the Promised Land? Are you aware that Moses tried several times to get God to change His position on the issue of his entry into Canaan, all to no avail? These lessons are coming up in the pages to follow.

Moses was the first leader of the nation of Israel. His life was a mixture of successes and disappointments. His successes greatly outnumbered his failures; yet because of his mistakes, he did not experience all the privileges he might have otherwise enjoyed.

The lives of Abraham, Moses, Joshua, David, and Elijah all contain lessons about how to lead God's people. Each of these men had a failure that limited his usefulness to God. We can learn from both their successes and their failures.

In this chapter, rather than look at all of Moses' dramatic, influential, and illustrious life, we will draw important lessons by examining just one of his failures and its unfortunate consequences.

Moses Models Transparency and Tells It Like It Is

Moses himself wrote the story of his anger in the wilderness of Zin. He was willing to tell of his weaknesses and failures just as readily as he told of his great accomplishments. Moses did not paint an idealistic picture of himself.

He did not avoid the narratives that show his vulnerability. Yet he is still highly honored by Jews and Christians as one of God's great leaders.

The works of God through us do not depend on our being perfect. The fact that God skillfully uses flawed human tools shows us more about God and His greatness than it does about any requirement of strength or wisdom necessary in the man or woman God uses. In telling the full story, Moses gives us hope that even though we have faults and weaknesses, God can use us.

> "The works of God through us do not depend on our being perfect."

Many Christians believe they cannot let other people, especially unbelievers, see any weaknesses or faults in their lives. They believe self-disclosures will make people turn away from them and from God if they find out Christians are less than perfect. This contributes to a misunderstanding of the grace of God. The people Christians know may begin to think that God demands perfection and will not tolerate any weakness or failure. As a result, they think that God will disqualify them as Christians if they do something wrong. Or they may consider themselves second- or third-rate Christians.

People need to know that failure is a normal part of our human existence and that God understands that. He is willing to forgive and help us continue growing to maturity.

When a Christian fails in some way, he or she should not attempt to hide from other people the fact that he or she is weak. If we admit our weaknesses and failures within the context of demonstrating God's grace for a repentant sinner, people will take courage that God will still love and forgive them if they fail.

For a Christian to publicly show vulnerability and weakness helps our hearers see that we recognize our imperfections. Admitting our sins creates an atmosphere in which others may feel more willing to admit theirs. Rarely will anyone be discouraged by our confessions. More likely, they will appreciate our honesty.

Naturally, we should not be too explicit when confessing our weaknesses.

We should not appear to be relishing or enjoying the memory of a sin or failure. Let's avoid making sin seem attractive or interesting.

Human Beings Have Great Needs

> In the first month the whole Israelite community arrived at the Desert of Zin, and they stayed at Kadesh. There Miriam died and was buried. Now there was no water for the community, and the people gathered in opposition to Moses and Aaron. (Numbers 20:1-2)

All human beings are needy. That is why God called us to minister to others. He selects and uses specific human "tools" to meet the needs of His people.

When the people we serve irritate us, we should remember that if they were perfect, they would not need us. God would not have called us to assist them. Because people have needs, we have opportunities to be useful.

The man or woman of God, as a tool in the hands of God, can be used to effectively meet other people's needs. God could meet their needs directly, but He often uses a human instrument to do it. This is cause for joy in being useful rather than a reason for complaint on our part. We should be honored to experience the joy of usefulness and service.

The people of Israel had a genuine need. They were thirsty and wanted water. People today are also thirsty — thirsty for the water of life, which is Jesus.

Even years after someone begins drinking of the water of salvation, the man or woman of God still longs to drink the waters of God. Our thirst continues and even grows the longer we walk with God. David said, "As the deer pants for streams of water, so my soul pants for you, my God. My soul thirsts for God, for the living God. When can I go and meet with God?" (Psalm 42:1-2). Isaiah said, "Come, all you who are thirsty, come to the waters; and you who have no money, come, buy, and eat!" (Isaiah 55:1). Jesus said, "Let anyone who is thirsty come to me and drink. Whoever believes in me, as Scripture has said, rivers of living water will flow from within them" (John 7:37-38). John gives the invitation in Revelation 22:17, "Let those who are thirsty come; and let all who wish take the free gift of the water of life." The thirsty Israelites symbolize thirsty humanity.

God has called us to serve others the water of life. We should never tire of meeting people's needs or complain about having to serve them. We are vessels taking the true water — Jesus — to them.

When people have needs, God can minister through us. That is our calling. We may become tired and impatient with people at times, as Moses apparently did. But let us not forget to be instruments in God's hands, wherever and whenever the need arises.

> "God has called us to serve others the water of life."

Humans Quarrel with and Oppose the Persons Best Able to Help Them

> They quarreled with Moses and said, "If only we had died when our brothers fell dead before the Lord! Why did you bring the Lord's community into this wilderness, that we and our livestock should die here? Why did you bring us up out of Egypt to this terrible place? It has no grain or figs, grapevines or pomegranates. And there is no water to drink!" (Number 25:3-5)

The thirsty Israelites complained to Aaron and Moses about their thirst. This illustrates the human tendency to blame others when problems occur. The instruments God chooses to minister to people often receive a misguided, unkind, and undeserved backlash as people resist God in their resentment of His authority. People want to be in control of their situations; they want to be their own gods, but they cannot be. They express their anger at God toward His chosen leaders, as though they would like to bring those people down.

You and I will sometimes be mistreated by those we are trying to help. Understanding this dynamic will help us exercise patience with God's people. Some will oppose us, but we are not the problem if we are walking in obedience to God's leading.

The accusations made by the Israelites in Number 25:4-5 are unfair. The people wanted to be free from slavery in Egypt. But when faced with the difficulties of life in the desert, they were quick to blame Moses and Aaron.

We are channels of God's solutions. Yet we are only one of the tools God uses to solve the problems of others.

The Bible says no weapon formed against us will prevail (Isaiah 54:17). No matter how often people oppose you, if you are obeying God, He will defend you. If you take matters into your own hands and try to vindicate yourself, more serious problems will arise. Time and time again throughout the travels to Canaan, God defended Moses when his followers complained. But in the wilderness of Zin, Moses took the matter into his own hands. We can learn from the sad outcome.

Moses taught the people, "Do not seek revenge or bear a grudge against anyone among your people, but love your neighbor as yourself. I am the Lord" (Leviticus 19:18). But Moses forgot what he himself had taught. Just before Israel crossed into Canaan, Moses said, "It is mine to avenge; I will repay" (Deuteronomy 32:35). In Romans 12:19, Paul quotes Moses when he says, "Do not take revenge, my dear friends, but leave room for God's wrath, for it is written: 'It is mine to avenge; I will repay,' says the Lord." David allowed God to defend him (1 Samuel 26:9-11).

Moses began well, but he reacted the wrong way.

The Success of God Pivots on Three Things

> Moses and Aaron went from the assembly to the entrance to the tent of meeting and fell facedown, and the glory of the Lord appeared to them. (Numbers 20:6)

As recorded in this verse, Moses did three things right.
- Moses left the people and went to God in prayer.
- Moses expressed his humility and dependence on God.
- Moses saw the glory of the Lord.

He is a good and duplicable model on each of these three behaviors. We too can do all three of these things. We just must decide that they are worth doing.

Moses Left the People and Went to God in Prayer

"Moses and Aaron went from the assembly to the entrance to the tent of meeting." We will fail if we stay in the arena of activity with people and try to pacify or deflect their anger, answer their questions, or solve their problems by our own strength, wisdom, or ability. We must sometimes get away from people in order to get alone with God. We don't remain away from them, nor do we avoid them endlessly. We must be approachable and available. But unless we sometimes get away from them and spend time alone with God, we will never obtain the help we and those we serve need from God. Even Jesus did this many times (Mark 1:35).

Moses Expressed His Humility and Dependence on God

Moses "fell facedown." The human face is a symbol of our identity; it is how others recognize us. God has created each of our faces differently. Orientals go to great lengths to "save face" and to help others do the same. But far from seeking to save his own face — maintain his own reputation — Moses got on his face before God.

God knows each of our faces. He knew Moses' face and talked to him face to face. "Since then, no prophet has risen in Israel like Moses, whom the Lord knew face to face" (Deuteronomy 34:10). Yet in the above narrative, Moses has his face to the ground. This is a posture of humility and desperation and is a model for intercessors today as well.

Moses Saw the Glory of the Lord

"The glory of the Lord appeared to them." God's glory is not always displayed in flashing colors and bright beams. Sometimes the glory of God is soft, subdued, and subtle. Elijah knew the glory of God in the cave when he heard the still, small voice of the Lord after the wind, earthquake, and fire had come and gone. If we want to see the glory of God, we must let Him show us whichever aspect of His glory He chooses to reveal at any given time. It is better to seek Him than to seek His glory; but in seeking Him, we may see His glory.

> *Our love for God's people may wane in the process of ministry to them.*

When we follow this pattern — leave people temporarily, fall on our faces before God, and pray faithfully until we see the glory of God — we will be able to minister to His people, love the unlovely, and lead God's people in God's paths God's way. Our love for God's people may wane in the process of ministry to them. But we are their fellow-servants and servants of God. We must never lose our sense of His glory. It is He whom we serve. He is the Source and End of all that we do.

God Gave Moses the Solution

> The Lord said to Moses, "Take the staff, and you and your brother Aaron gather the assembly together. Speak to that rock before their eyes and it will pour out its water. You will bring water out of the rock for the community so they and their livestock can drink." (Numbers 20:7-8)

God gave Moses specific directions. He directed him to take his staff and speak to the rock.

Many times in Scripture, we find God giving humans practical instructions. A good illustration of this is David at Ziklag (1 Samuel 30:6-8) when God told him to pursue the Amalekite raiding party. Another illustration is when Jehoshaphat moved into battle formation and then the sun reflected on the water, providing a miraculous deliverance (2 Kings 3:17-18).

We need practical solutions to ministry problems, and we also need personal comfort. God is a master at giving us both. God revealed His glory to Moses, then gave him specific instructions as to what to do. He will do the same for you.

Moses Followed God's Instructions

> Moses took the staff from the Lord's presence, just as he commanded him. (Numbers 20:9)

Moses started well. He took the staff and began to do what God said to do. What went wrong? How is it that Moses, the meekest man on earth besides Jesus Christ, lost control of his emotions and became angry and resentful? Starting well is not enough. We must begin and end correctly.

Moses Became Angry with God's People

> He and Aaron gathered the assembly together in front of the rock and Moses said to them, "Listen you rebels, must we bring you water out of this rock?" Then Moses raised his arm and struck the rock twice with his staff. (Numbers 20:10-11a)

In both Leviticus and Deuteronomy, Moses teaches against revenge and grudges. Yet in between those two books lies the book of Numbers, which records Moses' fleshly response of anger with God's people. Moses:

- Called the Israelites rebels
- Included himself in the miracle: "Must *we* bring you water?" (emphasis mine)
- Did not speak to the rock but struck it — twice

Bible archeology teaches us that in that area of wilderness, a crust can develop on the surface of the earth that makes the dirt hard and waterproof. The water is held inside the earth by the crust on the surface. Moses spent forty years in that desert; he knew how to find and release the water. By striking the rock, Moses resorted to a human ploy rather than just speaking to the rock and allowing God to receive all the glory.

Moses struck another rock some forty years before when people needed water. Exodus 17:5–6 tells us, "The Lord answered Moses, '… I will stand there before you by the rock at Horeb. Strike the rock, and water will come out of it for the people to drink.' So Moses did this in the sight of the elders of Israel." On that occasion, Moses did the right thing to strike the rock. This time, however, it was a flagrant disobedience to specific instructions. There is rich symbolism in these stories.

First Corinthians 10:4 tells us that rock represented Jesus. It symbolized His being smitten on the cross for our sins so that we may receive His water of life. He died once, and that was enough to give the water of life to all the thirsty of the world. He did not have to die twice. From the one-time-crucified Jesus flows the water of life to quench the spiritual thirst of all humanity. Jesus is the Rock of our salvation — the Rock that is our firm foundation, the Rock that is a shelter in the time of storm, the Rock in whose shadow humans find protection, comfort, and refreshment.

Moses did not have to strike the rock at all, not even once. He had only to speak to it. In the same way, we do not strike the Rock. Simply speak to Jesus, and you will be nourished.

Even after just having spent time in God's presence, seeing His glory, and receiving His detailed and specific instruction, Moses gave in to his emotions. He expressed his anger in ways that did not honor God or reverence His holiness. Moses' actions were irreverent; he did not treat

God respectfully. Moses' anger and lack of self-control greatly dishonored and displeased God.

And there were consequences to Moses' actions. Even though God did not immediately remove him from leadership, Moses was severely reprimanded by God.

Even so, God remained faithful to Moses, as shown in this word to Joshua: "As I was with Moses, so will I be with you; I will never leave you or forsake you" (Joshua 1:5).

We do not know if Moses' anger was influenced by God's anger at the complaint of the people. But even if Moses discerned that God was angry, it was not his prerogative to show anger, especially when He had clearly instructed him what to do.

Samuel was angry with the people of God when they wanted a king. But God said, "Give them a king." (I Samuel 8:22)

God was more gracious than either Moses or Samuel. He can be angry with His people; we should not.

Though God's Tool Was Faulty, God Still Cared for His People's Needs

> Water gushed out, and the community and their livestock drank. (Numbers 20:11b)

In spite of Moses' sin, God still gave the people the water they needed. Moses failed, but God did not. The human instrument took revenge, but God showed mercy. Moses entertained an ego-related desire for vindication and revenge. God cared for His people and met their needs. God's provision is more about what He does than what His instruments do.

It is not necessarily an indication that the human instrument is doing everything correctly when God continues to do His good work through His chosen servants for His people. Do not assume that God using you means you can relax and stop

> "God's provision is more about what He does than what His instruments do."

Choose Your Character

growing spiritually. God gave the Israelites water through a miracle produced by Moses' rod striking the rock twice — not because Moses did it right, but in spite of the fact that he did it wrong. Moses erred greatly in becoming angry and departing from the instructions God gave him to speak to the rock. But God still met the needs of the people.

God Pronounced an Irrevocable Punishment on Moses

> But the Lord said to Moses and Aaron, "Because you did not trust in me enough to honor me as holy in the sight of the Israelites, you will not bring this community into the land I give them." (Numbers 20:12)

We prefer to emphasize grace, mercy, love, forgiveness, and the encouraging aspects of God's character. Yet to have the whole picture of who God is and how He operates, we need to remember that He also has a firm side. He has authority. He is sovereign. We are to fear and respect Him. We must remain cautious in our strict obedience to His every command and instruction.

Moses disobeyed God and thus dishonored Him before the people he was leading. God wanted to bring water from the rock without it being struck. That would have brought greater glory to God than Moses striking the rock.

Paul cautioned his readers, "Consider therefore the kindness and sternness of God; sternness to those who fell, but kindness to you, provided that you continue in his kindness" (Romans 11:22). It is right that we do that. We often take courage from the fact that God keeps His promises of reward, comfort, blessing, healing, and forgiveness. However, He also keeps His promises of judgment, and we may experience the consequences of the mistakes we make for a long time. God is gracious and we experience favor, but we dare not ignore His sternness.

> But the Lord said to Moses and Aaron, "Because you did not trust in me enough to honor me as holy in the sight of the Israelites, you will not bring this community into the land I give them." (Numbers 20:12)

This sobering judgment from God is even more serious when we look at Moses' speech as the Israelites were about to enter the Promised Land:

> At that time I pleaded with the Lord: "Sovereign Lord, you have

begun to show to your servant your greatness and your strong hand. For what god is there in heaven or on earth who can do the deeds and mighty works you do? Let me go over and see the good land beyond the Jordan — that fine hill country and Lebanon."

But because of you the Lord was angry with me and would not listen to me. "That is enough," the Lord said. "Do not speak to me anymore about this matter. Go up to the top of Pisgah and look west and north and south and east. Look at the land with your own eyes, since you are not going to cross this Jordan. But commission Joshua, and encourage and strengthen him, for he will lead this people across and will cause them to inherit the land that you will see." (Deuteronomy 3:23-28)

Later in that same speech, Moses said to Israel:

The Lord was angry with me because of you, and he solemnly swore that I would not cross the Jordan and enter the good Land the Lord your God is giving you as your inheritance. I will die in this land; I will not cross the Jordan; but you are about to cross over and take possession of that good land. Be careful not to forget the covenant of the Lord your God that he made with you; do not make for yourselves an idol in the form of anything the Lord your God has forbidden. For the Lord your God is a consuming fire, a jealous God. (Deuteronomy 4:21-24)

> **Moses had a long and successful career, but it could have been even longer and more successful.**

Moses remembered the strictness of God because of his own experience. He reminded the Israelites that God has a stern side too.

Then Moses climbed Mount Nebo from the plains of Moab to the top of Pisgah, across from Jericho. There the Lord showed him the whole land — from Gilead to Dan, all of Naphtali, the territory of Ephraim and Manasseh, all the land of Judah as far as the Mediterranean Sea, the Negev and the whole region from the

Choose Your Character   83

Valley of Jericho, the City of Palms, as far as Zoar. Then the Lord said to him, "This is the land I promised on oath to Abraham, Isaac, and Jacob when I said, 'I will give it to your descendants.' I have let you see it with your eyes, but you will not cross over into it." And Moses the servant of the Lord died there in Moab, as the Lord had said. (Deuteronomy 34:1–5)

Moses had a long and successful career, but it could have been even longer and more successful. You too can have a rich, enduring, and effective ministry if you carefully obey every leading, instruction, and command of God. God keeps His promises.

The People's Quarrel Was with the Lord, Not Moses

These were the waters of Meribah, where the Israelites quarreled with the Lord and where he was proved holy among them. (Numbers 20:13)

Moses and Aaron bore the brunt of verbal abuse from the Israeli people. Numbers 20:3 says, "They quarreled with Moses." But Numbers 20:13 says, "… where the Israelites quarreled with the Lord and where he was proved holy among them."

Two things are important for us in this verse:

- The people's quarrel was not just with Moses. It was a complaint against God.
- God was proved holy by the judgment He pronounced.

> "If God allowed us to disobey and yet He continued to bless our ministry without measure, where would His holiness be?"

The first lesson is easy to understand. God's ministers can take great comfort from knowing that the complaints people have are not just against them but are also against God. Stay on God's side in a quarrel. He will defend you.

The second lesson is more subtle. Moses did not enter the Promised Land. By giving Moses a judgment for his disobedience that limited his ministry, God's holiness was maintained. If God allowed us to disobey and yet He continued to bless our ministry without measure, where would His holiness be? Where is the high standard of conduct for God's people if they can disobey and still have unhindered and lasting ministry? Moses' error and God's judgment teach us to be careful to obey fully, willingly, and if possible, cheerfully. Let's go all the way to the Promised Land.

For Further Thought

- In what ways do the people you serve reveal that they have great needs that God alone can meet?
- When people mistreat you, is it because of what you have done or because of their resistance toward God? What difference does that distinction make?
- How can you make use of the things Moses did correctly when you face challenges?
- Recall a time when God gave you the solution to a problem. As you meditate on that incident, ask yourself, "Can God always give me the solutions to my problems?"
- Recall a time when you started well but finished poorly. At what point in that event did you cross the line into disobedience? How can you avoid that in the future?
- Moses did four things wrong because he was angry. How does anger blind or confuse us so that we do not think correctly? What can you do to avoid Moses' serious error?
- Have you noticed that God continues to use you and your gifts even when you make mistakes? How can you avoid complacency when that happens?
- How do you feel about God's rigid requirements for those who represent Him?

CHAPTER 6
ZIPPORAH

Did you know that Moses left Egypt two times, once out of intense fear and once out of great faith? Has it ever occurred to you that God may have used Moses' conversations with his Midianite wife, Zipporah, to encourage him? Are you aware that Moses may have written the book of Genesis while in Midian? Did you know that the value of Zipporah's actions, which saved Moses' life on the way to Egypt, are lost to most Bible readers because of what she said about Moses? What part did Zipporah play in the secret drama of Moses' restoration on the back side of the desert? Let us take a closer look at this fascinating woman.

Zipporah has been largely overlooked by scholars who study Bible characters. Even when her story is examined, she has often been misunderstood. Many feel she is either an unimportant Bible character or an example of a problematic wife. Careful observation of the Bible narrative, however, reveals that she was likely a wise, courageous, perceptive, influential, and supportive wife.

I learned of this possibility while listening to a teaching my wife, Char, gave in Jos, Nigeria. She spoke in the main worship service in our host church, where she and I conducted an Empower Africa Christian Leadership Conference and participated in a Missions Summit. Some of the ideas in this chapter find their beginnings in that lesson.

Three Verses Are Enough

Most of our opinions about Zipporah are based on an incident that occurred as she traveled with her husband, Moses, and their two sons on the road from Midian to Egypt. Correctly interpreted, this incident provides an insight into the nobility of her character.

Not long after Moses' experience with the burning bush, he asked his father-in-law, Jethro, for permission to return to Egypt.

Then Moses went back to Jethro his father-in-law and said to him, "Let me return to my own people in Egypt to see if any of them are still alive."

Jethro said, "Go, and I wish you well."

Now the Lord had said to Moses in Midian, "Go back to Egypt, for all those who wanted to kill you are dead." So Moses took his wife and sons, put them on a donkey and started back to Egypt. And he took the staff of God in his hand.

> **In a time of Moses' weak faith and disobedience to the command of God to circumcise Israel's sons, Zipporah actually saved her husband's life.**

The Lord said to Moses, "When you return to Egypt, see that you perform before Pharaoh all the wonders I have given you the power to do. But I will harden his heart so that he will not let the people go. Then say to Pharaoh, 'This is what the Lord says: Israel is my firstborn son, and I told you, "Let my son go, so he may worship me." But you refused to let him go; so I will kill your firstborn son.'" (Exodus 4:18–23)

Traditionally, Bible scholars display a negative impression of Zipporah because of what she said to Moses on that trip to Egypt: "Surely you are a bridegroom of blood to me" (Exodus 4:25). But if we look at the complete story in context and what she *did*, we must reach another conclusion. In a time of Moses' weak faith and disobedience to the command of God to circumcise Israel's sons, Zipporah actually saved her husband's life.

At a lodging place on the way, the Lord met Moses and was about to kill him. But Zipporah took a flint knife, cut off her son's

> foreskin and touched Moses' feet with it. "Surely you are a bridegroom of blood to me," she said. So the Lord let him alone. [At that time she said "bridegroom of blood," referring to circumcision.] (Exodus 4:24–26)

In those three verses, we see enough of Zipporah's action to judge her character and appreciate the role she played in Moses' life.

The narrative continues:

> The Lord said to Aaron, "Go into the wilderness to meet Moses." So he met Moses at the mountain of God and kissed him. Then Moses told Aaron everything the Lord had sent him to say, and also about all the signs he had commanded him to perform.
>
> Moses and Aaron brought together all the elders of the Israelites, and Aaron told them everything the Lord had said to Moses. He also performed the signs before the people, and they believed. And when they heard that the Lord was concerned about them and had seen their misery, they bowed down and worshiped. (Exodus 4:27–31)

Aaron went to meet Moses at the same time Moses was traveling toward Egypt with his family. They met at the mountain of God. But the two brothers would never have met had Zipporah not saved Moses' life by her brave actions. Commentators often say that Zipporah went back to her father then, but the Bible does not say that here.

Moses Fled from Egypt the First Time in Fear, Not Faith

Forty years earlier, a younger, less cautious, more presumptuous Moses attempted to deliver the Israelite slaves in his own strength. At that time, Moses had not yet had his own personal encounter with God. He did not attempt to rescue all the Israelites, but he saved at least one Hebrew slave being mistreated by another.

> One day, after Moses had grown up, he went out to where his own people were and watched them at their hard labor. He saw an Egyptian beating a Hebrew, one of his own people. Glancing this way and that and seeing no one, he killed the Egyptian and hid him in the sand. The next day he went out and saw two

> Hebrews fighting. He asked the one in the wrong, "Why are you hitting your fellow Hebrew?"
>
> The man said, "Who made you ruler and judge over us? Are you thinking of killing me as you killed the Egyptian?" Then Moses was afraid and thought, "What I did must have become known."
>
> When Pharaoh heard of this, he tried to kill Moses, but Moses fled from Pharaoh and went to live in Midian, where he sat down by a well. (Exodus 2:11–15)

Moses was no longer the man he used to be. He was not the self-confident deliverer he had imagined himself to be just days earlier. He had run for his life. Nor was he yet the controlled and certain man who watched God perform many mighty miracles effecting Israel's escape from Egypt.

The book of Hebrews tells us that Moses left Egypt by faith. But his departure by faith was the second time he left Egypt. The first time, he was running for his life. He had been trying to save Israel by his strength, not by his faith in God. But his strength had proven inadequate. He arrived in Midian alone and despondent.

Moses had thought he was a deliverer, and he eventually became one. But when he reached Midian, he had no desire to be a national deliverer. He was only willing to deliver seven pretty shepherdesses from some unfair and aggressive shepherds.

One of those shepherdesses was the woman God chose to be his wife.

> Now a priest of Midian had seven daughters, and they came to draw water and fill the troughs to water their father's flock. Some shepherds came along and drove them away, but Moses got up and came to their rescue and watered their flock.
>
> When the girls returned to Reuel their father, he asked them, "Why have you returned so early today?"
>
> They answered, "An Egyptian rescued us from the shepherds. He even drew water for us and watered the flock."
>
> "And where is he?" he asked his daughters. "Why did you leave him? Invite him to have something to eat."
>
> Moses agreed to stay with the man, who gave his daughter Zipporah to Moses in marriage. (Exodus 2:16–21)

After he married Zipporah, the name Moses gave their first son does not suggest either hope for the future or despair because of the past. It is a neutral name, merely relaying the idea that he was living in a foreign land. "Zipporah gave birth to a son, and Moses named him Gershom, saying, 'I have become a foreigner in a foreign land'" (Exodus 2:22).

The Bible does not say how much time passed before the second son was born, but it does say that with Zipporah, Moses took his *sons* with him when he returned to Egypt (Exodus 4:20).

Some couples compete. Some argue; others fight. Some develop even warmer and more mature relationships than the good ones with which they began. The Bible does not tell us the nature of the rapport between Moses and Zipporah. Were they friends? We don't know, but it appears they had a good bond. We only need to read Genesis to guess what they talked about since all those events happened before Moses left Egypt and fled to Midian.

They had four decades to discuss all of this. Throughout the years of shepherding, family times, and life in the desert together, Moses and Zipporah undoubtedly discussed their varying cultural backgrounds. How many nights did they watch the stars where Moses told her of God's promise to Abraham, his ancestor — that Abraham's descendants would be innumerable like the stars?

Moses would have told her about Abraham's call, name change, and travels. He would have mentioned Isaac's disputes with the residents of Canaan over the wells Isaac dug and the local people claimed for themselves. He would have told of Jacob and Esau, Jacob's travels to Paddan Aram, and Jacob's wives and children. Zipporah would have learned about Joseph being sold as a slave and rising to the prime minister's position. She would have known the details of the migration of the entire family of Jacob from Canaan to Egypt. Moses would have narrated the years of Israeli slavery, his own experiences in the court and family of Pharaoh. He would have told her of his own failed attempt to deliver the Israelite slaves with his own strength.

Did Moses write Genesis in the desert after leaving Egypt? He had the time, but did he have the faith? Possibly Zipporah was inspired by the stories Moses told of his heritage. Could that have motivated her to defend her husband as he returned to Egypt?

Perhaps Jethro was also inspired. We don't know what god Jethro originally represented. Perhaps he maintained his career as priest and changed his god. Did Jethro's daughter (Moses' wife) have anything to do with her father's change in faith if there was a change? We know that Jethro eventually believed in the real God. Or did Jethro know God even before Moses arrived? Was he like Abimelek? Melchizedek? Job? Was he like them — a non-Jewish believer in the true God?

> **Possibly Zipporah was inspired by the stories Moses told of his heritage.**

While these questions go unanswered, we know Moses' faith was at low ebb at the burning bush. Still, during the forty years spent together, something from Moses evidently gave birth to faith in Zipporah.

Moses Resisted God's Plan for His Return to Egypt to Deliver Israel

After forty years of shepherding in the wilderness of Midian, Moses encountered the voice of God in a bush that burned but was not consumed. The burning of the bush was a miracle. God told Moses His name: "I am who I am" (Exodus 3:14). He promised Moses favor. He gave him the miraculous sign of the staff turning into a snake and back into a staff. God gave him the amazing sign of a hand becoming leprous and then clean again. The conversation between God and Moses was long and detailed. Yet all the while, Moses resisted God. Then he complained about his inability to speak:

> Moses said to the Lord, "Pardon your servant, Lord. I have never been eloquent, neither in the past nor since you have spoken to your servant. I am slow of speech and tongue."
>
> The Lord said to him, "Who gave human beings their mouths? Who makes them deaf or mute? Who gives them sight or makes them blind? Is it not I, the Lord? Now go; I will help you speak and will teach you what to say."
>
> But Moses said, "Pardon your servant, Lord. Please send someone else." (Exodus 4:10–13)

The narrative makes it clear that Moses was not eager to return to Egypt. He felt incapable. Yet centuries later, Stephen testified before the Sanhedrin:

> At that time Moses was born, and he was no ordinary child. For three months he was cared for in his parents' home. When he was placed outside, Pharaoh's daughter took him and brought him up as her own son. Moses was educated in all the wisdom of the Egyptians and was powerful in speech and action. (Acts 7:20-22)

According to Stephen, Moses was "powerful in speech and action." Yet at the burning bush, Moses claimed he was slow of speech. What made the difference between the fearful, hesitant Moses and the confident, brave man who eventually challenged Pharaoh and demanded that he let Israel go? What brought this uncertain, cautious man out of his pit into faith and trust in God again? Moses arrived in Midian apprehensive and discouraged, and forty years later he was still negative. What changed?

> "What brought this uncertain, cautious man out of his pit into faith and trust in God again?"

It would be an exaggeration to say that Zipporah, the faith-filled wife of Moses, made all the difference — that because of her support, this frightened, timid shepherd morphed into a mighty man of courage. But Zipporah filled an important role. She demonstrated support and displayed courage. She knew Israeli tradition and placed her faith in Moses and Moses' God. All of these factors certainly would have contributed to the restoration of Moses' confidence and would therefore influence the success of Moses' public life. She stepped in at a crucial juncture, and God used her.

What Really Happened on the Road to Egypt?

We do not know how long Moses was in Midian before he married Zipporah or how long they were married before they had children. It appears that Zipporah circumcised at least one of their sons on the way to Egypt. When God had Moses pinned down on the point of circumcision, she put the foreskin of one son at Moses' feet. The image of Zipporah as a supportive wife comes into focus when we view Zipporah's *action*, not just her words.

> But Zipporah took a flint knife, cut off her son's foreskin and touched Moses' feet with it. "Surely you are a bridegroom of blood to me," she said. (Exodus 4:25)

With her husband pinned down and his life threatened, Zipporah displayed perception, discernment, and wisdom. She had the courage to pull out a knife, require at least one of her possibly grown sons to expose his genitals, and cut off his foreskin. This would have been a bloody and painful experience for both mother and son, whatever their ages. She saw the death threat to Moses. Because she believed in the value and validity of his mission, she acted out her faith.

They had not casually decided to visit Egypt for a pleasant vacation. Zipporah was drawn by the history of Moses' people and by Abraham, Isaac, Jacob, and Joseph's confidence in a miracle-working God — the true God. This assignment to Egypt was to be another in a series of great moves of God among His people. God spoke to her husband in a burning bush, and he had signs to prove God was with him. Together, they were on an important and godly undertaking. Off went the clothes. Out came the knife. Off went the foreskin. Onward went the travelers.

> "Even the great Moses needed a Zipporah. Encouragement is valuable. Earn it. And give it liberally."

If you are married to a Christian leader, support your spouse. If your spouse is a spiritual leader, lend the support he or she needs from time to time. If you and your spouse are both Christian leaders, you can support each other. Your partnership will prove both strong and fruitful. Cast your vision so your spouse catches it, believes in what you are doing, and supports you. Take time to inspire your spouse with your dreams. Even the great Moses needed a Zipporah. Encouragement is valuable. Earn it. And give it liberally.

Zipporah's Role as Informant to Jethro

Moses' second son's name was Eliezer, which means "God is my helper." Moses stated, "My father's God was my helper; he saved me from the sword of Pharaoh" (Exodus 18:3-4). Eliezer's name gives glory to God. He was born later — perhaps after Moses (though still in Midian) regained some of his optimism.

The Bible does not clearly state how many years passed during the time of the ten plagues. It does not indicate or when or from where Zipporah left with her two sons to return to Jethro. But at some point, Moses sent her away. She later came back to Moses and the recently delivered Israelites in the wilderness. Her father, Jethro, and her sons, Gershom and Eliezer, also returned.

Some Bible readers feel that Zipporah returned to Midian during the chaos of the plagues in Egypt. It is more likely that she returned to her father in Midian after the exodus from Egypt. During the narrative of the plagues, there is no mention that Zipporah left. Zipporah's departure from Moses is recorded after the exodus occurred.

> Now Jethro, the priest of Midian and father-in-law of Moses, heard of everything God had done for Moses and for his people Israel, and how the Lord had brought Israel out of Egypt.
>
> After Moses had sent away his wife Zipporah, his father-in-law Jethro received her and her two sons. One son was named Gershom, for Moses said, "I have become a foreigner in a foreign land"; and the other was named Eliezer, for he said, "My father's God was my helper; he saved me from the sword of Pharaoh." (Exodus 18:1-4)

Zipporah is the most likely person to have been her father's informant. "Jethro, the priest of Midian and father-in-law of Moses, heard of everything God had done for Moses and for his people Israel, and how the Lord had brought Israel out of Egypt" (Exodus 18:1). How did he hear these wonderful words? Zipporah could only relate this to her father as a firsthand eyewitness if she had gone to and remained in Egypt with her husband throughout the months of the plagues.

Jethro heard of all that God had done. I can think of no more likely newscaster than the woman whom Jethro had given to Moses — the woman who heard the stories of the patriarchs, who believed in Moses' God, and who believed in Moses. Zipporah supported her man by relaying to her father the multiple mighty miracles God worked through him.

Wives, support your husbands. All men have feet of clay, and we all have times of weakness and discouragement. Your man may now be more like the defeated and terrified Moses who just arrived at Midian or the hesitant Moses who moved cautiously toward Egypt, than the brave Moses who left Egypt walking through the Red Sea on dry ground. In any case, you have an opportunity to further the work of the Lord by partnering with your husband, believing in him, supporting him, praying for him, and encouraging him.

Husbands, share your ministry dreams with your helpmate in such a way that she will believe in your God and in the validity of your ministry. If your wife is a minister, support her in her role as a spiritual leader. Protect her and provide for her the leadership God gives you in His Word as she cooperates with your leadership in the family. Support the man or woman of God in your family — that is the lesson we learn from Zipporah.

> *God's Word upholds the primacy of the marital relationship over all others.*

Moses wrote, "For this reason a man will leave his father and mother and be united to his wife, and they will become one flesh" (Genesis 2:24). The way Zipporah responded to Moses makes it apparent that Moses believed what he wrote. Enough human history had occurred by Moses' time that he could assess the disadvantages of emotionally bonding with other family members, neighbors, business associates, or friends more than with one's wife. He knew the value of "leaving" father and mother and uniting with one's wife.

Whether geographically or just emotionally, the husband and wife who recognize this principle and unite with each other experience many enormous personal benefits. Zipporah was blessed with a husband who understood and practiced this. By her supportive behavior, Zipporah indicates that she did too. God's Word upholds the primacy of the marital relationship over all others. Sociologists call it the husband/wife social dyad. Scripture clarifies its great worth. If we appreciate, defend, and prize it, we will enjoy it immensely.

We do not quickly associate learning about romance and teamwork in marriage with the story of Moses the law-giver. But these reflections on Zipporah enable us to reconsider the romances Moses recorded in Genesis: Adam and Eve, Abraham and Sarah, Isaac and Rebecca, Jacob and Rachel. He also includes Joseph's eventual marriage at age thirty to Asenath after he escaped the seductive temptations. Asenath was the daughter of Potiphera the priest of On.

Moses and Zipporah were a successful ministry team. They bonded emotionally and maintained a friendly relationship. We have reason to believe Mo and Zip got on well together.

Was Zipporah Moses' Cushite Wife?

Years after the exodus and many adventures in the wilderness, an incident occurred between Moses and his siblings, Miriam and Aaron, over his Cushite wife. Was this wife Zipporah or another woman? The Bible does not say. Here is what the Bible does say:

> Miriam and Aaron began to talk against Moses because of his Cushite wife, for he had married a Cushite. "Has the Lord spoken only through Moses?" they asked. "Hasn't he also spoken through us?" (Numbers 12:1-3)

At least three possibilities exist:

- Zipporah died and Moses remarried, this time to a Cushite (an African of Ethiopia).
- Moses married a second wife in addition to Zipporah.
- Zipporah had all along been a Cushite who lived in Midian.

Let's briefly explore these possibilities.

Zipporah Died and Moses Remarried, This Time to a Cushite

If this were the case, Miriam and Aaron would have exhibited small character to oppose Moses on the basis of his wife. That smallness in their character could, however, explain why God so quickly and decisively defended Moses. In doing so, he indirectly defended the Cushite wife as well. This part of the story would then uphold the idealism of predominance of the marriage relationship.

Moses Married a Second Wife in Addition to Zipporah

Miriam and Aaron may have been opposed to Moses having a second wife who, incidentally, was a Cushite. The Scripture does not say whether they opposed Moses because his Cushite wife was a Cushite or because she was a second wife. Many godly people in Israel, both before and after Moses, had more than one wife. It is therefore doubtful that Moses' siblings opposed him because the Cushite was a second wife. The skin of a Cushite was black. Is it possible that Miriam and Aaron were opposed to Moses because he married a second wife and because she was a black woman? In either case, God defended Moses — and the wife. In either case, the moral to learn is the importance of solidarity in marriage.

Zipporah Was a Cushite Who Lived in Midian

I was born in Indiana, and I went to school in Iowa. So I am both a Hoosier and a Hawkeye — nicknames for people from those two states. In the same way, it is possible that Jethro and his family were Cushites who lived in Midian. Then the Cushite wife God defended when He defended Moses would be Zipporah from Midian, the daughter of Jethro, the priest of Midian.

When Zipporah rejoined Moses at the Israeli camp in the wilderness, her successful role as wife, confidant, supporter, and helper to Moses may have aroused jealousy in Aaron and Miriam. Once Moses had his wife with him again, he no longer leaned emotionally on his sister and brother.

> **God defended Moses' wife against the verbal attacks of Moses' siblings, and Moses remained on the side of his spouse.**

Zipporah was a thinking person who had ideas of her own, which she shared with her husband. Resuming her constructive involvement in his career, she no doubt made suggestions and gave advice based on her experience as a desert shepherdess. That proved to be a greater help than Moses' sister and brother could provide.

God defended Moses' wife against the verbal attacks of Moses' siblings, and Moses remained on the side of his spouse. Your spouse needs your unconditional support too. You are one with your spouse, not your siblings. How many painful family arguments could be avoided if we understood this biblical principle?

For Further Thought

- Even after Moses' experience at the burning bush, Moses was still reluctant to help his people when they were slaves in Egypt. Do you see similarities to this within yourself?
- Have you experienced times when you were "pinned down" by God and your spouse came to your rescue with encouragement, counsel, correction, or practical help? How did that affect your relationship with God and your mate?
- Do you share your ministry vision with your spouse so that he or she can partner in that work with you? How can you improve in this area?
- In what way(s) could you be more supportive of your spouse?

CHAPTER 7
BALAAM

Did you know that the story of Balaam gives practical evidence for the reality of the invisible spiritual war that is going on all around us? Were you aware that Balaam did what God said, but since his heart was not in it, he fell into a trap? Do you realize that Balaam represents those of us who say and even do the right thing, but don't obey from our hearts?

Balaam symbolizes what happens when our ministry motives get tangled with carnal desires. The Bible is realistic, and though socioeconomic and geopolitical realities may differ from generation to generation, human nature does not.

The lessons we learn from this man's story are as relevant now as when Moses first recorded the interlocking of Balaam's failure with developments within Israel. The present generation of God's ministers needs a serious review of the warnings to be gleaned from Balaam's experience.

Balaam saw the spirit world with remarkable clarity but was blind to his own incorrect impetus. The extreme measures he took in pursuit of his personal goals differ from any Christian minister's materialistic motivations only in degree; a lesser form of Balaam's rationale may be lurking unknowingly in any of us.

The Spiritual Battle Is Real

"Whenever the ark set out, Moses said, 'Rise up, Lord! May your enemies be scattered; may your foes flee before you.' Whenever it came to rest, he said,

'Return, Lord, to the countless thousands of Israel'" (Numbers 10:35-36). Why did Moses concern himself with this kind of routine spiritual warfare? The story of Balaam provides part of the answer to that question.

> Then the Israelites traveled to the plains of Moab and camped along the Jordan across from Jericho.
>
> Now Balak son of Zippor saw all that Israel had done to the Amorites, and Moab was terrified because there were so many people. Indeed, Moab was filled with dread because of the Israelites.
>
> The Moabites said to the elders of Midian, "This horde is going to lick up everything around us, as an ox licks up the grass of the field."
>
> So Balak son of Zippor, who was king of Moab at that time, sent messengers to summon Balaam son of Beor, who was at Pethor, near the Euphrates River, in his native land. Balak said: "A people has come out of Egypt; they cover the face of the land and have settled next to me. Now come and put a curse on these people, because they are too powerful for me. Perhaps then I will be able to defeat them and drive them out of the land. For I know that whoever you bless is blessed, and whoever you curse is cursed."
>
> The elders of Moab and Midian left, taking with them the fee for divination. When they came to Balaam, they told him what Balak had said.
>
> "Spend the night here," Balaam said to them, "and I will report back to you with the answer the Lord gives me." So the Moabite officials stayed with him. (Numbers 22:1-8)

> **"Israel's own sin did to Israel what Balaam's curses could not do."**

Understanding the "other side" — the unseen enemy activity that is the background behind the visible drama — helps us better understand the nature of the battle. Here we see the causes for one of Israel's sins and the plague that broke out in the camp as a result. The story of Balak and Balaam reveals their roles in the seduction of Israel.

If we did not know about Balak and Balaam, we would not have the richer picture of the spiritual battle behind the moral battle. In the spiritual battle, blessings and cursings have some effect, but sin matters even more.

At the end of Balaam and Balak's eventual strategy to oppose Israel by enticing Israel to sin, Balak fought a partially successful battle. Because of Phinehas, God's people were spared an even worse plague. Balaam's curses from the mountains around the Israeli camp did not entirely destroy Israel. But enticing Israel to sin was, tragically, an effective plan. Israel's own sin did to Israel what Balaam's curses could not do. What a devilishly cunning battle strategy.

Balaam's Outward Start Was Right — But What of His Heart?

> God came to Balaam and asked, "Who are these men with you?"
>
> Balaam said to God, "Balak son of Zippor, king of Moab, sent me this message: 'A people that has come out of Egypt covers the face of the land. Now come and put a curse on them for me. Perhaps then I will be able to fight them and drive them away.'"
>
> But God said to Balaam, "Do not go with them. You must not put a curse on those people, because they are blessed."
>
> The next morning Balaam got up and said to Balak's officials, "Go back to your own country, for the Lord has refused to let me go with you."
>
> So the Moabite officials returned to Balak and said, "Balaam refused to come with us." (Numbers 22:9-14)

God's first word to Balaam was a statement of His will. "Don't go." This is comparable to a conversation God had with Moses. God had promised Abraham He would make a great nation of his descendants. This was God's original and unchanging plan, and Moses knew it. So Moses was able to resist temptation when God tested his moral character by offering to destroy the Israelites and make of Moses' descendants a great nation.

Balak was not pleased with Balaam's refusal. He sent more officials to persuade him to come. This time, as Balaam prayed, Jehovah God gave him permission to go, but he had to do only what God told him to do.

Unlike Moses, Balaam did not discern the difference between what God *says* and what God *intends*. It is possible that Balaam was experiencing an inner struggle, seeking both to obey God and to gain the monetary reward Balak was offering. Or Balaam's obedience may have been only outward as he inwardly looked for an opportunity to receive Balak's reward.

Balaam did not have the same discernment Moses had. If he had, he probably would not have taken the request back to God the second time. In going with Balak's envoy, Balaam evidently displeased God, even though Balaam's outward behavior conformed to what God instructed. "God was very angry when he went" (Numbers 22:22). God even used Balaam's donkey to communicate to Balaam His displeasure and a need for caution.

Twice God told Balaam to go. But there is a difference between what God told Balaam the second time and what He really wanted. In this case, Balaam did not discern the difference between what God said and what God intended, as Moses had done.

Do you know God well enough that He can speak to you in code form — a unique and personal way that only you and He know about — and you still understand His intent? Let us cultivate a close and trusting relationship with Him such that we know His will, and then do it.

Balaam Followed Through Correctly — At First

> When Balak heard that Balaam was coming, he went out to meet him at the Moabite town on the Arnon border, at the edge of his territory. Balak said to Balaam, "Did I not send you an urgent summons? Why didn't you come to me? Am I really not able to reward you?"
>
> "Well, I have come to you now," Balaam replied. "But I can't say whatever I please. I must speak only what God puts in my mouth."
>
> Then Balaam went with Balak to Kiriath Huzoth. Balak sacrificed cattle and sheep, and gave some to Balaam and the officials who were with him. The next morning Balak took Balaam up to Bamoth Baal, and from there he could see the outskirts of the Israelite camp.
>
> Balaam said, "Build me seven altars here, and prepare seven bulls

and seven rams for me." Balak did as Balaam said, and the two of them offered a bull and a ram on each altar.

Then Balaam said to Balak, "Stay here beside your offering while I go aside. Perhaps the Lord will come to meet with me. Whatever he reveals to me I will tell you." Then he went off to a barren height.

God met with him, and Balaam said, "I have prepared seven altars, and on each altar I have offered a bull and a ram."

The Lord put a word in Balaam's mouth and said, "Go back to Balak and give him this word."

So he went back to him and found him standing beside his offering, with all the Moabite officials. Then Balaam spoke his message:

Balak brought me from Aram, the king of Moab from the eastern mountains. "Come," he said, "curse Jacob for me; come, denounce Israel."

How can I curse those whom God has not cursed? How can I denounce those whom the Lord has not denounced? From the rocky peaks I see them, from the heights I view them. I see a people who live apart and do not consider themselves one of the nations. Who can count the dust of Jacob or number the fourth part of Israel? Let me die the death of the righteous, and may my final end be like theirs!

Balak said to Balaam, "What have you done to me? I brought you to curse my enemies, but you have done nothing but bless them!"

He answered, "Must I not speak what the Lord puts in my mouth?" (Numbers 22:36-23:12)

Balaam's first message was a blessing, not a curse. Evidently he gave God's whole message.

Notice a phrase that is part of Balaam's first blessing: "I see a people who live apart and do not consider themselves one of the nations" (Genesis 23:9). This was God's desire: that His people live apart from other nations and be separated — holy — unto Himself. This is why Israel's request for a king was so offensive to Samuel. They wanted to be like other nations. That was one of Israel's gravest errors.

Satan is the god of this world. To be separate from the world system — separated unto God — is a blessing. We have the best there is when we have God. Why would we want to be like other nations, like other people? Why are we so prone to conform to the patterns, expectations, and value systems of the world? Why are we so eager for acceptance with those in the world's system? Let's live in the blessing God pronounced on Israel through Balaam — the blessing of being separated from the world and separated to God.

> "Why are we so prone to conform to the patterns, expectations, and value systems of the world?"

A Review of Balaam's Second through Seventh Prophecies

Balaam's second prophecy includes statements about God being unchangeable. "God is not a human, that he should lie, not a human being, that he should change his mind. Does he speak and then not act? Does he promise and not fulfill? I have received a command to bless; he has blessed, and I cannot change it" (Numbers 23:19). These statements about the unchangeableness of God strike to the core of the issue before Balak — God had chosen to bless Israel, and God does not change His mind like humans do.

The second prophecy is longer, fuller, and stronger in its expression of God's blessings than the first one.

The third prophesy is still stronger and longer, revealing God's unchangeable intention to bless Israel.

Balaam gave his fourth through seventh prophecies on his own initiative, without Balak's invitation. The fourth prophecy says Israel will crush her enemies, which included Moab. This would not have pleased Balak, the king of Moab.

Then he spoke his message:

> The prophecy of Balaam son of Beor,
> the prophecy of one whose eye sees clearly,

the prophecy of one who hears the words of God,
who has knowledge from the Most High,
who sees a vision from the Almighty,
who falls prostrate, and whose eyes are opened:
I see him, but not now;

I behold him, but not near.
A star will come out of Jacob;
a scepter will rise out of Israel.
He will crush the foreheads of Moab,
the skulls of all the people of Sheth.

Edom will be conquered;
Seir, his enemy, will be conquered,
but Israel will grow strong.
A ruler will come out of Jacob
and destroy the survivors of the city. (Numbers 24:15-19)

The fifth prophecy said Amalek would be destroyed. "Then Balaam saw Amalek and spoke his message: 'Amalek was first among the nations, but they will come to ruin at last'" (Numbers 24:20).

The sixth prophecy said the Kenites would be destroyed. "Then he saw the Kenites and spoke his message: 'Your dwelling place is secure, your nest is set in a rock; yet you Kenites will be destroyed when Ashur takes you captive'" (Numbers 24:21-22).

> "Apparently there was a darker side of Balaam and his involvement in what happened."

The seventh prophecy said ships from Cyprus would also be destroyed. "Then he spoke his message: 'Ah, who can live when God does this? Ships will come from the shores of Cyprus; they will subdue Ashur and Eber, but they too will come to ruin'" (Numbers 24:23-24).

As Numbers 24 concludes, Balaam returned home, evidently without any reward, and Balak moved on. "Then Balaam got up and returned home, and Balak went his own way" (Numbers 24:25).

Here it appears that Balaam obeyed God at every step. However, from other Scriptures that we are about to look at, it becomes evident that

Balaam did not obey from his heart. That was a problem for him. Apparently there was a darker side of Balaam and his involvement in what happened. The king of Moab did not try to curse Israel anymore. He changed his strategy drastically by inviting Israel to sacrifice to their gods and engage in sexual immorality.

Moab Seduces Israel with Serious Consequences to Israel

After Balaam returned home, the Moabite women enticed Israeli men to their idolatrous sacrifices and sexual promiscuity. "While Israel was staying in Shittim, the men began to indulge in sexual immorality with Moabite women, who invited them to the sacrifices to their gods. The people ate the sacrificial meal and bowed down before these gods. So Israel yoked themselves to the Baal of Peor. And the Lord's anger burned against them" (Numbers 25:1-3).

So offensive was this and so dangerous to Israel that Moses took drastic and radical measures. He told Israel's judges to kill Israel's leaders publicly in order to turn away God's anger.

> The Lord said to Moses, "Take all the leaders of these people, kill them and expose them in broad daylight before the Lord, so that the Lord's fierce anger may turn away from Israel."
>
> So Moses said to Israel's judges, "Each of you must put to death those of your people who have yoked themselves to the Baal of Peor." (Numbers 25:4-5)

Phinehas is one of the heroes of this story because he stopped the plague. Zimri, an Israelite, took Kozbi, the daughter of Zur (a tribal chief of the Midianites) into the tabernacle. While they were having sex, Phinehas, the son of Aaron, killed them both with the same plunge of one spear. Twenty-four thousand Israelites had already been killed in the plague before Phinehas stopped it with his brave, bold, and righteous act.

The Numbers narrative of this event does not include Balaam. But as we will see, he was involved. He counseled Balak to have the Moabite women seduce Israel's men, and Israel's sin blocked the blessings and protection of God, bringing down the curse of a plague on Israel — the same Israel that Balaam had not been able to curse effectively. The enemy cannot touch us; we bring tragedy on ourselves by our sin.

Numerous Other Biblical References Fill in the Gaps

There are many other references throughout the Bible to the story of Balaam and Balak. They round out the narrative and thereby fill in the blanks between Numbers 24 and 25. These other Bible writers tell of Balaam giving moral lessons — or rather immoral lessons. Each reference adds another insight into Balaam's serious error.

Moses reports that Israel later took vengeance in Midian and killed Balaam. "They also killed Balaam son of Beor with the sword" (Number 31:8). Joshua reports, "In addition to those slain in battle, the Israelites had put to the sword Balaam son of Beor, who practiced divination" (Joshua 13:22).

The explanation for killing Balaam is given in Numbers 31:16. Moabite women enticed Israel to sin; they "followed Balaam's advice."

From Moses' explanation in Deuteronomy, it seems Balaam may have wanted to pronounce

> "We may notice verses in the Bible that affirm our desire for financial prosperity yet overlook the references to a simple lifestyle or to Balaam and his sin of using spiritual gifts for monetary gain."

curses, but God would not let him. Regarding the Moabites, he said, "For they did not come to meet you with bread and water on your way when you came out of Egypt, and they hired Balaam son of Beor from Pethor in Aram Naharaim to pronounce a curse on you. However, the Lord your God would not listen to Balaam but turned the curse into a blessing for you, because the Lord your God loves you. Do not seek a treaty of friendship with them as long as you live" (Deuteronomy 23:4–6).

Joshua spoke for God and explained spiritual warfare in his famous farewell speech near the end of his life. "When Balak son of Zippor, the king of Moab, prepared to fight against Israel, he sent for Balaam son of Beor to put a curse on you. But I would not listen to Balaam, so he blessed you again and again, and I delivered you out of his hand" (Joshua 24:9–10).

Nehemiah explained why Ammonites and Moabites were not allowed in the assembly. "No Ammonite or Moabite should ever be admitted into the assembly of God because they had not met the Israelites with food and water but had hired Balaam to call a curse down on them. (Our God, however, turned the curse into a blessing.)" (Nehemiah 13:1-2).

Micah reminded his generation of God's righteousness in the Balaam/Balak incident. "My people, remember what Balak king of Moab plotted and what Balaam son of Beor answered. Remember your journey from Shittim to Gilgal, that you may know the righteous acts of the Lord" (Micah 6:5).

Peter says that Balaam was already sinning before he went to Balak, even before his verbal exchange with the donkey. Balaam "loved the wages of wickedness" and was insane to pursue his course. He evidently only reluctantly obeyed God in delivering the prophecies God gave him to bless, not curse, Israel. Peter says, "They have left the straight way and wandered off to follow the way of Balaam son of Bezer, who loved the wages of wickedness. But he was rebuked for his wrongdoing by a donkey — and animal without speech — who spoke with a human voice and restrained the prophet's madness" (2 Peter 2:15-16).

Jude describes sinful people who reject God's way by using three examples from the Old Testament. "Woe to them! They have taken the way of Cain; they have rushed for profit into *Balaam's error*; they have been destroyed in Korah's rebellion" (Jude 11, emphasis mine).

John says in Revelation, "There are some among you who hold to the teaching of Balaam, *who taught Balak to entice the Israelites into sin* so that they ate food sacrificed to idols and committed sexual immorality" (Revelation 2:14, emphasis mine).

We can summarize Balaam in this way:
- Although Balaam appeared to fear Jehovah God, he also practiced divination, which is forbidden to God's people.
- He probably in his heart wanted to curse Israel, just as Balak wanted to.
- He was motivated by financial gain.
- He taught Balak to entice the Israelites into sin.
- Israel put Balaam to death for his part in this story.

Conclusions

Based on the colorful but sad story of Balaam, we reach twelve conclusions.

- The lessons we are to learn from Balaam's sin are pervasive throughout the Bible. God wants us to be duly warned about the possibility of Christian service being sidetracked by the love of money.
- Jesus was serious when He said, "You cannot serve both God and money" (Matthew 6:24).
- Balaam helps us see the extremes of evil to which one will stoop when motivated by the love of money. The love of money truly is the root of all kinds of evil (1 Timothy 6:10).
- Not everyone who speaks the truth about God and His people is a sincere follower of God's will. It is possible to have a great difference between your message, which can be very good, and the intents of your heart, which can be very evil. For a time you may be able to fool people, but God will eventually expose you. "Be not deceived: God cannot be mocked. People reap what they sow" (Galatians 6:7).
- God may mercifully use an unusual method to attempt to get our attention, to try to stop us from going against His will. We must learn to distinguish between adversity that we should prayerfully overcome and cautions that God graciously gives us for our protection and good.
- Sin gives the enemy room to work against us. Balak scored a certain but limited victory. Stay pure so you can fight successfully.
- Psychologists say we find what we are looking for — we find evidences that support what we believe. We may notice verses in the Bible that affirm our desire for financial prosperity yet overlook the references to a simple lifestyle or to Balaam and his sin of using spiritual gifts for monetary gain.
- Balaam's obedience may have been only outward as he inwardly looked for an opportunity to receive Balak's reward.
- Sexual temptations that are spiritually motivated by the enemy may succeed when other temptations do not and will ruin your ministry.
- We do not need to fear anyone's curse. God can turn curses into blessings.
- Spiritual warfare is a reality. God needs influential Christians who will discern the battle lines, enter into spiritual war, and gain victories over

a clever enemy. What would have happened had Moses not been doing spiritual warfare all those years?
- Our own sin blocks God's blessings and protection far more than our enemy's cursings.

For Further Thought

- What kind of warning signal does the conflict between what Balaam did (prophesy as God directed) and what he wanted to do (prophesy in such a way as to receive a monetary reward) send to you?
- Why isn't it good enough to say the right things when we are speaking for God?
- What have you learned in the story of Balaam about the place of sin in spiritual warfare?
- What did you learn from the story of Balaam about interpreting one part of the Bible with other parts of the Bible in mind?
- What do you believe about the conflict between love for money and love for God?
- What did you learn about the power (or lack of power) of a curse? When should Christians be cautious, and when should we be bold with the devil?
- What did you learn about the power of sin to block God's protection and blessings?

CHAPTER 8
JOSHUA

Were you aware that Joshua experienced many years of preparation for leadership under Moses? Did you realize that the story of Joshua confirms the importance of a leader hearing the voice of God? Do you know that Joshua teaches us by his example that it is wise to think and plan strategically — even in spiritual ministry?

It would be easy to overlook, minimize, or misunderstand the leadership of Joshua since he lived most of his public life in the shadow of his famous, intelligent, strong-willed, and illustrious mentor, Moses. However, Joshua was a great person in his own right. His life provides numerous lessons that are beneficial to Christians today.

Joshua Patiently Served as God Carefully Prepared Him

Joshua served, submitted to, and learned from the strong leadership of Moses for forty-plus years before receiving his own opportunity to serve God and lead His people. In our day, many people seek leadership positions without first proving that they are servants.

The following experiences prepared Joshua for leadership:

- Joshua was Moses' helper for many years. "Joshua son of Nun, who had been Moses' aide since youth, spoke up and said, 'Moses, my lord, stop them!'" (Numbers 11:28).
- Moses took Joshua with him when he went up the mountain of God. "Then Moses set out with Joshua his aide, and Moses went up on the mountain of God" (Exodus 24:13).

- On their way down the mountain, with the instructions for the tabernacle and its furniture and the stone tablets of the law, it was Joshua who first heard the sound of revelry in the camp and told Moses about it. "When Joshua heard the noise of the people shouting, he said to Moses, 'There is the sound of war in the camp'" (Exodus 32:17).

- Joshua stayed in the tent, the place for meeting with God. Either he was trusted with the responsibility of staying in the tent of the Lord, or he stayed there voluntarily because he wanted to be close to God. Either way, his staying in the tent speaks well of his early preparation for leadership. "The Lord would speak to Moses face to face, as one speaks to a friend. Then Moses would return to the camp, but his young aide Joshua son of Nun did not leave the tent" (Exodus 33:11).

- Joshua was commissioned to a military assignment early on in the adventures of crossing the wilderness. "Moses said to Joshua, 'Choose some of our men and go out to fight the Amalekites. Tomorrow I will stand on top of the hill with the staff of God in my hands.' So Joshua fought the Amalekites as Moses had ordered, and Moses, Aaron, and Hur went to the top of the hill" (Exodus 17:9-10). In the unseen drama on the mountaintop, Moses was praying, and Aaron and Hur held up Moses' tired arms. Joshua knew that the battle was the Lord's. Possibly from this experience, he learned to pray for and expect miracles in battle.

- Joshua won a victory. "So Joshua overcame the Amalekite army with the sword" (Exodus 17:13). And God wanted Joshua to remember it. "Then the Lord said to Moses, 'Write this on a scroll as something to be remembered and make sure that Joshua hears it, because I will completely blot out the name of Amalek from under heaven'" (Exodus 17:14).

- Moses sent Joshua with eleven other spies into Canaan. "These are the names of the men Moses sent to explore the land. (Moses gave Hoshea son of Nun the name Joshua.)" (Numbers 13:16). This name change may well have been wisdom on Moses' part. Hoshea means "salvation," whereas Joshua means "Jehovah is salvation" — which could have been a daily reminder to Joshua of his dependence on the Lord.

- Joshua and Caleb knew God and had faith that they could conquer the land of Canaan in spite of the giants and other hindrances. However, they were unsuccessful in urging the other Israelites to trust God and invade Canaan. "Joshua son of Nun and Caleb son of Jephunneh, who were among those who had explored the land, tore their clothes" (Numbers 14:6).

The path of development for God's leaders may seem long, but it is better to be prepared and therefore successful than to rush into leadership and fail.

Joshua Heard From and Obeyed God

Joshua heard from God shortly after Moses died. God told him to be strong and courageous, and Joshua obeyed. He spent the rest of his leadership years faithfully implementing God's instructions. Given that Moses was an outstandingly strong and dynamic leader, Joshua did well to receive the instruction from God, strengthen himself in the Lord, and exercise courage.

He obeyed so well that not only in Joshua's lifetime but into the next generation, people still followed God. We only have to compare Joshua's leadership with a long string of weaker judges who led Israel in subsequent generations to appreciate the strong and courageous leadership Joshua exercised.

> "Success that outlives the leader is true success."

> Israel served the Lord through the lifetime of Joshua and of the elders who outlived him and who had experienced everything the Lord had done for Israel. (Joshua 24:31)

Othniel was the next judge. It is written of his time, "So the land had peace for forty years, *until Othniel son of Kenaz died*" (Judges 3:11, emphasis mine).

Regarding Gideon's death, it is written, "Thus Midian was subdued before the Israelites and did not raise its head again. *During Gideon's lifetime,* the land had peace forty years" (Judges 8:28, emphasis mine). "No sooner had Gideon died than the Israelites again prostituted themselves to the Baals" (Judges 8:33).

These Scriptures could just as well be used to prove the wayward tendencies of the Israelites, but the point is that Joshua's success lasted into the next generation while the influence of subsequent leaders did not. Success that outlives the leader is true success. If an operation collapses when the leader dies or moves away, the leader did not build well; his leadership was too personality-centered. He did not build others; he did not build successors. A leader's success dies with him when he has not prepared a successor. Joshua's leadership style had lasting influence. After he died, the elders who had worked with him continued to lead well until they died.

Joshua Thought Ahead and Planned for the Next Steps

Joshua showed courage in significant ways.

- **He planned.** Before Israel crossed the Jordan into Canaan, Joshua secretly sent spies to Jericho. It is not unspiritual to plan ahead.
- **He knew when and how to keep secrets.** Joshua was not public about every aspect of his plans for the invasion of Canaan.
- **He thought.** He spent time thinking about the land of Jericho and the cities and villages he and Caleb and the other ten spies had visited.
- **He planned ahead and did research.** Following the example of Moses, who had sent twelve spies into Canaan earlier, Joshua also sent spies. He considered what his next steps should be.

Joshua Celebrated Important Spiritual Events

When the Israelites moved across the Jordan River, Joshua commemorated the occasion by setting up a memorial. He did not merely look backward; he thoughtfully observed the significance of an important spiritual event. He placed a marker on the spot where it happened, so it would be remembered.

He had a sense of history and realized that future generations should have a connection with history too. God's people need to see the bigger trans-generational picture in order to maintain perspective. Otherwise, we get lost in the difficulties of our own generation.

The stones carried from the bed of the Jordan and placed on the shore were "to serve as a sign among you … tell them that the flow of the Jordan was cut off" (Joshua 4:6–7). If we do not teach and emphasize the miracles we have experienced, we miss an opportunity to influence the next generation.

Do you celebrate and acknowledge spiritual milestones in the life of your church, your home, or your community? What spiritual victories and events do you feel God would have you begin to celebrate? Let's celebrate things worth celebrating. This can be a great encouragement to the people following us.

Joshua Solved Problems

At the crisis of Ai, Joshua proved himself as a problem-solver. He humbled himself, got on his face before God, and dealt severely and correctly with the difficulty of Achan's sin. Joshua's decisive actions paved the way for a victory at Ai; they also provided a sober lesson for all Israel regarding obedience to God.

> "He humbled himself, got on his face before God, and dealt severely and correctly with the difficulty of Achan's sin."

When the whole assembly stoned Achan, they could not have helped but be sobered and warned. Everyone had heard Joshua tell Israel not to take any spoils from Jericho. To treat this direct disobedience lightly would have been an error. Joshua seized the opportunity to make a spectacle of Achan at the beginning stages of a new nation in their own territory. This provided a strong lesson for all of Israel. In the New Testament, Peter dealt with Ananias and Sapphira. He illustrated the same sobering principle, giving the early church a strong lesson.

Joshua Experienced Recovery

Joshua and the elders of Israel made an error when they signed a treaty with the Gibeonites. However, Joshua did not let this error and its negative consequences derail his leadership or block him from obtaining his objectives. He honored his and the elders' promise, spared the Gibeonites, recovered, and moved forward.

A vast conceptual chasm divides these two types of people. Some of us look on our past and allow our failures and disappointments to influence our present. Others, with faith and expectancy, look forward to the potential good God can develop in their futures. Joshua's behavior demonstrates that he looked forward, not backward. Which direction you look will have enormous consequences in how you view life. Will you allow your past to discourage you or will you anticipate the good that God wants to bring to you? The choice is yours.

We all make mistakes. The question is, will we recover from them?

> "We all make mistakes. The question is, will we recover from them?"

The Bible does not paint a picture with no failures, difficulties, or isolation from troubles. Rather, it portrays a life of victory over the difficulties and preservation through the troubles. This was true for Joshua, and it can be true of us today. "The Lord makes firm the steps of those who delight in him; though he stumble, he will not fall, for the Lord upholds him with his hand" (Psalm 37:24).

Paul, in a great forward-looking statement of faith, progress, anticipation, and expectation, said:

> Not that I have already obtained all this, or have already arrived at my goal, but I press on to take hold of that for which Christ Jesus took hold of me. Brothers and sisters, I do not consider myself yet to have taken hold of it. But one thing I do: Forgetting what is behind and straining toward what is ahead, I press on toward the goal to win the prize for which God has called me heavenward in Christ Jesus. (Philippians 3:12–14)

Christians have many opportunities to direct the attention and faith of others into the future. We learn from errors and move on. That is part of the Christian walk.

Joshua Divided His Task into Small Parts

Joshua used wise military tactics. By conducting a central campaign first, he successfully divided the north and south parts of Canaan from each other. He thereby eliminated the possibility of a confederation of both northern and southern kingdoms simultaneously attacking the people of Israel. He took the challenge to defend the Gibeonites, to whom he had wrongly committed Israel. Yet this was an occasion for a great victory. The central area of Canaan came under Israeli control. This success was followed by triumphant campaigns in the south and then in the north.

A simple yet important lesson can be learned from this strategy. Cut your work into doable pieces. Huge tasks seem impossible. Divide them into many small parts. You can't save the world or Africa or even your community all in one week. But you can do a week-sized component if it is divided into day-sized sections.

> "Cut your work into doable pieces."

What can you get done today? What can you try to accomplish this week? What is a reasonable goal for this month? Pick out the most difficult task, define it, limit your projection to an achievable part of it, and do it. That is far better than the counterproductive exercise of hiding from the huge task or just worrying about it.

Joshua Experienced Miracles

Joshua commanded the sun to stand still, lengthening the time during which Israel was fighting a winning battle (Joshua 10:13). In that battle, large hailstones killed more of the enemy than the Israelites killed. "The Lord hurled large hailstones down on them, and more of them died from the hail than were killed by the swords of the Israelites" (Joshua 10:11). God fought for Israel. Joshua would not have succeeded without God's participation. And neither will we.

Joshua Carried Out God's Judgment

Joshua carried out the destruction of immoral, idolatrous nations. The annihilation of that wicked group was an act of mercy. Without that extermination, another generation would have been born and lived in sin, only to die and spend a horrible eternity in a lost condition. It is better not to exist than to be punished for eternity because you did not receive salvation.

We learned about God's corrective punishments stemming from His mercy in the story of Noah in the first chapter of this book. But in that case, *God* punished the unrighteous. In this instance, *Joshua* obeyed as a tool in God's hand.

Many people do not understand the wisdom of God in His acts of justice. But chastisements are acts of mercy to those who benefit from the lesson that can be drawn from the verdict. Punishments are corrections for the guilty; they are also warnings. They give us pause if we are contemplating doing something evil. Penalties are also preventatives. Judgments let us know that God keeps His Word even when His Word promises punishment. There will be fewer people in hell because of the warning power of righteous judgments in human history. And the children or staff members under your administration will love righteousness more if you give them corrections and penalties.

> "There will be fewer people in hell because of the warning power of righteous judgments in human history."

Joshua Challenged Others to Assume Responsibility

Joshua challenged people to grow in their self-reliance and self-determination. He wisely administered national affairs. He did not allow people to become dependent on the central government or to always expect others to help them when they should be helping themselves.

Joshua 17:14–18 is a sample of the wise administrative policies of Joshua:

> The people of Joseph said to Joshua, "Why have you given us only one allotment and one portion for an inheritance? We are a numerous people, and the Lord has blessed us abundantly."
>
> "If you are so numerous," Joshua answered, "and if the hill country of Ephraim is too small for you, go up into the forest and clear land for yourselves there in the land of the Perizzites and Rephaites."
>
> The people of Joseph replied, "The hill country is not enough for us, and all the Canaanites who live in the plain have chariots fitted with iron, both those in Beth Shan and its settlements and those in the Valley of Jezreel."
>
> But Joshua said to the house of Joseph — to Ephraim and Manasseh — "You are numerous and very powerful. You will have not only one allotment but the forested hill country as well. Clear it, and its farthest limits will be yours; though the Canaanites have chariots fitted with iron and though they are strong, you can drive them out."

We weaken people if we help them too much; we create dependency. Liberal handouts are not necessarily wise. Joshua was prudent on this point. Christians today may be tempted to enjoy the respect people give to their benefactors, but we ultimately do people a greater service when we help them achieve self-reliance than when we make them dependent on us.

> "We weaken people if we help them too much; we create dependency."

Joshua Led by Example

Joshua led all Israel in a commitment to worship and serve God. His method of challenging them was a clever and influential teaching method: using the example of his own family and household. His words of challenge to all Israel are some of the most powerful pro-Christian family rhetoric in the Bible. Joshua 24:14–28 contains the often-quoted phrases "Choose for yourselves this day whom you will serve … But as for me and my household we will serve the Lord."

> "His words of challenge to all Israel are some of the most powerful pro-Christian family rhetoric in the Bible."

May the Lord grant us the wisdom to lead our families well and then allow Him to use us to illustrate the gospel message in the fabric of daily life. Then our Christian leadership will stem from our private lives as well as the public successes we experience in our preaching and teaching ministries.

Here are the words to a song I wrote for my grandson Joshua.

> God gave a promise to His children
> To give them a beautiful land.
> He needed a man who would lead them there.
> Joshua was the man.
>
> Lead us to the Promised Land, Joshua. Not to the left or the right.

Lead us to the Promised Land, Joshua. Lead us on in God's light.
The land is good and the land is bright. Oh, what a beautiful sight!
Lead us to the Promised Land, Joshua. Lead us on in God's light.

Today God promises us a beautiful land.
He loves us and has a good plan.
He needs a man who will lead us there.
Who, this time, is God's man?

Lead us to the Promised Land, Joshua. Not to the left or the right.
Lead us to the Promised Land, Joshua. Lead us on in God's light.
The land is good and the land is bright. Oh, what a beautiful sight!
Lead us to the Promised Land, Joshua. Lead us on in God's light.

For Further Thought

- What can you learn from Joshua about patient preparation for leadership?
- What spiritual milestones have you passed without due observation or celebration? What will you do about this in the future?
- What can you learn about problem-solving and recovery from Joshua and his experience with the Gibeonites?
- How might you make use of Joshua's strategy of dividing a large task into smaller parts and doing the small parts one at a time?
- What encouragement to pray for and expect miracles did you receive from this chapter?
- What do you believe about Joshua's policy to destroy the idolatrous people of Canaan? What application of this principle should or should not be made today?
- What do you need to do for those who are following your leadership so that they do not become dependent on you, but rather accept challenges and responsibilities on their own?
- How will you make use of Joshua's teaching method when he said, "Choose for yourselves this day whom you will serve ... But as for me and my household we will serve the Lord"?

CHAPTER 9
SAMUEL

Would you like to have had a praying mother like Samuel had? Did you know that Samuel probably founded an institution of prophets? What would it be like to hear the voice of the Lord as Samuel did? Do you realize that you can?

Samuel was not born into the priesthood or in a kingly line. Yet he was a man of prayer. This man of God — on the sheer merits of the fact that he walked with God, heard from God, spoke for God, and served God with consistency — exercised tremendous influence over Israel. And he affected Israel's safety from the Philistines.

The school of the prophets was founded by Samuel and lasted for several centuries. Through times of corruption and moral decay in Israel's leadership, it exercised godly influence. Priests or kings were the "established" leaders of Israel in that day. But for many generations, this informal band of prophets stepped courageously to the forefront and challenged Israel to serve God.

The Advantages of Having Godly Parents

Samuel arrived in this world as an answer to prayer. His parents went to the house of God to offer sacrifice and to worship God. "Once when they had finished eating and drinking in Shiloh, Hannah stood up. Now Eli the priest was sitting on his chair by the doorpost of the Lord's house. In her deep anguish Hannah prayed to the Lord, weeping bitterly. And she made a vow saying, Lord Almighty, if you will only look on your servant's misery and remember me, and not forget your servant but give her a son, then I will give him to the Lord for all the days of his life, and no razor will ever be used on his head" (1 Samuel 1:9–11). Samuel was dedicated even before birth.

Hannah kept her vow and took Samuel to the tabernacle at Shiloh at a very early age.

> After he was weaned, she took the boy with her, young as he was, along with a three-year-old bull, an ephah of flour and a skin of wine, and brought him to the house of the Lord at Shiloh. When the bull had been sacrificed, they brought the boy to Eli, and she said to him; "Pardon me, my lord, as surely as you live, I am the woman who stood here beside you praying to the Lord. I prayed for this child, and the Lord has granted me what I asked of him. So now I give him to the Lord. For his whole life he will be given over to the Lord." And he worshiped the Lord there. (1 Samuel 1:24–28)

Samuel's affirming and loving mother gave him a new coat every year. "Each year his mother made him a little robe and took it to him when she went up with her husband to offer the annual sacrifice" (1 Samuel 2:19).

Following his mother's line of thought and action, Samuel ministered in the tabernacle. "Samuel was ministering before the Lord — a boy wearing a linen ephod" (1 Samuel 2:18). While still a child, Samuel experienced an outstanding call by God and learned to hear the voice of God.

> **Israel needed a Samuel, but to produce one, God needed a Hannah.**

Parents have a great opportunity to raise their children for God. We should create the most conducive spiritual atmosphere possible in our lives and homes. We should do all we can to encourage our children to have deep experiences with God for themselves.

Israel needed a Samuel, but to produce one, God needed a Hannah. The next generation needs godly citizens, and God is using you and me to produce, pray for, and instruct them. One of the reasons God makes couples one is to produce godly offspring. "Has not the Lord made the two of you one? You belong to him in body and spirit. And why has he made you one? Because he was seeking godly offspring. So be on your guard, and do not be unfaithful to the wife of your youth" (Malachi 2:15). Let's do what we can to give many "Samuels" to the next generation.

Samuel Learned Early How to Discern God's Voice

Just as people have differing degrees of physical strength and intelligence quotients, so we are gifted with varying spiritual abilities. In the atmosphere of living in the tabernacle, Samuel had the ability and opportunity to develop a sensitive ear to hear the voice of the Lord.

> Then the Lord called Samuel.
>
> Samuel answered, "Here I am." And he ran to Eli and said, "Here I am; you called me."
>
> But Eli said, "I did not call; go back and lie down." So he went and lay down.
>
> Again the Lord called, "Samuel!" And Samuel got up and went to Eli and said, "Here I am; you called me."
>
> "My son," Eli said, "I did not call; go back and lie down."
>
> Now Samuel did not yet know the Lord: The word of the Lord had not yet been revealed to him.
>
> A third time the Lord called, "Samuel!" And Samuel got up and went to Eli and said, "Here I am; you called me."
>
> Then Eli realized that the Lord was calling the boy. So Eli told Samuel, "Go and lie down, and if he calls you, say, 'Speak, Lord, for your servant is listening.'" So Samuel went and lay down in his place.
>
> The Lord came and stood there, calling as at the other times, "Samuel! Samuel!"
>
> Then Samuel said, "Speak, for your servant is listening."
> (1 Samuel 3:4–10)

We may not all be as gifted as Samuel was in our ability to hear the voice of God, but we each have the opportunity to choose what we value. If we really want to hear from God and sincerely value His word to us, He will speak. So the question is not "Do I naturally have the spiritual ability to hear God's voice?" Rather it is, "Do I value it enough that I will wait, pray, fast, listen, and focus my attention on God so that I will hear His voice when He speaks?"

Any of us can hear the voice of God if we are listening. We must value, seek, and pursue the word of the Lord. If we do our part, God will do His. He is waiting for us. He will respond.

> **"Any of us can hear the voice of God if we are listening."**

The Lord was with Samuel as he grew up, and he let none of Samuel's words fall to the ground. And all Israel from Dan to Beersheba recognized that Samuel was attested as a prophet of the Lord. The Lord continued to appear at Shiloh, and there he revealed himself to Samuel through his word. And Samuel's word came to all Israel. (1 Samuel 3:19–4:1)

As a young man, Samuel gained the reputation that none of his words fell to the ground. What do we have to do to gain such a reputation? Speak less? Wait before God more? Discern God's voice? Get away from other voices? Value God's voice? Not speak unless or until we hear God's voice? Focus on listening? Yes. All of that.

A Stern Warning about Disciplining Children

God's first message to Samuel was a sober one:

> And the Lord said to Samuel: "See, I am about to do something in Israel that will make the ears of everyone who hears about it tingle. At that time I will carry out against Eli everything I spoke against his family — from beginning to end. For I told him that I would judge his family forever because of the sin he knew about; his sons blasphemed God, and he failed to restrain them. Therefore I swore to the house of Eli, 'The guilt of Eli's house will never be atoned for by sacrifice or offering.'" (1 Samuel 3:11–14)

Christian parents, correct and discipline your children. Eli, Samuel, and David all failed to raise their children to serve God in a godly way. Perhaps it was because of them that Paul — the Old Testament scholar and New Testament writer — gave us this qualification for leadership in God's church: "He must manage his own family well and see that his children obey him, and he must do so in a manner worthy of full respect. (If anyone does not know how to manage his own family, how can he take care of God's church?)" (1 Timothy 3:4-5).

Chapter 10 of my book *Habits of Highly Effective Christians* is entitled "How to Raise Obedient Children." It contains sixteen guidelines for administrating loving, fair, and firm correction for children. These combine to provide a practical, useful, and biblical methodology for training and instructing our children. When Char and I conduct Leadership Empowerment Conferences, this is one of the subjects that stimulates the best discussions and raises many questions.

Samuel heard God's stern warning about the wickedness of Eli's sons. It seems strange that Samuel would not have improved in rearing his own children. Yet his sons proved unfit as judges.

> When Samuel grew old, he appointed his sons as Israel's leaders. The name of his firstborn was Joel and the name of his second was Abijah, and they served at Beersheba. But his sons did not follow his ways. They turned aside after dishonest gain and accepted bribes and perverted justice.
>
> So all the elders of Israel gathered together and came to Samuel at Ramah. They said to him, "You are old, and your sons do not follow your ways; now appoint a king to lead us, such as all the other nations have." (1 Samuel 8:1-5)

Samuel was certainly not a failure as a godly man in his generation, but he did have this flaw: his sons were ungodly. Did Samuel follow Eli's poor example as a father to his own children? On the other hand, if Eli raised Samuel, how was it that Samuel turned out so much better than Eli's own sons? Does this show us the power of Hannah's prayerful influence on Samuel?

Samuel had a second family-related flaw caused by his regard for his sons: he was blind to their lack of qualifications for leadership positions. Nepotism, in this case, stemmed from the natural blindness of the parent. We see sins in others more readily than we see them in our own children. This gives us all the more reason to raise our children to be obedient, godly, and honest citizens.

Prayer Was an Important Part of Samuel's Ministry

Business leaders used to emphasize the need for managers to write down and prioritize all the tasks they need to accomplish in a day. Now, a new emphasis encourages the effective leader to determine his own priorities and take care of them before circumstances demand attention. Schedule your priorities. Do the *important* and you will not be controlled by the tyranny of the *urgent*.

For the Christian, nothing should take priority over prayer. If we don't spend ample time in prayer, we will be ineffective in ministry and in life. None of us can be any more successful than our prayer lives allow.

> "Do the *important* and you will not be controlled by the tyranny of the *urgent*. For the Christian, nothing should take priority over prayer."

No one has the right to tell another how much to pray, so you are free to set your own schedule. I will only say that I have doubled my amount of daily prayer time twice in my adult years. In each increase, I experienced profound results.

How much time you spend in prayer indicates how important prayer is to you. It is not a question of how much time you have, because we all have twenty-four hours each day.

Schedule prayer as a part of your work time. Do not hurriedly pray and then go to work. Make a specific length of time in prayer your first item of business. Think of this in whatever way helps you feel comfortable and justified spending this time in prayer.

Keep your prayer appointments with God. Shut off your cell phone. You must de-prioritize some things in order to prioritize others. Strategically and selectively plan what you will *neglect* so you have time for what you prioritize. God will not rush in and order you to pray the way people do when they knock on your door or call you on the phone.

It is not irresponsible to get alone for extended times of prayer. Given that we cannot solve human problems with human solutions, prayer is the most responsible way for men and women of God to conduct their ministries and their lives. Of course, we need to be available to people. But we also desperately need to be available to God.

Prayer is important, but prayer waits for you. Supervise yourself. If you don't make yourself pray, you won't do it. If you pray only as long as it is convenient, you are allowing circumstances, not your priority, to control your schedule.

What if you knew that the number of times the Lord would speak to you was proportionate to how much time you spent with Him? Would you spend more time with Him? How much do you want to hear from Him?

Look at Samuel's prayer log:

- "I will intercede with the Lord for you" (1 Samuel 7:5).
- "He cried out to the Lord on Israel's behalf, and the Lord answered him" (1 Samuel 7:9).
- "So the Philistines were subdued and they stopped invading Israel's territory. Throughout Samuel's lifetime, the hand of the Lord was against the Philistines" (1 Samuel 7:13).
- "He built an altar there to the Lord" (1 Samuel 7:17).
- "As for me, far be it from me that I should sin against the Lord by failing to pray for you" (1 Samuel 12:23).

Prayer was a vital part of Samuel's ministry. If he did not do it, he would have felt like a failure before God. If God says to pray, then it is a sin to not pray. For Samuel, prayerlessness was sin.

Contrast that with the two times God told Jeremiah *not* to pray:

> Do not pray for this people or offer any plea or petition for them, because I will not listen when they call to me in the time of their distress. (Jeremiah 11:14)

> Then the Lord said to me: "Even if Moses and Samuel were to stand before me, my heart would not go out to this people. Send them away from my presence! Let them go!" (Jeremiah 15:1)

After years of the people of Judah rejecting the prophets God sent, God gave up on Judah. He told Jeremiah *not* to pray for them.

Moses and Samuel had reputations as men of prayer. This reputation was so well-established that God used them as illustrations of prayerful persons. Even though they were powerful intercessors, even they could not have changed God's mind and canceled the punishment God intended for Judah.

We can learn two lessons here. First, Samuel was a man of influence because of his prayers. He was a powerful intercessor worthy to be used as an illustration. Second, sensitive men and women of God do not just exert energy in mindless prayer. They know when they should pray and when they should not. They are efficient in their use of prayer time. They do not waste their energies praying for something that God does not want to do.

Samuel refused to "sin against the Lord by failing to pray" (1 Samuel 12:23). What God wanted to do in Samuel's day required prayer for Israel, and Samuel was the man for the job. On the other hand, what God needed to do in Jeremiah's day required his obedient servant to *not* pray for Judah. Prayer is such a powerful tool that it should not be used capriciously. To pray a lot is not the goal, but rather to pray according to God's current plan.

The Leader of the School of Prophets

Among other great accomplishments, Samuel probably founded an enduring theological institution — the school of prophets. It is not mentioned in Scripture anytime earlier than this. In today's terms, Samuel was likely the founding president of a Bible college, which was later directed by such luminaries as Elijah and Elisha.

> When David had fled and made his escape, he went to Samuel at Ramah and told him all that Saul had done to him. Then he and Samuel went to Naioth and stayed there. Word came to Saul: "David is in Naioth at Ramah"; so he sent men to capture him. But when they saw a group of prophets prophesying, with *Samuel standing there as their leader,* the Spirit of God came on Saul's men, and they also prophesied. Saul was told about it, and he sent more men, and they prophesied too. Saul sent men a third time, and they also prophesied. Finally, he himself left for Ramah and went to the great cistern at Seku. And he asked, "Where are Samuel and David?"
>
> "Over in Naioth at Ramah," they said.
>
> So Saul went to Naioth at Ramah. But the Spirit of God came even on him, and he walked along prophesying until he came to Naioth.

He stripped off his garments, and he too prophesied in Samuel's presence. He lay naked all that day and all that night. This is why people say, "Is Saul also among the prophets?" (1 Samuel 19:18-24, emphasis mine)

It is unfortunate that Saul was not a better student in Samuel's school. Nevertheless, Samuel's ministry teaches us that hearing from God is more important than being in either political or religious structures. Samuel was neither a priest nor a king, but who would deny that he led Israel? And who would deny the value of Israel's prophets after reading the history of Israel?

> Samuel was neither a priest nor a king, but who would deny that he led Israel?

Samuel founded an informal organization of men who sought the Lord, wanted to hear from God, and spoke repeatedly to the people of God by delivering His Word to them. Through the school of prophets, we can appreciate Samuel's ministry and his far-reaching influence. Successive generations of his students continued to influence Israel.

We will look at the school of prophets again in later chapters, when we examine the lives of Elijah and Elisha.

Samuel Was Fruitful

As a result of his prayer life, Samuel was a useful tool in the hand of the Lord. He was the last of the judges and the first of the prophets. Notice the great accomplishments of this man of prayer:

- He effectively judged and led Israel many years. (1 Samuel 12:1-5)
- He provided safety for Israel through prayer. (1 Samuel 7:13)
- He anointed Saul. (1 Samuel 10:1-9)
- He defended his own integrity. (1 Samuel 12:1-5)
- He predicted Saul's eventual failure. (1 Samuel 15:1-29)
- He anointed David as future king of Israel. (1 Samuel 16:1-13)
- He established the first school of the prophets. (1 Samuel 19:18-24)
- He was mourned by all Israel at his death. (1 Samuel 25:1)

Samuel was a seer. He saw things because he spent time with God. And God used him mightily.

God is looking for tools He can use today. Will you be a Samuel? Will you spend time with God? Will you learn to listen to Him? Will you discern His voice? Will you deliver His messages? Will you make yourself available to God? Will you raise your children so they are available to God?

For Further Thought

- In what way(s) would you like to benefit your nation and your children the way Hannah benefited Israel and Samuel?
- How valuable is it to you to hear the voice of the Lord?
- Why do you think Samuel could hear God's stinging rebuke of Eli's sons yet not be very successful as a father himself? What does this teach us about human nature?
- Is prayer as important to you as it was to Samuel?
- What are you doing to raise up Christian leaders for the next generation?
- What changes would you like to make in your life patterns so that you can serve effectively for many years, as Samuel did?

CHAPTER 10

SAUL

Did you know that Saul had several significant early successes and yet remained humble? Do you realize that Saul was a mighty warrior and a fine leader of soldiers in his early experiences as Israel's first king? Were you aware that Saul failed as king because of his own poor choices, not because he was destined to fail? What can we learn from Saul?

I do not like what Saul did. I don't like what he became. I disagree with the choices he made. I do not want be like Saul. I try hard not to be like him. I pray that I may not be like him. Nevertheless, there are ways in which I am like Saul. I make decisions like he did and do things like he did. Sometimes I act selfishly and foolishly. Other times, I throw spears (figuratively) at those with whom I am upset or disappointed.

I can — I *must* — learn from Saul. I must learn how *not* to be like him. Saul's story is a description of what we must not become, rather than a prescription of things we should do.

Saul's ego was his worst enemy. Saul disqualified himself from being a godly leader and eventually destroyed himself. After many years of self-destruction, Saul eventually completed the task by taking his own life. "A gazelle lies slain on your heights, Israel. How the mighty have fallen!" (2 Samuel 1:19).

Saul Was God's Choice at the Beginning

A long string of impressive advantages, blessings, and positive signs accompanied Saul's selection as king and his presentation to Israel. First Samuel 8:2–10:7 records a detailed and impressive narrative explaining God's sovereign involvement:

- God told Samuel to give Israel a king. (1 Samuel 8:21–22)
- God providentially brought Saul to Samuel. (1 Samuel 9:1–18)
- Samuel understood it was God's will to anoint Saul. (1 Samuel 9:19–20)
- Saul apparently had genuine self-effacement and humility. (1 Samuel 9:21)
- Samuel honored Saul publicly in word and deed. (1 Samuel 9:22–24)
- Samuel gave Saul a night-long conference. (1 Samuel 9:25–26)
- Samuel gave a promise to Saul for direction from God. (1 Samuel 9:27–10:8)
- God changed Saul's heart. (1 Samuel 10:9–16)
- Samuel boasted about Saul as he presented Israel's new king: "Do you see the man the Lord has chosen? There is no one like him among all the people." (1 Samuel 10:24)
- The people enthusiastically accepted and approved of Saul. (1 Samuel 10:24)
- Samuel explained to Saul the rights and duties of kingship. (1 Samuel 10:25)
- God touched the hearts of valiant men to follow Saul. (1 Samuel 10:26)
- Saul humbly refused to retaliate against the scoundrels who despised him and spoke unkindly about him. (1 Samuel 10:27)

Saul was God's choice. He began well. He had every opportunity to succeed as Israel's king. Prior to his selection, Saul had no ambition to be king. However, his ego took over after he became king.

Because we know the end of his story, we may be critical of Saul's early life — before he began making big mistakes. Part of this may be due to our preference for his replacement, our darling David. In the early part of Saul's story, he was the right choice. He could have succeeded.

But Saul failed.

People who take the philosophical position of determinism assume that Saul was destined to fail. That assumption does an injustice to God, Saul, and the role of personal responsibility. Saul could only be guilty of sin if he were free to not sin. He could not be guilty of failure unless he were free to not fail; failure would have been his destiny.

But Saul was not a mere puppet, controlled by powers greater and stronger than his. His freedom to not fail makes him guilty.

Determinism's view is the wrong way to look at Saul and God and our own lives. In order to understand the big lesson of this chapter, we must understand that Saul had a good beginning. He could have continued to do well, but he freely made poor choices.

> "He began well. He had every opportunity to succeed as Israel's king."

Saul's First Military Venture

Shortly after he was selected as king, Saul had a choice to make. He could allow the enemy of Israel to disgrace his people and his nation by gouging out the eyes of a part of the Israelites — the Gileadites. Or he could muster the rest of the people of Israel to fight and rescue them. He made the right choice. Saul and his army marched all night and rescued the people of Jabesh Gilead from the threatening Ammonites.

> Nahash the Ammonite went up and besieged Jabesh Gilead. And all the men of Jabesh said to him, "Make a treaty with us, and we will be subject to you."
>
> But Nahash the Ammonite replied, "I will make a treaty with you only on the condition that I gouge out the right eye of every one of you and so bring disgrace on all Israel."
>
> The elders of Jabesh said to him, "Give us seven days so we can send messengers throughout Israel; if no one comes to rescue us, we will surrender to you."
>
> When the messengers came to Gibeah of Saul and reported these terms to the people, they all wept aloud. Just then Saul was returning from the fields, behind his oxen, and he asked, "What is wrong with everyone? Why are they weeping?" Then they repeated to him what the men of Jabesh had said.

> When Saul heard their words, the Spirit of God came on him in power, and he burned with anger. He took a pair of oxen, cut them into pieces, and sent the pieces by messengers throughout Israel, proclaiming, "This is what will be done to the oxen of anyone who does not follow Saul and Samuel."
>
> Then the terror of the Lord fell on the people, and they turned out with one accord. When Saul mustered them at Bezek, the men of Israel numbered three hundred thousand and those of Judah thirty thousand.
>
> They told the messengers who had come, "Say to the men of Jabesh Gilead, 'By the time the sun is hot tomorrow, you will be rescued.'"
>
> When the messengers went and reported this to the men of Jabesh, they were elated. They said to the Ammonites, "Tomorrow we will surrender to you, and you can do to us whatever you like."
>
> The next day Saul separated his men into three divisions; during the last watch of the night they broke into the camp of the Ammonites and slaughtered them until the heat of the day. Those who survived were scattered, so that no two of them were left together. (1 Samuel 11:1–11)

Notice how God led Saul in this matter and even confirmed his actions. Saul "burned with anger" after the Spirit of God came on him in power. And when Saul called for the men of war to come, the "terror of the Lord fell on the people." God was truly with Saul in this military venture and gave him great success.

After this, Saul was confirmed as king. Earlier, some had thought little of Saul, and Saul's new supporters wanted to do away with them. However, Saul graciously forgave them.

> The people then said to Samuel, "Who was it that asked, 'Shall Saul reign over us?' Turn these men over to us so that we may put them to death." But Saul said, "No one will be put to death today, for this day the Lord has rescued Israel."
>
> Then Samuel said to the people, "Come, let us go to Gilgal and there renew the kingship." So all the people went to Gilgal and

made Saul king in the presence of the Lord. There they sacrificed fellowship offerings before the Lord, and Saul and all the Israelites held a great celebration. (1 Samuel 11:12-15)

God had changed Saul's heart (1 Samuel 10:9-16). He began well, had potential for being a good king, and had every opportunity for success. His first military victory confirmed this. But his very next battle sowed the seeds of his gradual downfall.

Saul Presumptuously Offered Sacrifices

Saul responded to geopolitical events beyond his control and attacked the Philistines. No problem there. But then, in an event within his control, Saul acted presumptuously.

> The Philistines assembled to fight Israel, with three thousand chariots, six thousand charioteers, and soldiers as numerous as the sand on the seashore. They went up and camped at Mikmash, east of Beth Aven. When the Israelites saw that their situation was critical and that their army was hard pressed, they hid in caves and thickets, among the rocks, and in pits and cisterns. Some Hebrews even crossed the Jordan to the land of Gad and Gilead.
>
> Saul remained at Gilgal, and all the troops with him were quaking with fear. He waited seven days, the time set by Samuel; but Samuel did not come to Gilgal, and Saul's men began to scatter. So he said, "Bring me the burnt offering and the fellowship offerings." And Saul offered up the burnt offering. Just as he finished making the offering, Samuel arrived, and Saul went out to greet him.
>
> "What have you done?" asked Samuel.
>
> Saul replied, "When I saw that the men were scattering, and that you did not come at the set time, and that the Philistines were assembling at Mikmash, I thought, 'Now the Philistines will come down against me at Gilgal, and I have not sought the Lord's favor.' So I felt compelled to offer the burnt offering."
>
> "You have done a foolish thing," Samuel said. "You have not kept the command the Lord your God gave you; if you had, he would have established your kingdom over Israel for all time. But now

your kingdom will not endure; the Lord has sought out a man after his own heart and appointed him ruler of his people, because you have not kept the Lord's command."

Then Samuel left Gilgal and went up to Gibeah in Benjamin, and Saul counted the men who were with him. They numbered about six hundred. (1 Samuel 13:5-15)

Samuel instructed Saul to wait for him to come to offer sacrifices. It was inappropriate for Saul to offer a sacrifice since he was neither a priest nor a prophet. Saul made a foolish and presumptuous decision when he did not wait for Samuel.

God responded to what Saul did and informed him of his mistake through Samuel.

> *Saul made a foolish and presumptuous decision when he did not wait for Samuel.*

Samuel said to Saul, "I am the one the Lord sent to anoint you king over his people Israel; so listen now to the message from the Lord. This is what the Lord Almighty says: 'I will punish the Amalekites for what they did to Israel when they waylaid them as they came up from Egypt. Now go, attack the Amalekites and totally destroy all that belongs to them. Do not spare them; put to death men and women, children and infants, cattle and sheep, camels and donkeys.'" (1 Samuel 15:1-3)

God gave Saul another chance, but a tendency toward disobedience had already developed.

Saul Failed the Second Test

Had Saul obeyed Samuel's word during this second opportunity, he could have proceeded with a successful career. But Saul disobeyed again, this time by not exterminating the Amalakites. It was Saul's own behavior that made God sorry he made Saul king. God made his choice for Saul. But when Saul made bad choices, God responded accordingly.

So Saul summoned the men and mustered them at Telaim — two hundred thousand foot soldiers and ten thousand from Judah.

> Saul went to the city of Amalek and set an ambush in the ravine. Then he said to the Kenites, "Go away, leave the Amalekites so that I do not destroy you along with them; for you showed kindness to all the Israelites when they came up out of Egypt." So the Kenites moved away from the Amalekites.
>
> Then Saul attacked the Amalekites all the way from Havilah to Shur, near the eastern border of Egypt. He took Agag king of the Amalekites alive, and all his people he totally destroyed with the sword. But Saul and the army spared Agag and the best of the sheep and cattle, the fat calves and lambs — everything that was good. These they were unwilling to destroy completely, but everything that was despised and weak they totally destroyed. (1 Samuel 15:6-9)

God did not manipulate Saul. Likewise, God does not program the whole drama of our lives in advance. He watches what we do and responds, acts, helps, hinders, guides, blesses, or refrains from blessing, according to our behavior. Notice God's response to Saul's actions.

> *Then* the word of the Lord came to Samuel: "I regret that I have made Saul king, because he has turned away from me and has not carried out my instructions." Samuel was angry, and he cried out to the Lord all that night.
>
> Early in the morning Samuel got up and went to meet Saul, but he was told, "Saul has gone to Carmel. There *he has set up a monument in his own honor* and has turned and gone on down to Gilgal."
>
> When Samuel reached him, Saul said, "The Lord bless you! I have carried out the Lord's instructions."
>
> But Samuel said, "What then is this bleating of sheep in my ears? What is this lowing of cattle that I hear?"
>
> Saul answered, "The soldiers brought them from the Amalekites; they spared the best of the sheep and cattle to sacrifice to the Lord your God, but we totally destroyed the rest."
>
> "Enough!" Samuel said to Saul. "Let me tell you what the Lord said to me last night."
>
> "Tell me," Saul replied.

Samuel said, "Although you were once small in your own eyes, did you not become the head of the tribes of Israel? The Lord anointed you king over Israel. And he sent you on a mission, saying, 'Go and completely destroy those wicked people, the Amalekites; make war on them until you have wiped them out.' Why did you not obey the Lord? Why did you pounce on the plunder and do evil in the eyes of the Lord?" "But I did obey the Lord," Saul said. "I went on the mission the Lord assigned me. I completely destroyed the Amalekites and brought back Agag their king. The soldiers took sheep and cattle from the plunder, the best of what was devoted to God, in order to sacrifice them to the Lord your God at Gilgal."

But Samuel replied: "Does the Lord delight in burnt offerings and sacrifices as much as in obeying the Lord? *To obey is better* than sacrifice, and *to heed is better* than the fat of rams. For rebellion is like the sin of divination, and arrogance like the evil of idolatry. *Because you have rejected the word of the Lord, he has rejected you as king.*"

Then Saul said to Samuel, "I have sinned. I violated the Lord's command and your instructions. I was afraid of the men and so I gave in to them. Now I beg you, forgive my sin and come back with me, so that I may worship the Lord."

But Samuel said to him, "I will not go back with you. *You have rejected the word of the Lord, and the Lord has rejected you as king over Israel!*" (1 Samuel 15:9–23, emphasis mine)

Saul's biggest problem was willfulness. He was willing to disobey God. Obedience is difficult if one does not have a contrite and yielded heart. People tend to admire such things as intelligence, ability, persistence, endurance, willingness to suffer or experience pain and inconvenience, physical strength, and charm. However, no human qualities are as important as obedience.

Saul was more interested in setting up a monument to himself than in doing what God said. So Saul did not obey, even when God gave him a second chance.

> "Obedience is difficult if one does not have a contrite and yielded heart."

If you are unwilling to obey the Lord, you too will end up with Saul's problem. The Lord cannot use you. Success in God's eyes — real success — is measured by the degree to which you are doing what God has asked you to do. Obedience is success. God's rejection of disobedient servants is therefore merely an outcome of our decisions.

Saul Became Jealous of David

Saul himself appointed David as court musician and captain in his army. Yet Saul soon became jealous of the person he had appointed.

> Whatever mission Saul sent him on, David was so successful that Saul gave him a high rank in the army. This pleased all the troops, and Saul's officers as well. (1 Samuel 18:5)

> As they danced, they sang: "Saul has slain his thousands, and David his tens of thousands." Saul was very angry; this refrain displeased him. (1 Samuel 18:7-8)

> In everything he did he had great success, because the Lord was with him. (1 Samuel 18:14)

> The Philistine commanders continued to go out to battle, and as often as they did, David met with more success than the rest of Saul's officers, and his name became well known. (1 Samuel 18:30)

Scoundrels actively spoke against Saul earlier, and he did not allow anyone to punish them. To the contrary, David was doing Saul no harm; he was serving him. But David's success became a threat to Saul's ego. He did not like it when the women sang of David's superior accomplishments. Saul's good character proved to be short-lived.

> "Must you always be the best at everything?"

Do you show how magnanimous you are by tolerating criticism from those who cannot hurt you, only to harbor jealousy toward those who may succeed more than you? Must you always be the best at everything? Or are you big enough in character to surround yourself with people more capable than you in their areas of expertise and rejoice in their successes? That takes self-confidence — God-given self-confidence. God-confidence can help you handle the success of those around you.

Saul Was Plagued by an Evil Spirit

Saul's experience was excessive. However, the advantage of an extreme picture in literature is that the lesson is clear. It was clear enough in this case to reveal the sin in Saul. The ability to recognize it helps us avoid it in our own lives. His experience helps us today focus on the issue of professional or positional jealousy.

What choices are you making today that impact the attitudes you will have tomorrow? What do you need to think, say, and do now so that your attitude is sweet, encouraging, and godly in the future? When we make decisions, we are not only affecting the present, we are also moving in the direction of becoming something else. What are you becoming?

Saul was not evil at first. And his change wasn't sudden. Through a series of decisions he made, an evil presence developed and eventually predominated. He did not like it when the women sang of David's superior accomplishments. The following verses paint a picture of Saul's downfall:

> Now the Spirit of the Lord had departed from Saul, and an evil spirit from the Lord tormented him. (1 Samuel 16:14)

> Saul's attendants said to him, "See, an evil spirit from God is tormenting you." (1 Samuel 16:15)

> "Let our lord command his servants here to search for someone who can play the lyre. He will play when the evil spirit from God comes on you, and you will feel better." (1 Samuel 16:16)

> Whenever the spirit from God came on Saul, David would take up his lyre and play. Then relief would come to Saul; he would feel better, and the evil spirit would leave him. (1 Samuel 16:23)

> The next day an evil spirit from God came forcefully on Saul. He was prophesying in his house, while David was playing the lyre, as he usually did. Saul had a spear in his hand. (1 Samuel 18:10)

> But an evil spirit from the Lord came on Saul as he was sitting in his house with his spear in his hand ... David was playing the lyre. (1 Samuel 19:9)

Through his series of choices and behaviors, Saul's heart closed toward God. Because of Saul's ego, God removed Himself from him. Saul's own choices opened him to the influences of evil spirits that tormented him. He was unable to successfully wrestle against them. At this stage, King Saul was trying to live with the successful David in his court and wrestling with an unseen spiritual enemy. He was merely living with the consequences of earlier poor choices.

Men and women of God must be careful to keep every thought under captivity. If not, we run the chance that some evil spirit will get into our spirits and confuse us, make us jealous, or disturb our relationships with those around us. Second Corinthians 10:5 says, "We demolish arguments and every pretension that sets itself up against the knowledge of God, and we take captive every thought to make it obedient to Christ."

If we harbor evil thoughts, we expose ourselves to satanic attacks or other evil influences. Demons take advantage of the open door, enter our hearts and minds, attempt to control our wills, and eventually defile us. The Bible cautions us this way: "See to it that no one falls short of the grace of God and that no bitter root grows up to cause trouble and defile many" (Hebrews 12:15). If our minds are defiled, we will not see clearly. We will become jealous, act foolishly and selfishly, and throw virtual spears at our supposed enemies.

> **Fight to keep a clean heart or you will become useless.**

If we are contaminated, defiled, and influenced by evil spirits, we are manipulated by powers greater than we are. We can't be loving, affirming, and big-hearted. Instead, we are jealous, self-centered, suspicious, and narrow-minded. This will ruin the ministry of any man or woman of God. Fight to keep a clean heart or you will become useless. You may not become as useless as Saul, but to the degree you allow evil influences into your mind, you will decrease your usefulness to God.

You may think this is so obvious and elementary that it should not be in this book. Unfortunately, I have seen pastors, Christian leaders, and even myself become too much like Saul. I have struggled plenty of times against being confused by an evil spirit, giving in to lust, or becoming bitter. I have fought not to be jealous and prayed earnestly that I would be forgiving and affirming even to those who have hurt me. Christians today are all subject to these kinds of problems. Let us do our best not to give place to the devil.

Saul's Self-destructive Behavior

Instead of seeking God, Saul sought Satan. The Philistines assembled against Israel. Saul, after failing to reach God, resorted to the self-destructive measure of consulting evil spirits through a witch.

> Now Samuel was dead, and all Israel had mourned for him and buried him in his own town of Ramah. Saul had expelled the mediums and spiritists from the land. The Philistines assembled and came and set up camp at Shunem, while Saul gathered all Israel and set up camp at Gilboa. When Saul saw the Philistine army, he was afraid; terror filled his heart. He inquired of the Lord, but the Lord did not answer him by dreams or Urim or prophets. Saul then said to his attendants, "Find me a woman who is a medium, so I may go and inquire of her." (1 Samuel 28:3–7)

It was wrong for Saul to consult demons through a medium. But God allowed an apparition of the departed Samuel to appear before him.

> Samuel said to Saul, "Why have you disturbed me by bringing me up?"
>
> "I am in great distress," Saul said. "The Philistines are fighting against me, and God has departed from me. He no longer answers me, either by prophets or by dreams. So I have called on you to tell me what to do."
>
> Samuel said, "Why do you consult me, now that the Lord has departed from you and become your enemy? The Lord has done what he predicted through me. The Lord has torn the kingdom out of your hands and given it to one of your neighbors — to David. Because you did not obey the Lord or carry out his fierce wrath against the Amalekites, the Lord has done this to you today. The Lord will deliver both Israel and you into the hands of the Philistines, and tomorrow you and your sons will be with me. The Lord will also give the army of Israel into the hands of the Philistines." (1 Samuel 28:15–19)

Was the appearance that seemed to be Samuel really Samuel, or was it an evil spirit? If it was Samuel, why did God allow the wicked Saul to disturb the godly Samuel? If it wasn't Samuel, does God allow evil spirits to successfully pretend to be someone else? Does He allow them to speak? If they speak, do they always (or ever) speak the truth?

Demons have no desire to tell the truth except to establish credibility so they can deceive in greater measure. Their greatest deceit is that they, not God, should be consulted. When summoned, they will respond. They will say, "God may hide his plans, but we demons will tell you whatever you want to know. Call on us. We are there for you."

> **Their greatest deceit is that they, not God, should be consulted.**

While some of the above questions must go unanswered, this much we can assume: If the apparition Saul saw was anything other than the Samuel to which the narrative refers, the Bible would not be telling us the truth. If the text says it was Samuel, it was Samuel. If it had been an evil spirit, the Scripture would have said it was an evil spirit pretending to be Samuel. It evidently was Samuel, and he could be depended on to tell the stunning truth; his words would not drop to the ground, even now. Saul was doomed. It was too late for him to repent. The Philistines would win.

If Saul knew the Philistines would win the battle, why did he not at least beg them for peace? Why did he choose self-destruction and take Jonathan, the army, and Israel's reputation with him? Saul was selfish to the end. He killed himself the next day on the battlefield. He destroyed not only himself but others for whom he should have been protective and caring. This is poor leadership at its worst.

> **We can learn, even from Saul, how not to be like Saul.**

What are we to learn from the tragedy of Saul's failure? If we realize that we too, having begun well, have the potential for becoming self-destructive through disobedience, we can benefit from the warning Saul's life provides for us. Let us courageously and quickly identify any ego-related self-preservative attitudes within us. Jesus said, "For whoever wants to save their life will lose it but whoever loses their life for me and the gospel will save it." (Matthew 16:25)

May God give us the grace to heed the warning of Saul's failures and serve His people humbly and obediently. Then the story of Saul will have had its proper effect. We can learn, even from Saul, how not to be like Saul.

For Further Thought

- The privileges of representing God, serving Him, delivering God's Word, and standing before Him as intercessors have caused spiritually unqualified persons to seek that office. Saul was presumptuous. Are you also presumptuous in any way?
- Which do you tend to fear more, people's opinions or God's evaluation of your character? How can you address any improper balance you may have in this area?
- Are you jealous of more successful Christians, or do you encourage them? Give examples.
- How do you feel when you think the Holy Spirit has left you for a period of time?
- Do you have a tendency to pamper your ego and thereby kill your ministry? How do you plan to kill your ego instead?

CHAPTER 11
DAVID

Did you know that David lived, grew up, and developed a relationship with the Lord in obscure sheep fields? How do you suppose he cultivated an ability to trust in and focus on God by watching sheep? Could the sheep he led have taught him not to fight back or seek revenge?

David was gifted, perhaps a genius. He was a musician, poet, athlete, military strategist, ethicist, statesman, leader, and king. He is one of the most prominent figures in the history of the world and the most famous ancestor of Jesus, who is called the Son of David. No Bible character offers such a full range of human successes and failures as David.

The highlights of David's life are recorded in 1 Samuel 16 through 1 Kings 2:11 and in 1 Chronicles 10:14 through 29:30. There we learn this man after God's own heart (1 Samuel 13:14) allowed sin in his sons without correcting them. He also loved God passionately yet had an affair with a married woman. And he was a loyal soldier and beloved military leader who betrayed one of his finest warriors and closest friends.

David's life falls into three phases: his years of preparation for leadership, the successful years of his reign, and the years of difficulty following his moral failure. Fewer chapters record his successful years than record the events of his preparatory or difficult years.

We often think that as soon as David got past his training under the discipline of Saul, his successful kingly career began and continued for a long time. But Scripture indicates his successful years were limited.

Trouble, adversity, and embarrassment awaited him in his latter years as a result of his moral failure, not correcting his sons, and trusting in the flesh.

Obscurity Is No Problem for God

When Samuel visited Jesse's home in search of the next king for Israel, Jesse overlooked David. If this is any indication of the family's posture toward David, it is clear the family had little regard for the youngest son. Assuming that David wrote the 116th Psalm, he refers favorably there to the formative example of his mother. "Truly I am your servant, Lord; I am your servant, as was my mother before me; you have loosed my bonds of affliction" (Psalm 116:16). Though disregarded by his father and his brothers (who followed Jesse's example), David was nevertheless encouraged by his mother's love for God.

We do not know how many years (or how many months in each year) David spent alone, watching the sheep. His references in the psalms to his sheep-watching responsibilities suggest that shepherding was a major part of his young life. In any event, he used those hours well, worshipping, developing the performing arts in his musical abilities, and practicing with his sling, killing a bear and a lion. Most important, he used the contemplative opportunity to develop his personal philosophy of life (Psalm 23). In the lonely valleys near Bethlehem, God built Israel's most famous and beloved king.

I am a runner. In mid-2005, I ran my regular early-morning ten kilometers numerous times in Bethlehem, just down the hill from the traditional home of Jesse's family. I waved greetings to young shepherd boys watching their sheep in the fields on those hills and valleys. The ample rocks and barrenness suggested to me that David had plenty of unoccupied hours. I suspect any shepherd would gladly seek profitable pastimes provided he possessed imagination. David evidently did.

David was like Moses as a leader-in-training. Moses was banished from the king's court and fled for his life. David was disregarded by his family and assigned to watching the sheep. Both leaders developed while watching sheep in obscurity. In due time, they were discovered and brought into public leadership.

You may think you live in obscurity and no one knows you even exist. That is a wonderful place to be because God knows exactly where you are. Be content, and do not waste the valuable training time God is giving you for contemplation, prayer, and self-development. Obscurity is not a problem for God. If you sulk in your obscurity, you may remain there. Instead, seek God and prepare yourself for greater service. God found Moses, and God found David. He will find you too.

> *God found Moses, and God found David. He will find you too.*

Jesse neglected David, but God helped Samuel find him (1 Samuel 16). "For the eyes of the Lord range throughout the earth to strengthen those whose hearts are fully committed to him" (2 Chronicles 16:9). What are you doing to develop yourself while you're waiting for Him to discover you?

The Basis for Confidence

Jesse sent his son David with instructions to take food supplies to his soldier brothers serving in Saul's army. When he arrived, his brothers scorned him rather than welcoming him. "When Eliab, David's oldest brother heard him speaking with the men, he burned with anger at him and asked, 'Why have you come down here? And with whom did you leave those few sheep in the wilderness? I know how conceited you are and how wicked your heart is; you came down only to watch the battle'" (1 Samuel 17:28). David was not discouraged by this treatment, however. He pursued his interest in the battle, Goliath, and God's reputation.

Later, as David approached the giant, Goliath cursed him by his gods. David ignored the giant's disdain and his slanderous remarks, and replied with his own mature statement of his philosophy of war:

> You come against me with sword and spear and javelin, but I come against you in the name of the Lord Almighty, the God of the armies of Israel, whom you have defied. This day the Lord will deliver you into my hands, and I'll strike you down and cut off your head. This very day I will give the carcasses of the Philistine army to the birds and the wild animals, and the whole world will know that there is a God in Israel. All those gathered here will know that it is not by sword or spear that the Lord

saves; for the battle is the Lord's and he will give all of you into our hands. (1 Samuel 17:45-47)

Goliath was formidable, but David placed his faith in God and His power, and he won the victory.

David's God-focused philosophy of war was right on target. It enabled him to fight successfully for many years.

Submitting to God's Training Program

Samuel secretly anointed David to become king. Soon after that, God began the developmental process through which He prepared David. At Saul's invitation, David became Saul's harpist and began to observe life at the king's court. After returning to his home, presumably because of Israel's war with the Philistines, David's father sent him to his brothers at the battlefront with cheese and foodstuffs.

Jealous Saul was a difficult mentor. David escaped the king's spear twice and his army twice. But through adversity after adversity at the hand of Saul, David learned to not fight back. He refused to oppose God's anointed.

David fled from Jerusalem when his son Absalom, an illegitimate and self-proclaimed leader, entered the city. He left his home rather than see a civil war destroy Jerusalem. Even against the silly and powerless fool Shimei, David would not fight (as recorded in 2 Samuel 16:10-14).

> *David, the ethicist, held to a higher level of behavior than Moses had taught.*

The imprecatory Psalms, which include cursing against enemies, are sometimes misunderstood. But when we realize that David trusted God to defend him rather than taking revenge himself, we can appreciate the high ethical standard David maintained. David, the ethicist, held to a higher level of behavior than Moses had taught. Moses only instructed that one should limit one's vengeance to repaying in kind the treatment of the original offender.

If we do not fight for ourselves but rather let God do our fighting for us, we will have learned a valuable lesson from David.

David Was a Wise Leader of Soldiers

David's victory over Goliath catapulted him into a successful military career. He had victories everywhere he turned. "David was so successful that Saul gave him a high rank in the army" (1 Samuel 18:5). "In everything he did he had great success, because the Lord was with him" (1 Samuel 18:14). "David met with more success than the rest of Saul's officers, and his name became well known" (1 Samuel 18:30).

Later at Nob, he fled from Saul. David sought direction from God, relying on the priests there to assist him. "Ahimelek inquired of the Lord for him" (1 Samuel 22:10). Saul learned of the priest's assistance and became extremely angry. Ahimelek responded to Saul, "Was that day the first time I inquired of God for him? Of course not!" (1 Samuel 22:15). Saul had eighty-five priests killed that day. This did not stop David from inquiring of the Lord often.

Because he habitually sought the Lord, God gave David military intelligence for his protection many times. At Keilah, as he continued to flee from Saul, "he inquired of the Lord saying, 'Shall I go and attack these Philistines?'" (1 Samuel 23:2). "Once again David inquired of the Lord" (1 Samuel 23:4). "Again David asked, 'Will the citizens of Keilah surrender me and my men to Saul?' And the Lord said, 'They will'" (1 Samuel 23:12). David was protected time and time again.

> "Because he habitually sought the Lord, God gave David military intelligence for his protection many times."

When David became king, the Philistines invaded Israeli territory, "so David inquired of the Lord, 'Shall I go and attack the Philistines? Will you deliver them into my hands?'" (2 Samuel 5:19). The Philistines attacked again, "so David inquired of the Lord, and he answered, 'Do not go straight up, but circle around behind them and attack them in front of the poplar trees. As soon as you hear the sound of marching in the tops of the poplar trees, move quickly, because that will mean the Lord has gone out in front of you to strike the Philistine army'" (2 Samuel 5:23-24).

It is little wonder David could say, "With your help I can advance against a troop; with my God I can scale a wall" (2 Samuel 22:30).

David's guiding principle of continually inquiring of the Lord, coupled with his faith in God as the source for military victories, was the reason for his repeated successes. What if you and I were to apply that policy to the work we do for God? What difference would it make in our homes, businesses, careers, churches, communities, and nations?

David's Heart for God

One has only to read David's psalms to find ample poetic evidence of his strong desire for the Lord.

The celebrative manner in which David directed and participated in the procession to Jerusalem with the ark is just one example of his public and private passion for God (2 Samuel 6:1-11). David was not ashamed of his zeal for the Lord, as evidenced by his scorning of the ridicule his wife (Saul's daughter) gave him. "David said to Michal, 'It was before the Lord, who chose me rather than your father or anyone from his house when he appointed me ruler over the Lord's people Israel — I will celebrate before the Lord. I will become even more undignified than this, and I will be humiliated in my own eyes. But by these slave girls you spoke of, I will be held in honor'" (2 Samuel 6:21-22).

David's penitence after his sin with Bathsheba and against Uriah also reveals David's love for God.

> Against you, you only have I sinned and done what is evil in your sight; so you are right in your verdict and justified when you judge ... Cleanse me with hyssop, and I will be clean; wash me, and I will be whiter than snow. Let me hear joy and gladness; let the bones you have crushed rejoice ... Create in me a pure heart, O God, and renew a steadfast spirit within me. Do not cast me from your presence or take your Holy Spirit from me. Restore to me the joy of your salvation and grant me a willing spirit, to sustain me ... You do not delight in sacrifice, or I would bring it; you do not take pleasure in burnt offering. My sacrifice, O God, is a broken spirit; a broken and contrite heart you, God, will not despise. (Psalm 51:4, 7-8, 10-12, 16-17)

Let us too have a heart toward God.

Beginning Well Is Not Enough

David was Israel's greatest king. He was the founder of the dynasty in which Jesus Christ was born. Yet only ten chapters record David's triumphant years. For sixteen chapters, he was in training. For ten chapters, he was a triumphant king. These are followed by fourteen chapters that record his sin, its consequences, and his constant struggle against various difficulties until he died.

David had three major strengths that were offset later in life by three major failures. If he had used any one of his strengths, he could have avoided all three of the following failures:

- **David did not correct his children.** David was soft on the sin in his own family. He failed to discipline his sons, three of whom most certainly should have been punished: Amnon, Absolom, and Adonijah. Amnon raped his sister Tamar. Absalom revolted against his father and tried to take the entire kingdom. When David did nothing about it, Joab took matters into his own hands, killed Absalom, and eventually rebuked David. Just prior to David's death, Adonijah also tried to usurp the throne. Scripture says, "His father had never rebuked him by asking, 'Why do you behave as you do?'" (1 Kings 1:6). David did not discipline his sons; Israel suffered shame as a result.

- **David sinned with Bathsheba and murdered Uriah.** Some Bible scholars believe that when David sinned with Bathsheba, he should not have been in Jerusalem in the first place, but rather on the battlefield. As a soldier and leader of soldiers, the sin of David murdering one of his mighty men is unconscionable.

- **David showed his dependence on human strength by numbering his army, contrary to God's Word.** David's final mistake was to trust in the power of his own army rather than trust in God. God told Israel through Moses not to count soldiers, which was a way of expressing the need to trust God, not the arm of flesh. Yet David insisted, against Joab's advice, on enrolling the fighting men.

David could have utilized these major strengths against those failures:

- **He believed in God for military victory.** Why did David not trust God for victory toward the end of his life? Earlier, he had inquired of the Lord regarding military questions and gained numerous victories. Could God not give him further victories without relying on a strong army of many soldiers? Could God's strength in battle not also have helped David raise obedient children?

- **He inquired of the Lord regarding military matters.** Why didn't David inquire of the Lord regarding his children's disobedience? Why not ask the Lord what to do with the problem of the woman in his neighborhood bathing within view of the royal palace? Couldn't he inquire of the Lord regarding the decision to number Israel's army?
- **He had a passionate love for God.** If David loved God so intensely, why did he allow disobedience in his family? How could he have an affair with a neighbor's wife? How could he send Uriah to his death? How could he trust human military might and disobey God's command not to number his army?

> "His faith in God's power to deliver, his policy of regularly seeking God's counsel, and his love for God were in operation only selectively later in his life."

It seems the older David grew, and the more comfortable he became as king, the more his moral and spiritual strength declined. His faith in God's power to deliver, his policy of regularly seeking God's counsel, and his love for God were in operation only selectively later in his life. This can be a lesson to help us avoid becoming too comfortable — and less dependent on God. David did not finish well. Will you?

For Further Thought

- Are you willing to inquire of the Lord for success everywhere you turn? How will you cultivate this practice in your daily life?
- What does it mean to have a heart toward God? Are you developing this trait in yourself?
- How can you use your personal strengths to help you triumph over your weaknesses?
- What steps do you need to take today so that you will still thrive as you enter your golden years? What are you doing currently to position yourself to finish well?

CHAPTER 12
ELIJAH

You may not feel like the mighty Elijah, but did you know that the Bible says Elijah was a human being just like we are? Were you aware that the prestigious and powerful Elijah was content with common things? What was Elijah really like? What do we need to know if we want to be an Elijah?

There are similarities between the spiritual condition of Israel in Elijah's day and that of our world today. We, like Israel, are under attack by a hateful spiritual enemy who wants to destroy us. Israel needed an Elijah; today's nations need men and women like Elijah.

Notice what Elisha did and said when Elijah, his mentor, was caught up into heaven:

> He picked up the cloak that had fallen from Elijah and went back and stood on the bank of the Jordan. Then he took the cloak that had fallen from him and struck the water with it. "Where is the Lord, the God of Elijah?" he asked. When he struck the water, it divided to the right and to the left, and he crossed over.
> (2 Kings 2:13–14)

Elisha asked, "Where is the Lord?" The answer is "On His throne, listening to prayer, performing miracles, just as he has always been." The more important question is "Where are the Elijahs of God?" Will you be one?

Elijah Was a Human Being Like Us

Elijah was one of the most powerful men in the Old Testament. He set an example through his prayer life, miracles, courage, and the powerful showdown in the contest with Baal and Asheroth in opposition to Yahweh on Mount Carmel. It is recorded in some of the most picturesque literature in the Bible. He was a great man who did great things together with God.

If Elijah were different from us, we would be excused from doing or even trying to do what he did. The justification for not being as powerful an influence in our day as Elijah was in his day is effectively removed, however, by James 5:17. It says, "Elijah was a human being, even as we are." This statement challenges us. Since Elijah was like us, we could, and by implication should, do exploits like he did.

> **If Elijah were different from us, we would be excused from doing or even trying to do what he did.**

Elijah faced the same kinds of situations we face. I can imagine Elijah's little boy running to him, crying, "Daddy, Daddy, my puppy is lost. Where is he? How can I find him?" Or Elijah's wife coming to him, saying, "El, the water in the creek is so muddy I can't get the laundry clean. I wash and wash and the clothes get muddier and muddier. What can I do?" Or Elijah's neighbor demanding, "Elijah, your sheep and goats are disturbing my family. If you don't get them out of my field, I'm going to have one for dinner." Elijah had domestic challenges like ours, and he was a person like us. Yet he lived a godly life of prayer and spiritual accomplishment. We can too.

Even though you are a normal human being and have daily responsibilities, will you take time to be spiritual?

Elijah Was Not Enamored or Preoccupied with Earthly Finery

Second Kings 1:7–8 says, "The king asked them, 'What kind of man was it who came to meet you and told you this?' They replied, 'He was a man with a garment of hair and with a leather belt around his waist.'"

Is it really important for us to know what kind of clothes Elijah wore? No. But it is important that we understand what kind of character Elijah had.

The clothes he wore give us some indication of that. What he wore reflects his value system.

We find many references in the Old Testament to fine clothes. We know they existed and that some people valued them.

Jacob gave Joseph a beautiful coat of many colors. This may have been unwise, because it set Joseph up to be a point of jealousy for his brothers. It would not have been wrong for Joseph to wear the gift. But according to the story, he bragged about his dreams. That indicated Joseph was self-impressed — perhaps, partly, because of his beautiful garment.

Achan hid a beautiful Babylonian robe taken from the rubble of Jericho in the floor of his tent along with stolen silver coins and a wedge of gold. He paid for that mistake with his life. It was not wrong to have nice clothes or even to value nice clothes. But it was wrong to steal them and pretend the theft did not happen. Achan would not have even been tempted with those clothes except that he valued them — too much. His strong desire for them was the deeper motivational difficulty.

Gehazi had the same problem. He ran after Naaman's chariot and lied in order to receive beautiful Babylonian garments. His wrong value system led him into temptation.

Both Daniel and Mordecai were given royal robes to wear. But in neither of those cases did the clothes reflect the value system of the person wearing them. They were gifts given by someone else who valued them.

> "Jesus also taught the value of living simply."

Wearing nice clothes is not wrong; we all ought to look our best for God's glory. After all, the Bible says that man looks on the outward appearance; the first impressions we give about ourselves are usually based on what people see. Our clothes are important statements about our tastes. However, we should not be preoccupied with finery. Elijah, had he chosen, could have made a priority of wearing long, flowing, beautiful robes. Yet he was content with a garment of hair and a leather belt.

The Bible describes a position of balance in which our supply is adequate. Financial blessings do come to God's people — some more than others.

Hard work, honesty, and clean habits, combined with avoiding the expenses of bad habits, give economic advantages to God's people. John wished blessings for his readers when he wrote, "I pray that you may enjoy good health and that all may go well with you, even as your soul is getting along well" (3 John 1:2). The Bible definition of *prosperity* is for the road to be open and smooth — for things to go well — which includes much more than just financial or material blessings. And the blessings God gives to those who tithe and give liberally to God's work are also well known.

Nevertheless, Jesus also taught the value of living simply. He said, "Do not store up for yourselves treasures on earth, where moth and rust destroy, and where thieves break in and steal." He also said, "No one can serve two masters. Either he will hate the one and love the other, or he will be devoted to the one and despise the other. You cannot serve both God and money." In addition, He said, "But seek first His kingdom and his righteousness, and all these things will be given to you as well" (Matthew 6:19, 24, 33).

> "Among the people of 'corrupt mind,' to avoid were those 'who *think that godliness is a means to financial gain.*'"

Paul warned Timothy about errors believed by those who do "not agree with the sound instruction of our Lord Jesus Christ and godly teaching" (1 Timothy 6:3). Along with people of "corrupt mind" to avoid were those "who *think that godliness is a means to financial gain.* But godliness with contentment is great gain ... For the love of money is a root of all kinds of evil ... not to be arrogant nor to put their hope in wealth, which is so uncertain, but to put their hope in God, who richly provides us with everything for our enjoyment" (1 Timothy 6:5-6, 10, 17, emphasis mine). Some Christians today teach that we can use godliness or selected Bible practices to gain financially. However, this is not consistent with the teaching of the whole Bible; Paul said it is not "sound instruction" or "godly teaching."

I grew up in the 1950s with "poverty theology." "Prosperity theology" was popular when we came back to the U.S. from China in the 1990s. Both were out of balance. We are to use money to serve God, not use God to serve money. Rejoice in what God gives you and don't be embarrassed about it. But neither be preoccupied with it nor possessed by it. If you talk often about material possessions, that could be a sign that you value them too much.

I see three problems with prosperity theology:

- It causes those who prosper materially and financially to become proud and arrogant. Such arrogance hinders their ministries.
- It causes those who do not prosper materially and financially to feel inferior or to lose confidence. This reduces or hinders their joy in ministry.
- Prosperity theology is not consistent with the balanced teachings of the Bible.

Where are those who will not be caught up in the pursuit of financial prosperity, but rather seek first the kingdom of God? Will you be one?

Elijah Spent Much Time Alone with God

First Kings 17:1-5 says, "Now Elijah the Tishbite, from Tisbe in Gilead, said to Ahab, 'As the Lord, the God of Israel lives, whom I serve, there will be neither dew nor rain in the next few years except at my word.' Then the word of the Lord came to Elijah: 'Leave here, turn eastward and hide in the Kerith Ravine, east of the Jordan. You will drink from the brook, and I have ordered the ravens to feed you there.' So he did what the Lord had told him."

Elijah faced domestic responsibilities at home. However, the time came when he needed to get away from normal daily activities in order to have an extended time alone with God. We do not know how much time passed between Elijah delivering his message to the king and his departure for the Kerith Ravine. But of the three and one-half years between Elijah's announcement and the contest on Mount Carmel, we might guess Elijah spent a number of months alone with God at Kerith.

On July 9, 2002, I significantly increased the amount of daily time I spend in prayer. Since then, I have experienced deeper insights into the truth of God's Word. I now have greater liberty and authority in teaching and preaching, along with more opportunities to serve, teach, and preach.

Additionally, I have experienced increased fine-tuning of flawed character traits. When I pray more, God works more. I want God to work a lot in my life. So I will pray a lot in order to see God more involved. I have long said that the most important thing I do in any day is pray, but now I am practicing that. I routinely spend more time in prayer than any other one thing I do each day.

> "When I pray more, God works more."

Have you discovered the value and productivity of spending lengths of time alone with God in prayer?

Elijah Discerned God's Plan and Prayed Accordingly

James 5:17b–18 says, "He prayed earnestly that it would not rain, and it did not rain on the land for three and a half years. Again he prayed, and the heavens gave rain, and the earth produced its crops."

Elijah was so "powerful and effective" (James 5:16) in his prayer life because he cooperated with God in prayer and prayed according to God's plan. He listened to God, who told him what He was planning to do, and Elijah prayed accordingly.

Based on God's agenda, Elijah prayed that rain would not fall. That seems like a strange prayer. When we haven't had rain for a while, we usually pray *for* rain. What kind of prophet would pray that rain will *not* fall? A prophet who knows God's plan. God wanted to defame Baal, the Canaanite rain god.

God's plan worked perfectly. The prophets of Baal could produce neither rain in the valleys nor fire on the mountain. When God's purpose in the drought was complete, and Elijah and God had everyone's attention, he prayed according to the next phase of God's plan — that rain *would* fall.

The second phase required Elijah to completely reverse his direction in prayer. What kind of prophet would pray one way one day and then pray exactly the opposite the next day? A prophet who knows how to move with God through the phases and stages of His plan; a prophet who partners with God and prays according to His plan. In each instance, Elijah was following God's agenda for that specific time.

The wisdom of God is far superior to the ideas of men. This is why we should submit our wills to His and seek His plan.

Some of us do the will of God — what God has shown us to do — too long. We have to be sensitive to changes in God's direction. We have no right to assume that we will always be where we are now or that we will always do what we are doing today. We must stay up-to-date with God. We should be ready, as Elijah was, to move to the next phase, pray a new way, and do new things whenever God directs a change.

What is God's plan for your community? For your church? For your family? For your career? What would happen if you began to pray according to God's plan? What would your church or community be like ten years from now if you prayed according to God's agenda for the next ten years? Mount Carmel illustrates the power that can be released in the heavens and in the affairs of humans when a person of God prays according to God's plan. The result is far greater than what human imaginations can produce. God is "able to do immeasurably more than we can ask or imagine" (Ephesians 3:20).

God is even more eager than you are for you to pray according to His agenda. He is searching for those who will be more concerned about His desires than their own. God is very pleased when we ask Him to reveal His will to us so that we can pray in cooperation with it. He wants us to know His will. Therefore, we ought to be either praying according to God's will or praying that we may know His will so that we can pray in agreement with it.

Will you find out what God wants to do through you? Are you willing to pray and move with God as His cooperative partner when you know?

Elijah Publicly Challenged the Political and Religious Systems

In 1 Kings 18:19, Elijah challenged Ahab, "Now summon the people from all over Israel to meet me on Mount Carmel. And bring the four hundred and fifty prophets of Baal and the four hundred prophets of Asherah, who eat at Jezebel's table." The following story illustrates this kind of miracle can also happen now if we pray.

While in Madagascar in mid-2004, I heard about a witch doctor in a village who could cause a person to levitate. He had so much influence in the community that some Christians reverted to their superstitious ways. It made many nonbelievers afraid to become Christians. To counter this, a concerned and prayerful group of Christians moved into action. They publicly announced that the true God would hinder the witch doctor so he could not cause a person to levitate. The Christians prayed. The villagers gathered around. When the witch doctor was unable to conduct his usual ceremonies, observers saw that God's power was superior to that of the evil spirits.

Bible stories like Elijah's may seem long ago and far away. Yet what happened on Mount Carmel can still occur today. The powerful encounters that are recorded in the book of Acts are possible for those who are willing to follow God closely.

After spending months alone with God in prayer, Elijah had the courage to publicly confront the established religious system of his day. He had the daring to taunt the prophets of Baal while they prayed. He also had the confidence to pour scarce water on the sacrifice he was about to offer to God — three times! He had the nerve to order the 450 prophets of Baal and the 400 prophets of Asherah killed. After this, he again ascended Mount Carmel and began to pray for rain.

At the end of the day, everyone knew which god was the true God. They recognized that He was a God of might and power. All this was possible because God found a partner who was willing to be a vessel used by a mighty God.

Christians are not to put God to the test in unwise, humanly imagined contests. That is foolish and presumptuous. But Elijah was moving in the will of God. He was led by God in this public demonstration of His superiority. When God leads us and gives us the courage, we too can bring glory to Him by moving obediently and boldly.

Will you take the time to find out what God wants to do and then publicly, obediently, and boldly represent Him?

Elijah Addressed Important National Issues

First Kings 18:18 says, "'I have not made trouble for Israel,' Elijah replied. 'But you and your father's family have. You have abandoned the Lord's commands and have followed the Baals.'" Second Kings 1:3-4 says, "The angel of the Lord said to Elijah the Tishbite, 'Go up and meet the messengers of the king of Samaria and ask them, "Is it because there is no God in Israel that you are going off to consult Baal-Zebub, the god of Ekron?" Therefore this is what the Lord says: "You will not leave the bed you are lying on. You will certainly die!"'"

Elijah understood God's perspective about events of national importance to Israel. Elijahs today should prepare sermons with the Bible in one hand and the newspaper in the other. We need to know Scripture *and* what it says about current events. We must skillfully use the Bible so our sermons instruct with authority that ensures "This is what the Lord says." But unless we are also reading the newspaper or listening to the news, we will not know the important issues of the day. We will not give the Holy Spirit an opportunity to lay the burden of His concerns about current events on our hearts.

> "Unless we are also reading the newspaper or listening to the news, we will not know the important issues of the day."

Elijahs today need to know what is going on around them in their society and nation. We need to be concerned about those issues. We need to know what God has to say about these concerns and be able to speak "the very words of God" (1 Peter 4:11). This will require constant prayer and Bible study along with keeping up on the news. You may need to spend time sharing these things in prayer and study together with other wise men and women of God. There is wisdom in doing so.

If you want to be an Elijah in your area of ministry, seek God's perspective on important issues facing you and the people around you. Then courageously speak out in the name of the Lord. Know the problems. Have an informed opinion. Be knowledgeable about how the Bible speaks to contemporary concerns. Then gather the courage to speak out from Scripture on meaningful subjects.

What do you think about Christians becoming involved in politics? What do you think of corruption in public administration? What is your position on sex education in public schools? How can your city and state convert the wealth from the precious stones, gold, silver, and copper in your mountains into roads, bridges, schools, and hospitals? Have you thought this through? Do you pray about these things? Do you discuss and study such issues with other men and women of God? Do you seek God's wisdom? Have you ever expressed your views to your public leaders?

Will you become aware of local, national, contemporary issues, find God's will in the matter, and speak out for Him with wisdom and authority?

Elijah Received Encouragement from God in a Moment of Weakness

The excitement of Mount Carmel must have been tremendous. The fire coming down from heaven to consume the sacrifice, the slaying of 850 false prophets, the miraculous and timely rain — each would have made a powerful impression on any observer. But it especially impacted Elijah. It was also emotionally and physically exhausting. How did Elijah handle the emotion of the next few days? Evidently his thoughts turned in upon himself, as he fled from a wicked and angry queen intent on killing him. The thrill of yesterday's excitement was gone.

Where was the strong spiritual leader Israel needed? He was hiding in a cave. First Kings 19:9–13 says:

> There he went into a cave and spent the night. And the word of the Lord came to him: "What are you doing here, Elijah?"
>
> He replied, "… I am the only one left, and now they are trying to kill me too" …
>
> Then a great and powerful wind … but the Lord was not in the wind … there was an earthquake, but the Lord was not in the earthquake. After the earthquake came a fire, but the Lord was not in the fire. And after the fire came a gentle whisper. When Elijah heard it, he pulled his cloak over his face and went out and stood at the mouth of the cave.
>
> Then a voice said to him, "What are you doing here, Elijah?"

When the congregation is gathered, it is easy to be caught up in the glory of the presence of the Lord. The musical instruments are playing, the dancers are dancing, the tambourines are playing, and the crowd is worshipping with joy. In such a spiritually buoyant atmosphere, God's anointing sometimes enables preachers to teach far better than they could if success depended just on their own knowledge and understanding or verbal and rhetoric skills. We rejoice in the glorious presence of God on Sunday morning.

But when Monday arrives, our emotions often take a dive. Sunday's excitement seems long ago and far away. People in ministry probably should not make any important career decisions on Mondays because they are in an emotional cave.

> *We humans are not designed to fly high with emotional excitement day after day.*

We humans are not designed to fly high with emotional excitement day after day. We must be able to hear the encouraging voice of the Holy Spirit on Monday if we want to minister and be ministered to the following Sunday. Cultivate the ability to work your way through the valleys if you want to celebrate the joy of the Lord with God's people at church again. Give yourself time to recuperate after exhausting and emotionally draining times of spiritual work. This will ensure you will be ready for the next opportunity.

The Bible records how God spoke through winds at the Red Sea and on Pentecost. He spoke in earthquakes in front of Korah's tents and at Phillipi. He spoke through fires on Mount Sinai and in the upper room. Elijah was able to discern which of the sounds he heard at the cave contained the voice of the Lord. This time in the cave, God's voice was not in the wind, earthquake, or fire, but in a whisper. When Elijah heard the whisper, he went to the mouth of the cave and God spoke to him. Let us too listen for God's whispers.

Will you hear the voice of the Lord in the emotional valley that follows the mountaintop experience? Will you hold steady through the emotional ups and downs of the Christian life?

Elijah Was Involved in International Developments

In 1 Kings 19:15-18, God said to Elijah, "Anoint Hazael king over Aram. Also, anoint Jehu son of Nimshi king over Israel, and anoint Elisha son of Shaphat from Abel Mehoiah to succeed you as prophet. Jehu will put to death any who escape the sword of Hazael, and Elisha will put to death any who escape the sword of Jehu. Yet I reserve seven thousand in Israel — all whose knees have not bowed down to Baal and all whose mouths have not kissed him."

You may think that not everyone can be involved in international ministry. Not so. God will use you differently than He used Elijah, but still your regular place of prayer can become your world center for international intercession.

When I lived in the United States, I prayed in my garage before and after breakfast. I placed numerous verses about prayer on the garage walls. I didn't read all of them every day, but I often referred to them as I prayed. Now that I travel most of the time, I find a different place to pray everywhere I go. But I still remember the Scriptures I had on the walls. Here are some of them:

> Then Jesus told ... a parable to show them that they should always pray and not give up. (Luke 18:1)
>
> If you remain in me and my words remain in you, ask whatever you wish, and it will be given you. (John 14:7)
>
> You may ask me for anything in my name, and I will do it. (John 14:14)
>
> I tell you the truth, my Father will give you whatever you ask in my name. (John 16:23)
>
> This is the confidence we have in approaching God: that if we ask anything according to his will, he hears us. And if we know that he hears us — whatever we ask — we know that we have what we asked of him. (1 John 5:14-15)
>
> The prayer of a righteous man is powerful and effective. (James 5:16)
>
> Rise up, O Lord! May your enemies be scattered; may your foes flee before you. (Numbers 10:35)

They will never be silent day or night. You who call on the Lord, give yourselves no rest, and give him no rest until he establishes. (Isaiah 62:6–7)

… to him who is able to do immeasurably more than all we ask or imagine. (Ephesians 3:20)

Ask of me and I will make the nations your inheritance, the ends of the earth your possession. (Psalm 2:8)

What is impossible with men is possible with God. (Luke 18:27)

Bless me and enlarge my territory! Let your hand be with me. (1 Chronicles 4:10)

I will not let you go unless you bless me. (Genesis 32:27)

Elijah, Daniel, Isaiah, and Jeremiah all had messages, not only for Israel but for other nations as well. Why should we pray just for our own country? Look at a globe or a world map, and make a list of the nations. In my weekly routine, I begin with Iceland and pray my way through every nation of North America, Central America, the Caribbean, South America, Africa, Europe, the Middle East, Asia, and the Pacific regions. I pray for the pastors, churches, missionaries, people groups, Christians, prisoners, prison keepers, educators, media, entertainers, and other types of people in societies, tribes, and governments in each of those regions.

> *In prayer, you can travel the world from nation to nation anytime you want to.*

Regardless of the nation I am in at the time, I have a "world center for international intercession" as I walk on the early morning streets of Africa's cities or quieter rural roads. You can have an international ministry too. Your job, health, age, or other factors and responsibilities may hinder you from physically going abroad, but prayer knows no boundaries. In prayer, you can travel the world from nation to nation anytime you want.

Will you look at the nations of the world and become a part of God's army of intercessors?

Elijah Trained Future Ministers and Mentored a Successor

First Kings 19:19-21 says, "Elijah went from there and found Elisha son of Shaphat ... Then he set out to follow Elijah and became his servant." Second Kings 2:3, 5 says, "The company of the prophets at Bethel came out to Elisha and asked ... The company of the prophets at Jericho went up to Elisha and asked ..."

Even though Elijah was a busy prophet, he took the time to train a successor. He also spent time with groups of prophets at Bethel, Gilgal, and Jericho. Activities like this take time, but if we want to influence not only our generation but also the next one, we must make this investment.

God's work is vast. We will possibly not finish the job while we are alive. We must deliberately allow the next cohort of ministers to stand on our shoulders and do a better job than we did. By being transparent, we can help them avoid making some of the same mistakes we made. When we make fewer mistakes, the Holy Spirit can do His work better. As we mature in ministry, we learn that we will not always be the "sage on the stage." The time comes for senior ministers to be the "guides on the side."

Are you giving opportunities to those you are training? Is a desire to develop younger leaders reflected in your choice of leaders at home group meetings? Do you take time to mentor younger servants of the Lord so they can carry on the work in the next generation?

Elijah Was Worth Chariots and Horsemen

Second Kings 2:11-12 says, "As they were walking along and talking together, suddenly a chariot of fire and horses of fire appeared and separated the two of them, and Elijah went up to heaven in a whirlwind. Elisha saw this and cried out, 'My father! My father! The chariots and horsemen of Israel!' And Elisha saw him no more. Then he took hold of his own clothes and tore them apart."

Elisha was not merely saying that he *saw* chariots and horsemen. He was actually calling Elijah "the chariots and horsemen of Israel." What is the symbolism of Elijah being called chariots and horsemen?

Here is my understanding. Chariots were powerful weapons of warfare in Elijah's day. Archers could shoot arrows, and spearmen could throw spears from elevated positions safe within the protective sides of chariots. The chariots themselves were also weapons, to say nothing of the war horses out front, striking with powerful hooves. On the wheels of some chariots were blades capable of cutting down many foot soldiers. Elisha was implying that Elijah was a strong spiritual weapon for Israel.

How would we illustrate this today? One powerful modern weapon is the Patriot missile. This strictly defensive weapon can hit an incoming intercontinental ballistic missile while it is still in the air headed toward its target. God needs "chariots" (us) to be spiritual weapons much like a Patriot missile that can bring down the fiery darts of the enemy before they reach our nations.

Today, as in Elijah's time, we are under attack by invisible forces of unrighteousness. These evil spirits intend the destruction of God's people and His church. These unseen spiritual forces are responsible for the blinding and binding of many non-Christians and even some believers. God needs men and women today who, like Elijah, will be powerful, effective weapons, rushing to the defense of all that is precious to God. The militant church must fight against the spirits of jealousy that breed discontent. They need to fight lusts that urge people into various forms of perverse sexual sins or marital unfaithfulness. They need to do spiritual battle against false religions that lure people into demon and devil worship. They must stand strong against deceptive spirits that lead to witchcraft, materialism, atheism, and numerous doctrines of devils.

> "God needs men and women today who, like Elijah, will be powerful, effective weapons."

Will you do today for your nation what Elijah did in his day for his nation? Will you become a strong spiritual weapon that God can use to tear down the forces of unrighteousness? If you are willing to do the difficult spiritual work in the invisible realm, you will be doing the work of an Elijah. You too will be "chariots and horsemen."

Will you enter into an invisible spiritual war and bring destruction to those forces that are trying to destroy your nation? Will you be an Elijah today?

For Further Thought

- What practical steps do you need to take to stay in contact with local and national issues?
- What are you doing to guarantee that you have ample time alone with God?
- Are you intentionally seeking to know what to pray about and how to pray before you begin to pray for specific things?
- What superstitions or societal situations need to be confronted in your community? What are you doing to know whether or not God would have you confront them?
- When you have been through a highly energetic and exciting time of ministry, do you give yourself some time to recuperate spiritually?
- What are you doing to influence the nations of the world through your world center for international intercession — your place of prayer?
- What do you need to do to invest yourself and your influence in raising up leaders for the next generation?
- In what ways are you seeking to be a powerful weapon of spiritual warfare?

CHAPTER 13
ELISHA

Did you know that Elisha was a wealthy man, but gave up everything to become Elijah's protégé? Were you aware that Elisha began his new career as a humble servant?

What is your value system? What do you seek first? What do you like to talk about most? Who do you aspire to become? These are important questions if you want to be used by God.

Elisha is considered by many to be similar to Elijah, his mentor. Yet the differences between these two mighty men of God provide additional lessons from this unique Bible character.

Elisha Valued the Role of a Prophet

Elisha had been a successful career man, employer, and land baron.

> Elijah went from there and found Elisha son of Shaphat. He was plowing with twelve yoke of oxen, and he himself was driving the twelfth pair. Elijah went up to him and threw his cloak around him. Elisha then left his oxen and ran after Elijah. "Let me kiss my father and mother good-bye," he said, "and then I will come with you."
>
> "Go back," Elijah replied. "What have I done to you?"
>
> So Elisha left him and went back. He took his yoke of oxen and slaughtered them. He burned the plowing equipment to cook the meat and gave it to the people, and they ate. Then he set out to follow Elijah and became his servant. (1 Kings 19:19-21)

Elisha was plowing with twelve yoke of oxen. One man alone cannot drive twelve pair of oxen at the same time. Elisha had to have had at least eleven employees, each driving a pair of oxen. He also drove a pair himself; he was a "hands on" man. He was obviously a successful farmer.

When presented with the opportunity to serve as Elijah's assistant, he immediately accepted the task. He asked only that he might part properly from his parents. Elijah gave him permission. At the same time, he released Elisha from any obligation. "'Go back,' Elijah replied. 'What have I done to you?'" (1 Kings 19:20). Elisha killed one pair of oxen, offered meat to everyone nearby, burned the plow, and began to follow Elijah.

> There is no greater work than to help depopulate hell and populate heaven.

Over the centuries, other men have left their careers to follow the Lord. Amos left his sheep. Peter and John left their nets. Surely we can and should serve God in other careers. Whatever vocation God leads us to follow, we ought to do it with all our hearts, and as unto the Lord (see Ephesians 6:7).

Full-time Christian leaders are not the only ones who are serving the Lord and an eternal purpose. But they do have the distinction of giving their entire energies to an eternal cause. There is no greater work than to help depopulate hell and populate heaven. Elisha evidently understood this.

Elisha Served

"Then he set out to follow Elijah and became his servant" (1 Kings 19:21). It is one thing to become a servant. It is another thing to have a servant's heart and serve from the heart. Many servants are referred to in the Bible. Not all of them followed in their masters' footsteps. But Elisha did.

Later, Elisha had his own servant, Gehazi, but Gehazi did not pursue God under Elisha's leadership as Elisha had under Elijah's leadership. Gehazi's poor performance provides a stark contrast with Elisha, who served fully and sincerely.

Later, in Dothan, Scripture tells us Elisha had a servant. We do not know who that servant was. It could have been Gehazi. Or, if Gehazi had died by then, this could be someone else.

After being Elijah's faithful servant, Elisha was granted the position of leading prophet. Not all servants are promoted like that. Was Elisha given this honor because of his desire for prophetic ministry and the value he placed on spiritual realities?

> *Seeking the God of the mighty man is better than seeking the mighty man of God.*

Just being close to a great man or woman of God is not enough for you to become one yourself. Seeking the God of the mighty man is better than seeking the mighty man of God. Elisha served a mighty man, but his behavior, attitude, and later ministry show us that he also sought the mighty God.

Later in the story, Elisha is introduced to Jehoshaphat as the one who served Elijah.

> Jehoshaphat asked, "Is there no prophet of the Lord here, through whom we may inquire of the Lord?"
>
> An officer of the king of Israel answered, "Elisha son of Shaphat is here. He used to pour water on the hands of Elijah." (2 Kings 3:11)

As Joshua worked for Moses and as Elisha ministered to Elijah, so we are to serve Jesus. This is not an easy task. A serving heart does not come easily, but God can give one to us if we ask Him. We naturally want to follow our own ideas. But if we subdue our personal wishes and maintain a desire for the heart of a servant, God will help us.

Elisha Sought Spiritual Things

In those days, it was customary for each son in a family to receive an equal share of his father's possessions. The exception was the oldest son, who accepted the responsibilities of leadership in the family. He inherited twice as much as the other children. When Elisha asked Elijah for a "double portion," he was not asking for twice what Elijah had. He was asking for a double portion of what he thought the other sons of the prophet would receive. He was not grasping for personal greatness in a selfish, ambitious, or egotistical sense. Elisha wanted to inherit the leadership and responsibility for the family of prophets. Elisha wanted spiritual leadership opportunities and was willing to accept the consequent responsibilities and obligations.

> Elijah said to Elisha, "Tell me, what can I do for you before I am taken from you?"
>
> "Let me inherit a double portion of your spirit," Elisha replied.
>
> "You have asked a difficult thing," Elijah said, "yet if you see me when I am taken from you, it will be yours — otherwise, it will not." (2 Kings 2:9–10)

God honored Elisha's desire for spiritual things. Elisha was present when Elijah was taken, and he did receive a great anointing from God.

Elisha Called Down a Curse on the Youth Who Jeered at Him

> From there Elisha went up to Bethel. As he was walking along the road, some boys came out of the town and jeered at him. "Get out of here, baldy!" they said. "Get out of here, baldy!" He turned around, looked at them and called down a curse on them in the name of the Lord. Then two bears came out of the woods and mauled forty-two of the boys. (2 Kings 2:23–24)

As soon as Elisha's career was launched and miracles began to happen, some boys came along and made fun of him. Elisha called down a curse on them, and the boys were punished.

This curious story raises questions about the place of cursing, if any, in the life of the modern man or woman of God. If Elisha cursed those who ridiculed him, should God's servants today also do that? Several observations may help us understand Elisha's situation. They enable us to judge for ourselves whether we should follow his example.

This incident happened early in Elisha's career. It may not be the way he would have handled the problem after he had mellowed over time. Ministers tend to be less vindictive after years of experience has taught them how to deal better with people.

Another consideration is the age of these "boys." The Hebrew language indicates that they were not children of eight or nine years. They were youths, probably teens or older. Their jeers would have stemmed not so much from childish immaturity as from a deliberate, thoughtful, and perhaps even hateful disrespect for the man of God. Elisha was dealing with a more serious situation than little boys innocently making fun of a bald man.

A more important factor to consider in determining the validity of calling down curses on people is the stage of ethical developments in Elisha's generation.

Prior to Moses, it was customary in most cultures to exceed an original offense with stronger, more severe retribution. Moses taught that revenge should be limited to the severity of the original offense. If someone takes your eye, take only an eye; if someone takes your oxen, take the same number of oxen. Perhaps Moses' progressive view will be more clear if we insert some words: "[only an] eye for [an] eye, [only a] tooth for [a] tooth, [only a] hand for [a] hand, [and only a] foot for [a] foot" (see Exodus 21:24). The one who inflicted the injury should suffer only the same injury (Leviticus 24:20). Revenge had to be controlled and limited.

Generations later, David carried ethical development forward a huge step by asking God to take revenge. He would not seek vengeance himself, but committed the punishment of his enemies into God's care. In the following imprecatory psalm, David prays for a curse on his enemies:

> Contend, Lord, with those who contend with me; fight against those who fight against me. Take up shield and armor; arise and come to my aid. Brandish spear and javelin against those who pursue me. Say to me, "I am your salvation."
>
> May those who seek my life be disgraced and put to shame; may those who plot my ruin be turned back in dismay. May they be like chaff before the wind, with the angel of the Lord driving them away; may their path be dark and slippery, with the angel of the Lord pursuing them. Since they hid their net for me without cause and without cause dug a pit for me, may ruin overtake them by surprise — may the net they hid entangle them, may they fall into the pit, to their ruin.
>
> Then my soul will rejoice in the Lord and delight in his salvation.

> My whole being will exclaim, "Who is like you, Lord? You rescue the poor from those too strong for them, the poor and needy from those who rob them." (Psalm 35:1–10)

Centuries later, Jesus taught us to not seek revenge at all. He said we are to "turn the other cheek" (Matthew 5:39). We are to give our shirt to the one who demands our coat (Luke 6:29). "If someone slaps you on one cheek, turn the other also. If someone takes your coat, do not withhold your shirt." (Luke 6:29). This was yet another big ethical improvement.

In the epistles, Paul raised the bar still further. He taught us to help our enemies recognize their error by proactively doing good things to those who do evil to us. "On the contrary: If your enemy is hungry, feed him; if he is thirsty, give him something to drink. In doing this, you will heap burning coals on his head" (Romans 12:20).

In the series of ethical progressions described above, Elisha lived between David and Jesus. He had the Psalms to guide his thoughts. He knew Moses' teachings not to be overly vindictive and David's instructions not to seek his own revenge. He committed the jeering youths to God, letting Him punish them. The expression "in the name of the Lord" tells us that God had already authorized this curse for His own purposes. Elisha was merely acting as God's personal representative in this matter.

Elisha's behavior — even calling a curse down on the youths in the name of the Lord — was appropriate according to the ethical standard of his day and according to his perception of how God wanted to act in this situation. His behavior was "phase specific," which was acceptable for that time.

Should God's servants today curse those who ridicule them? As Christians, we are to follow the teachings of Jesus. He said:

> You have heard that it was said, "Love your neighbor and hate your enemy." But I tell you, love your enemies and pray for those who persecute you, that you may be children of your Father in heaven. He causes his sun to rise on the evil and the good, and sends rain on the righteous and the unrighteous. If you love those who love you, what reward will you get? Are not even the tax collectors doing that? And if you greet only your own people, what are you doing more than others? Do not even pagans do

that? Be perfect, therefore, as your heavenly Father is perfect. (Matthew 5:43–48)

Love your enemies, do good to those who hate you. (Luke 6:27)

We also have the high standards outlined in Paul's writings:

Bless those who persecute you; bless and do not curse. (Romans 12:14)

We work hard with our own hands. When we are cursed, we bless; when we are persecuted, we endure it. (1 Corinthians 4:12)

The Lord came to take away our curse, to set prisoners free of curses. To be like Him, we must follow His lead and do the same. We have a high standard to achieve. What may have been acceptable for Elisha in his day is not necessarily appropriate for us to do in ours. Let us behave and think the way God wants us to. The fact that a Christian would even *want* to call down a curse on someone brings that Christian's character into question.

> "What may have been acceptable for Elisha in his day is not necessarily appropriate for us to do in ours."

If Elisha had lived after Jesus, his love for the Lord would have dictated different behavior. It is understandable for the inexperienced prophet just beginning his career in the period of time in which he lived.

Elisha Was Not Enamored by Strong, Influential Political Figures

Naaman, commander of the army of the king of Aram, went to visit Elisha. "So Naaman went with his horses and chariots and stopped at the door of Elisha's house. Elisha sent a messenger to say to him, 'Go, wash yourself seven times in the Jordan, and your flesh will be restored and you will be cleansed'" (2 Kings 5:9–10).

Elisha did not even go out to meet the well-positioned, important Naaman, but sent Ghazi with a message for him. Contrast this behavior with the way he treated the members of the school of prophets when they asked him to accompany them to the Jordan. Elisha was available to the no-name people in the school of prophets, but not to Naaman. He had his priorities correct.

Do we overly enjoy the company of people of great magnitude? What opportunities might we miss to teach, mentor, or help younger believers if we are busy trying to associate with important people?

Elisha Understood Cross-Cultural Issues

In 2 Kings 5, Elisha actually gave Naaman permission to kneel in the house of a heathen god, Rimmon. After repeatedly urging Elisha to accept the gifts he offered, Naaman finally gave up. Then Naaman made a strange request:

> "If you will not," said Naaman, "please let me, your servant, be given as much earth as a pair of mules can carry, for your servant will never again make burnt offerings and sacrifices to any other god but the Lord. But may the Lord forgive your servant for this one thing: when my master enters the temple of Rimmon to bow down and he is leaning on my arm and I have to bow there also — when I bow down in the temple of Rimmon, may the Lord forgive your servant for this."
>
> "Go in peace," Elisha said. (2 Kings 5:17-19)

Why did Naaman want to escort his king into a heathen temple and not be guilty of idolatry? And how do we interpret Elisha's response? There is a significant lesson in the incident recorded in 2 Kings 5.

Elisha understood that the condition of the mind and heart is more important than the position of the body. For Naaman to bow outwardly when he was not really worshipping the false god spiritually was not a problem to God. "Go in peace," Elisha said. We can interpret this to mean, "Do your vocational duty, and fulfill the responsibilities of your profession. I know you will not be really worshipping as you bow." Naaman would *bow*, but he would not *worship*. Elisha knew the difference between an outward form of worship and the meaning any action had to the doer. God looks on the heart.

> "Naaman would *bow*, but he would not *worship*."

The reverse application of this principle can also be made. Not all people who raise their hands, dance, and sing in a Christian church service are really worshipping. We must have our minds and hearts focused on the Lord for true worship to occur. Let's use the atmosphere of praise to advantage but actually adore God from our hearts. Words, hands, and songs can help, but they are not worship.

> "Words, hands, and songs can help, but they are not worship."

Elisha Presided Over a Flourishing School of Prophets

Student enrollment was evidently up, and new buildings were needed. The success of the company of prophets under the leadership of Elisha is indicated in the following conversation between Elisha and his students:

> The company of the prophets said to Elisha, "Look, the place where we meet with you is too small for us. Let us go to the Jordan, where each of us can get a pole; and let us build a place there for us to meet."
>
> And he said, "Go." (2 Kings 6:1-2)

Did the school of prophets flourish at this time because of Elisha's gifts? His leadership? His charismatic persona? Was it because Elisha had better people skills than the abrupt, outspoken Elijah demonstrated? Was Elisha a better administrator? These questions remain unanswered, but we know from the above verses that the school experienced growth under Elisha's leadership.

We also know that Elisha's students wanted him to join them as they sought to expand their school. Evidently Elisha was approachable. This may be a factor in why the school prospered during his years at the helm.

Elisha submitted to the request of the prophets. They went together to the Jordan.

> Then one of them said, "Won't you please come with your servants?"
>
> "I will," Elisha replied. And he went with them. They went to the Jordan and began to cut down trees. (2 Kings 6:3-4)

Either the school of prophets or Elisha, or both, had a good reputation in the community. Is this another reason the school was flourishing? Otherwise, no one would have loaned one of them a valuable ax. "As one of them was cutting down a tree, the iron ax head fell into the water. 'Oh no, my lord!' he cried out. 'It was borrowed!'" (2 Kings 6:4–5)

God is growing His church the world over. People are getting saved. Congregations are being started and are growing. The number of believers needing to be discipled continues to increase. Pastors are being called and appointed. Some step into responsibility because there is no one else to do the work. Still others start churches themselves.

The education of God's prophets was an important matter in the days of Samuel, Elijah, and Elisha, as it is for God's servants and ministers today. Formal studies (attending accredited classes at Bible institutes, Bible colleges, and seminaries), informal learning (such as in a conversation), and nonformal professional improvements (conferences and seminars) are all vital forms of education and training for pastors and Christian leaders. Accredited degrees (for those prepared academically to pursue them) and basic training (for beginner leaders) are both necessary.

Over the centuries, it has not been the scholars from academia who have broadly influenced the common people and their societies to move toward God at the grass-roots level. Samuel, Elijah, and Elisha seem to have understood this. They were successful prophets themselves, and they took time to develop and encourage others. Jesus trained fishermen and other non-clergy for ministry, side-stepping the entire Levitical system and Aaronic priesthood organizations of His day. Ezekiel and Jeremiah were both priests, but not one of Jesus' disciples had been a priest before becoming a follower.

We don't usually think of "school" and "prophets" in the same sentence. However, Samuel's, Elijah's, and Elisha's schools of prophets were not contradictions in terms. Some church leaders tend to choose either power or knowledge. Such a choice is not necessary. Christian leaders must balance spiritual power and education. If you are a prayerful, anointed, and inspired man or woman of God, add information and knowledge to your power by studying. If you are the scholarly type or have already received theological training or ministry-related academic instruction, empower your information by getting on your knees before God.

Char and I conduct Leadership Empowerment Conferences in the cities of Africa. We teach participants both to pray and to study, to fast and to get an education. We encourage them to get on their faces before God in extended times of pursuing His anointing, while disciplining themselves to study God's Word. We empower them to prepare spiritually and to preach content-rich sermons. It is not enough to stand in front of the congregation, shout hallelujah, and aim for a strong emotional response. Nor is it enough to inform people with dry, unmoving, impractical, theoretical rhetoric. If ministers do not have both the power of God and good information in their public ministry, they will not experience their full potential. We do not have to choose between emotion, good content, and the anointing of the Holy Spirit. We can and must have all three.

My wife and I lived in Korea from 1973 until 1986. We often went to the famous "prayer mountains" where our Korean brothers and sisters poured out their hearts in earnest prayer for their land and their churches. These prayer mountains are one important factor in the revival and growth of the church in that nation. The Koreans value and seek education, but they also recognize the power and results of prayer.

> "The Koreans value and seek education, but they also recognize the power and results of prayer."

I served in academia in the United States for ten years, from 1996 until 2006. My students were pursuing either master's or doctor of ministry degrees. I salute those who pursue higher education and advanced training. Char and I felt convicted that pastors and leaders needed training while they remain on the job in their place of ministry. Too many times, well-intentioned ministerial candidates go to the big city or a faraway country for theological education and never return to the places of ministry that desperately need them. This prompted us to sell our home and cars in 2007 and move to Africa to conduct Leadership Empowerment Conferences. Our leadership conferences are similar to what Samuel, Elijah, and Elisha did as they moved from Ramah to Gilgal and Jericho to teach, mentor, and disciple prophets in multiple locations.

Elisha Saw Clearly into the Spirit World

The king of Aram was unable to defeat the Israeli army because Elisha kept informing Israel's king of his enemy's campaigns. Knowing he must first deal with Elisha, the king of Aram sent his army to pursue him in Dothan. Elisha's servant was alarmed the next morning to see the army with horses and chariots surrounding the city. Understandably, he panicked.

> Then he [the king of Aram] sent horses and chariots and a strong force there. They went by night and surrounded the city. When the servant of the man of God got up and went out early the next morning, an army with horses and chariots had surrounded the city. "Oh no, my lord! What shall we do?" the servant asked.
>
> "Don't be afraid," the prophet answered. "Those who are with us are more than those who are with them." And Elisha prayed, "Open his eyes, Lord, so that he may see." Then the Lord opened the servant's eyes, and he looked and saw the hills full of horses and chariots of fire all around Elisha. (2 Kings 6:14–17)

Why was Elisha not afraid? Did he already see the superior number of heavenly forces? Did he not need to see it to know it was there? Even if Elisha knew this, he understood that the servant needed to see it in order to understand it.

How would our lives be affected if we could see the spirit world? What if we could see the enemy lurking at a distance? What if we knew the superior number and power of the forces of righteousness — defending, protecting, ready to rescue, present and prepared for battle? Each of us envisions spiritual realities differently. But whether we see them or not, we can know, as Elisha did, that the forces of righteousness are greater in quantity, strength, authority, and ability to win the fight.

Elisha Recognized the Ministry Value of Music

We conclude this chapter on a musical note. Elisha recognized the value of the ministry of music in creating a spiritual atmosphere.

> Elisha said, "As surely as the Lord Almighty lives, whom I serve, if I did not have respect for the presence of Jehoshaphat king of Judah, I would not pay any attention to you. But now bring me a

harpist." While the harpist was playing, the hand of the Lord came on Elisha. (2 Kings 3:14-15)

The word *music* appears in Today's New International Version of the Bible 128 times, *song* appears 110 times, *sing* 158 times, *sang* 21 times, *choir* 5 times, and *instrument* (referring to musical instrument or instruments) 23 times. These combined 445 references give us an idea of the importance of music to God's people. We have more reasons to sing than anyone else in the world.

Satan scores some victories when he robs Christians of their song. Satan also scores victories when he gets Christians to sing the wrong songs. The world is full of music stolen from God to use for evil purposes. Some music is sensual, sexual, satanic, or hateful. Other types of music promote violence or encourage various forms of an ungodly lifestyle. But music is a gift from God to us. Let us sing *of* God and sing *to* God. When we give our voices back to Him in worshipful song, we rejoice before the Lord. In times of prayer, a song sung to the Lord has great power to uplift and edify.

> But music is a gift from God to us. Let us sing of God and sing to God.

The Bible in general, and the book of Psalms particularly, have numerous references to music. Here is one excellent example:

> It is good to praise the Lord and make music to your name, O Most High, proclaiming your love in the morning and your faithfulness at night, to the music of the ten-stringed lyre and the melody of the harp. For you make me glad by your deeds, Lord; I sing for joy at what your hands have done. (Psalm 92:1-4)

Paul instructed his readers to sing, "Speaking to one another with psalms, hymns and songs from the Spirit. Sing and make music from your heart to the Lord" (Ephesians 5:19).

One dry day, Joram, the king of Israel, and Jehoshaphat, king of Judah, agreed to confederate with the king of Edom to attack Moab, which had rebelled against Israel. After a seven-day march through the desert of Edom, the combined armies ran out of water — not a drop for either soldiers or animals.

> Jehoshaphat asked, "Is there no prophet of the Lord here, through whom we may inquire of the Lord?"
>
> An officer of the king of Israel answered, "Elisha son of Shaphat is here. He used to pour water on the hands of Elijah."
>
> Jehoshaphat said, "The word of the Lord is with him." So the king of Israel and Jehoshaphat and the king of Edom went down to him. (2 Kings 3:11–12)

Elisha asked a strange thing; he asked for a harpist. Then he focused his attention on God. *"While the harpist was playing,* the hand of the Lord came on Elisha" (2 Kings 3:15, emphasis mine). Through Elisha, the Lord showed the three kings He would supply them with plenty of water. In addition, He would also enable them to defeat Moab.

When we are faced with impossible situations, we should calm ourselves, sing, worship, and allow the Lord to speak to us. Music is one of God's gifts to us. He knows we need to be uplifted. He created the unique combination of music and music appreciation so that could happen.

Christian leaders carry a heavy load with their concern for the work of God, the condition of their flocks, and efforts to rescue the lost sheep. Understandably, they will not feel light-hearted all the time. No Christian will. But if we never sing or rejoice before the Lord in private times of prayer and praise as well as in corporate worship, we will not fully realize the power of singing to the Lord.

For Further Thought

- Do you seek to only bless and never curse? What sinister or delusional motive may be behind a desire for a man or woman of God to curse another person?
- What political people are you acquainted with? Can you be relaxed with them and minister to them respectfully without being intimidated by their power or position?
- What cross-cultural issues do you need to understand in order to reduce the potential for misunderstanding between yourself and those of another country?
- What can you learn about spiritual leadership by observing how Elisha led the school of prophets during his tenure?
- What are you doing to make certain your communication with people is both content rich and spiritually anointed?
- Can you see into the spirit world? What do you see? How is that helpful to you?
- Do you sing to the Lord? Why or why not?

CHAPTER 14
ESTHER

Did you know that Esther was an orphan who possessed a submissive, cooperative attitude? Did you realize that Esther's physical beauty was enhanced by her helpful attitude and concern for others? Do you understand how intelligent, clever, and wise Esther was?

Good literature includes subtleties that arouse the reader's curiosity. The book of Esther meets this criterion. The story has intrigue, a sinister plot, divine involvement, and deliverance. Numerous moral lessons are cleverly couched throughout. We enjoy the story of Esther because we like adventure, action, drama, romance, plots and counter-plots, success stories, and justice.

King Xerxes ruled over the Medes and Persians' 127 provinces from Eastern Africa to India, but he could not rule his wife Vashti. She would not cooperate with him. It deeply angered him when she refused to display her beauty. When he ordered a kind of "beauty contest" to find a suitable replacement, Esther was among the candidates. The record states, "Now the king was attracted to Esther more than to any of the other women, and she won his favor and approval more than any of the other virgins. So he set a royal crown on her head and made her queen instead of Vashti" (Esther 2:17).

What qualities caused the king to be attracted to Esther? Though she was certainly blessed with physical beauty, we need to look deeper than that to profit fully from this character study. Esther's lesson-packed action drama illustrates the power of submission over tyranny. It was displayed by her self-control, poise, courage, willingness to use the means at hand, and firm contention for justice.

Esther Was Submissive

Esther was beautiful both outwardly and inwardly. "Mordecai had a cousin named Hadassah, whom he had brought up because she had neither father nor mother. This young woman, who was also known as Esther, had a lovely figure and was beautiful. Mordecai had taken her as his own daughter when her father and mother died" (Esther 2:7).

Esther was obedient to her uncle. "Esther had kept secret her family background and nationality just as Mordecai had told her to do, for she continued to follow Mordecai's instructions as she had done when he was bringing her up" (Esther 2:20). She learned at an early age the virtue and importance of obedience.

This trait of obedience, however, was not exercised exclusively toward her original mentor, Mordecai. A spirit of submission and cooperation had evidently become a part of who Esther was. This is shown by the fact that she maintained it in the king's harem. "When the turn came for Esther (the young woman Mordecai had adopted, the daughter of his uncle Abihail) to go to the king, she asked for nothing other than what Hegai, the king's eunuch who was in charge of the harem, suggested. And Esther won the favor of everyone who saw her" (Esther 2:15).

> The Bible says that obedience is beautiful.

The Bible says that obedience is beautiful. "Your beauty ... should be that of your inner self, the unfading beauty of a gentle and quiet spirit, which is of great worth in God's sight" (1 Peter 3:3-4).

Imagine being in the dressmaker's shop, between the perfumed oil bath and the hair salon in the harem's central beautification district. Three ladies have been outfitted with new gowns by the chief dressmaker. When the first new addition to the harem looks at her new gown, her beautiful face contorts into an ugly frown. "I don't like this color," she complains. "It never looks good on me. Besides, the texture is too rough, and it doesn't slide freely on my hips and legs. This will never do."

The second "beauty" tries on her new gown, purses her lips in a sulk, and whines, "Well, this is the color I agreed to, but the dress is too tight around my shoulders and too loose around my hips. Why can't you get it right?"

A third young woman arrives. She smiles, greets the dressmaker, and waits her turn. When presented with her gown, she thanks him. When she emerges from the dressing room for his review, he says, "Oh, the waist is not quite right."

"I am sure you can fix that with no difficulty," she replies. "You are a professional. I like the rest of it. You do a wonderful job of making us look good."

Which of the three do you think was the most beautiful?

Imagine further that everywhere she went — eating in the dining room, receiving a pedicure and manicure at the beauty parlor, or getting her eyebrows trimmed and eyelashes curled — Esther's humble and gracious attitude brought respect and appreciation. Attitude is an important part of beauty.

Esther's submissive, obedient, and cooperative spirit is not to be mistaken for weakness or a lack of her own well-developed opinions. Esther had courage and a strong will, as is shown later in the story when she risks her life and states her case before the king. She even dared to accuse Haman, who was present at the time. Esther was no coward or silly beauty. She had courage and character. She knew how to be in command of her will for beneficial purposes. She exhibited power under control.

Esther was beautiful and found favor with everyone. She could have become conceited, demanding, and/or self-impressed. She evidently resisted those temptations.

Esther Showed Concern for Others

One day, as Esther was going about her duties as the new queen, the eunuchs and her female attendants came to her. They told her that Mordecai was outside the gates of the palace, grieving in sackcloth and ashes.

Esther received favor and she had the attention of the king. She was involved in the activities of the court and the affairs of the ladies of the court. Esther could have become more preoccupied with other matters than her cousin out by the gate. But when she heard about Mordecai, she not only cared, but "was in great distress" (Esther 4:4). She sent clothes for him to put on instead of his sackcloth, but he would not accept them.

Esther had no idea the issue troubling her relative would affect her too. For all she knew, Mordecai had a personal difficulty that he thought perhaps she could help him with.

When Esther's offer of new clothes did not console him, she "summoned Hathak, one of the king's eunuchs assigned to attend her, and ordered him to find out what was troubling Mordecai and why" (Esther 4:4–5). When he returned, he told Esther that Mordecai had learned of a wicked plan. Haman, one of the king's top advisors, devised a plan to exterminate all the Jews in the kingdom. This massive tragedy would mean an end to the entire nation of the Jewish people.

Mordecai instructed her to make a plea with the king for her people.

Esther sent this reply to Mordecai: "Go, gather together all the Jews who are in Susa, and fast for me. Do not eat or drink for three days, night or day. I and my attendants will fast as you do. When this is done, I will go to the king, even though it is against the law. And if I perish, I perish" (Esther 4:15–16).

Esther did not sidestep the problem or abdicate her responsibility. Rather, she complied with Mordecai's instruction, knowing it could mean her own death.

Esther Resisted the Temptations of the Successful

Problems often reveal one's character. When the pressure is on, the true nature of an individual is revealed more clearly than when life is moving along normally and all seems well. On the other end of the spectrum, however, is a different kind of temptation. Success also provides an opportunity to view one's character. Accomplishment corrupts some people. It allows further development of arrogance, contributing to an inflated ego and a superiority complex.

Why must the man or woman of God be particularly concerned about this? John 15:7–8 says that Jesus wants us to be fruitful in our lives, our characters, and our ministries. This brings glory to God. As we abide in Christ, we can ask God for fruitfulness and He will grant our request. But if our fruitfulness makes us successful in life, we will be tempted by pride.

Esther avoided that temptation. She provides for us a model of a person who, in spite of beauty and success, remembered her roots and struggled on behalf of her people.

> "If our fruitfulness makes us successful in life, we will be tempted by pride."

Esther Fought Her Battle by Praying

Esther and her attendants did a difficult thing; they conducted a three-day absolute fast — going without food and water. She asked Mordecai and the Jews at Susa to do the same. Then she put her life on the line by appearing without invitation before the king. She prayed, but she also planned and developed a wise strategy.

Nowhere in this book are the words *pray, prayed,* or *prayer* to be found. If Esther and her friends fasted, didn't they also pray? Certainly. And if they fasted and prayed, to whom did they pray? God, of course. No prayers to Him are mentioned in Esther, but they are unquestionably implied.

This seems rather like real life. We don't see God. We can't hear the private prayers of others. Prayer, if done in secret as Jesus said, is invisible, as is the God to whom we pray. Yet the results of His involvement in response to prayer abound.

God's active presence in our lives can be just as pervasive as demonstrated in the story of Esther. Even if we do not talk a lot about our prayer lives, we can see that He is involved and that He provides "grace to help us in our time of need" (Hebrews 4:16).

> On the third day Esther put on her royal robes and stood in the inner court of the palace, in front of the king's hall. The king was sitting on his royal throne in the hall, facing the entrance. When he saw Queen Esther standing in the court, he was pleased with her and held out to her the gold scepter that was in his hand. So Esther approached and touched the tip of the scepter. (Esther 5:1-2)

It is never wrong to pray about the evils in political arenas. Let us not ignore our moral obligation to prayerfully oppose evil wherever it exists in government or society. Out of supposed political correctness or social tolerance, some Christians sidestep opportunities to be an influence. God is willing to be involved in geopolitical conflict on the side of righteousness. The story of Esther illustrates that He recognizes the reality of evil and desires to help us be victorious over it.

God has political opinions. One side can be right and the other side wrong. And when politically correct but morally wrong policies, agendas, party platforms, or ethical issues become evident, they must be opposed by prayer.

Do not be afraid to have a political opinion and to pray about it. If you know the mind of God and how to pray in a given situation, you must oppose evil through prayer. You may not be a queen, but you, your family, and your loved ones will be affected by political outcomes.

> "God is willing to be involved in geo-political conflict on the side of righteousness."

Esther Planned Carefully and Did Not Hurry

In addition to praying, Esther planned. While she and her people were fasting these three days, Esther was strategizing how she should approach the king with her request. More than likely, she consulted certain trusted advisors.

Too many Christians, even leaders and ministers, believe the Holy Spirit only acts spontaneously. But there are times when we must plan ahead in order to do the right things God's way. Esther understood how important this was.

The king extended his scepter when Esther approached. She touched its tip, undoubtedly relieved that God had graciously brought her safe thus far. She could have immediately expressed her request at this point. But wisely, she did not. She instead mentioned a banquet she had prepared for him and Haman even before she approached the king. That took planning and effort. The king was suitably impressed by her preparations.

God Answered Esther's Prayers Even Before She Prayed

Esther is not the only one in the story who prepared in advance. Years before this crucial moment in time, God arranged for Mordecai to overhear two men, Bigthana and Teresh, conspiring to assassinate the king. The night after Esther invited the king and Haman to her prepared banquet, God kept the king from sleeping. The boring records in the archives were brought out and read to him. God led the scribe to read at that very time the particular section that brought Mordecai's good deed to light. He even arranged for Haman to be waiting at the door to enter the king's room just after Mordecai's good deed was revealed.

When the king asked his trusted advisor what should be done for a man who had served the king well, Haman proudly assumed he was that man. So he described in detail the most public honor he could think of. Imagine his distress when the king gave this very honor to Haman's enemy, Mordecai.

It is not hard to see God's hand in these events.

Esther Exercised Patience

At the banquet, Esther still declined the opportunity to express her complaint.

> Bring Haman at once," the king said, "so that we may do what Esther asks." So the king and Haman went to the banquet Esther had prepared. As they were drinking wine, the king again asked Esther, "Now what is your petition? It will be given you. And what is your request? Even up to half the kingdom, it will be granted."
>
> Esther replied, "My petition and my request is this: If the king regards me with favor and if it pleases the king to grant my petition and fulfill my request, let the king and Haman come tomorrow to the banquet I will prepare for them. Then I will answer the king's question." (Esther 5:5–8)

Esther was no empty-headed, vindictive, or emotional woman. The issue at hand meant life or death to her people. Yet she declined the opportunity to immediately express her desire to the king. That required strength of character. She evidently understood human nature quite well and decided to show honor to the king before making her request.

This delay gave time for the king's curiosity to be fully aroused. First she postponed her answer until later that same day. That would give her a chance to honor him at a banquet she had prepared. Then, Esther again put off her response until yet another day and the next banquet. She showed patience and wisdom by requesting these delays. She also certainly had the attention of the king.

> God never seems to hurry and is never late. Could we learn to be more like Him on this point?

In our impatience, do we fail to honor God? Is our desire for hasty results motivated by faith or a lack of faith? God never seems to hurry and is never late. Could we learn to be more like Him on this point? Wise Esther seems to have known that taking a slower pace allows for more reflection and satisfactory results.

Esther Remained Objective

We have arrived at the pivotal part of the drama. Esther did not blink, flinch, or hold back. At the right time, she spoke courageously. Notice how poised, measured, confident, yet entreating her words are.

> So the king and Haman went to Queen Esther's banquet, and as they were drinking wine on the second day, the king again asked, "Queen Esther, what is your petition? It will be given you. What is your request? Even up to half the kingdom, it will be granted."
>
> Then Queen Esther answered, "If I have found favor with you, Your Majesty, and if it pleases you, grant me my life — this is my petition. And spare my people — this is my request. For I and my people have been sold to be destroyed, killed and annihilated. If we had merely been sold as male and female slaves, I would have kept quiet, because no such distress would justify disturbing the king."
>
> King Xerxes asked Queen Esther, "Who is he? Where is he — the man who has dared to do such a thing"

Esther said, "An adversary and enemy! This vile Haman!"
(Esther 7:1-6)

Esther focused on protection of herself and her people, not on hatred of her enemy. First, she tactfully asked for her people to be saved. Only when the king asked the identity of the man who had dared to do such a thing did she spring the trap on Haman.

> Then Haman was terrified before the king and queen. The king got up in a rage, left his wine and went out into the palace garden. But Haman, realizing that the king had already decided his fate, stayed behind to beg Queen Esther for his life.
>
> Then Haman was terrified before the king returned from the palace garden to the banquet hall, Haman was falling on the couch where Esther was reclining.
>
> The king exclaimed, "Will he even molest the queen while she is with me in the house?"
>
> As soon as the word left the king's mouth, they covered Haman's face. Then Harbona, one of the eunuchs attending the king, said, "A pole reaching to a height of fifty cubits stands by Haman's house. He had it set up for Mordecai, who spoke up to help the king."
>
> The king said, "Impale him on it!" So they impaled Haman on the pole he had set up for Mordecai. Then the king's fury subsided.
> (Esther 7:6-10)

> "Esther showed no weakness. At the crucial moment, she spoke with undeniable courage."

Esther did not back down even when the king commanded Haman to be impaled on the pole he had set up for Mordecai. Esther showed no weakness. At the crucial moment, she spoke with undeniable courage.

Justice requires wisdom and firmness. Mercy at the right times can be a result of wisdom and strength. But, unfortunately, mercy is too often merely a result of weak character — unwillingness to uphold righteousness and preserve justice. Esther's firmness and consistency in maintaining justice in this instance are qualities to be admired and emulated.

Esther Boldly Pressed Her Advantage

The day after the king gave the estate of Haman to Esther, the drama continued.

Esther again pleaded with the king, falling at his feet and weeping. She begged him to put an end to the evil plan of Haman the Agagite, which he had devised against the Jews. Then the king extended the gold scepter to Esther and she arose and stood before him.

"If it pleases the king," she said, "and if he regards me with favor and thinks it the right thing to do, and if he is pleased with me, let an order be written overruling the dispatches that Haman son of Hammedatha, the Agagite, devised and wrote to destroy the Jews in all the king's provinces. For how can I bear to see disaster fall on my people? How can I bear to see the destruction of my family?"

King Xerxes replied to Queen Esther and to Mordecai the Jew, "Because Haman attacked the Jews, I have given his estate to Esther, and they have impaled him on the pole he set up. Now write another decree in the king's name in behalf of the Jews as seems best to you, and seal it with the king's signet ring — for no document written in the king's name and sealed with his ring can be revoked."

At once the royal secretaries were summoned — on the twenty-third day of the third month, the month of Sivan. They wrote out all Mordecai's orders to the Jews, and to the satraps, governors, and nobles of the 127 provinces stretching from India to Cush. These orders were written in the script of each province and the language of each people and also to the Jews in their own script and language. Mordecai wrote in the name of King Xerxes, sealed the dispatches with the king's signet ring, and sent them by mounted couriers, who rode fast horses especially bred for the king.

The king's edict granted the Jews in every city the right to assemble and protect themselves; to destroy, kill and annihilate the armed men of any nationality or province who might attack them and their women and children, and to plunder the property of their enemies. The day appointed for the Jews to do this in all the provinces of King Xerxes was the thirteenth day of the twelfth month, the month of Adar. A copy of the text of the edict was to be issued as law in every province and made known to the people of every nationality so that the Jews would be ready on that day to avenge themselves on their enemies. (Esther 8:3–14)

God does not approve of personal revenge. We are to be forgiving. So how are we to interpret Esther's behavior? She requested permission for the Jews to defend themselves and plunder the property of their enemies. Was this act pleasing to God?

Centuries earlier, Saul had failed to press his advantage against King Agag, whom Saul was to destroy, and whom Samuel eventually had to kill. Haman was an Agagite, a descendent of this wicked king. Esther was not weak like Saul. She acted more decisively and wisely than he.

Corrective punishment to rid the earth of evil is not the same as personal revenge. Men and women of God must follow God's example in His love for justice. They must understand the rightness of justice and uphold justice in the administrative affairs of our churches and ministries. Of course, we cannot approve of vengeance. Justice breeds respect for right and distaste for wrong, while personal payback elicits still more hatred.

> "Corrective punishment to rid the earth of evil is not the same as personal revenge."

The Bible Supports National Defense

God miraculously provided the means of self-defense for the Jews. He used judges, armies, and kings for this purpose in previous centuries. This time, he used the king's edict. This would not have happened if God were not in favor of countries protecting themselves. National defense is not revenge. It is the attempt to stop the aggressor and prevent further evil.

Every country that maintains a strong military for national defense contributes to the prevalence of peace in the world. Evil nations do not attack strong nations. A strong defense, therefore, is a deterrent to war. Christians who are serving their nations as soldiers are not soldiering because they want war, but because they *do not* want war. They are defending their nations and families against aggressors who do not recognize the rights of free people.

If God were anti-military, John the Baptist would have spoken to the Roman soldiers of his day on that subject instead of merely instructing them to not complain about their wages. "Some soldiers asked him, 'And what should we do?' He replied, 'Don't extort money and don't accuse people falsely — be content with your pay'" (Luke 3:14).

> "National defense is not revenge. It is the attempt to stop the aggressor and prevent further evil."

In Esther's time, God did not destroy the enemies of the Jews with hailstones, lightning, or thunder. He gave them the means to defend themselves. God's answer to our prayer for protection may be to provide us with the ability to protect ourselves. There is nothing wrong with using the defensive measures He has given us.

Esther was a beautiful, wise, poised, self-controlled, intelligent, considerate, and firm young woman who kept her power under control, put her life on the line, and became a savior for her people. Could it be that God has given you similar traits "for such a time as this" (Esther 4:14)?

For Further Thought

- What does Esther's continued humility in her success say to you about greatness?
- What did you learn from Esther's sincere praying?
- What are you doing to be deliberate and strategic in your planning?
- How do you remain emotionally steady and objective when dealing with explosive issues?
- What does Esther's life say to us about pressing our advantage when God gives us one?
- What lessons can you apply to your life by noting that God gave Esther and the Jews of her day military equipment and permission to use it?

CHAPTER 15
JOB

Did you know that God was proud of Job and defended him? Were you aware that God eventually required Job's three critical friends to go to him to receive the benefits of his prayers? Did you realize that Job's statement of personal ethics is one of the most noble, comprehensive, and exemplary proclamations in the Bible?

In the previous chapter, we studied a Bible character in a book that made no mention of either God or prayer. The opposite happens in Job. The words, thoughts, and actions of God are carefully described. We even see some pictures of God's activities that are not described in such detail in any other book of the Bible. God's conversations with the devil and His involvement in the invisible, behind-the-scenes spiritual drama make this book uniquely helpful to the Christian warrior. This study, like the story of Balaam, reveals the reality of the spiritual forces involved in humans' lives. Yet the lessons from Job are quite different from those learned from Balaam. These lessons are rich in meaning and lead to greater intimacy with God.

None of us wants to endure the sufferings of Job. We do not wish to experience anything even remotely comparable. Yet any one of us would be glad to experience the vindications, revelations, and victories he received. Job teaches us lessons of patience, courage, faithfulness, and perseverance.

In 2005 and 2006, my wife and I were involved in lengthy talks with the director of an international missions group. Char had been invited to serve as a trainer for missionary candidates. She would also be a consultant to the numerous Bible colleges and institutes operated in more than eighty nations. Meanwhile, I would serve as the coordinator of continuing education for career missionaries and the pastors of churches in those nations. In response to this invitation, I resigned my graduate missions professor position in the university where I had been teaching. I also resigned my job as associate pastor of English ministries in a local Chinese church. Char and I visited the community where these new opportunities were based and began searching for a home to purchase.

After the house shopping began, we received a phone call saying that the offer was being withdrawn. That same day, bursitis and a staph infection crippled my left elbow. Several days later, Char discovered she had two infected teeth that needed root canals. We found ourselves facing the loss of two jobs, bursitis, staph infection, and two abscessed teeth. Since I had resigned my two positions, I was no longer employed. We felt like two Jobs.

I will return to my personal story at the end of this chapter. In the meantime, let's look at what you and I can learn from this book of Job that will help us next time we suffer.

The Four Pillars of Job's Righteous Life

Job was blameless and upright; he feared God and shunned evil. But suffering can happen to anyone — even the most righteous.

> In the land of Uz there lived a man whose name was Job. This man was blameless and upright; he feared God and shunned evil. He had seven sons and three daughters, and he owned seven thousand sheep, three thousand camels, five hundred yoke of oxen and five hundred donkeys, and had a large number of servants. He was the greatest man among all the people of the East.
>
> His sons used to hold feasts in their homes on their birthdays, and they would invite their three sisters to eat and drink with them. When a period of feasting had run its course, Job would make arrangements for them to be purified. Early in the morning he would sacrifice a burnt offering for each of them, thinking, "Perhaps my children have sinned and cursed God in their hearts." This was Job's regular custom. (Job 1:1-5)

Job's righteousness is further displayed in his response to his wife when she suggested that he give up. He replied, "You are talking like a foolish woman. Shall we accept good from God, and not trouble?" (Job 2:10).

Even Job's friend Eliphaz, in his first speech leading up to his many accusations against Job, testified to Job's righteousness: "Think how you have instructed many, how you have strengthened feeble hands. Your words have supported those who stumbled; you have strengthened faltering knees" (Job 4:3-4). Throughout the book of Job, Eliphaz emphasizes that Job's suffering is due to his sin. Yet even he was forced to acknowledge Job's virtues.

God Himself defended Job to his accusing friends: "After the Lord had said these things to Job, he said to Eliphaz the Temanite, 'I am angry with you and your two friends, because you have not spoken of me what is right, as my servant Job has'" (Job 42:7).

> "Job was righteous, and yet he suffered."

Job was the richest man in the East. Wealth often corrupts a person, but not in his case. Job shows us that one can be prosperous and yet blameless and upright. His systematic intercession for his children also attests to his high level of moral uprightness. Job was righteous, and yet he suffered.

The devil is our accuser. He brought charges against Job before God. He further indicted Job via his friends. Instead of comforting Job, they repeatedly argued that he brought his suffering upon himself.

In the midst of the barrage of guilt hurled at him, Job maintained his righteousness. Even in the New Testament, God praises Job as a great example of righteousness and patience. James considered him a model of godliness, not as an illustration of punishment of evil:

> Brothers and sisters, as an example of patience in the face of suffering, take the prophets who spoke in the name of the Lord. As you know, we count as blessed those who have persevered. You have heard of Job's perseverance and have seen what the Lord finally brought about. The Lord is full of compassion and mercy. (James 5:10-11)

If the enemy can cause us to believe that we are suffering because we are evil, he gains an advantage inasmuch as our courage is undermined. We think we are suffering because we deserve to suffer, so why try to escape it? Suffering may, but does not always, indicate that God is dealing with a sin in our lives. According to James 1:2–5, when we do not understand the trials we are facing, we are to ask God for wisdom, and He will give it to us.

If we recognize that righteous people suffer too, we can defend ourselves against the accusations we often feel when we go through trials. A direct correlation between sin and suffering undermines the confidence we need to pass the tests. May the Lord help us focus on His purpose in the circumstances He has allowed in our lives.

God Took Pleasure in Job's Righteousness

> "One day the angels came to present themselves before the Lord, and Satan also came with them" (Job 1:6).

Though the meeting was initiated by Satan, God raised the subject of Job and his righteousness. "Then the Lord said to Satan, 'Have you considered my servant Job? There is no one on earth like him; he is blameless and upright, a man who fears God and shuns evil'" (Job 1:8). God took pleasure in boasting to Satan about Job.

After Job passed the first round of the tests Satan brought on him, God again pointed to Job with pride. "Then the Lord said to Satan, 'Have you considered my servant Job? There is no one on earth like him; he is blameless and upright, a man who fears God and shuns evil. And he still maintains his integrity, though you incited me against him to ruin him without any reason'" (Job 2:3).

> **We often use the expression 'please the Lord,' but we may not appreciate the depth of this phrase.**

We bring God great pleasure when we do right. We often use the expression "please the Lord," but we may not appreciate the depth of this phrase. Evidently, even under the duress of his sufferings, Job continued to please the Lord.

God Had a Protective Hedge around Job

> "Does Job fear God for nothing?" Satan replied. "Have you not put a hedge around him and his household and everything he has? You have blessed the work of his hands, so that his flocks and herds are spread throughout the land. But now stretch out your hand and strike everything he has, and he will surely curse you to your face."
>
> The Lord said to Satan, "Very well, then, everything he has is in your power, but on the man himself do not lay a finger."
>
> Then Satan went out from the presence of the Lord. (Job 1:9–12)

God put a protective hedge around Job, his household, and his possessions. He blessed the work of his hands, his flocks, and his herds. Satan could not penetrate the hedge or block the blessings. This was the accuser's complaint as he argued with God regarding Job's righteousness. Satan does not like it when God protects us from him. He wants access to us, but he cannot have it unless God or our sin allows it.

Why did Job's three friends assume that God was displeased with Job? Did they not realize that it was God's approval and favor upon Job that led Him to protect and bless him?

We have the "inside scoop" — the invisible part of the story. We know God was pleased with Job. That was the whole issue of the argument between God and Satan. Job's friends didn't have that insight.

Just as it was improper for Job's friends to assume that Job's sin brought on his sufferings, so we should not assume God is displeased with us just because we are suffering. Trials provide us with valuable time for reflection and self-examination. They give us an opportunity to confess sin if we have done something wrong and receive forgiveness and cleansing from God. But times of suffering should not be occasions for self-condemnation. "There is now no condemnation for those who are in Christ Jesus" (Romans 8:1). God forgives us so completely that if we mention a confessed sin a second time, He may ask, "What sin are you talking about?" Knowing we are forgiven is a great basis for confidence in the face of suffering.

God Knew Job's Ability

God knows the strength of the steel He is testing. He will never let us experience more difficulties than we can handle. First Corinthians 10:13 presents us with the principle of God's perfect tempering process: "No temptation has seized you except what is common to man. And God is faithful; he will not let you be tempted beyond what you can bear. But when you are tempted, he will also provide a way out so that you can stand up under it."

> "God knows the strength of the steel He is testing."

God knew the strength of Job's endurance. Because of that, He allowed Satan to bring on him the sudden calamities that destroyed oxen, sheep, camels, and Job's children.

How did Job react to all his losses?

> At this, Job got up and tore his robe and shaved his head. Then he fell to the ground in worship and said: "Naked I came from my mother's womb, and naked I will depart. The Lord gave and the Lord has taken away; may the name of the Lord be praised." In all this, Job did not sin by charging God with wrongdoing. (Job 1:20–22)

Job proved himself worthy of God's compliment.

Having passed that test, Job then faced the second round. Satan obtained God's permission to afflict Job's body:

> Satan went out from the presence of the Lord and afflicted Job with painful sores from the soles of his feet to the crown of his head. Then Job took a piece of broken pottery and scraped himself with it as he sat among the ashes.
>
> His wife said to him, "Are you still maintaining your integrity? Curse God and die!"
>
> He replied, "You are talking like a foolish woman. Shall we accept good from God, and not trouble?"
>
> In all this, Job did not sin in what he said. (Job 2:7–10)

Both times that God gave Satan permission to bring difficulties to Job,

God was right about Job's ability to endure. In both instances, God's confidence in Job's faith, patience, and endurance was justified.

Suffering is not meaningless. God is refining, developing, maturing, and preparing us for an eternal purpose. In order to purify and advance his workers, God brings them through affliction. No other religion gives its believers such a lofty and eternally valuable reason for enduring distress. Some religions advise adherents to embrace pain. Others recommend abandoning desire. Only Christianity promises positive results to believers through suffering.

Needless suffering is difficult to endure, but purposeful, result-oriented difficulty is easier to handle. And suffering known to be bearable becomes manageable.

Behaviorists have experimented with rats to determine the effects of hope when suffering or facing death. Rodents that swim around a tank enough to learn there is no escape quickly abandon any further effort to maintain their lives. They give up, stop swimming, and sink.

But rats that are rescued just before they would have given up (based on the timing of the earlier rats abandoning hope) swim on until they are saved. Knowing they will be picked out of the water gives them the courage to swim until they are helped. They swim much longer than the rats that were not taught by *being* rescued that they *would be* rescued.

> **He knows we will fight on and on, enduring whatever suffering comes our way, if we know we can.**

If you know that you will not be given a test or temptation that you cannot handle, you have the courage and hope you need in order to win the test of faith. The principle in 1 Corinthians 10:13 gives us the encouragement we need to endure. God wants to develop a hardy spiritual army of persevering soldiers. He knows we will fight on and on — enduring whatever suffering comes our way — if we know we can. The suffering He allows is a statement of His confidence in us; it is a compliment. Knowing we will be rescued empowers us to endure until we are rescued. Only those who quit do not finish. You can win if you keep going.

The High Purpose in Human Suffering (Scriptures)

The following verses from the Epistles and Revelation talk about suffering:

> We also glory in our sufferings, because we know that suffering produces perseverance. (Romans 5:3)

> Now if we are children, then we are heirs — heirs of God and co-heirs with Christ, if indeed we share in his sufferings in order that we may also share in his glory. I consider that our present sufferings are not worth comparing with the glory that will be revealed in us. (Romans 8:17–18)

> For just as we share abundantly in the sufferings of Christ, so also our comfort abounds through Christ. If we are distressed, it is for your comfort and salvation; if we are comforted, it is for your comfort, which produces in you patient endurance of the same sufferings we suffer. And our hope for you is firm, because we know that just as you share in our sufferings, so also you share in our comfort. (2 Corinthians 1:5–7)

> I ask you, therefore, not to be discouraged because of my sufferings for you, which are your glory. (Ephesians 3:13)

> I want to know Christ — yes, to know the power of his resurrection and participation in his sufferings, becoming like him in his death. (Philippians 3:10)

> Now I rejoice in what I am suffering for you, and I fill up in my flesh what is still lacking in regard to Christ's afflictions, for the sake of his body, which is the church. (Colossians 1:24)

> You became imitators of us and of the Lord, for you welcomed the message in the midst of severe suffering with the joy given by the Holy Spirit. (1 Thessalonians 1:6)

> All this is evidence that God's judgment is right, and as a result you will be counted worthy of the kingdom of God, for which you are suffering. (2 Thessalonians 1:5)

> So do not be ashamed of the testimony about our Lord or of me his prisoner. But join with me in suffering for the gospel, by the power of God. (2 Timothy 1:8)

That is why I am suffering as I am. Yet this is no cause for shame, because I know whom I have believed, and am convinced that he is able to guard what I have entrusted to him until that day. (2 Timothy 1:12)

Join with me in suffering, like a good soldier of Christ Jesus. (2 Timothy 2:3)

I am suffering even to the point of being chained like a criminal. But God's word is not chained. (2 Timothy 2:9)

… persecutions, sufferings — what kinds of things happened to me in Antioch, Iconium and Lystra, the persecutions I endured. Yet the Lord rescued me from all of them. (2 Timothy 3:11)

Remember those earlier days after you had received the light, when you endured in a great conflict full of suffering. (Hebrews 10:32)

Continue to remember those in prison as if you were together with them in prison, and those who are mistreated as if you yourselves were suffering. (Hebrews 13:3)

Brothers and sisters, as an example of patience in the face of suffering, take the prophets who spoke in the name of the Lord. As you know, we count as blessed those who have persevered. You have heard of Job's perseverance and have seen what the Lord finally brought about. The Lord is full of compassion and mercy. (James 5:10–11)

… trying to find out the time and circumstances to which the Spirit of Christ in them was pointing when he predicted the sufferings of Christ and the glories that would follow. (1 Peter 1:11)

For it is commendable if you bear up under the pain of unjust suffering because you are conscious of God. (1 Peter 2:19)

Dear friends, do not be surprised at the fiery ordeal that has come on you to test you, as though something strange were happening to you. But rejoice inasmuch as you participate in the sufferings of Christ, so that you may be overjoyed when his glory is revealed … However, if you suffer as a Christian, do not be ashamed, but praise God that you bear that name. (1 Peter 4:12–13, 16)

> To the elders among you, I appeal as a fellow elder and a witness of Christ's sufferings who also will share in the glory to be revealed. (1 Peter 5:1)
>
> Resist him, standing firm in the faith, because you know that your fellow believers throughout the world are undergoing the same kind of sufferings. And the God of all grace, who called you to his eternal glory in Christ, after you have suffered a little while, will himself restore you and make you strong, firm and steadfast. (1 Peter 5:9–10)
>
> I, John, your brother and companion in the suffering and kingdom and patient endurance that are ours in Jesus, was on the island of Patmos because of the word of God and the testimony of Jesus. (Revelation 1:9)

Not one of these verses leads us to believe that suffering is due to sin in the life of the sufferer.

Suffering's High Purposes (Theological Statements)

The following theological statements demonstrate suffering's high purposes:

- No automatic correlation exists between personal sin and suffering. Sometimes good people suffer; the distress has nothing to do with sin. On the other hand, sometimes wicked people whom one might think ought to experience pain do not. Psalm 37:7 says, "Be still before the Lord and wait patiently for him; do not fret when people succeed in their ways, when they carry out their wicked schemes."

- The cause or nature of an incident of suffering is inconsequential when compared to what it produces in our lives. Affliction or persecution — whether accidental or coincidental; physical, mental, or emotional — enables us to be partakers of Christ's suffering, become one with Him, and grow in character.

- Distress is only temporary because this earthly life is temporary. Suffering is not our focus. Rather, we look for the results, to identify with Jesus and experience His intended fruit of pain.

- Our attitude is to be one of joy. This does not happen automatically, and it may be difficult to maintain. Yet happiness stems from the opportunity to share in Christ's sufferings.

- A joyful attitude in difficulty is not natural. Yet if we yield ourselves to Jesus and His developmental process in our lives, our sufferings will produce spiritual growth and greater intimacy with Him.
- Our distresses, though painful, are less than the reward. They cannot be compared with the exceeding and great glory that shall be revealed in us.
- Affliction is unavoidable, so prepare to accept and embrace it. Look for its spiritual benefits.
- All Christians experience pain, though we hear about some persons' afflictions more than that of others.
- While not all distress is discipline for wrongdoing, some is. "Endure hardship as discipline; God is treating you as his children. For what children are not disciplined by their father? ... No discipline seems pleasant at the time, but painful. Later on, however, it produces a harvest of righteousness and peace for those who have been trained by it" (Hebrews 12:7, 11).

Job Maintained His Righteousness

How did Job endure? He fixed his eyes on God and maintained his own appraisal of himself, rejecting the accusations of his "friends."

"Though he slay me, yet will I hope in him" (Job 13:15). "I know that my redeemer lives, and that in the end he will stand in the earth. And after my skin has been destroyed, yet in my flesh I will see God" (Job 19:25-26). Job could never have endured his ordeals if he had not fixed his eyes on God and trusted God to treat him fairly. Nothing Satan threw at Job could tear him away from the Lord.

> "In the end, Job was justified, not his friends."

Some take a judgmental view of Job. They side with Job's three companions, who unrelentingly attacked him with harsh words. In defense against his friends' accusations, Job strayed precariously close to pride, displayed in a pious claim for innocence. But in the end, Job was justified, not his friends.

If, in maintaining his own righteousness, Job was clinging to his hope in God, we can celebrate it and follow his example. If Job was arrogantly claiming he had no sin at all, we must avoid doing the same. Each sufferer will have to sort out which of the two is true in his or her case.

If Job had agreed that he had sinned as all men have, but that he did not believe his suffering was due to sin, the lengthy conversation recorded in Job 3 through 37 would have been quite different. The self-righteousness in Job would not have intensified, and the accusations would have softened.

We cannot rewrite Job's story, but we can rewrite our own. When you face accusations, real or imagined, admit that you are not perfect. But don't assume that the suffering is due to your sin. Something more is likely going on.

Job's Personal Ethics Policy

Within the lengthy conversation between Job and his friends, Job's ethical code appears (Job 31). In view of our emphasis in this study of Job's character and integrity, let's look at his list of rules as a model. Each one of us has our own moral standards. Not all will be as well-defined as Job's, but we can each learn something from Job's personal rules:

- He determined not to look lustfully at women.

    > I made a covenant with my eyes not to look lustfully at a virgin. For what is our lot from God above, our heritage from the Almighty on high? Is it not ruin for the wicked, disaster for those who do wrong? Does he not see my ways and count my every step? (Job 31:1–4)

    > If my heart has been enticed by a woman, or if I have lurked at my neighbor's door, then may my wife grind another man's grain, and may other men sleep with her. For that would have been wicked, a sin to be judged. It is a fire that burns to Destruction; it would have uprooted my harvest. (Job 31:9–12)

- He determined to treat employees with justice, as equals.

    > If I have denied justice to any of my servants, whether male or female, when they had a grievance against me, what will I do when God confronts me? What will I answer when called to account? Did not he who made me in the womb make them? Did not the same one form us both within our mothers? (Job 31:13–15)

- He sought to be generous and helpful to the poor.

    If I have denied the desires of the poor or let the eyes of the widow grow weary, if I have kept my bread to myself, not sharing it with the fatherless — but from my youth I reared them as a father would, and from my birth I guided the widow — if I have seen anyone perishing for lack of clothing, or the needy without garments, and their hearts did not bless me for warming them with the fleece from my sheep, if I have raised my hand against the fatherless, knowing that I had influence in court, then let my arm fall from the shoulder, let it be broken off at the joint. For I dreaded destruction from God, and for fear of his splendor I could not do such things. (Job 31:16-23)

- Gold or gods were not to be served or trusted.

    If I have put my trust in gold or said to pure gold, "You are my security," if I have rejoiced over my great wealth, the fortune my hands had gained, if I have regarded the sun in its radiance or the moon moving in splendor, so that my heart was secretly enticed and my hand offered them a kiss of homage, then these also would be sins to be judged, for I would have been unfaithful to God on high. (Job 31:24-28)

- He determined not to curse his enemies but to help the traveler.

    If I have rejoiced at my enemies' misfortune or gloated over the trouble that came to them — I have not allowed my mouth to sin by invoking a curse against their life — if those of my household have never said, "Who has not been filled with Job's meat?" — but no stranger had to spend the night in the street, for my door was always open to the traveler. (Job 31:29-32)

- Job did not hide his sin, but dealt with it openly and transparently.

    If I have concealed my sin as people do, by hiding my guilt in my heart because I so feared the crowd and so dreaded the contempt of the clans that I kept silent and would not go outside — (Oh, that I had someone to hear me! I sign now my defense — let the Almighty answer me; let my accuser put his indictment in writing. Surely I would wear it on my shoulder, I would put it on like a crown. I would give him an account of my every step; I would present it to him as to a ruler.) — (Job 31:33-37)

- Job determined to have an attitude of stewardship toward his land.

> If my land cries out against me and all its furrows are wet with tears, if I have devoured its yield without payment or broken the spirit of its tenants, then let briers come up instead of wheat and stinkweed instead of barley." (Job 31:38-40)

It would be possible to be critical of Job, thinking that all his moral and ethical rhetoric was bravado, boasting, and self-defense against the accusations of his three visitors. Is it not equally possible to see Job as an upright, moral, and ethical model to follow? Is it not possible that the godly character demonstrated in this record of Job's ethics is one of the Bible's patterns to which godly people in other generations can also adhere?

Job Repented When God Showed Him a Clearer Picture

Much about Job's character can be learned by examining his response to the personal revelations God gave him (recorded in Job 38-41). Did Job defend himself? Did he boast? What attitude did Job display?

> Job replied to the Lord: "I know that you can do all things; no purpose of yours can be thwarted. You asked, 'Who is this that obscures my plans without knowledge?' Surely I spoke of things I did not understand, things too wonderful for me to know. You said, 'Listen now, and I will speak; I will question you, and you shall answer me.' My ears had heard of you but now my eyes have seen you. Therefore I despise myself and repent in dust and ashes." (Job 42:1-6)

> "When God in His grandeur spoke, Job humbled himself quickly and thoroughly."

These are not the words of an arrogant sinner pretentiously denying his sin. Job's self-defense included (in the narrative of Job 6-37) his response to the accusations of his friends. When God in His grandeur spoke, Job humbled himself quickly and thoroughly.

Covering a sin is worse than the sin that is covered. Acknowledging sin is the way to obtain forgiveness and cleansing.

The lengthy discussion between Job and his friends focused on the friends' attempts to explain the reason for Job's suffering: his sin. Job repeatedly reacted with self-defense. God's revelation, however, reminded Job of His greatness and perfection. Compared to God, Job was nothing. When God revealed Himself to Job, he had no more questions.

An Optimistic Application to Ourselves

Let's take a magnanimous attitude toward Job and bear the following in mind:

- Job did not have the advantage we have today of the numerous Scriptures that teach us of God's lofty purposes and how suffering serves those purposes.
- Job did not have our Bible-based theological understanding on the subject of suffering.
- In one day, without notice or explanation, Job lost all his children, oxen, sheep, and camels.
- Job's body was wracked with painful sores that undoubtedly made him more pessimistic than usual.
- Job did not know about the unseen and unheard conversations between God and the devil, as we do.
- Job's friends, instead of comforting him, repeatedly accused him of committing a sin that brought on the suffering. Their interpretation of suffering as punishment from God was an unfair judgment against Job.
- The combined forces of the preceding six factors would wear down the patience and endurance of any man.
- God told Job's friends they had not spoken of "what was right." He suggested they ask Job to pray for them, saying, "I will accept his prayer and not deal with you according to your folly" (Job 42:7). This indicates that God was more pleased with Job than Job knew.

These observations lead us to the following personal applications:

- When you and I go through reversals and difficulties, when the accuser throws our sins into our faces, when our friends don't understand, when we think we are alone in our pain and sorrow, when we don't see the spiritual activities of our accuser or the intervention of our invisible Defender — we should remember this lesson from Job: God is more pleased with us than we realize.

- We cannot understand everything in this life. Too many unknowable factors exist. "A person's steps are directed by the Lord. How then can anyone understand their own way?" (Proverbs 20:24). Let us not needlessly add to whatever we are suffering by judging ourselves too harshly. Paul said, "I care very little if I am judged by you or by any human court; indeed, I do not even judge myself. My conscience is clear, but that does not make me innocent. It is the Lord who judges me" (1 Corinthians 4:3-4).

> "God is more pleased with us than we realize."

Remember the personal story I shared in the beginning of this chapter? It listed the difficulties Char and I experienced when we thought we were transitioning from academia to missionary continuing-education ministries. I know now that God used the two resignations, and the suspense of not knowing what to do or where to turn, to guide us to the exciting opportunity to train Christian leaders in Africa. He moved us from the relative comforts of academia to the challenges of travel throughout southern Africa.

I also realize now that Satan daily added his accusations to this horrible experience. For many months, he lied to me. He said my problems happened because we were not fit for the positions with the mission.

If I had it to do over, I would try harder to throw off the self-condemnation. I would attempt to focus on the career decisions before us. The accusations I experienced at that time were the most difficult part of my suffering — and they were all untrue.

If we acknowledge that we cannot understand everything in this life, we will be able to move on with greater confidence. Job teaches us not to allow the devil's accusations to compound the trouble God has allowed for our development. Job felt God was far away and indifferent during his trials. However, God was probably closer and more attentive in that time of his life than He had ever been.

For Further Thought

- How does acknowledgment of God's lofty purpose of refinement and development help carry you through times of suffering?
- What do you think about the statement that God usually allows suffering for a noble purpose, occasionally as necessary discipline, but never for revenge?
- How would you react if you thought God was boasting about you the way He boasted about Job?
- Do you feel that the hedge of protection God placed around Job is different from the protection He offers you? Explain.
- What help is it to be aware that God knows your ability to endure and He will never let you experience a difficulty He realizes you cannot handle?
- How could Job have avoided the criticism that he was being self-righteous when he defended himself?
- What was the biggest surprise you experienced when you read Job's personal ethical standards for behavior?
- When God revealed Himself to Job, what does Job's spontaneous repentance tell you about his character?
- Do you agree with the concept that God is more pleased with us than we realize? How does this idea change the way you view your life?

CHAPTER 16
ISAIAH

Did you know that Isaiah volunteered for service? Were you aware that Isaiah described personal peace as a benefit of faith in God possibly more clearly than any other writer? Did you realize that Isaiah the poet penned some of the most lofty prose in the Bible describing the Messiah?

Isaiah prophesied in Judah and Jerusalem during the years of decline in Israel, the northern kingdom. During the year Uzziah died in Jerusalem, Isaiah volunteered to serve. Uzziah reigned for fifty-two years. Most of those years, he was a godly leader and enjoyed success. But things changed at the end of his reign. He became proud, usurped the authority of a priest, and burned incense in the temple. As punishment, leprosy broke out on his forehead, eventually leading to his death. His son reigned in his place until Uzziah died. Then Jotham became king.

Isaiah saw visions during the reigns of Uzziah, Jotham, Ahaz, and Hezekiah. Why didn't he prophesy during the time of Hezekiah's son Manasseh? Was Isaiah active only until Hezekiah died? Tradition says Manasseh had Isaiah sawn in two. That would stop visions! Did Manasseh kill Isaiah soon after beginning to reign? That's unlikely since Manasseh was only twelve years old at the time. Many of these questions must remain unanswered. But this is the political setting in which Isaiah served.

Isaiah Responded to a Need and God's Question

> In the year that King Uzziah died, I saw the Lord seated on a throne, high and exalted, and the train of his robe filled the

temple. Above him were seraphs, each with six wings: with two wings they covered their faces, with two they covered their feet, and with two they were flying. And they were calling to one another: "Holy, holy, holy is the Lord Almighty; the whole earth is full of his glory."

At the sound of their voices the doorposts and thresholds shook and the temple was filled with smoke. "Woe to me!" I cried. "I am ruined! For I am a man of unclean lips, and I live among a people of unclean lips, and my eyes have seen the King, the Lord Almighty."

Then one of the seraphs flew to me with a live coal in his hand, which he had taken with tongs from the altar. With it he touched my mouth and said, "See, this has touched your lips; your guilt is taken away and your sin atoned for."

Then I heard the voice of the Lord saying, "Whom shall I send? And who will go for us?"

And I said, "Here am I. Send me!" (Isaiah 6:1-8)

God in His glory revealed Himself to Isaiah. God filled the temple. Angels sang and the whole place shook. In that setting, Isaiah recognized his own personal inadequacy. An angel announced his forgiveness. When Isaiah heard the Lord ask, "Whom shall I send? And who will go for us?" he promptly volunteered for service.

Like many other instances in biblical and church history, Isaiah saw a need coupled with an awareness that God was speaking about it. It constituted a call. This happened, for example, to William Carey. Carey was a shoe cobbler, but he could not escape the world map on the wall of his cobbler's shop. He saw a need. Eventually, he started the Protestant missionary movement by writing a book. It was about the use of practical means (such as missionary societies) to raise funds for doing missions work. It awakened his generation. He also served many fruitful years in India.

Isaiah's experience teaches us that the response to a need can be a call. When we see a need, we should ask ourselves, "Is meeting this need my call?" In Isaiah's case, the need he observed was accompanied by a question from God: "Whom shall I send? And who will go for us?" (Isaiah 6:8).

Isaiah's experience also teaches that righteousness is not a requirement for a call. Isaiah's reaction when he saw the Lord filling the temple was to acknowledge his own sinfulness and unworthiness. God forgave him and cleansed him, just as God cleans up each of the tools He uses.

Isaiah's next response was to volunteer. Two major issues are illustrated in Isaiah's call:

- Recognizing a need accompanied by the witness of the Spirit can constitute a call.
- You don't have to be perfect to be called.

> "When we see a need, we should ask ourselves, 'Is meeting this need my call?'"

What needs do you see in your church, community, city, or nation? Is it possible that God will use your sensitivity to that need to stir you up to Christian service? Isaiah, Nehemiah, and William Carey each saw needs and responded. What needs do you see? Will you repeat Isaiah's famous words, "Here am I. Send me"? Or will you listen to the accuser as he tells you that you are not good enough and are not qualified to be called by God?

Isaiah Understood the Rewards of Faith

Godly virtues often have personal reward built into them. Patience, for example, is its own reward; peace is the reward for patience. The patient person does not have to struggle with the emotional discomfort of frustration — he feels none or little of that *because* of his patience. In a similar vein, Isaiah understood the relationship between faith in God and personal peace. He said, "If you do not stand firm in your faith, you will not stand at all" (Isaiah 7:9). He also said, "You [God] will keep in perfect peace those whose minds are steadfast, because they trust in you" (Isaiah 26:3).

In addition, Isaiah penned these well-known words: "He gives strength to the weary and increases the power of the weak. Even youths grow tired and weary, and young men stumble and fall; but those who hope in the Lord will renew their strength. They will soar on wings like eagles; they will run and not grow weary, they will walk and not be faint" (Isaiah 40:29-31).

The person who trusts in God enjoys the tranquil quietness of spirit that accompanies such trust. He also enjoys renewed strength when he is weary. Isaiah understood this. For him, faith and trust was the only way to experience peace of mind.

Isaiah Enjoyed a Picturesque Understanding of the Messiah

Isaiah not only was very poetic, he also had an acute sense of what God was saying. Notice the following announcement, which includes the familiar words we hear so often at Christmas time:

> Nevertheless, there will be no more gloom for those who were in distress. In the past he humbled the land of Zebulun and the land of Naphtali, but in the future he will honor Galilee of the nations, by the Way of the Sea, beyond the Jordan —
>
> The people walking in darkness have seen a great light; on those living in the land of deep darkness a light has dawned. You have enlarged the nation and increased their joy; they rejoice before you as people rejoice at the harvest, as soldiers rejoice when dividing the plunder.
>
> For as in the day of Midian's defeat, you have shattered the yoke that burdens them, the bar across their shoulders, the rod of their oppressor. Every warrior's boot used in battle and every garment rolled in blood will be destined for burning, will be fuel for the fire.
>
> For to us a child is born, to us a son is given, and the government will be on his shoulders. And he will be called Wonderful Counselor, Mighty God, Everlasting Father, Prince of Peace. Of the increase of his government and peace there will be no end. He will reign on David's throne and over his kingdom, establishing and upholding it with justice and righteousness from that time on and forever. The zeal of the Lord Almighty will accomplish this. (Isaiah 9:1-7)

The poetic picture of the greatness of the Messiah in Isaiah 9:1-7, and the pathos and sensitive sentiment of Isaiah's description of the suffering Messiah in Isaiah 53:1-12, reveal deep insights into the life and ministry of Jesus. These often-quoted verses display ideas that help us interpret the historic record of Jesus' ministry as described in the Gospels. The written narrative of Jesus' life causes us to feel certain emotions, but not like Isaiah's insightful prophecies.

How could Isaiah make such accurate yet broad-sweeping, emotionally connecting, and profound interpretive statements about the Messiah when he lived hundreds of years before the Messiah would appear? How profound is the prophetic Word of God!

> "The written narrative of Jesus' life causes us to feel certain emotions, but not like Isaiah's insightful prophecies."

Who has believed our message and to whom has the arm of the Lord been revealed? He grew up before him like a tender shoot, and like a root out of dry ground. He had no beauty or majesty to attract us to him, nothing in his appearance that we should desire him. He was despised and rejected by others, a man of suffering, and familiar with pain. Like one from whom people hide their faces he was despised, and we held him in low esteem.

Surely he took up our pain and bore our suffering, yet we considered him punished by God, stricken by him, and afflicted. But he was pierced for our transgressions, he was crushed for our iniquities; the punishment that brought us peace was on him, and by his wounds we are healed. We all, like sheep, have gone astray, each of us has turned to our own way; and the Lord has laid on him the iniquity of us all. He was oppressed and afflicted, yet he did not open his mouth; he was led like a lamb to the slaughter, and as a sheep before its shearers is silent, so he did not open his mouth.

By oppression and judgment he was taken away. Yet who of his generation protested? For he was cut off from the land of the living; for the transgression of my people he was punished. He was assigned a grave with the wicked, and with the rich in his death, though he had done no violence, nor was any deceit in his mouth.

Yet it was the Lord's will to crush him and cause him to suffer, and though the Lord makes his life an offering for sin, he will see his offspring and prolong his days, and the will of the Lord will prosper in his hand.

After he has suffered, he will see the light of life and be satisfied; by his knowledge my righteous servant will justify many, and he will bear their iniquities. Therefore I will give him a portion among the great, and he will divide the spoils with the strong, because he poured out his life unto death, and was numbered with the transgressors. For he bore the sin of many, and made intercession for the transgressors. (Isaiah 53:1–12)

Matthew, Mark, Luke, and John each wrote his own history of the life of Jesus. They give us some background, the facts, the context, the conversations, and descriptions of the events in Jesus' life. But the powerful expressions in Isaiah 53:1–12 surpass their historical records. They provide a poetic and moving description of the love of the Savior and the greatness of His character. Isaiah best described Jesus, who took our place in suffering; Isaiah blessed us with the inside story. Now, as a consequence, we "rejoice before you as people rejoice at the harvest, as soldiers rejoice when dividing the plunder" (Isaiah 9:3).

Isaiah Understood the Paradox in the Divine and Human Partnership

"All that we have accomplished you have done for us" (Isaiah 26:12). Partnership with God is marvelous. He works through our personalities, vocabularies, and temperaments in an amazing blend of the divine with our human elements. We are sometimes tempted to think it is we who preach, teach, heal, comfort, counsel, and minister effectively. But whatever we appear to accomplish, God actually does.

A similar paradox is found in God's promise to Joshua. "I will give you every place where you set your foot, as I promised Moses" (Joshua 1:3). Joshua and the people of Israel walked on the land and fought for it, but it was God who gave it to them.

Eleazar, son of Dodai and one of David's mighty men, had an experience of a close blend of the human and divine working together. "Then the Israelites retreated, but Eleazar stood his ground and struck down the Philistines till *his hand grew tired and froze to the sword.* The Lord brought about a great victory that day. The troops returned to Eleazar, but only to strip the dead" (2 Samuel 23:9–10, emphasis mine).

The Lord worked so mightily through Eleazar that it was impossible to determine where the human hand stopped and the sword began. God worked through the man, and God worked through the sword. The sword and the man were both used by God. Eleazar did it, and God did it.

> "Whatever we appear to accomplish, God actually does."

Later, Paul restated this concept. Today's New International Version of the Bible helps us understand this more clearly than other translations: "I can do all this through him who gives me strength" (Philippians 4:13). Some translations render this verse, "I can do all things," apparently indicating that we can do anything. But surely the Bible does not literally teach this. We cannot fly. Nor can one Christian minister alone save the world or even one nation in his or her lifetime. It is more consistent with the teaching of the whole Bible to believe that what we do, we do through His strength. "All that we have accomplished you have done for us" (Isaiah 26:12). We do it, but only with His enabling strength. The human and the divine work together. God uses the tool. The spirit of the prophet is subject to the prophet.

The same concept is included in the action of placing crowns at the feet of the One on the throne in heaven:

> Whenever the living creatures give glory, honor and thanks to him who sits on the throne and who lives forever and ever, the twenty-four elders fall down before him who sits on the throne and worship him who lives for ever and ever. They lay their crowns before the throne and say: "You are worthy, our Lord and God, to receive glory and honor and power, for you created all things, and by your will they were created and have their being." (Revelation 4:9–11)

When we get to heaven, we too will likely lay our crowns at His feet, acknowledging that it was He who made it all possible.

When we realize the impossibility of our ministry situations, we need to be serious and intentional. We must pray sincerely that God will be involved and help us and then state that we will be careful to give Him all the glory. God does work miraculously through us. He works so cleverly, naturally, and in ways perfectly consistent with our own personalities, temperaments, vocabularies, training, and intellectual gifts, we may think it is we who are doing the ministry so well. If we could grasp the danger of this handicap and get out of God's way, wouldn't He work even more mightily through us?

Isaiah Allowed His Readers to Interpret Conflicting Messages

The latter part of Hezekiah's life included Jerusalem's miraculous deliverance from Assyria and the added fifteen years of Hezekiah's life. It also included Hezekiah's pride and political mistakes in his last years before his death. These fifteen years would have occurred during the latter part of Isaiah's life, after forty-six years of experience as a prophet. During this time, dramatic and sad changes took place in Hezekiah's attitude. Isaiah recorded this period, with one great difference between his record and the accounts in Kings and Chronicles.

Three different texts in Scripture describe the prayer for healing, the healing itself, and the subsequent public events in Hezekiah's life and developments in Jerusalem: 2 Kings 20, 2 Chronicles 32, and Isaiah 38–39. These historical records are almost identical in sequence and detail. Yet each text contains important differences. Second Chronicles 32:25 refers more overtly to Hezekiah's pride: "Hezekiah's heart was proud and he did not respond to the kindness shown him; therefore the Lord's wrath was on him and on Judah and Jerusalem." Chronicles is more clear in its reference to Hezekiah's pride than 2 Kings, though 2 Kings does mention it.

Second Chronicles 32:31 indicates that God left Hezekiah to see what he would do: "When envoys were sent by the rulers of Babylon to ask him about the miraculous sign that had occurred in the land, God left him to test him and to know everything that was in his heart." Chronicles adds that God was testing Hezekiah.

The biggest difference in these three records, however, is the addition of the song Isaiah includes. Kings and Chronicles omit the beautiful song of praise that Hezekiah wrote after he was healed. Read its lovely and uplifting lyrics, and compare what Hezekiah wrote to what he did and thought. These Scriptures enable us to appreciate Isaiah's ability to write good literature and trust his readers to get the message.

Here is what Isaiah records that 2 Kings and 2 Chronicles omit:

> A writing of Hezekiah king of Judah after his illness and recovery:
>
> I said, "In the prime of my life must I go through the gates of death and be robbed of the rest of my years?"
>
> I said, "I will not again see the Lord, the Lord, in the land of the living; no longer will I look on my fellow mortals, or be with those who now dwell in this world. Like a shepherd's tent my house has been pulled down and taken from me. Like a weaver I have rolled up my life, and he has cut me off from the loom; day and night you made an end of me. I waited patiently till dawn, but like a lion he broke all my bones; day and night you made an end of me. I cried like a swift or thrush, I moaned like a mourning dove. My eyes grew weak as I looked to the heavens. I am being threatened; Lord, come to my aid!"
>
> But what can I say? He has spoken to me, and he himself has done this. I will walk humbly all my years because of this anguish of my soul. Lord, by such things people live; and my spirit finds life in them too. You restored me to health and let me live.
>
> Surely it was for my benefit that I suffered such anguish. In your love you kept me from the pit of destruction; you have put all my sins behind your back. For the grave cannot praise you, death cannot sing your praise; those who go down to the pit cannot hope for your faithfulness.
>
> The living, the living — they praise you, as I am doing today; parents tell their children about your faithfulness. The Lord will save me, and we will sing with stringed instruments all the days of our lives in the temple of the Lord. (Isaiah 38:9-20)

The song is theologically sound and self-effacing. It gives God praise, acknowledging human weakness and God's power. The problem with Hezekiah's beautiful song is that he did not match it with his life. It is inconsistent with what he did and what he thought. Hezekiah did not have his systems of thought, word, and action integrated. He thought and acted selfishly even immediately after penning his lovely expressions of humility in noble-sounding poetry.

It is possible that the reason the historians left Hezekiah's song of praise out of their narratives was that they knew Hezekiah did not live up to his beautiful words.

Many modern interpreters of Hezekiah's life story take his song recorded in Isaiah at face value and assume that Hezekiah was genuine. Presuming that what a person does speaks more loudly than what that person says, we arrive at a different interpretation of Hezekiah's latter years. We must compare Isaiah 38:9–20, the record of Hezekiah's good words, to what he did (Isaiah 38:2–3) and thought (Isaiah 39:8).

Hezekiah's problem of resisting Isaiah's word to him and praying his willful prayer is discussed in detail elsewhere. For a complete treatment and its implication for learning how to pray more effectively by praying according to God's will, please refer to "The Power and Danger of Prayer," Chapter 2 in my book *Rise to Seek Him: The Joy of Effective Prayer*.

Hezekiah prayed a wonderful prayer for deliverance of Jerusalem from the invading Assyrians, then became proud. When directed by Isaiah to prepare to die, he prayed the opposite of what Isaiah had instructed, bragged in his prayer, and was bitter and arrogant. The result of his prayer was that God gave him fifteen more years, but they were filled with political mistakes. The years brought needless tragedies to Judah for more than seventy years. This series of sorrowful events does not demonstrate that God is weak, but that God is a good teacher who lets people make mistakes and hopes they will learn from them (see 2 Kings 20, 2 Chronicles 32, and Isaiah 38–39).

Isaiah told Hezekiah that the next generation would be carried off to Babylon to serve as eunuchs in a heathen kingdom. Hezekiah said Isaiah's word was good. What? Who would say that was good? Only someone who was glad there would be only peace *in his time*. Hezekiah's thinking further exposed his lack of care for God's people and his preoccupation with selfish desires.

Hezekiah was righteous and successful during the first fourteen years of his ministry. That record and his beautiful song recorded in Isaiah have misled some people to think of him as a mighty man of God. But Hezekiah's song was different from his behavior.

Today, people are still being misled by men and women of God who say all the right things but are not genuine. If we discern the true message Isaiah wanted to communicate, we will see Hezekiah for the errant king he became and learn from his errors.

Good literature leaves something for the reader to discover. Isaiah was a clever writer. In addition to telling Hezekiah's story, as Kings and Chronicles do, he includes Hezekiah's song. This song serves as an illustration of the pious-sounding sermons of preachers who say all the right things. Their public messages are beautiful and their words are true, even if not backed up by the speaker's personal life. They do not mislead their hearers by what they *say*. They mislead their hearers into thinking either that preachers are phonies or that it doesn't matter if a speaker says one thing publicly and lives another way privately. Hezekiah was not doing what God wanted him to do. Even if he truly believed the words of his song at the time he wrote them, the fact that he did not act and think consistently makes him a contradictory leader.

> "Hezekiah's song was different from his behavior."

Tradition states that Isaiah was sawn in two during the reign of the evil king Manasseh, Hezekiah's son. Hebrews 11:37 says that some of the heroes of faith were "sawed in two … The world was not worthy of them. These were all commended for their faith, yet none of them received what had been promised. God had planned something better for us so that only together with us would they be made perfect" (Hebrews 11:37–41).

Isaiah Understood God's Willingness to Engage Humans Intellectually

We are in a battle of ideas, and God will help us win. He has given us the ability to discern right and wrong and to cast down evil imaginations and accusations. He will help us argue in the classic sense of argument as in intellectual debate. He will help us understand. He will help us defeat the evil forces of unrighteousness — fallen angels, which He also created.

Isaiah was a thinker, and he describes a thinking God who wants to engage us mentally.

Isaiah portrayed God as fighting wrong ideas with right ones. God is concerned about concepts. He is interested in worldviews. He Himself invites us to reason: "'Come now, let us reason together,' says the Lord. 'Though your sins are like scarlet, they shall be as white as snow; though they are red as crimson, they shall be like wool'" (Isaiah 1:18).

Reasoning with the Lord as pictured in the above Scripture is not an isolated idea. It is borne out in other writings of Isaiah. For example:

> "Review the past for me, let us argue the matter together; state the case for your innocence." (Isaiah 43:26)

> "'See, it is I who created the blacksmith who fans the coals into flame and forges a weapon fit for its work. And it is I who have created the destroyer to work havoc; no weapon forged against you will prevail, and you will refute every tongue that accuses you. This is the heritage of the servants of the Lord, and this is their vindication from me,' declares the Lord." (Isaiah 54:16-17)

Weapons can be concrete, physical arms like the military hardware described in Isaiah 54:16. They can also be abstract, intellectual, and conceptual, as implied in Isaiah 54:17. Ideas are weapons. Some ideas are attack weapons; other ideas are defensive weapons. Isaiah said his readers would "refute every tongue that accuses." Throughout sixty-six chapters, we see Isaiah organizing his thoughts, expressing them logically, and appealing to his hearers and readers persuasively. Isaiah was engaged in the war of ideas. He invites God's servants today to be engaged in this war.

> "Ideas are weapons. Some ideas are attack weapons; other ideas are defensive weapons."

Wrong ideas must be refuted. The philosophies of man are inferior to the philosophy of God. Today, we observe a plethora of differing worldviews: animists, Shintoists, Communists, Muslims, Hindus, Latinos, European secularists, to name a few. Christians have their own worldview. Let us not be afraid to speak of it. Our system of thought, if it is true to God's Word, is intellectually solid because it is God's.

In today's shrinking world, the clash of civilizations is becoming more intense. Scholars discuss modern culture wars. We talk about change agents, early adopters, and late adopters. All these new terms help us modernize the notion that one person's way of thinking can be radically different from another's. And they help us understand that worldviews can change. God's way of thinking is different from human thinking and is worth learning about. It is even worth going to war — the intellectual cultural war — over. The Christian's ideas can win.

How does Christ relate to culture? Does He work against it, through it, above it, in it, or in spite of it? Culture matters a lot because it determines how we think. And how we think matters enormously. Our development or underdevelopment depends largely on the state of our minds. And the development or underdevelopment of a nation is a result of the collective state of the minds of its people. A simple exercise to employ when considering this question is this: How does the influence television has on you and your family compare to how the Bible influences you?

Wrestling in prayer is one way we engage in the war of ideas. "We demolish arguments and every pretension that sets itself up against the knowledge of God, and we take captive every thought to make it obedient to Christ" (2 Corinthians 10:5). Men's pretentious philosophies need to be cast down through prayer. These wrong ideas can be refuted by truth.

God wants to reason with us. He wants to engage us both intellectually and spiritually. We insult Him when we consider our opinions as superior to the truth and wisdom in His Word. God offers us a wonderfully superior alternative to human thoughts and ways: His thoughts and ways.

Isaiah Understood the Superiority of God's Thoughts and Ways

Isaiah, more than other writers of the Bible, distinguished clearly between human intellect and God's knowledge. Notice the contrast:

> Seek the Lord while he may be found; call on him while he is near. Let the wicked forsake their *ways* and the unrighteous their *thoughts*. Let them turn to the Lord, and he will have mercy on them, and

to our God, for he will freely pardon. "For my *thoughts* are not your *thoughts*, neither are your *ways* my *ways*," declares the Lord. "As the heavens are higher than the earth, so are my *ways* higher than your *ways* and my *thoughts* than your *thoughts*. As the rain and the snow come down from heaven, and do not return to it without watering the earth and making it bud and flourish, so that it yields seed for the sower and bread for the eater, so is my word that goes out from my mouth: It will not return to me empty, but will accomplish what I desire and achieve the purpose for which I sent it. You will go out in joy and be led forth in peace; the mountains and hills will burst into song before you, and all the trees of the field will clap their hands." (Isaiah 55:6–12, emphasis mine)

Isaiah was convinced that God's superior ways and thoughts would eventually win. The Word of God will accomplish its intended purpose. That is why God wants us to study His Word, know His heart, learn how to communicate, and engage people in meaningful conversations.

Peter was not the intellectual that Isaiah was, but even this fisherman-turned-apostle knew the importance of reason. "But in your hearts revere Christ as Lord. Always be prepared to give an answer to everyone who asks you to give the reason for the hope that you have. But do this with gentleness and respect" (1 Peter 3:15).

There may have been many times when Isaiah questioned what God was doing. But he acknowledged that God's ways are superior. That's a good thing to realize if you plan to trust Him. Whether asking for wisdom to understand how to pray the right way in complex situations, or reasoning with people who do not yet know the Lord, relying on God's wisdom rather than our own is wisdom.

> "Isaiah was convinced that God's superior ways and thoughts would eventually win."

Isaiah Understood Death Is Sometimes the Most Gracious Gift

The Bible presents the world with an optimistic, hope-filled, and meaningful concept of death. It is radically different from any other worldview. Isaiah does not stand alone among the writers of the Bible in declaring the beauty of death for the righteous. However, he does make a clear and positive statement regarding the passage we call death:

> The righteous perish, and no one takes it to heart; the devout are taken away, and no one understands that the righteous are taken away to be spared from evil. Those who walk uprightly enter into peace; they find rest as they lie in death. (Isaiah 57:1-2)

Isaiah said the righteous are "spared from evil." Hezekiah might have been one example in Isaiah's mind. Hezekiah could have spared Jerusalem from suffering a lot of evil had he put his house in order and prepared to die as Isaiah had told him. Instead, Hezekiah's political blunderings in the fifteen years that were added to his life led to great moral deterioration. They precipitated more sorrow, immorality, idolatry, and ruin during the reign of his son Manasseh. Manasseh was born during Hezekiah's extended fifteen years and was not part of God's original plan.

Perhaps Isaiah, in speaking of death, remembered David's Psalm 116: "Precious in the sight of the Lord is the death of those faithful to him" (Psalm 116:15).

Hosea was a contemporary of Isaiah's, but he began to prophesy earlier than Isaiah. Hosea had said, "I will deliver them from the power of the grave; I will redeem them from death. Where, O death, are your plagues? Where, O grave, is your destruction?" (Hosea 13:14).

> "When we grieve over the loss of our loved ones, we need to remember Isaiah's insightful and objective perspective."

Centuries later, Paul quoted Hosea as he scorned the power of death, emphasized the resurrection, and gave hope to Christian believers:

> When the perishable has been clothed with the imperishable, and the mortal with immortality, then the saying that is written will come true: "Death has been swallowed up in victory."
>
> "Where, O death, is your victory? Where, O death, is your sting?" The sting of death is sin, and the power of sin is the law.
> (1 Corinthians 15:54-56)

When we grieve over the loss of our loved ones, we need to remember Isaiah's insightful and objective perspective. Of course, we who remain miss the people we love. But looking at life from their perspective, they may be escaping, at God's gracious provision, horrible evil. There is amazing wisdom in these words: "The righteous are taken away to be spared from evil" (Isaiah 57:1).

Isaiah Understood the Need for Constant Prayer

> I have posted watchmen on your walls, Jerusalem; they will never be silent day or night. You who call on the Lord, give yourselves no rest, and give him no rest till he establishes Jerusalem and makes her the praise of the earth. (Isaiah 62:6–7)

Christians sometimes talk about faith, rest, and peace, claiming that resting in Him means we should present our petitions to the Lord and leave them with Him. There is a place for resting, trusting, and enjoying His peace, but those beliefs must be consistent with the whole counsel of God. Our theology of prayer and trust versus prayer and persistence must be biblical. To do so, it must consider the Scriptures that urge us to be persistent, determined, consistent, faithful, and insistent when we pray, as well as the ones that tell us to pray, trust, and rest. "Jesus told them a parable to show them that they should always pray and not give up" (Luke 18:1).

> "One of the ways we fight wrong ideas with good ideas is by wrestling in prayer."

Isaiah counseled the intercessors of his day to not rest but to keep praying. In doing so, he also teaches us that. Balance the Scriptures about resting in the Lord with this one about not resting and you will have a biblical view on this issue.

One of the ways we fight wrong ideas with good ideas is by wrestling in prayer. In prayer, we engage in a very real struggle. If we refuse to join this invisible struggle, we will never be the influence or success we could be. Nor will the pretensions Satan uses as weapons be refuted to the glory of God and the liberation of the people who are in bondage.

For Further Thought

- What are the implications of the statement that ministry is a partnership of the divine and human?
- How does Isaiah's record of Hezekiah's song add intrigue to the drama of interpreting the life of Hezekiah?
- What are your thoughts regarding Isaiah's emphasis on God inviting man to reason with Him?
- In what way does Isaiah challenge people to lift their thoughts up higher than human thoughts to God's thoughts?
- What new insights did you gain from God's perspective on death as a release from evil?
- What do you think about not resting but persevering in prayer?

CHAPTER 17
JEREMIAH

Did you know that Jeremiah never married? Did you realize that God told him not to marry? Were you aware that even though Jeremiah was not to marry, in the spirit he understood idolatry as spiritual adultery? Did you realize that getting rid of hindrances to ministry is one of the important preparations for service to the Lord?

The development of high ethical and moral standards helps Christians become trustworthy. If a Christian is not trustworthy, how can anyone follow his or her leadership? If a minister of the gospel is not consistent and persistent in the pursuit of righteousness, how will anyone consider him or her worthy of being followed?

It appears that no one in Scripture, other than Jesus, suffered more for the sake of his message and yet was as true to his calling than Jeremiah. No one in Scripture more perfectly exemplifies how to be faithful to a difficult vocation of public ministry with perseverance and steadfastness. By how he lived and what he wrote, Jeremiah still speaks to godly leaders today.

What did Jeremiah know that enabled him to be so consistent? How could he stand strong in the face of the difficulties, adversities, personal persecution, death threats, and imprisonments he experienced? What about this man made him such a stalwart tower of unshakable strength? Is there something in his belief system that we can learn and adopt? If we think like Jeremiah thought, could we too become bold, brave, and courageous?

Jeremiah Understood His Call

Jeremiah knew that God was intimately involved in his pre-birth creation and development. "Before *I formed you in the womb* I knew you, before you were born I set you apart; I appointed you as a prophet to the nations" (Jeremiah 1:5, emphasis mine).

David had the same insight. "For you created my inmost being; you knit me together in my mother's womb. I praise you because I am fearfully and wonderfully made; your works are wonderful, I know that full well. My frame was not hidden from you when I was made in the secret place. When I was woven together in the depths of the earth, your eyes saw my unformed body" (Psalm 139:13-16).

Isaiah said the same thing about Jacob. "But now listen, Jacob, my servant, Israel, whom I have chosen. This is what the Lord says — *he who made you, who formed you in the womb,* and who will help you: do not be afraid, Jacob, my servant, Jeshurun, whom I have chosen" (Isaiah 44:1-2, emphasis mine).

Isaiah believed it about himself as well. "And now the Lord says — *he who formed me in the womb* to be his servant to bring Jacob back to him and gather Israel to himself, for I am honored in the eyes of the Lord and my God has been my strength" (Isaiah 49:5, emphasis mine).

Isaiah also believed it was inappropriate to be critical of the Creator. "Woe to those who quarrel with their Maker, those who are nothing but potsherds among the potsherds on the ground. Does the clay say to the potter, 'What are you making?' Does your work say, 'The potter has no hands'? Woe to those who say to their father, 'What have you begotten?' or to their mother, 'What have you brought to birth?' This is what the Lord says — the Holy One of Israel, and its Maker: concerning things to come, do you question me about my children, or give me orders about the work of my hands?" (Isaiah 45:9-11). Isaiah believed in self-acceptance.

> "God is in control of every intricate detail of the creation of each new baby."

From a biological standpoint, we understand the human reproductive process today much more clearly than Jeremiah, David, or Isaiah did. But those ancient men knew something that many do not know: that God is in control of every intricate detail of the creation of each new baby. You only need to compare yourself with your siblings to catch a glimpse of the vast possibilities of differences, even when siblings are produced by the same biological parents. Who made you the way you are?

Every baby girl is born with hundreds of thousands of eggs in her ovaries. Each has the potential to be fertilized and become a living human being. Beginning at puberty, one or more of these eggs move down fallopian tubes from the ovaries to the womb each month and position themselves to be fertilized by a sperm. Who decides which egg becomes a baby? A man's body can produce 500 million sperm in a day. From 75 to 900 million sperm are deposited in a woman's body at one time. A man's body will produce millions of billions of sperm in his lifetime. Each one has the potential to fertilize a human egg. Who decides which sperm will reach the egg first? Consider the number of eggs produced by your mother, multiplied by the number of sperm produced by your father. There was one chance in trillions that you would be precisely the way you are. Yet it happened. You are the only person just like you.

Jeremiah, David, and Isaiah stated that God personally creates every baby. Am I to believe that Jeremiah was created by God and that I am a mistake? Do you believe that God made David the way He wanted David to be, but there's something inherently wrong with you? Each of us is a unique creation, masterfully designed, just the way God intended us to be. When you get a chance, tell someone, "God did a good job when He made me. He did a good job when He made you too."

Throw your shoulders back, and hold your head up high. You are a masterpiece, intentionally placed in your generation in your geographic location. Paul preached that God "marked out their appointed times in history and the boundaries of their lands" (Acts 17:26). You are God's person, placed in God's chosen timing in history and in the exact setting God planned for you. Do not let any person or any spiritual being rob you of the dignity, joy, confidence, and courage God intends for you to enjoy as you go about fulfilling His purposes for your life. What you do with what God made you to be is your choice and responsibility, but God did a good job. So be confident. Be strong.

God's plan for Jeremiah's life included being single. "Then the word of the Lord came to me: 'You must not marry and have sons or daughters in this place.' For this is what the Lord says about the sons and daughters born in this land and about the women who are their mothers and the men who are their fathers: 'They will die of deadly diseases. They will not be mourned or buried but will be like dung lying on the ground. They will perish by sword and famine, and their dead bodies will become food for the birds and the wild animals'" (Jeremiah 16:1–4).

Jeremiah shows character, submission, contrition, and strength by his obedience to God's command.

Jeremiah Understood Tearing Down as Preparation for Building

> "See, today I appoint you over nations and kingdoms to uproot and tear down, to destroy and overthrow, to build and to plant" (Jeremiah 1:10).

Jeremiah understood a simple principle: before you build, you must tear down whatever is on the current site. Before the home you live in now was constructed, the land had to be cleared; whatever was on the land had to be removed. It may have been trees, rocks, a mound of dirt, or an earlier structure. Only after the ground was cleared and prepared for the foundation was it possible to start building. Otherwise, the new structure would either have to be built around the obstacle or it would crumble for lack of good foundation.

The same is true of building God's church or a Christian life that has strength, beauty, and stability. Spiritual forces occupy each geographic area of the world. They do not yield easily to an invasion by an agent representing the kingdom of God. These invisible forces arrayed in their assigned territories against God's kingdom and Church must be dealt with before we can gain entrance into their territory. They must be uprooted, torn down, destroyed, and overthrown.

According to 2 Corinthians 10:4–5, we are able to cast down every evil imagination that exalts itself against God. "The weapons we fight with are not the weapons of the world. On the contrary, they have divine power to demolish strongholds. We demolish arguments and every pretension that sets itself up against the knowledge of God, and we take captive every thought to make it obedient to Christ." If we do not demolish the dark forces before we proceed, we cannot successfully build the kingdom of God.

On the island of Cyprus (Acts 13:6-11) and in the city of Philippi (Acts 16:16-18), Paul had to deal with evil spirits in order to make progress in his work.

According to Jesus, the advance of the Church will continue in the face of spiritual resistance. The gates of hell shall not prevail against it. "I will build my church, and the gates of death will not overcome it" (Matthew 16:18). But those statements are made on the assumption that the Church is on the move, on the offensive, taking territory. We are the aggressors, and we shall win. The gates of hell (death) cannot resist God's Church. We wrestle against rulers, authorities, and powers of this dark world. We do battle against the spiritual forces of evil in the heavenly realms. As we do so, we prepare the spiritual atmosphere to give place to the building of the kingdom of God and the Church. This spiritual preparation must take place first. Only then, can we fully succeed in church planting, evangelism without reversion, permanent kingdom growth, physical health, and victory.

> "We are the aggressors, and we shall win. The gates of hell (death) cannot resist God's Church."

An alternate interpretation of Matthew 16:18 suggests these verses refer to the grave or Hades, the place of the dead. In that case, it means death will not triumph over the Church in the last day. The gates of Hades will open, and the Church will be resurrected. Such an interpretation is consistent with other teachings in the Bible. The interpretation I mentioned is also consistent with the teachings of the Bible and yet has a more encouraging and applicable message.

The same principle of tearing down before constructing anew applies to the individual who wants to become a disciple and soldier of Christ. It will help him build strong character, unshaken and unshakable faith, confidence in God, and continuing and prevailing maturity, growth, and development in Christ. Works of the flesh must first be uprooted, destroyed, and overthrown. In a New Testament parallel passage, Paul says, "You were taught with regard to your former way of life, to put off your old self, which is being corrupted by its deceitful desires; to be made new in the attitude of your minds; and to put on the new self, created to be like God in true righteousness and holiness" (Ephesians 4:22–24). Any attempt to build character on a cluttered or unprepared site, where evil characteristics linger, will result in a shaky foundation or malformation.

To bear the fruit of the Spirit and glorify God with good works throughout your long and fruitful life, you must deal with the negative issues and hindrances. You must build the positive characteristics and beautiful behaviors that glorify God. It is essential to tear down some sinful strongholds before you construct an edifice that honors God. First prepare the site, then build the building. Jeremiah understood this. That is one of the reasons he was strong.

Jeremiah Understood Idolatry as Spiritual Adultery

> Go and proclaim in the hearing of Jerusalem: "This is what the Lord says: 'I remember the devotion of your youth, how as a bride you loved me and followed me through the wilderness, through a land not sown.'" (Jeremiah 2:2)

> How can you say, "I am not defiled; I have not run after the Baals"? See how you behaved in the valley; consider what you have done. You are a swift she-camel running here and there, a wild donkey accustomed to the desert, sniffing the wind in her craving — in her heat who can restrain her? Any males that pursue her need not tire themselves; at mating time they will find her. Do not run until your feet are bare and your throat is dry. But you said, "It's no use! I love foreign gods, and I must go after them.'" (Jeremiah 2:23–25)

Jeremiah understood that sexual adultery was an appropriate illustration of idolatry. He is not alone in understanding that our intimate relationship with God is illustrated in marriage fidelity. Solomon, Isaiah, Ezekiel, Hosea, Zephaniah, Paul, and John all portrayed believers as the wife or bride of Christ and adultery as an illustration of idolatry.

Jeremiah is just as graphic as other writers, but no more so. In his writings, Israel is first presented as the young bride who loved and followed her Lover through the wilderness. Later in the same chapter, Israel is the unfaithful wife who, like a wild donkey or she-camel, is sniffing and running after other lovers. With such language, Jeremiah pled with Israel to return to her God. His message was largely rejected. However, we can catch from it a glimpse of the motivation of Jeremiah's unflinching, unwavering fidelity. He was absolutely faithful through all the struggles.

When we understand this marital metaphor, you and I will also want to be God's faithful partners.

Many Christians are in love with the things of the world. Some are tempted, for example, to turn to witchcraft to get their own way when God refuses or delays to grant their requests. In some places, believers practice New Age methodologies or other Eastern religions. These modern-day idolatries are spiritual adultery. The man or woman of God has no business pursuing any idol or false religion. Let us keep our hearts and minds pure, focused only on God and His ways.

Jeremiah Had a Strong Message from God and Could Not Help but Speak

Therefore this is what the Lord God Almighty says: "Because the people have spoken these words, I will make my words in your mouth a fire and these people the wood it consumes." (Jeremiah 5:14)

> **God's anointing is not the same as emotion, but it is often communicated with emotion.**

You deceived me, Lord, and I was deceived; you overpowered me and prevailed. I am ridiculed all day long; everyone mocks me. Whenever I speak, I cry out proclaiming violence and destruction. So the word of the Lord has brought me insult and reproach all day long. But if I say, "I will not mention his word or speak anymore in his name," his word is in my heart like a fire, a fire shut up in my bones. I am weary of holding it in; indeed, I cannot. (Jeremiah 20:7–9)

The power of Jeremiah's message was strong, not insipid or merely professional. We must present strong messages, not just loud messages.

Let's have fire in our bones that determines our words and sermons. Let the power of the message of God come through in what we say and how we say it.

God's anointing is not the same as emotion, but it is often communicated with emotion. How much emotion do you put into your conversations, teachings, or sermons about God? Do you ever weep as you speak? Does your voice ever crack? Or are you always composed and in total control of your emotions? As a result, do you come across as dry, monotone, unfeeling, cold, calculated, and boring? I am not saying that every sermon or discussion about God needs to be presented with tears running down our cheeks. But if weeks go by and we are never emotional at any point, we may have become so professional that the prophetic element is lacking. We may be missing the touch of God in our own hearts. People are fearful, suffering, angry, in pain, grieving, without hope, and bound by forces of darkness. Others are lulled to sleep by complacency. You and I have the word of life that can change lives. First, let it change yours. Then, allow the life-giving power of God change others.

If you are a pastor or church leader, I assume that you are studying and preparing messages with significant content. But careful examination of the text tends to make us academic in our approach and presentation. After the study, do you add conviction and energy to the good content? Are you convicted yourself? Do you say something strong, provocative, stimulating, motivating, stinging, or convicting to the passive in your congregation? To the troubled, do you say something calming, relieving, and comforting? After all your preparation is complete, ask God to put power, energy, and force in your life and in your message.

I am not speaking of volume or empty emotion. The anointing of the Holy Spirit on good content is one thing. It is vastly different than employing shallow human emotion to attempt to compensate for lack of content or deep convictions with mere emotion, volume, or play-acting.

Jeremiah Appreciated the Difference between God's and Human's Value Systems

Each of us makes decisions about how we spend time and money based on our personal sense of values. A sports enthusiast will use his free hours reading and talking about sports. If he has the money, he will spend it attending a sporting event. If someone values education, she will use her time attending classes, reading, and studying. If she can afford it, she will spend her money in pursuit of education. If a person highly values family, he or she will spend time accordingly and use financial resources in a way consistent with that value.

Of course, God has a different sense of values from ours. Humans may see certain things on earth as important. But God knows the only things that are of real value are those that will last into eternity. Human beings may value pleasure, recognition, position, material possessions, physical strength, athletic ability, human knowledge, or the intellect to assimilate and use knowledge. But what if we were able in this life to know what God valued? Imagine it were possible to make decisions now based on what we will value in heaven. When we left this life and entered into the next one, we would have no regrets about what we valued, what we held lightly, and how we used our time and money while here.

> *Wisdom, strength, and riches can glorify God when used correctly.*

The Bible says we are to get wisdom, so wisdom itself is not wrong; it is valuable. The promises of God include physical healing, which implies that health and physical strength are of value. God's promises of provision include financial blessings if we seek first the kingdom of God and His righteousness. We must use our finances in God-glorifying ways and not make obtaining money our major goal in life. So having money is not wrong. But notice the wisdom of these words from Jeremiah:

> This is what the Lord says: "Let not the wise boast of their wisdom or the strong boast of their strength or the rich boast of their riches, but let those who boast boast about this: that they understand and know me, that I am the Lord, who exercises kindness, justice and righteousness on earth, for in these I delight," declares the Lord. (Jeremiah 9:23-24)

Wisdom, strength, and riches can glorify God when used correctly. But God's Word says that none of these three is worth boasting about. If we are going to boast, it should be in our understanding and knowledge of God. He delights in kindness, justice, and righteousness.

God likes it when we help people and are nice to them. He is pleased when we are just, which includes punishing wrong as well as rewarding right deeds. God takes pleasure in our doing right things. Romans 13:1–4 says that the government — including policemen if they are acting righteously — exists to enforce rightness. Right living is more valuable to God than earthly wisdom, strength, and riches. Valuing it will bring us to heaven with no regrets about what we cherished in this life.

Jeremiah understood this. That is how he could serve God so tenaciously in spite of the severe opposition he faced. Jeremiah's sense of values was consistent with God's, so he kept serving and speaking faithfully. Because he was renewed from within, he could resist conformity to exterior social pressures.

Jeremiah Submitted to God's Plan and Wanted God's Correction

"Discipline me, Lord, but only in due measure — not in your anger, or you will reduce me to nothing" (Jeremiah 10: 24). "The heart is deceitful above all things and beyond cure. Who can understand it?" (Jeremiah 17:9). In these two verses, Jeremiah tells us how to deal with our own deceiving hearts. By example, he recommends asking God to discipline us.

It is to our advantage to receive God's refining corrections. Would you rather have the ego-satisfying feeling you get from insisting you are right even when you are wrong, or be corrected so that you become more useful to God? We all like to *feel* right. But wouldn't you rather *be* right — even though the process of becoming right is painful and humbling — than to continue to only *feel* right?

Jeremiah tells us our hearts are so deceitful, we do not adequately comprehend how deceived by them we are. There are faults and sins in our lives of which we are not aware. Jeremiah had the courage and wisdom to ask God to shine His light into every corner, box, closet, and cupboard of his heart so that he might be rid of them. "Discipline me, Lord," he asked. Our accuser, the devil, is happy to tell us how bad we are, but he intends our destruction. It is far more productive to ask God to reveal our sin to us, because He will forgive and cleanse us. Then we can be more fruitful for Him.

If you join Jeremiah in asking God to discipline you in due measure, you have access to the most accurate insight, the wisest counsel, the kindest critique, and the gentlest correction. It is the most perfectly well-intended and executed refinement process ever known in human experience.

I fear correction. But I fear fruitlessness even more. I dread being told I am wrong. But I dread even more being less than I could be. I do not like finding out what I have been doing wrong. But I like even less pridefully continuing behaviors or actions I could change if God were to correct me, even if He corrects me through another person. I would rather someone tell me what I *need* to hear than for someone to tell me what he or she thinks I *want* to hear. If I have the reputation of being easy to correct, there is a better chance that people will tell me what I need to know. If I have the reputation of stubbornly clinging to my own thought patterns, behaviors, and opinions, I'm likely not to find out at all.

> "I fear correction. But I fear fruitlessness even more."

Jeremiah Understood Development through Difficulties

Do you want to eventually have more influence than you have now? Do you want to eventually be more successful than you are now? Do you want to eventually handle bigger tasks and carry more responsibility than you do now? If so, you need to know the process God uses to get you from where you are now to where He and you want you to be.

> If you have raced with people on foot and they have worn you out, how can you compete with horses? If you stumble in safe country, how will you manage in the thickets by the Jordan? (Jeremiah 12:5)

Jeremiah uses a logical sequence in contrasting two things that are relatively easy with two things that are more difficult. The lesson in both of the comparisons is the same, but the imagery is different. In the first image, a runner races against other runners more easily than he runs against horses. In the second image, a runner runs more easily in the safe country than he can run through the thick bush. In both instances, God is saying that the present level of difficulty we are experiencing is easy compared to the race we must run if we expect to have more influence, success, or responsibility.

One of my students told me he wanted to move forward to a more difficult level of scholarly achievement. So when he complained to me about a professor who was giving him trouble with his term paper, I confronted him. "You tell me you want to advance to doctoral studies and earn a PhD. If you can't handle your professor's critique of your master's-level term paper, how do you expect to ever write a doctoral thesis?" He thanked me for the question.

> **Develop the ability to cooperate with God's plan for your development.**

We each need to learn to handle our present challenges without complaining. God is only complimenting us when he provides a training program that will stretch us to become more influential, successful, and useful to Him. Learn how to interpret adversity. Develop the ability to cooperate with God's plan for your development. Experience how God builds His Church and His people, and work with His plan without complaining.

Jeremiah's Word for Pastors: Love and Care for Sheep

God loves, defends, and provides for pastors. Pastors are very close to His heart because they represent Him and serve as His under-shepherds. But the shepherds are there for the sheep, not the reverse. Jesus loves shepherds because He loves sheep. He provides for the care of sheep by appointing His called and chosen servants to follow His example in serving them.

Some pastors have these roles turned around. They want to be served by the sheep. They enjoy too much the respect that goes with their office. Some pastors beat the sheep. Some scold the sheep. These "servants" would enjoy their work much more if they learned to serve from the heart.

Jesus is the model Shepherd. He served His sheep, and we are to follow His example. Jeremiah and Peter have excellent instructions for us on these points.

> "Woe to the shepherds who are destroying and scattering the sheep of my pasture!" declares the Lord. Therefore this is what the Lord, the God of Israel, says to the shepherds who tend my people: "Because you have scattered my flock and driven them away and have not bestowed care on them, I will bestow

punishment on you for the evil you have done," declares the Lord. "I myself will gather the remnant of my flock out of all the countries where I have driven them and will bring them back to their pasture, where they will be fruitful and increase in number. I

> "Jesus is the model Shepherd. He served His sheep and we are to follow His example."

will place shepherds over them who will tend them, and they will no longer be afraid or terrified, nor will any be missing," declares the Lord. (Jeremiah 23:1-4)

Be shepherds of God's flock that is under your care, watching over them — not because you must, but because you are willing, as God wants you to be; not pursuing dishonest gain, but eager to serve; not lording it over those entrusted to you, but being examples to the flock. And when the Chief Shepherd appears, you will receive the crown of glory that will never fade away." (1 Peter 5:2-4)

If you as a church leader find yourself valuing your prestige or position more than your people, you need to repent. Ask God to change your heart and give you a love for your people. If you want to be like Christ, you will be willing to lay down your time, interests, attention — your life — for the sheep He gives you. If you find yourself lacking in the qualities of love and caring, submit your heart to God. Let Him make you into the shepherd He wants you to be.

Jeremiah Preached Timely and Specific Messages

Sometimes Jeremiah preached that things would go well. Sometimes he preached doom. Each message was accurately and appropriately presented to the right target audience. He did not have automatic messages that were often repeated. He always spoke with clarity and specificity.

Jeremiah sent a message to the Jews in Babylon that pertained to the Jews who had obeyed God by submitting to the Babylonian government and were settling down in Babylon. "'For I know the plans I have for you,' declares the Lord, 'plans to prosper you and not to harm you, plans to give you hope and a future'" (Jeremiah 29:11).

To the Jews and leaders in Mizpah left behind in the land serving the Babylonian government's interest, Jeremiah sent this message: "Gedaliah son of Ahikam, the son of Shaphan, took an oath to reassure them and their men. 'Do not be afraid to serve the Babylonians,' he said. 'Settle down in the land and serve the king of Babylon, and it will go well with you. I myself will stay at Mizpah to serve the Babylonians who come to us, but you are to harvest the wine, summer fruit and olive oil, and put them in your storage jars, and live in the town you have taken over'" (Jeremiah 40:9–10). This was not a welcome word, but Jeremiah preached it as God's message for those people at that time.

It is easy for Christian teachers to get stuck in a rut. We teach our favorite subjects based on earlier revelation and tend to think of one solution as the cure-all for every problem. Jeremiah teaches us to stay sensitive to what the Lord's message is for any specific group of people. The Greek language helps us with this issue by having two words for *word*. *Logos* means "word" in the general sense, and *rhema* means a specific word directed to a specific situation. We need to know both. We teach and preach general truth about God, man, and the relationship between them. We also deliver specific messages to specific groups.

> "Jeremiah teaches us to stay sensitive to what the Lord's message is for any specific group of people."

Jeremiah Knew the Faithfulness of God

Jeremiah's message was repeatedly rejected. Rare were the times when anyone listened to him. When his ministry was rejected, Jeremiah felt rejected. Rejection when you are wrong is understandable. Even though it is painful, rejection can be helpful. But to be rejected for delivering a righteous message of truth from God can be a bitter experience.

Jeremiah endured personal persecution. His listeners turned on him again and again, even while contemporary history was proving that his messages had been accurate.

Jeremiah observed Judah's intense suffering. All the grievous hardships described in Lamentations and Jeremiah were unnecessary. Had his listeners received his message, those sufferings could have been avoided. "Yet this I call to mind and therefore I have hope: because of the Lord's great love we are not consumed, for his compassions never fail. They are new every morning; great is your faithfulness" (Lamentations 3:21-23).

In spite of all the difficulties, Jeremiah saw the mercy, goodness, and faithfulness of God. Can you see them, too, even in the face of all the trials in your life? To serve God consistently and fruitfully, you must have the same faith that allowed Jeremiah to see the faithfulness of God in the face of overwhelming adversity. God needs you to be a Jeremiah today. He will make you strong. And He will show you His steadfast love in the difficulties.

Jeremiah Learned through Suffering

Jeremiah was arrested under false charges. He suffered humiliation and physical difficulties for having obeyed God.

> After the Babylonian army had withdrawn from Jerusalem because of Pharaoh's army, Jeremiah started to leave the city to go to the territory of Benjamin to get his share of the property among the people there. But when he reached the Benjamin Gate, the captain of the guard, whose name was Irijah son of Shelemiah, the son of Hananiah, arrested him and said, "You are deserting to the Babylonians!"
>
> "That's not true!" Jeremiah said. "I am not deserting to the Babylonians."
>
> But Irijah would not listen to him; instead, he arrested Jeremiah and brought him to the officials. They were angry with Jeremiah and had him beaten and imprisoned in the house of Jonathan the secretary, which they had made into a prison. Jeremiah was put into a vaulted cell in a dungeon, where he remained a long time.
>
> Then King Zedekiah sent for him and had him brought to the

palace, where he asked him privately, "Is there any word from the Lord?"

"Yes," Jeremiah replied, "you will be delivered into the hands of the king of Babylon."

Then Jeremiah said to King Zedekiah, "What crime have I committed against you or your attendants or this people, that you have put me in prison? Where are your prophets who prophesied to you, 'The king of Babylon will not attack you or this land?' But now, my lord the king, please listen. Let me bring my petition before you: do not send me back to the house of Jonathan the secretary, or I will die there."

King Zedekiah then gave orders for Jeremiah to be placed in the courtyard of the guard and given a loaf of bread from the street of the bakers each day until all the bread in the city was gone. So Jeremiah remained in the courtyard of the guard. (Jeremiah 37:11-21)

Even Jesus learned through suffering. "Son though he was, he learned obedience from what he suffered" (Hebrews 5:8). Do you think the disciple is greater than his Master?

The apostle Paul suffered perhaps more than any New Testament person other than Jesus according to Paul's own record. God even gave him advance notice that he would suffer for the Lord: "I will show him how much he must suffer for my name" (Acts 9:16).

"Not only so, but we also glory in our sufferings, because we know that suffering produces perseverance; perseverance, character; and character, hope" (Romans 5:3-4).

Jeremiah was willing to suffer for his message and his Master. An influential Christian has a difficult assignment. People look up to and sometimes lean on him or her, but the rewards are eternal.

Jeremiah Knew the Value of Humbling Himself before God

God was developing leaders long before we came up with the clever idea of leadership development. In Jeremiah's case, one of the learning tools God used was suffering.

There is a pattern in the suffering experienced by some of the Bible's greatest leaders. David was afflicted under Saul and learned how to entrust his career to the hands of the Lord. Jeremiah knew that if he humbly submitted to God's training program, God would eventually raise him up.

> It is good for people to bear the yoke while they are young. Let them sit alone in silence, for the Lord has laid it on them. Let them bury their faces in the dust — there may yet be hope. Let them offer their cheeks to one who would strike them, and let them be filled with disgrace. For people are not cast off by the Lord forever. Though he brings grief, he will show compassion, so great is his unfailing love. For he does not willingly bring affliction or grief to any human being. (Lamentations 3:27–33)

If we servants of God fight with the sheep He has assigned us to serve, or are egotistical, proud, bossy, or demanding, God cannot use us mightily. He allows difficulties to correct and train us. How did Jeremiah know it was good for a young man to humble himself if he did not learn this through personal experience? When he was afflicted, he further humbled himself in the self-affliction of fasting and sincere repentance before God. The resulting rewards of restoration, lifting, and usefulness taught him so he could teach others.

> *He allows difficulties to correct and train us.*

When God allows suffering to come your way, do you immediately try to reject it? Or do you ask God to use it in your life to make you what He wants you to be? Are you a Jeremiah?

For Further Thought

- Have you ever felt your message so strongly that you knew you couldn't not give it? What did you do?
- How do you plan to align your value system more closely with God's now that you know the three things about which Jeremiah says we should not boast?
- Have you experienced enough of God's helpful corrections that you realize it is a great advantage to be corrected by a perfectly wise and perfectly loving God? How did you react when you acknowledged this?
- How do you plan to make use of Jeremiah's teaching about God developing us through difficulties?
- Has God ever had to defend His sheep against you? If so, how well did you listen to Him?
- Meditate on a time when God gave you a specific message for a certain group of people. How did they respond? How did you feel after delivering that message?
- Have there been times when God revealed His great faithfulness to you?
- In what respect would you like to follow Jeremiah's example in learning through suffering?
- If you have ever humbled yourself in an extreme way, such as prolonged fasting or praying all night, in a special effort to seek God, how did He respond to you?

CHAPTER 18
EZEKIEL

This chapter is different from the other chapters of this book in that it focuses more on Ezekiel's message than his life. Here we spotlight Ezekiel's end-time prophecy, particularly as related in chapters 38 and 39. Ezekiel does have lessons for us from his life. By example, he teaches us about having faith in spite of being an exile and that sin has consequences and leads eventually to destruction. It is a message regarding hopefulness in spite of the devastation he saw coming to Israel. But the heart of this chapter is end-time prophecy.

Ezekiel's perspective is more international and universal than other Hebrew prophets. Furthermore, he addresses issues involving more centuries of human history than other biblical prophecies. He speaks to his generation in a number of parables, sermons, and appeals. However, because of his long-range international scope and his significant contribution to our understanding of eschatology (the doctrine of future things), we will focus on the future aspect of his messages.

Ezekiel's prophecies are uniquely time-related, sequential, and tied to Israel's central place among the nations of the world. They comprise a lens through which to view and interpret recent-past and current events. This chapter can be useful in understanding today's international geopolitical developments, especially in the Middle East. Prophecy includes forth-telling and foretelling, but here we will predominately examine the latter type.

Ezekiel Was a Prophetic Priest in Exile in Babylon

> In my thirtieth year, in the fourth month on the fifth day, while I was among the exiles by the Kebar River, the heavens were opened and I saw visions of God. On the fifth of the month — it was the fifth year of the exile of King Jehoiachin — the word of the Lord came to Ezekiel the priest, the son of Buzi, by the Kebar River in the land of the Babylonians. There the hand of the Lord was on him. (Ezekiel 1:1–3)

Ezekiel was a contemporary of Jeremiah. Like Jeremiah, he was both a priest and a prophet. But unlike Jeremiah, who prophesied in Jerusalem during Judah's final years, Ezekiel was among the exiles already in Babylon. Several deportations took place during the declining years of Judea. Ezekiel evidently was in one of the earlier groups of deportees.

Many times, truth about God and His ways is glaringly clear in Scripture. When it comes to prophecy, however, the events predicted and the message about them are sufficiently revealed in the Bible so the inquirer can find it with effort. It is also sufficiently hidden so the unbeliever cannot — will not — find it. The student of prophecy is working with material that is intentionally unclear.

> "The student of prophecy is working with material that is intentionally unclear."

Not everything is revealed, but enough is. It's like a puzzle. It's not conclusively clear, but clear enough. What do I mean by clear enough?

The CEO of a large and successful international corporation recently directed her company through a complicated merger with another corporation. In the negotiation process, she told her board that the suitability of the merger was "perfect enough." We often strive for perfection, and when it is not attained, we back away from the proposal. But few are the times when a perfect partnership is accomplished. We usually have to be satisfied with sufficient commonality that unity can be achieved eventually. The phrase the CEO coined described this sentiment as she referred to the merger plan this way: "It is not perfect, but you can't find perfect." The potential for a successful merger, she stated, was "perfect enough."

Using that logic, the prophecies and interpretations presented here are not perfectly clear, but they are clear enough. As events unfold before our natural eyes, we may recall that Ezekiel, Isaiah, and Jeremiah saw those events centuries ago with their spiritual eyes. All can be well with our souls; God is in control of international developments.

This chapter does not give a full view of eschatology. We will concern ourselves with just one of the major focuses of Ezekiel: what happens to Israel in the last days? If eschatology is an interesting subject to you, check out some of the many helpful books available today discussing Bible prophecy and especially end-time prophecy. We will look at Ezekiel's prophecies here and bring alongside a few other Hebrew prophets. Our purpose is to open our eyes to the magnitude of the plans the Sovereign Lord has for the world. We will learn how He uniquely uses Israel to fulfill those plans. We are in the center of confusing military activities and geopolitical developments in the world today. But we can draw comfort, insight, and courage from knowing that God knew in advance and planned the events Ezekiel described. Nothing surprises Him.

Ezekiel used the phrase *Sovereign Lord* again and again. It was evidently his favorite name for God. According to Today's New English Version, Ezekiel used this name for God 210 times. In all the other books of the Bible, this name for God appears only 79 more times. With the numerous foretelling prophecies given by Ezekiel, it is easy to see he had an unusual awareness of God's control and involvement in human history. Perhaps he liked to use *Sovereign Lord* because of his keen sensitivity to God's involvement in the current events of his own time.

The Sovereign Lord, speaking through a prophet in exile, gave comfort, insight, and courage to Israel in Ezekiel's day and to observant believers in subsequent generations. Israelites and those interested in Israel can comfort one another with Ezekiel's words, just as Paul told the Thessalonians to comfort one another with his words (see 1 Thessalonians 4:13-18). Right understanding of the sovereignty of a loving God, who stays involved in the affairs of humans, gives believers comfort, insight, and courage. All of these are good results from the prophetic Word.

Here is how Jeremiah stated it: "'So then, the days are coming,' declares the Lord, 'when people will no longer say, "As surely as the Lord lives, who brought the Israelites up out of Egypt," but they will say, "As surely as the Lord lives, who brought the descendants of Israel up out of the land of the north and out of all the countries where he had banished them." Then they will live in their own land'" (Jeremiah 23:7–8). These are comforting words indeed.

Israel Is Favored among the Nations

God began with Abraham to build a nation through which He intended to bless the world. "I will make you into a great nation, and I will bless you; I will make your name great, and you will be a blessing. I will bless those who bless you, and whoever curses you I will curse; and all peoples on earth will be blessed through you" (Genesis 12:2–3).

Israel gave the world a Savior and the Old Testament. For centuries, the rest of the nations have gained from Israel's contributions to their ethical, spiritual, and moral progress. Other civilizations have received many benefits from Israel. Even for all the recorded sins and rebellions of Israel against her God, Israel's high standard challenges the world. What other nation recorded so candidly her past faults so that future generations could learn from them? What other great man in history was as transparent as Moses was in writing the Pentateuch, in which he does not portray himself ideally, but realistically? What other civilization incorporates the immoral affairs of her most beloved king as Israel's literature includes regarding King David? What other nation would add in a book like Jonah, which shows not only the eventual obedience of the reluctant prophetic missionary, but also the inner wrestling he underwent before finally obeying God's command?

> "Even for all the recorded sins and rebellions of Israel against her God, Israel's high standard challenges the world."

What other nation today has developed a desert into a garden in less than half a century? What other nation remains unrecognized as a legitimate neighbor among hostile neighbors? What other land endures constant bombardment and threats, yet exercises such restraint in an attempt not to antagonize her neighbors? Just as God promised to Abraham, all nations of the earth are being blessed through his descendants. The biggest blessing Israel gave us was the Savior. Even today, many advances are made in science and computer technology due to research by the Israelis.

God's Plans for Israel Are Set Aside for a Time Because of Her Sin

God originally desired to make Israel a special nation, outstanding among other kingdoms, in order for other nations to see His glory and be drawn to Himself. "This is what the Sovereign Lord says: 'This is Jerusalem, which I have set in the center of the nations, with countries all around her'" (Ezekiel 5:5).

However, centuries of willful sin and rejection of God, God's Word, and God's prophets are well documented in Kings and Chronicles, Israel's own literature. God sent many prophets to call Israel back to Him, but the efforts were in vain. Ezekiel joined his predecessors in predicting that God would punish Israel greatly for her sin, almost destroying her.

> Therefore this is what the Sovereign Lord says: I myself am against you, Jerusalem, and I will inflict punishment on you in the sight of the nations. Because of all your detestable idols, I will do to you what I have never done before and will never do again. Therefore in your midst parents will eat their children, and children will eat their parents. I will inflict punishment on you and will scatter all your survivors to the winds. Therefore as surely as I live, declares the Sovereign Lord, because you have defiled my sanctuary with all your vile images and detestable practices, I myself will shave you; I will not look on you with pity or spare you. A third of your people will die of the plague or perish by famine inside you; a third will fall by the sword outside your walls; and a third I will scatter to the winds and pursue with drawn sword. (Ezekiel 5:8–12)

So great would be the downfall of Israel that other nations would gloat. "This is what the Sovereign Lord says: 'The enemy said of you, "Aha! The ancient heights have become our possession"'" (Ezekiel 36:2).

Ezekiel Predicted Israel Would Regather After Punishment

After God's punishment, God would bring Israel back to her homeland. Ezekiel, along with Jeremiah and other prophets, predicted Israel's restoration. Through to the end of chapter 36, numerous Scriptures indicate God's favor on Israel. Here is a sample.

> This is what the Sovereign Lord says: "When I gather the people of Israel from the nations where they have been scattered, I will be proved holy through them in the sight of the nations. Then they will live in their own land, which I gave to my servant Jacob." (Ezekiel 28:25)

The future prosperity would surpass the past, Ezekiel predicted:

> I will multiply the number of people living on you, even the whole house of Israel. The towns will be inhabited and the ruins rebuilt. I will increase the number of people and animals living on you, and they will be fruitful and become numerous. I will settle people on you as in the past and will make you prosper more than before. Then you will know that I am the Lord. (Ezekiel 36:10–11)

God would work for Israel, but the reason was to glorify His own name among the nations. God was concerned about His reputation:

> Therefore say to the house of Israel, "This is what the Sovereign Lord says: It is not for your sake, house of Israel, that I am going to do these things, but for the sake of my holy name, which you have profaned among the nations where you have gone. I will show the holiness of my great name, which has been profaned among the nations, the name you have profaned among them. Then the nations will know that I am the Lord, declares the Sovereign Lord, when I am proved holy through you before their eyes." (Ezekiel 36:22–23).

> **"I will gather you from all the countries and bring you back into your own land."**

Ezekiel repeated the prediction numerous times: "For I will take you out of the nations; I will gather you from all the countries and bring you back into your own land" (Ezekiel 36:24).

God would, in favor to His people, bless them with internal spiritual changes: "I will give you a new heart and put a new spirit in you; I will remove from you your heart of stone and give you a heart of flesh. And I will put my Spirit in you and move you to follow my decrees and be careful to keep my laws" (Ezekiel 36:26-27).

Ezekiel Is Famous for This Prophecy Regarding Israel's Restoration

> The hand of the Lord was on me, and he brought me out by the Spirit of the Lord and set me in the middle of a valley; it was full of bones. He led me back and forth among them, and I saw a great many bones on the floor of the valley, bones that were very dry. He asked me, "Son of man, can these bones live?"
>
> I said, "Sovereign Lord, you alone know."
>
> Then he said to me, "Prophesy to these bones and say to them, 'Dry bones, hear the word of the Lord! This is what the Sovereign Lord says to these bones: I will make breath enter you, and you will come to life. I will attach tendons to you and make flesh come upon you and cover you with skin; I will put breath in you, and you will come to life. Then you will know that I am the Lord.'"
>
> So I prophesied as I was commanded. And as I was prophesying, there was a noise, a rattling sound, and the bones came together, bone to bone. I looked, and tendons and flesh appeared on them and skin covered them, but there was no breath in them.
>
> Then he said to me, "Prophesy to the breath; prophesy, son of man, and say to it, 'This is what the Sovereign Lord says: Come, breath, from the four winds and breathe into these slain, that they may live.'" So I prophesied as he commanded me, and breath entered them; they came to life and stood up on their feet — a vast army.
>
> Then he said to me: "Son of man, these bones are the whole house of Israel. They say, 'Our bones are dried up and our hope is gone; we are cut off.'" (Ezekiel 37:1-11)

Not only would Israel be restored politically and nationally, Ezekiel said the restoration would also include a spiritual element. "They will no longer defile themselves with their idols and vile images or with any of their offenses, for I will save them from all their sinful backsliding, and I will cleanse them. They will be my people, and I will be their God" (Ezekiel 37:23).

> Then the nations will know that I the Lord make Israel holy, when my sanctuary is among them forever. (Ezekiel 37:28)

From 1948 onward, the world has witnessed the fulfillment of these verses. The amazing restoration of Israel to her homeland is the fulfillment of Ezekiel's vision of the bones living again.

If we skipped Ezekiel 38 and 39 and move on to Ezekiel 40 to the end of book, it would seem that heaven came down. Indeed, there are many parallels between the description of the Holy City in John's Revelation at the end of the Bible and Ezekiel 40 through 48. We will make some observations about that later, but we must first look at the events described in Ezekiel 38 and 39.

After Israel's Restoration, Gog and Magog Wage a Great War on Israel

The war of Gog and Magog fits into the category of extraordinary and spectacular events. An unchanging God does work through cataclysmic events when necessary. He sent a universal flood, visited ten plagues on Egypt, caused the earth to open up and "swallow" rebellious persons, and parted the waters four times (for Moses, Joshua, Elijah, and Elisha). He rained hailstones on the Canaanites, stopped the sun, and fed thousands. And

> "An unchanging God does work through cataclysmic events when necessary."

according to Peter, He will burn the entire earth with fire. In view of this record, it is not unbelievable that God would literally do what Ezekiel predicts. For the honor of His name, He will defend Israel after gathering her back from nations all over the world. The deliverance of Israel from the coalition of armies allied against her certainly qualifies as a cataclysmic intervention. God is a self-revealing Being. The deliverance from her attackers recorded in Ezekiel 38 and 39 unquestionably would be a spectacular revelation.

Israel's six-day war of 1967 and the Yom Kippur War of 1973 illustrate God's willingness to be as involved in geopolitical military events as He was in Bible days. In more recent years, a two-day wind storm in Iraq blew away the sand in which hundreds of deadly explosives were buried. When the wind died down, soldiers could safely drive around each of the hundreds of recently exposed land mines.

In the Gog and Magog war, all nations will see another even more spectacular, awesome, timely deliverance. The more disproportionate the military ability of Israel and the attacking coalition, the greater the deliverance. Many nations are in the attacking coalition, while, by contrast, no allies of Israel are named. God promised Abraham that He would bless the world through his descendants. In the Gog and Magog war, this will be done with extraordinary fireworks.

> "The more disproportionate the military ability of Israel and the attacking coalition, the greater the deliverance."

We do not know how much time will pass between the restoration of Israel recorded in Ezekiel 37 and the war of Gog and Magog that is recorded in Ezekiel 38 and 39. But considerable detail is given regarding an attack against Israel by nations to the north. Bible scholars generally agree that ancient Magog, Rosh, Mesheck, and Tubal are present-day Russia and the former Soviet republics.

> Son of man, set your face against Gog, of the land of Magog, the chief prince of Meshek and Tubal; prophesy against him and say: "This is what the Sovereign Lord says: I am against you, Gog, chief prince of Meshek and Tubal. I will turn you around, put hooks in your jaws and bring you out with your whole army — your horses, your horsemen fully armed, and a great horde with large and small shields, all of them brandishing their swords." (Ezekiel 38:2-4)

Ezekiel gives us many details. Notice these five important revelations regarding the Russian-led coalition's make-up and the nature of their plan of attack:

- The leader of Russia will devise a political and military scheme.
- The Russian leader will conduct elaborate preparations.
- A large and powerful multinational army will be gathered. (Notice that neither Egypt nor Iraq are included.)
- God will oppose this Russian leader.
- Throughout the description, the nations that join the coalition are identified.

Ezekiel 38:4–10 says, "I will turn you around, put hooks in your jaws and bring you out with your whole army — your horses, your horsemen fully armed, and a great horde with large and small shields, all of them brandishing their swords. Persia, Cush and Put will be with them, all with shields and helmets, also Gomer with all its troops, and Beth Togarmah from the far north with all its troops — the many nations with you."

The generally accepted modern-day names of the nations identified by Ezekiel in the above text are as follows. As you can see, this is a vast array of nations.

- Persia is Iran.
- Cush is Sudan, Ethiopia, and possibly Eritrea.
- Put is Libya, Algeria, and Tunisia.
- Gomer is Turkey and possibly Germany and Austria.
- Beth Togarmah is Turkey, Armenia, and the Turkic-speaking peoples of Asia Minor and central Asia.

> Get ready; be prepared, you and all the hordes gathered about you, and take command of them. After many days you will be called to arms. In future years you will invade a land that has recovered from war, whose people were gathered from many nations to the mountains of Israel, which had long been desolate. They had been brought out from the nations, and now all of them live in safety. You and all your troops and the many nations with you will go up, advancing like a storm; you will be like a cloud covering the land. This is what the Sovereign Lord says: On that

> day thoughts will come into your mind and you will devise an evil scheme. (Ezekiel 38:4-10)
>
> This is what will happen in that day: When Gog attacks the land of Israel, my hot anger will be aroused, declares the Sovereign Lord. In my zeal and fiery wrath I declare that at that time there shall be a great earthquake in the land of Israel. (Ezekiel 38:18-19)

We can watch contemporary events to see the coalition gradually begin to form. Already Russia is on good terms with Iran and some of the other nations mentioned as members of the coalition. The disdain those nations harbor toward Israel is also apparent.

That War Has Not Yet Occurred

Neither the Six-Day War of 1967 nor the Yom Kippur War of 1973 match the above prophecy. They were smaller, shorter wars, and Israel was enabled to defend herself. There were no spectacular or supernatural phenomena that compare with Ezekiel 38 and 39. We must watch for a later, larger-scale war against Israel coming principally from the north.

> After many days you will be called to arms. In future years you will invade a land that has recovered from war, whose people were gathered from many nations to the mountains of Israel, which had long been desolate. They had been brought out from the nations, and now all of them live in safety. (Ezekiel 38:8)

Before the invasion occurs, Israel will be living in relative safety and peace.

> You will say, "I will invade a land of unwalled villages; I will attack a peaceful and unsuspecting people — all of them living without walls and without gates and bars. I will plunder and loot and turn my hand against the resettled ruins and the people gathered from the nations, rich in livestock and goods, living at the center of the land." Sheba and Dedan and the merchants of Tarshish and all her villages will say to you, "Have you come to plunder? Have you gathered your hordes to loot, to carry off silver and gold, to take away livestock and goods and to seize much plunder?" (Ezekiel 38:11-13)

Ezekiel's narrative states that God will publicly call this war into being so all the nations will see. "You will come from your place in the far north, you and many nations with you, all of them riding on horses, a great horde, a mighty army. You will advance against my people Israel like a cloud that covers the land. In days to come, Gog, I will bring you against my land, so that the nations may know me when I am proved holy through you before their eyes" (Ezekiel 38:15-16).

God's purpose for organizing this war is to prove Himself holy to these nations. God plans to bring glory to Himself through this as He brings destruction on His enemies.

> **God's purpose for organizing this war is to prove Himself holy to these nations.**

Amazing and Unprecedented Destruction Will Fall on the Attacking Army

A timely earthquake that is part of the phenomena that defeat Gog and Magog will be centered in Israel. "This is what will happen in that day: When Gog attacks the land of Israel, my hot anger will be aroused, declares the Sovereign Lord. In my zeal and fiery wrath I declare that at that time *there shall be a great earthquake in the land of Israel*. The fish in the sea, the birds in the sky, the beasts of the field, every creature that moves along the ground, and all the people on the face of the earth will tremble at my presence. The mountains will be overturned, the cliffs will crumble and every wall will fall to the ground" (Ezekiel 38:18-20, emphasis mine).

The world will witness an amazing spectacle. Notice the combination of catastrophic happenings that must originate from high in the sky — torrents of rain, hailstones, and burning sulfur — as well as the earthquake from below: "I will execute judgment on him with plague and bloodshed; I will pour down torrents of rain, hailstones and burning sulfur on him and on his troops and on the many nations with him" (Ezekiel 38:22).

> I will send fire on Magog and on those who live in safety in the coastlands, and they will know that I am the Lord. I will make known my holy name among my people Israel. I will no longer let my holy name be profaned, and the nations will know that I the Lord am the Holy One in Israel. (Ezekiel 39:6-7)

Notice the remains of soldiers and military equipment after the battle is over. It would be difficult to imagine anything worse than the public display of God's power on an earthly army than this.

> Son of man, this is what the Sovereign Lord says: "Call out to every kind of bird and all the wild animals: 'Assemble and come together from all around to the sacrifice I am preparing for you, the great sacrifice on the mountains of Israel. There you will eat flesh and drink blood. You will eat the flesh of mighty men and drink the blood of the princes of the earth as if they were rams and lambs, goats and bulls — all of them fattened animals from Bashan. At the sacrifice I am preparing for you, you will eat fat till you are glutted and drink blood till you are drunk. At my table you will eat your fill of horses and riders, mighty men and soldiers of every kind,'" declares the Sovereign Lord.
>
> I will display my glory among the nations, and all the nations will see the punishment I inflict and the hand I lay on them. From that day forward the house of Israel will know that I am the Lord their God. (Ezekiel 39:17-22)

The breadth and intensity of the destruction in the world's most catastrophic battle is without precedent. Chapter 39 concludes with a summary description of Israel's deliverance by God:

> Therefore this is what the Sovereign Lord says: I will now restore the fortunes of Jacob and will have compassion on all the people of Israel, and I will be zealous for my holy name. They will forget their shame and all the unfaithfulness they showed toward me when they lived in safety in their land with no one to make them afraid. When I have brought them back from the nations and have gathered them from the countries of their enemies, I will be proved holy through them in the sight of many nations. Then they will know that I am the Lord their God, for though I sent them into exile among the nations, I will gather them to their own land, not leaving any behind. I will no longer hide my face from them, for I will pour out my Spirit on the house of Israel, declares the Sovereign Lord. (Ezekiel 39:25-29)

God will use these events to exalt Himself in Israel for Israel's benefit and also to impress the nations with His glory.

Does Oil Lie Buried beneath Israel's Surface?

Why would Russia attack Israel? What motive would be pervasive enough to attract such a large-scale coalition? Could it be petroleum wealth that has not yet surfaced? Scripture reveals such a possibility.

In late 1962, as a first-year student in a small Bible college, I took a course on the Pentateuch. That was when I first heard about Jacob and Moses prophesying oil beneath Israel's surface. Reading *Epicenter* by Joel Rosenberg forty-four years later confirmed those beliefs. The following references to treasures beneath the surface are included in Scripture's specific promises of blessings to the twelve sons of Jacob and their descendants.

> "What motive would be pervasive enough to attract such a large-scale coalition?"

Shortly before he died, Jacob called for his sons and said to them, "Gather around so I can tell you what will happen to you in days to come" (Genesis 49:1). One of the blessings Jacob foretold for Joseph was this: "Because of the Almighty, who blesses you with blessings of the heavens above, *blessings of the deep that lies below,* blessings of the breast and womb" (Genesis 49:25, emphasis mine).

Moses also prophesied about Joseph: "May the Lord bless his land with the precious dew from heaven above and *with the deep waters that lie below*" (Deuteronomy 33:13, emphasis mine).

Moses foretold regarding Zebulun: "They will summon peoples to the mountain and there offer the sacrifices of the righteous; they will feast on the abundance of the seas, on the *treasures hidden in the sand*" (Deuteronomy 33:19, emphasis mine).

About Asher, Moses said: "Most blessed of sons is Asher; let him be favored by his brothers, and *let him bathe his feet in oil*" (Deuteronomy 33:24, emphasis mine).

Regarding all of Israel, Moses said: "The Lord alone led him; no foreign god was with him. He made him ride on the heights of the land and fed him with the fruit of the fields. He nourished him with *honey from the rock, and with oil from the flinty crag*" (Deuteronomy 32:12–13, emphasis mine).

God said through Isaiah: "I will give you the treasures of darkness, *riches stored in secret places,* so that you may know that I am the Lord, the God of Israel, who summons you by name" (Isaiah 45:3, emphasis mine).

Is it likely that Israel will discover oil? Is it possible that oil is one of the major reasons the coalition of Ezekiel 38 and 39 is eager to swallow the defenseless nation? We cannot know for certain, but oil exploration is now progressing in Israel in the vicinity of the base of what might be called Asher's foot. It is an area just south of the ancient land assignment to the tribe of Asher. The discovery of oil there would clearly coincide with Moses' prediction that Asher would "bathe his feet in oil." If this exploration is productive, we may see further events unfold in accordance with the prophecy of Ezekiel. If we take Jacob and Moses seriously, we can look for Israel to discover oil.

Ezekiel Describes the Return of Temple Worship

Ezekiel 38 and 39 describe the battle of Gog and Magog. The next nine chapters describe the temple area, the gates to the temple court, rooms for preparing sacrifices, rooms for the priests, the new temple, the return of God's glory, the restoration of the priesthood, and Israel's full restoration.

The presence of the Dome of the Rock and the Al-Aksa Mosque on the temple mount in Jerusalem today is certainly a barrier to the construction of the Jewish temple described in Ezekiel 40 through 48. Could it be that the war of Gog and Magog, with its widespread destruction, accounts for the removal of all physical and political obstacles. Will that open the way for the restoration of the Jewish temple on that site?

What about the priesthood in that day? Kings Saul and Uzziah were punished because they usurped the privilege of the priest in their days. However, the New Testament tells us God has raised up a new priesthood, which includes you and me. The last nine chapters of Ezekiel may describe the setting for that priesthood for believers who anticipate it. Believers will be given the joy of serving as priests of God on that day.

The New Testament says this about the roles of priests at the time described recorded by Ezekiel 40–48:

> You also, like living stones, are being built into a spiritual house

> to be a holy priesthood, offering spiritual sacrifices acceptable to God through Jesus Christ. (1 Peter 2:5)

> But you are a chosen people, a royal priesthood, a holy nation, God's special possession, that you may declare the praises of him who called you out of darkness into his wonderful light. (1 Peter 2:9)

> … and has made us to be a kingdom and priests to serve his God and Father — to him be glory and power for ever and ever! Amen. (Revelation 1:6)

> You have made them to be a kingdom and priests to serve our God, and they will reign on the earth. (Revelation 5:10)

> Blessed and holy are those who have part in the first resurrection. The second death has no power over them, but they will be priests of God and of Christ and will reign with him for a thousand years. (Revelation 20:6)

Is it possible that believers will be given the joy of serving as priests of God on that day? If so, the roles of priests and the setting of the temple described in the last chapters of Ezekiel would be of particular interest to us.

Israel's Glorious State Surpasses Former Glories

Isaiah and other prophets join Ezekiel in attesting to the restoration of Israel's house of worship, along with unprecedented international influence:

> In the last days the mountain of the Lord's temple will be established as the highest of the mountains; it will be exalted above the hills, and all nations will stream to it.
>
> Many peoples will come and say, "Come, let us go up to the mountain of the Lord, to the house of the God of Jacob. He will teach us his ways, so that we may walk in his paths." The law will go out from Zion, the word of the Lord from Jerusalem.
>
> He will judge between the nations and will settle disputes for many peoples. They will beat their swords into plowshares and their spears into pruning hooks. Nation will not take up sword against nation, nor will they train for war anymore. (Isaiah 2:2-4)

The river flowing from the temple is described along with the trees at the water's edge: "Fruit trees of all kinds will grow on both banks of the river. Their leaves will not wither, nor will their fruit fail. Every month they will bear fruit, because the water from the sanctuary flows to them. Their fruit will serve for food and their leaves for healing" (Ezekiel 47:12).

Ezekiel's river gives another perspective. It provides a parallel description for the river described in the last chapter of the Bible written by the apostle John: "... down the middle of the great street of the city. On each side of the river stood the tree of life, bearing twelve crops of fruit, yielding its fruit every month. And the leaves of the tree are for the healing of the nations" (Revelation 22:2). Put the descriptions of the rivers of Ezekiel 47 and Revelation 22 together, and we have a glorious picture — beauty and depth in the water, healing and health from all kinds of fruit trees, and many types of fish.

Here is another detail of the restored Jerusalem in the Bible. Is it possible that the ark of the covenant and other treasured items from the temple will be restored to it? The following prophecy of Jeremiah suggests that. "Yes, this is what the Lord Almighty, the God of Israel, says about the things that are left in the house of the Lord and in the palace of the king of Judah and in Jerusalem: 'They will be taken to Babylon and there they will remain *until the day I come for them*,' declares the Lord. 'Then I will bring them back and *restore them to this place*'" (Jeremiah 27:21-22, emphasis mine).

Ezekiel, the foreteller of events involving Israel at the center of international developments, provides the insight, comfort, and courage Christians need as we watch geopolitical phenomena unfold before our eyes. If the events spoken of by Ezekiel actually take place in

> **Those who know and believe Bible prophecy can be calm and confident in our God.**

our lifetimes, we can rest assured that the Sovereign Lord to whom Ezekiel referred is indeed in control and working His purpose in the world. Those who do not know the Lord or the prophecies of the Bible may feel that the fate of the human race has spun out of control. But those who know and believe Bible prophecy can be calm and confident in our

God. Ezekiel provides the prophecy that gives us assurance through times of tumultuous geopolitical developments.

Ezekiel's prophecy will afford comfort, insight, and courage to persons living in these troubled times of cataclysmic events. Ezekiel teaches that the Lord is sovereign. He will restore and protect Israel, and us, because He takes care of His own. This lesson from Ezekiel's prophecy is uniquely valuable to us today.

For Further Thought

- How has this chapter drawn a closer connection in your mind between what you are doing now to serve the Lord and what you will do to serve Him as a king and priest in His eventual kingdom?
- In what way does the study of future things encourage you?
- What does Israel's favored position among the nations teach about our duty to pray for Israel and Jerusalem? Do you now, more than before you read this chapter, feel the need to pray for these countries?
- What lesson can we learn from the fact that God set Israel aside for her sin?
- Do you see a similarity between current events and what God said through Ezekiel centuries ago?
- What new insights did you receive by looking at Israel's restoration as portrayed in Ezekiel's valley of dry bones and the subsequent chapters?
- What is happening today that looks similar to Ezekiel 38-39?
- What comes to your mind when you try to imagine the catastrophic events in God's deliverance of Israel as recorded in Ezekiel 38-39?
- What does the discovery of oil in Israel mean to you?
- Do you see yourself participating in the temple activities and worship described in Ezekiel 40-48?

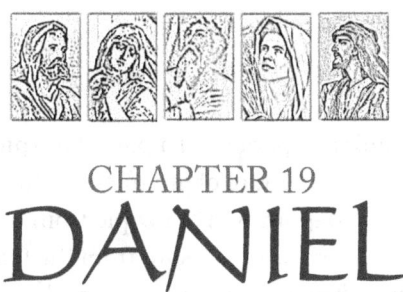

CHAPTER 19
DANIEL

Are you aware that Daniel is the only major personality in the Bible besides Jesus Christ of whom there is no sin recorded? No mention is ever made of Daniel's wife or family. Was Daniel a eunuch? Did you know Daniel loved God more than the king's dainty food?

Ezra 6:1-12 relates a fascinating record of an amazing source of support for the Jewish nation during a time of restoration. Three successive kings of Persia all supported the reconstruction of the temple and the restoration of worship to "the God of heaven." How is it that God's people in Judea experienced such favor from a heathen and ungodly kingdom far to the east?

Ezra 6:14 is difficult to explain: "So the elders of the Jews continued to build and prosper under the preaching of Haggai the prophet and Zechariah, a descendant of Iddo. They finished building the temple according to the command of the God of Israel and the decrees of Cyrus, Darius and Artaxerxes, kings of Persia." How is it the Israelites were supported like this? The answer is found in another book. God had a man serving His interests in the courts of that heathen kingdom. His name was Daniel.

Daniel is a type of Christ. The Bible says that all have sinned, but no sins are recorded of this dedicated, wise, noble, scholarly, courageous, humble, faithful, and obedient man of God.

Our nation needs Daniels today. We need the salt of godly influence in the leadership of the government. Our influence could be great, but there is a price to pay, just as Daniel paid a price for the influence he exercised in his day. I will make seven observations about Daniel in this chapter.

Daniel Was Moved Involuntarily from the Familiar to the Foreign

In Daniel's lifetime, Judah experienced a period of spiritual decline. So God judged this nation. God's tool of judgment — the king of Babylon — demanded a massive deportation of people from Judea and also confiscated many articles used in worship from the temple of Jerusalem. Through circumstances beyond his control, Daniel was moved from Judah to Babylon. Daniel and his friends were selected for training in political science in a foreign nation. He lived in Babylon against his will, yet he served God's purpose there.

> "He lived in Babylon against his will, yet he served God's purpose there."

You may have been born in, lived in, or are now living in circumstances you would not have chosen, that you did not want, or that you do not like. Your circumstances may place you with people you would rather not be with or in a political or social situation you do not like. If that is true, remember Daniel. It wasn't his choice to be a foreigner living in exile in the courts of idolatrous, haughty kings. He did not choose to be thrust among the jealous, power-hungry, ungodly government officials who surrounded him. Yet Daniel sought the Lord and His will in that inconvenient situation. He dealt wisely with the circumstances that were given to him. From the time he arrived in the foreign nation to which God sent him, he resolved to uncompromisingly maintain his convictions and serve his God.

For three years, Daniel submitted to Babylonian language lessons, education in Babylonian literature, and training in governmental administration. He sought God's purpose for him in that atmosphere. God had a plan for Daniel, and He has a plan for you in your national, social, educational, religious, and family situation. Will you dare to be a Daniel and find God's purpose in your generation and circumstances, no matter how complex, difficult, and adverse they may be? Will you watch God work miracles to use you in ways you would never dream of?

Daniel Valued Spiritual Things More Than the Food of the King's Court

The normal reaction to the promotion, opportunity, and honor that Daniel received, according to man's secular outlook, is to glory in it, receive it, and enjoy it. Daniel did not.

Daniel and his friends had no physical defects. They were handsome, well-informed, and quick to learn. They were qualified to serve in the king's court. This could have led to pride, but not for Daniel. He placed greater value on godly living than on the luxury of human pleasures like eating royal food and drinking royal wine. Daniel submitted to three years of rigorous training for life in the king's court, but he preferred not to eat the dainty foods offered to him.

I do not tell people what they should or should not eat. But I do use Daniel's example to illustrate a truth I apply to myself. God comes before food. Deciding what, how much, and when to eat — and when to voluntarily choose not to take meals — is a serious discipline for high-achieving Christians who want to keep their bodies fit and their minds clear to seek God and serve His people. First Corinthians 6:19-20 says, "Do you not know that your bodies are temples of the Holy Spirit, who is in you, whom you have received from God? You are not your own; you were bought at a price. Therefore honor God with your bodies."

> **The Holy Spirit will show you when, what, and how much to eat if you ask Him.**

Our bodies are temples of the Holy Spirit. What we put into them affects how healthy we are, how well we sleep, how much we weigh, how agile we are, and how long we will live. Examining our eating choices may cause divisive discussions. The Holy Spirit will show you when, what, and how much to eat if you ask Him. You can also consult health books or people in the medical profession. Basically, eat healthy foods, stay away from foods known to be unhealthy, and avoid excesses.

The Bible portrays those who are undisciplined in what they eat in an unfavorable light. "Their god is their stomach, and their glory is in their shame. Their mind is set on earthly things" (Philippians 3:19). If we want to serve God to the greatest extent possible, our love for Him will affect our eating patterns.

Honor God with your meals. Then watch how this discipline helps bring order and self-control into other areas of your life. Daniel valued his pursuit of God more than eating pleasant things. Will you dare to be like Daniel, who showed his love for God in what he did and didn't eat?

Daniel Was Methodical in Prayer

Daniel's jealous peers in government could find only one thing that might enable them to trap him into the king's disfavor. It was his attitude and behavior with reference to his God, specifically his methodical prayer life. These evil officials convinced the king to make an edict to kill anyone who requested anything from anyone other than him.

Yet even after the obvious trap was set, "three times a day he got down on his knees and prayed, giving thanks to his God, just as he had done before" (Daniel 6:10). The story of the political snare and Daniel's deliverance from the lions' den is a lesson on courage. But the reference to Daniel's systematic prayer life reveals an insight into the possible basis for all the other character strengths displayed throughout his life. *Daniel prayed.* He was a man of prayer. Daniel was intentional about praying. Nothing, not even a death threat, interrupted his prayer routine. If Daniel lived today, he would turn off his cell phone when he went to prayer.

> **If Daniel lived today, he would turn off his cell phone when he went to prayer.**

Daniel valued prayer so much that he developed a habit that guaranteed he was certain to pray. Do you schedule times for focused prayer? Will you dare to be like Daniel in systematic prayer?

Daniel Was Courageous

Daniel showed unusual courage in speaking hard messages to the kings he served. He even continued to pray regularly despite having a death threat over his head.

The officials who plotted against Daniel were his peers. Daniel could not have been entirely insensitive to the peer pressure or to the fact that they opposed him. He may have been tempted to compromise, appease them, or create a situation that allowed him to avoid conflict with them.

Daniel found himself surrounded by the pressure of pomp, royalty, power, and authority. Yet Daniel fearlessly spoke the truth with tact, wisdom, and accuracy. Daniel repeatedly interpreted dreams to kings, even when the message placed him in the precarious position of being critical of the king. Notice the diplomacy in the statement Daniel made before he delivered a message of judgment to Nebuchadnezzar: "My lord, if only your dream applied to your enemies and its meaning to your adversaries" (Daniel 4:19).

Daniel learned how to tell even difficult truths tactfully and wisely. Will you develop the courage to say what needs to be said even when it is a difficult message?

Daniel Identified with Others When He Prayed

Daniel demonstrated close identification with others in his prayer reading the prophecy of Jeremiah. He discovered the prediction of the Jews' restoration to their homeland after seventy years. He "turned to the Lord God and pleaded with him in prayer and petition, in fasting, and in sackcloth and ashes" (Daniel 9:3).

Throughout the narrative of his prayer (Daniel 9:4-14) Daniel repeatedly used the plural pronouns *we, our,* and *us.* He did not place himself above those for whom he prayed. He identified with his people. He included himself with them. He included them with himself.

> *Daniel repeatedly used the plural pronouns we, our, and us. He did not place himself above those for whom he prayed.*

Jesus, in the Lord's Prayer, taught us to pray using the first person plural. Many today use *I, me,* and *my,* but it is closer to the humble attitude Jesus wants us to have to use *we, our,* and *us.* As we lead in group prayer, saying "we pray" acknowledges the others around us who are also praying. This combination of inclusiveness and humility contributes to unity and invites others' participation in our prayers.

Daniel humbly threw himself on God's mercy. He acknowledged that he and his generation did not deserve an answer to the prayers they were praying. He said, "We do not make requests of you because we are righteous, but because of your great mercy" (Daniel 9:18). This contrasts with the proud prayer of Hezekiah who "turned his face to the wall and prayed to the Lord, 'Remember, Lord how I have walked before you faithfully and with wholehearted devotion and have done what is good in your eyes'" (2 Kings 20:3). Daniel prayed regularly and with humility. Will you dare to be like Daniel and humbly include others in your prayers?

Daniel's Experience Gives Us Insight into the Realities of Spiritual Warfare

Daniel 10:12–11:1 records a conversation Daniel had with the Lord in a vision.

> Then he continued, "Do not be afraid, Daniel. Since the first day that you set your mind to gain understanding and to humble yourself before your God, your words were heard, and I have come in response to them. But the prince of the Persian kingdom resisted me twenty-one days. Then Michael, one of the chief princes, came to help me, because I was detained there with the king of Persia. Now I have come to explain to you what will happen to your people in the future, for the vision concerns a time yet to come."
>
> While he was saying this to me, I bowed with my face toward the ground and was speechless. Then one who looked like a man touched my lips, and I opened my mouth and began to speak. I said to the one standing before me, "I am overcome with anguish because of the vision, my lord, and I feel very weak. How can I, your servant, talk with you, my lord? My strength is gone and I can hardly breathe." Again the one who looked like a man touched me and gave me strength. "Do not be afraid, you who are highly esteemed," he said. "Peace! Be strong now; be strong."
>
> When he spoke to me, I was strengthened and said, "Speak, my lord, since you have given me strength." So he said, "Do you know why I have come to you? Soon I will return to fight against

the prince of Persia, and when I go, the prince of Greece will come; but first I will tell you what is written in the Book of Truth. (No one supports me against them except Michael, your prince. And in the first year of Darius the Mede, I took my stand to support and protect him.)"

From this, we learn the following important lessons about spiritual warfare. These can help us become more-informed and therefore better-prepared prayer warriors:

- Behind visible phenomena is an invisible spiritual world.
- A spiritual prince has authority over a specific geographical area.
- Demons and evil spirits are organized.
- Spiritual princes have the ability to hinder God's messengers.

> "Our prayers make a difference. There are things that God does because I pray that He would not do if I didn't pray."

- The angel Michael is able to successfully fight the prince of the geographical area in which we are conducting spiritual warfare, but we must remain in prayer.
- Our prayers make a difference. There are things that God does because I pray that He would not do if I didn't pray. I do not know which prayers fit into this category, so I pray as though they all do (see Ephesians 6:12 and 2 Corinthians 5:3–5).
- Tenacious, fervent, and systematic prayer is not for the weak. It requires commitment and effort.

Daniel was not afraid to engage in spiritual warfare in order to understand the spiritual realities behind his visible troubles. He persevered. Will you dare to be like Daniel in persevering prayer?

Daniel Prophesied about the Eventual Triumph of the Kingdom of God

> In the time of those kings, the God of heaven will set up a kingdom that will never be destroyed, nor will it be left to another people.

> It will crush all those kingdoms and bring them to an end, but it will itself endure forever. This is the meaning of the vision of the rock cut out of a mountain, but not by human hands — a rock that broke the iron, the bronze, the clay, the silver and the gold to pieces. The great God has shown the king what will take place in the future. The dream is true and its interpretation is trustworthy. (Daniel 2:44–45)

All the earthly kingdoms symbolized by the huge statue of gold, silver, brass, iron, and clay developed and subsequently weakened. Afterward, Daniel saw a stone that was hewn out of the mountain that broke the statue and filled the earth. This may symbolize one of two things:

- The coming kingdom of Jesus Christ on earth, which will replace all the preceding earthly kingdoms and last for eternity
- The gradual coming of the invisible kingdom of God, as people all over the earth yield to the kingship of Jesus Christ as their Lord and the kingdom of God becomes evident in an increasing number of human situations all over the earth.

In either case, the kingdom comes in answer to our prayer that God's kingdom will come and His will be done on earth as it is in heaven. Daniel lived in a non-Jewish, heathen, perverse society. Yet he saw through time to the triumphant, glorious kingdom days. They have been a hope and encouragement to God's people through the ages as we anticipate, pray for, and work toward the future. Daniel interpreted the king's dream only to the king he served. But because his words were recorded, people in every subsequent generation have been able to know in advance the eventual triumph of God's kingdom.

After reading Jeremiah's prophecy, Daniel began to pray that this prophecy would come to pass. We should follow Daniel's example of praying that what God says will happen shall happen. We can pray that God will work in today's socioeconomic and geopolitical situations to create the circumstances that will best allow the kingdom of God to grow and fill the earth. A similar prayer is to ask God to produce here and now an atmosphere in which Jesus can best build His Church, which He said He would do. God can work in contemporary human history, creating situations that soften the hearts of humans. He can also produce circumstances in nations that provide the financial and human resources necessary to see His kingdom grow and His church established.

Other places in the Bible, following Daniel, also express the encouraging theme of the eventual success of God's kingdom.

> "Will you give kingdom hope to your otherwise hopeless and helpless nation and generation?"

For example, Matthew 16:18 says, "I tell you that you are Peter, and on this rock I will build my church, and the gates of death will not overcome it."

Daniel is an example of presenting a positive kingdom message of hope and expectation even in the midst of difficulties. Will you give kingdom hope to your otherwise hopeless and helpless nation and generation? Will you pray that God works in human history to establish His kingdom and Christ's church? Will you dare to be involved in international prayer ministry?

For Further Thought

- What can we learn from Daniel's systematic praying?
- What lesson about courage can you learn from Daniel's example?
- When we pray for sinners and the lost, what advantage is it to pray in the first person plural (*we, us*)? How does it help to identify closely with those for whom you are praying?
- What image do you see when you envision the reality, rank, organization, and powers of the spiritual forces of darkness when you pray?
- What lesson have you learned from Daniel's vision of the rock that was hewn out of the mountain growing and filling the earth? How will you share that knowledge with others?

CHAPTER 20
HOSEA

Do you realize that Hosea was a kind of living metaphor? Were you aware that God asked him to marry a harlot? And did you know that even after bearing a child for Hosea, when his wife, Gomer, ran after other men, God told Hosea to bring her back again? You might be surprised to learn that Hosea's message focused primarily on spiritual adultery.

The human inclination to serve gods other than the one true God — idolatry — is no less important in the spiritual realm than adultery is in a human marriage. Marriage is a metaphor that teaches us about commitment, faithfulness, and fruitful productivity. Hosea's life graphically teaches this by the negative illustration of Gomer's adultery.

More than any other man, God required that Hosea's personal life, attitude, and conduct prove and illustrate the reality and truth of His message. His marriage to Gomer, his love and care for her, the names of his children, and his pursuit of his repeatedly wayward, promiscuous wife all vividly illustrate God's deep love for us. He has a strong desire for a close personal relationship with us, and He will even forgive our idolatry.

The subject of intimate experiences in marriage is only indirectly raised by Hosea's metaphor. However, this subject is taken up in this chapter because the whole counsel of God includes instruction in it. Beyond that, understanding the joys of physical intimacy and the spiritual lessons in it adds depth to our love for God. It gives us a realistic grasp of the awfulness of idolatry.

Hosea's wayward wife provides an example of how *not* to treat God.

Fidelity in marriage, by indirect implication from Gomer's error, is an illustration of how to be faithful to God.

Understanding Metaphors

Metaphors help us understand abstract truths by comparing them to concrete items; the known illustrates the unknown. They are used often in the Bible to help us understand the relationship between God and humans. Some metaphors describing God are Rock, Shepherd, Light, Father, King, and Hen. Because of the beauty and complexity of our relationship with God, many metaphors are needed. Each one shows a different aspect of the relationship, but never the whole relationship. Each metaphor has limitations; there are some things about each that do not apply to our understanding of God.

Take, for example, "God is my Rock." A rock is solid, dependable, unshaken, and unshakable; it protects and is secure. You can build your house on it. God too is solid, dependable, unshaken, and unshakable; He protects and is secure. You can build your life on Him. But there are ways in which God is not like a rock. He is not hard, unfeeling, cold, and totally unaware that we are even there. Unlike a rock, He is warm and caring. A metaphor has the strength of rapid communication and quick perception. But we must be discerning or it could be misunderstood.

Here's another example: "The Lord is my Shepherd." Our Good Shepherd is our provider, protector, and leader. He guides us and, if necessary, He will rescue us. But there are ways in which the Lord is not like a shepherd. We don't put our brightest students out in the fields with the sheep and goats. And the young shepherds who watch animals in the bush all day aren't the most informed about current events. In contrast to that, Jesus, our Shepherd, is very clever and fully aware of current events. Some things are true about shepherds that are true of God, and others are not. We must distinguish carefully in order to appreciate the value of the metaphor and apply only the applicable aspects.

One metaphor that is found repeatedly throughout the Bible has been largely, if not entirely, overlooked. The reason for this may be that it could lead to misunderstanding the relationship between ourselves and God. This is the metaphor of God as our Husband and Lover. He loves us very much. A close relationship with Him is satisfying and produces fruit.

But the physical aspect of human intimacy is totally absent in our relationship with God. To think our relationship with God had anything to do with sensual or sexual matters would be a gross misconstruction.

Misconceptions about the meanings of words can produce serious misunderstandings. The word *intercourse*, for example, is usually linked with sex. However, its broader meaning refers to the voluntary mutual exchange of words, goods, or ideas that produces new benefits. For instance, social intercourse produces friendships, academic intercourse produces richer understandings, and commercial intercourse produces exchanges of goods. Sexual intercourse produces physical pleasure and children. Prayer is spiritual interaction (intercourse) with God. It produces creativity, the fruit of the Spirit, spiritual offspring, and great ongoing satisfaction.

The word for "knowledge" or "to know" in the Old Testament is *yada*. This same word in the Hebrew language is used to indicate physical intimacy between a man and wife. Adam knew Eve, and Cain was born. Abraham knew Sarah, and Isaac was born. The same word is used in this verse: "Knowledge of the Holy One is understanding" (Proverbs 9:10).

> **As a result of times of intimacy with the Father, God — the Holy One — gives us understanding.**

To appreciate the metaphor of God as our Husband, we must understand that knowing God goes much deeper than any physical experience. "To the pure, all things are pure, but to those who are corrupted and do not believe, nothing is pure. In fact, both their minds and consciences are corrupted" (Titus 1:15).

In order to properly understand God's desire for spiritual intimacy, relational fidelity, and personal faithfulness in a close relationship with Him, let us attempt to correctly understand the metaphor of God as our Husband.

Some religions in the past, like Canaanite cults, used sex as a part of worship. Some religions in the present do the same, such as the worship of Kali in Calcutta, India. This is clear from the temple prostitution that surrounds "worship" in those religions. The Bible-believing Christian will have none of that.

Many times, we do not know what to do with the challenges we face. Our creativity runs dry. We face complex questions and problems and do not have the answers or solutions. We must preach, but do not know what to say. We must instruct, but do not know what to teach. In those times, we need the understanding that comes from being intimate with God. As a result of times of intimacy with the Father, God — the Holy One — gives us understanding. This is the central benefit we will discuss in this chapter: the fruitfulness of being intimate with God.

Hosea's Marriage Is a Metaphor

The message of the book of Hosea is that Israel committed idolatry, turning her back on the one true God and following after other gods. God's faithful love for Israel was illustrated by Hosea's patient behavior with his wayward wife. He repeatedly welcomed her back. Hosea is a picture of God as the loving, patient, waiting, and forgiving husband to whom Israel and we should return.

God told Hosea to marry a harlot. "When the Lord began to speak through Hosea, the Lord said to him, 'Go, marry a promiscuous woman and have children with her, for like an adulterous wife this land is guilty of unfaithfulness to the Lord.' So he married Gomer daughter of Diblaim, and she conceived and bore him a son" (Hosea 1:2-3).

God's message to Israel, illustrated by Hosea's marriage, was, "You have broken your marriage vows."

Hosea said to Israel, "Rebuke your mother, rebuke her, for she is not my wife, and I am not her husband. Let her remove the adulterous look from her face and the unfaithfulness from between her breasts. Otherwise I will strip her naked and make her as bare as on the day she was born; I will make her like a desert, turn her into a parched land, and slay her with thirst" (Hosea 2:2-3).

Israel's Husband was God, and Hosea predicted she would return to Him. "She will chase after her lovers but not catch them. Then she will say, 'I will go back to my husband as at first, for then I was better off than now'" (Hosea 2:7).

Hosea illustrates God's faithfulness even when He was rejected. In obedience to God, he bought unfaithful Gomer back and loved her again.

> The Lord said to me, "Go, show your love to your wife again, though she is loved by another and is an adulteress. Love her as the Lord loves the Israelites, though they turn to other gods and love the sacred raisin cakes." So I bought her for fifteen shekels of silver and about a homer and a lethek of barley. Then I told her, "You are to live with me many days; you must not be a prostitute or be intimate with any man, and I will behave the same way toward you." (Hosea 3:1-3)

Imagine brokenhearted Hosea pleading for his wayward wife to return to the security, provision, and faithful love he offered her. "Come home to me, sweetheart. Those other men don't really love you, respect you, or care about you. They are just using you. But the children and I love you and miss you. Let's have a happy family again. I will take care of you. " This is a touching picture of God pleading for us to return to Him and to the security, provision, and faithfulness He offers. His love for us is great, and He desires to forgive us and welcome us back to Him.

God repeatedly brought His charges against Israel:

> They will eat but not have enough; they will engage in prostitution but not increase, because they have deserted the Lord to give themselves to prostitution; old wine and new wine take away their understanding. My people consult a wooden idol and are answered by a stick of wood. A spirit of prostitution leads them astray; they are unfaithful to their God. They sacrifice on the mountaintops and burn offerings on the hills, under oak, poplar and terebinth, where the shade is pleasant. Therefore your daughters turn to prostitution and your daughters-in-law to adultery. (Hosea 4:10-13)

Hosea predicted that God would judge Israel, His unfaithful wife. "They are unfaithful to the Lord; they give birth to illegitimate children. When they celebrate their New Moon feasts, he will devour their fields" (Hosea 5:7).

God intended to marry His people. "I will betroth you to me forever; I will betroth you in righteousness and justice, in love and compassion. I will betroth you in faithfulness, and you will acknowledge the Lord" (Hosea 2:19-20).

"I will plant her for myself in the land; I will show my love to the one I called 'Not my loved one.' I will say to those called 'Not my people,' 'You are my people": and they will say, 'You are my God'" (Hosea 2:23).

An attitude of prostitution takes people away from God. "A spirit of prostitution leads them away; they are unfaithful to their God" (Hosea 4:12)." A spirit of prostitution is in their heart; they do not acknowledge the Lord" (Hosea 5:4). The proper way to relate to our true Lover and Husband is to enjoy spiritual intimacy with Him, not embracing other ideologies or attractions.

But Israel was intent on going after other lovers. "They have gone up to Assyria like a wild donkey wandering alone. Ephraim has sold herself to lovers" (Hosea 8:9).

Israel was so calloused in their spirits that they were unaware of, or at least insensitive to, the hurt they were causing their offended Lover. "Do not rejoice, Israel; do not be jubilant like the other nations. For you have been unfaithful to your God; you love the wages of a prostitute at every threshing floor" (Hosea 9:1).

> "The proper way to relate to our true Lover and Husband is to enjoy spiritual intimacy with Him, not embracing other ideologies or attractions."

If Israel would return to her God, Hosea said that the previous metaphor of Master would be replaced by the metaphor of Husband. "'In that day,' declares the Lord, 'you will call me "my husband"; you will no longer call me "my master"'" (Hosea 2:16).

The Metaphor of God as Husband Elevates the Role of Physical Intimacy in Marriage

God is practical. He often uses something good to teach about something else that is good. Sex, correctly understood and experienced, was originally pure. And it still can be. God created the human race in such a way that love, moral character, intimacy, and fidelity are built into the marriage relationship. This union does not only coincidentally or secondarily illustrate our relationship with God. The marriage relationship was originally *created* in order to provide a suitable metaphor to illustrate our association with God.

God could have made the human race capable of reproduction in nonpersonal ways. Fish, for example, do not even have physical contact. The male spreads sperm on eggs laid on the river or ocean bottom. But God draws married partners together in heart, mind, and soul. Physical contact, pleasure, and satisfaction are important aspects of human marriage. Furthermore, between occasions of physical contact in lovemaking are periods of contentment, pleasant memories, and joyful anticipation.

Genesis 2:18 says, "The Lord God said, 'It is not good for the man to be alone. I will make a helper suitable for him.'" God initiated marriage. Many things in the natural world are illustrations of some aspect of God's greatness. Why shouldn't marriage, including the act of intimacy, illustrate something abstract that is even more profound than the concrete action, pleasures, satisfaction, and fruitfulness of marriage? Marriage is good. Physical contact is good. God made it so.

> "God has more to say in the Song of Solomon than that a king loved a shepherdess."

The Song of Solomon is a love story between a king and a shepherdess. But there is a deeper layer to the understanding of that book. God has more to say in the Song of Solomon than that a king loved a shepherdess. This poem uses graphic sexual and sensual expressions to communicate a message about God's love for us and our loving responses to Him.

> "His left arm is under my head and his right arm embraces me" (Song of Solomon 2:6).

> "Your lips drop sweetness as the honeycomb, my bride; milk and honey are under your tongue" (Song of Solomon 4:11).

> "Your stature is like that of the palm, and your breasts like clusters of fruit. I said, 'I will climb the palm tree; I will take hold of its fruit. May your breasts be like clusters of grapes on the vine, the fragrance of your breath like apples, and your mouth like the best wine.' (She responds by saying:) 'May the wine go straight to my beloved, flowing gently over lips and teeth'" (Song of Solomon 7:7-9).

The Bible uses the experiences enjoyed by happily married spouses to illustrate God's love. That says something about the correctness and purity of lovemaking.

Sex is pleasurable and beneficial for far more than just procreative purposes. It includes intense and satisfying mutual pleasure between two married persons. The sensual expressions used in the Song of Solomon demonstrate the legitimacy of enjoying sexual intercourse in marriage. God would not have used physical lovemaking to illustrate intense mutual love between God and humans if lovemaking were bad or evil.

Husbands and wives are taught in Scripture to considerately and lovingly meet their spouses' sexual needs. First Corinthians 7:2-5 says:

> Since sexual immorality is occurring, each man should have sexual relations with his own wife, and each woman with her own husband. The husband should fulfill his marital duty to his wife, and likewise the wife to her husband. The wife does not have authority over her own body but yields it to her husband. In the same way, the husband does not have authority over his own body but yields it to his wife. Do not deprive each other except perhaps by mutual consent and for a time, so that you may devote yourselves to prayer. Then come together again so that Satan will not tempt you because of your lack of self-control.

If the human marriage relationship is a metaphorical illustration of intimacy with God, the relationship should not be one of use, abuse, or conquest. Rather, it will unselfishly focus on the happiness and contentment of the other party. The husband who is only concerned about his own physical gratification is selfish. He should proceed at a slow, gentle pace so that his wife is fulfilled as well as he is. When husbands lovingly, gently fondle and caress their wives so that their wives are fully satisfied, both partners benefit. The husband gets pleasure from the fulfillment of his manhood, and the wife benefits from the experience so much she wants it again and again.

We are to be happy with our mates and celebrate the attraction of our spouses' physical bodies. Here is the easiest verse in the Bible to obey: "May you rejoice in the wife of your youth. A loving doe, a graceful deer — may her breasts satisfy you always, may you ever be intoxicated with her love" (Proverbs 5:18-19). This enjoyment is real. It also symbolizes a rich spiritual truth about God.

Whoever has a wife is blessed. Proverbs 18:22 says, "He who finds a wife finds what is good and receives favor from the Lord."

Physical intimacy in marriage is sheer joy, without any stain or impurity. Hebrews 13:4 says, "Marriage should be honored by all, and the marriage bed kept pure, for God will judge the adulterer and all the sexually immoral" (Hebrews 13:4). This verse is often translated as a command, but Greek grammar allows that it could accurately be translated as a statement. In that case, the "should be" would be replaced by "is." Then it would be rendered, "Marriage is honored by all and the marriage bed pure." The statement is stronger than the command. The command requires us to do something; the statement affirms a truth.

God wants the human race to produce children to populate the earth. This too is part of the goodness of sex in marriage. Genesis 1:28 says, "Be fruitful and increase in number." Adam and Eve were instructed to have children, evidently lots of them.

In sexual intercourse, each married partner has the opportunity to give the most intense and exciting physical human experience possible to the mate they love. Married partners can be drawn closer together through this experience. Similarly in times of reflection, we appreciate the spiritual lessons that can be learned about God.

The aspects of satisfaction and fruitfulness in physical human intimacy are both part of the metaphor symbolizing our intimate union with God, our Lover and Husband. God uses the most stimulating human experience possible to demonstrate His great desire for a close relationship with us.

In order to fully appreciate this line of thought, we must avoid concepts of lust, evil, misuse, abuse, and selfishness in sex. Only in innocence, purity, holiness, and discovery can we enjoy marital intimacy in all the grandeur, holiness, and mutual satisfaction God intended. In such a relationship, there is no embarrassment, shame, or holding back.

The misuse of sex as a conquest or seduction outside of marriage is a violation of the marriage vow and an illustration of idolatry. God hates both. Let's flee from the disgrace, humiliation, guilt, and regrets inherent in illicit sex. Do not conform to the outside world, but be transformed by the renewing of your mind by the Holy Spirit from within (see Romans 12:2).

The satisfaction and security of loving and being loved endures during the time between incidents of intimacy. This is true in human marriage and in our relationship with God. We become "intoxicated with ... love" (Proverbs 5:19). Having a good marriage relationship helps us understand our relationship with God better.

The Metaphor of God as Husband Teaches the Fruitfulness of Intimacy with God

Jesus taught us to get alone with the Father in prayer. "When you pray, go into your room" (Matthew 6:6). The word for *room* in this verse can be translated "bedchamber." In the privacy of our places of prayer, we can have intimate times of fellowship with God. We can unashamedly pour out our hearts to Him. We can confess all our inner thoughts. God will show us His love. He will comfort us and encourage us. He will give us creative ideas that enable us to produce things for Him that look like Him.

Paul refers to the beginning of this wonderful relationship by referring to marriage. "I am jealous for you with a godly jealousy. I promised you to one husband, to Christ, so that I might present you as a pure virgin to him" (2 Corinthians 11:2).

As a result of spending intimate time with God in prayer, worship, and fellowship, His creative ideas fill our hearts. These thoughts eventually come to fruition. But even before they do, the ideas in our spirits make us more prone to behave in ways pleasing to Him and less likely to yield to temptation.

I wondered for many years why John referred to God's "seed" being in us. Understanding the metaphor of God as Husband enables us to comprehend another dimension of the truth. Notice the vocabulary John uses to express that God's life is in His own. "Those who are born of God will not continue to sin, because *God's seed remains in them*; they cannot go on sinning, because they have been born of God" (1 John 3:9, emphasis mine).

The usual interpretation of the above verse centers on the sonship aspect of our relationship with God. This interpretation of *seed* communicates the fact that born-again Christians have His genes: He has given us His nature, and we are His offspring. What we produce will then be an extension of His life and creative energy. He is our Father; we are His sons and daughters. His life, energy, and life-giving power are in us.

The Word of God is rich. It can have multiple interpretations and applications, and each of them communicates a valuable truth. I suggest that there is a second sense in which His vivacity, being, energy, and revitalizing power is maintained and increased. His life in us is also illustrated by a metaphor that emphasizes continuing intimacy. Closeness with Him is vital. Spending time alone with God in prayer is necessary to continually replenish that creativity and invigorating power we received as God's sons and daughters. Sonship *creates* His life in us; intimacy in prayer *maintains* it. Intimacy with God in prayer allows His life to dwell deep within our spirits. It makes us fruitful so we are able to pass life on to others as we minister to them.

> Being saturated with God's ideas in our spirits can help us resist the attraction of any would-be suitors.

God's seed — His life-producing and creative energy in us — acts as a preventative to sin. When we are filled with God's life, we don't want or need any other. Intimacy with God produces resistance to sin; we do not want to offend the Lover with whom we spend intimate time. Being saturated with God's ideas in our spirits can help us resist the attraction of any would-be suitors.

Just as "satisfaction" in adultery is short-lived, shallow, and guilt-ridden, so is the dissatisfaction of idolatry. The relationship with our divine Husband is satisfying. No other lover offers this.

God, our strong Soldier Husband, saves us, loves us, and sings joyfully over us. "The Lord your God is with you, the Mighty Warrior who saves. He will take great delight in you; in his love he will no longer rebuke you, but will rejoice over you with singing" (Zephaniah 3:17). Just as a husband sings of his love to his wife, so God sings over us. Even though I have been married to Char since April 1969, I still sing romantic songs to her. I want to keep our marriage fresh, romantic, and exciting. God, our Husband, is so in love with us He rejoices over us with love songs.

When Jesus came to earth and died for us, He came to find, win, and purchase His bride with His own blood. Envision His life on earth as a proposal for marriage. "Will you marry Me? I will die for you. Will you be My bride?" If you say yes, the Father and Son will shout with joy at the marriage supper of the Lamb. "To him who is able to keep you from stumbling and to present you before his glorious presence without fault and with great joy ..." (Jude 1:24). Jesus says to the Father, "I have bought her with my blood. Isn't she beautiful?"

The saints of God in the New Jerusalem are the bride of the Lamb. "Let us rejoice and be glad and give him glory! For the wedding of the Lamb has come, and his bride has made herself ready" (Revelation 19:7). "One of the seven angels who had the seven bowls full of the seven last plagues came and said to me, 'Come, I will show you the bride, the wife of the Lamb'" (Revelation 21:9). No one person is individually married to Jesus; collectively we all make up the bride of Christ. On that great day, we all will be the marriage partner in the greatest wedding and longest-lasting happy relationship imaginable. There is nothing non-masculine about being a part of that joyful and celebrating crowd.

Meanwhile, we become fruitful for God here on earth as a result of being intimate with Him. We are filled with His ideas and bear fruit for Him. Believers have God's life-giving, creative seed in them. God's seed symbolizes new life, energy, creative ideas, visions, hopes, and understanding. It is right for us to want God to saturate us with His thoughts. Intimacy with God is worth seeking, and it is productive. When we have been intimate with God, the productive dreams and life-giving energy of God permeate our being. After the gestation period is over and the idea He planted in us has been born, we find the offspring looks amazingly like Him, while it also looks like us. The divine and the human have partnered. The project has God's fingerprints all over it. It is a work of art that God produced.

Yet that fruit was borne out by us. Our sermons, teachings, and writings — though planted in our spirits by God — have our likeness on them too. Our personalities and vocabularies are not overlooked. The "children" look and sound like us. So when God produces through you a good sermon or Bible lesson or any other product of godly fruitfulness, do not compare your "child" with another's. Your prophecy or Bible lesson will have your personality in it. This is as it should be. Be fruitful and multiply. Produce many good projects for God.

The Metaphor of God as Husband Demonstrates God's Jealousy

Hosea is not the only prophet who uses this metaphor. Isaiah says, "As a young man marries a young woman, so will your Builder marry you; as a bridegroom rejoices over his bride, so will your God rejoice over you" (Isaiah 62:5).

Jeremiah adds, "I remember the devotion of your youth, how as a bride you loved me" (Jeremiah 2:2). Then notice the change in Jeremiah 2:23-25: "You are a swift she-camel running here and there, a wild donkey accustomed to the desert, sniffing the wind in her craving — in her heat who can restrain her? Any males that pursue her need not tire themselves; at mating time they will find her. Do not run until your feet are bare and your throat is dry. But you said, 'It's no use! I love foreign gods, and I must go after them.'"

Jerusalem is the adulterous wife in Ezekiel's imagery. It illustrates that idolatry is spiritual adultery — being unfaithful to our divine Lover and Husband. Ezekiel 16, especially verses 25 and 26, is graphic. "At every street corner you built your lofty shrines and degraded your beauty, spreading your legs with increasing promiscuity to anyone who passed by. You engaged in prostitution with the Egyptians, your neighbors with large genitals, and aroused my anger with your increasing promiscuity."

We do not know fully now the nature of the intimacy that is possible with God, but we can and should seek to be intimate with Him. After all, God initiates the offer of intimacy; let us not spurn His gift.

Loving anything more than we love God is foolish and counterproductive. God is very loving and very jealous.

Different cultures have different representations to symbolize loyalty in marriage. For example, long hair in Corinth (1 Corinthians 11:2-16), wedding rings in the West, and leather skirts in parts of Africa. To honor our marriage to God, we should figuratively keep our hair long, wear our wedding rings, and keep our skirts down and our legs together. In other words, we will do everything necessary to show by our attitude and behavior that we are faithful to our Lover. "Do not love the world or anything in the world. If you love the world, love for the Father is not in you" (1 John 2:15). We will not love the world or the things in the world; we will be loyal to our divine Husband.

Everyone understands a jilted husband's jealousy. While customs of courtship, wedding practices, and marriage laws vary in each culture, the justified anger and hurt that a betrayed spouse feels is understood and recognized in them all. If idolatry is like adultery, anyone, in any culture, can readily understand what God feels when we commit idolatry.

> "If idolatry is like adultery, anyone, in any culture, can readily understand what God feels when we commit idolatry."

In the lobby of a hotel in Antananarivo, Madagascar, in mid-2004, a pretty prostitute approached me and suggested I should let her be my wife while I was there. I took out my wallet and showed her a picture of Char. I told her, "I am married to the most wonderful and beautiful woman in the world. If you think I would throw this away for a short time with you, you have no idea of the trust and happiness my wife and I enjoy together." Then I walked away. We are to do the same thing when something of the world's system attracts or distracts us from loving God.

Casting idolatry in the framework of spiritual adultery enables us to see how offensive, inappropriate, and hurtful idolatry is and how it breaks God's heart. Our divine Husband weeps over our foolishness in leaving Him, the injury we inflict upon ourselves as a result, and His own loss of someone He loves dearly.

This Metaphor Is Fully Developed in Christ and His Church

Paul the apostle joins other Bible writers to teach about our relationship with God by using the metaphor of marriage. Lessons about Christ and the Church can also explain the relationship between husband and wife.

> Submit to one another out of reverence for Christ. Wives, submit yourselves to your own husbands as you do to the Lord. For the husband is the head of the wife as Christ is the head of the

church, his body, of which he is the Savior. Now as the church submits to Christ, so also wives should submit to their husbands in everything.

Husbands, love your wives, just as Christ loved the church and gave himself up for her to make her holy, cleansing her by the washing with water through the word, and to present her to himself as a radiant church, without stain or wrinkle or any other blemish, but holy and blameless. In this same way, husbands ought to love their wives as their own bodies. He who loves his wife loves himself. After all, people have never hated their own bodies, but they feed and care for them, just as Christ does the church — for we are members of his body. (Ephesians 5:21-30)

In Paul's treatment of marriage, he uses Jesus and the Church to illustrate the obligations each partner has. Jesus gave Himself for the Church. The Church responds by submitting, obeying, and cooperating with Him as Savior, Lord, and Leader. Likewise, the husband is to give himself for his wife — nourishing her, encouraging her, caring for her, and bearing burdens for her. Following Jesus' example, he takes responsibility to help solve problems instead of blaming her for them.

Paul uses each relationship to illustrate the other. The husband-and-wife relationship helps us understand the relationship between Christ and the Church. Jesus gives Himself for her and the Church submits to His leadership. The relationship illustrates how husbands and wives should relate to each other.

Christ and the Church are united, and the husband and his wife are united. "'For this reason will a man leave his father and mother and be united to his wife, and the two will become one flesh.' This is a profound mystery — but I am talking about Christ and the church. However, each one of you also must love his wife as he loves himself, and the wife must respect her husband" (Ephesians 5:31-33). Husbands are to love their wives as they love themselves and as Christ loves the Church. The Lord loves us as He loves Himself. How awesome is that? All of the redeemed beloved of God are privileged to be intimate with their divine Husband.

For too long, we have avoided using this metaphor in an understandable but unnecessary effort to avoid possible confusion. My hope is that raising these delicate subjects may open your mind more fully to the challenge to know God at ever deeper levels. Knowledge of Him is understanding, and many are the times when we need understanding.

If we neglect the metaphor of God as Husband, we miss part of the biblical emphasis on love, satisfaction, and creativity as a result of intimacy with Him. On the other hand, if we overly focus on it and confuse worship and sex, we risk a horrible misinterpretation of worship. Some non-Christian religions make this mistake when they encourage temple prostitution.

Jesus will return in the clouds one day to take His bride away to celebrate the marriage supper of the Lamb. After, that we will live with Him forever in the house He is now preparing for us. You'll never find a more romantic love story than that.

For Further Thought

- Has God ever asked you to do something in your life to illustrate spiritual truth to those around you?
- In what way would you like to improve your relationship with your spouse as a result of this chapter?
- What does it mean to you that God planted His life in you when you were born again and now maintains and increases it through your intimate relationship with Him?
- How has the idea of a romantic God impressed you?
- In what way do you plan to increase intimacy with God and experience greater fruitfulness?
- How do marital fidelity and adultery help us understand how much God loves us?
- How does Jesus' treatment of the church exemplify the way husbands should treat their wives?

CHAPTER 21
MARY

Did you realize that Mary was almost surely not revered in her generation as she is today? Did you know that Mary, even early in life, was probably not a giddy, silly girl, but a thinker? You may be surprised to learn that Mary would never have been able to marry Joseph if God had not intervened.

Mary's life teaches us some of the most profound lessons that can be learned from a human being. She yielded herself to God's plan for her, even among the myriad of questions that filled her young, thoughtful mind. She wondered about the mysterious meaning of the events that developed around and within her. Her willingness to obey and trust God with the unsolvable mysteries and irreconcilable contradictions of her life is a wonderful example for us to follow. In what ways are you like Mary? In what ways are you unlike her?

The Bible tells us to meditate — think on — the Word of God. The narratives of Mary repeatedly tell us that she "pondered" and "treasured" what she observed and heard. Viewing Mary as a reflective and contemplative person can help us appreciate why she was willing to experience the sword that pierced her soul.

Mary Willingly Subjected Herself to Potential Ridicule and Scorn

> In the sixth month of Elizabeth's pregnancy, God sent the angel Gabriel to Nazareth, a town in Galilee, to a virgin pledged to be married to a man named Joseph, a descendant of David. The

virgin's name was Mary. The angel went to her and said, "Greetings, you who are highly favored! The Lord is with you."

Mary was greatly troubled at his words and wondered what kind of greeting this might be. But the angel said to her, "Do not be afraid, Mary, you have found favor with God. You will conceive and give birth to a son, and you are to call him Jesus. He will be great and will be called the Son of the Most High. The Lord God will give him the throne of his father David, and he will reign over the house of Jacob forever; his kingdom will never end."

"How will this be," Mary asked the angel, "since I am a virgin?"

The angel answered, "The Holy Spirit will come on you, and the power of the Most High will overshadow you. So the holy one to be born will be called the Son of God. Even Elizabeth your relative is going to have a child in her old age, and she who was said to be unable to conceive is in her sixth month. For no word from God will ever fail."

"I am the Lord's servant," Mary answered. "May it be to me according to your word." Then the angel left her. (Luke 1:26–38)

God had promised that a virgin would be with child and give the world a Savior. This presented a practical problem, however. What married woman remains a virgin? And even if she remained a virgin, who would believe it? So God could not have used a married person. An unmarried person perhaps? If an unwed woman produced a child, the child would be labeled a bastard and she a promiscuous woman. What kind of reputation or living situation would that be from which to present a Savior to the world? Who in those days, besides Hosea who married a harlot because God told him to, would marry and care for a woman who had a child out of wedlock? How was God going to find a virgin willing to be the mother of the Savior? So our all-wise God found an engaged, but not yet married, virgin. Her name was Mary.

> "What married woman remains a virgin? And even if she remained a virgin, who would believe it?"

Perhaps "May it be to me according to your word" was her motto. If it had not already been, perhaps it became her slogan from that day forward. It certainly was her practice.

Besides the fact that she was talking with a celestial creature, Mary had a more profound reason to be greatly troubled and afraid. Tradition says she was about sixteen years of age. The Bible gives us enough information to know that she valued her reputation as a virtuous woman. How could she live in disgrace, guilt, or the perceived guilt of fornication? She was a virgin. She had kept herself pure and holy. Had she been a careless or reckless woman, she would not have cared about that. But she had not been careless, and she did care about that. What would her family think? Would her father publicly disgrace her? What about the neighbors? What would her girlfriends think? What would the young men in Nazareth think? How could she possibly face the public again once the news of her pregnancy got out? Whatever reputation she developed would be with her for life, and she knew it.

But in obedience and trust, she abandoned all her good reasons for caution. She submitted herself to the word of the Lord spoken to her through the angel. Had the angel not said that "no word from God will ever fail"? She was willing, but what would Joseph think? We don't know the depth of her friendship with him at that time. Had their marriage been arranged? We only know she had agreed to marry him.

God Spoke Supernaturally to Joseph on Her Behalf

> This is how the birth of Jesus the Messiah came about: His mother Mary was pledged to be married to Joseph, but before they came together, she was found to be pregnant through the Holy Spirit. Because Joseph her husband was a righteous man and did not want to expose her to public disgrace, he had in mind to divorce her quietly.
>
> But after he had considered this, an angel of the Lord appeared to him in a dream and said, "Joseph son of David, do not be afraid to take Mary home as your wife, because what is conceived in her is from the Holy Spirit. She will give birth to a son, and you are to give him the name Jesus, because he will save his people from their sins."

All this took place to fulfill what the Lord had said through the prophet: "The virgin will conceive and give birth to a son, and they will call him Immanuel" (which means "God with us").

When Joseph woke up, he did what the angel of the Lord had commanded him and took Mary home as his wife. But he had no union with her until she gave birth to a son. And he gave him the name Jesus. (Matthew 1:18-25)

Joseph would share Mary's risk. Apparently he cared for her, for he had asked her to marry him. The Scripture says he was not willing to embarrass or disgrace her. He had the true picture from heaven's messenger, and whatever people thought would not be as important as obeying God. So with great relief, he went to Mary with the comforting words of the angel's message to him. Together, the couple would carry their burden, endure whatever hardships became necessary, and provide emotional support to each other.

Mary Saw the Bigger Picture

The angel told Mary that her cousin Elizabeth was in her sixth month of pregnancy (Luke 1:36). After making the trip to the hill country of Judea to visit her, Mary stayed with Elizabeth for about three months (Luke 1:56). Evidently, Mary stayed with Elizabeth until just before or until the birth of John the Baptist. Not much time could have passed between Mary receiving her announcement about Jesus and her trip to visit Elizabeth. Scripture says, "*At that time* Mary got ready and *hurried* to a town in the hill country of Judea where she entered Zechariah's home and greeted Elizabeth" (Luke 1:39-40, emphasis mine).

She didn't have much time to reflect on the news that she would give birth to the Son of God and Savior of the world. But when this teenage girl arrived at Elizabeth's house, she uttered a song of praise with amazingly rich content, depth of understanding, and breadth of insight. Mary said:

> My soul glorifies the Lord and my spirit rejoices in God my Savior, for he has been mindful of the humble state of his servant. From now on all generations will call me blessed, for the Mighty One has done great things for me — holy is his name. His mercy extends to those who fear him, from generation to generation. He

has performed *mighty deeds* with his arm; he has *scattered those who are proud* in their inmost thoughts. He has *brought down rulers* from their thrones but has *lifted up the humble*. He has *filled the hungry* with good things but has *sent the rich away empty*. He has helped his servant Israel, remembering to be merciful to Abraham and his descendants forever, just as he promised our ancestors. (Luke 1:46–55, emphasis mine).

No ordinary teenage girl in Nazareth would have the lofty thoughts that came from Mary's heart to her mouth. God had done mighty things. He would lift some and lower others. The proud would be scattered. All generations would be influenced. The rich would be sent away empty, and the poor would be filled with good things.

> **No ordinary teenage girl in Nazareth would have the lofty thoughts that came from Mary's heart to her mouth.**

Mary attended synagogue on Sabbath days. She listened and learned. She did not flirt with the boys, giggle with the girls, or daydream as the rabbi taught from the Scriptures week after week. Mary knew the promises of God, and she understood the importance of her role. She was not preoccupied with her own subjective reflections about what it would be like to be a mother so soon and what people might think.

The accurate portrayal of rich theological content in Mary's song is astonishing. How could a layperson understand these profound truths — especially a young girl in a society in which women were not educated at the same level with men? She either spoke as a prophetess or she was an exceptionally informed and intelligent young woman who clearly understood the promises of God to her ancestors and knew that those promises were about to be fulfilled. She was no common scatterbrained teenager. God chose well.

Mary Was Warned of Personal Suffering

Months after the angel's announcement, Joseph and Mary went to Bethlehem for tax-registration purposes. Jesus was born while they were there. Shepherds visited, with their story of the angels' announcement and songs of praise on the hillside below. The contemplative and intelligent Mary took to heart all these supernatural events. "But Mary treasured up all these things and pondered them in her heart" (Luke 2:19).

A religious rite was performed within a few days. "When the time came for the purification rites required by the Law of Moses, Joseph and Mary took him to Jerusalem to present him to the Lord" (Luke 2:22). In the temple, Mary was warned of impending sorrows. "Simeon blessed them and said to Mary, 'This child is destined to cause the falling and rising of many in Israel, and to be a sign that will be spoken against, so that the thoughts of many hearts will be revealed. And a sword will pierce your own soul too'" (Luke 2:34-35).

Simeon, a Jerusalem citizen, had received the promise that he would see the Messiah before he died. If he studied the Scriptures, he may have known the Messiah would cause people to stumble and fall (Isaiah 8:14) and save the weak and needy (Psalm 72:13). Perhaps he understood that the stone rejected would become the cornerstone (Psalm 118:22). But would young Mary from Nazareth have known that her Son was the One who would be either a stepping-stone — lifting some from sin to forgiveness and acceptance with the Father — or a stumbling stone that would dash the proud hopelessly to the ground? Might Mary have wanted to ask about this, but held back? The eternal destiny of every person on earth would be determined by what they decided to do with her Son, Jesus. She may have also wondered what it meant that a sword would pierce her heart.

Mary, Joseph, and Jesus Received Supernatural Provision and Protection

After the trip of six miles (ten kilometers) to Jerusalem for the purification rites and circumcision, the family evidently returned to Bethlehem. They were no longer in the stable by the time the magi arrived; they were in a house. And Jesus was no longer an infant, but a child. "On coming to the house, they saw the child with his mother Mary, and they bowed down and worshiped him. Then they opened their treasures and presented him with gifts of gold, frankincense and myrrh" (Matthew 2:11).

Before Joseph and Mary even knew they would need to make a rush trip to Egypt, God arranged for and delivered their provisions for that trip by using the wealth of others who had made another trip. We know from Scripture that Joseph was not a wealthy man, even though some have speculated that he was. The Old Testament gave instructions as to what to do if someone could not afford a lamb for the purification ceremony (Leviticus 12:8). Joseph and Mary fit the economic category for those who were to bring "a pair of doves, or two young pigeons" (Luke 2:24). The gifts of gold, frankincense, and myrrh were therefore a timely provision. The magi were indirectly responsible for the death threat to the baby Jesus, because they told Herod about the birth of the new king. But their gifts made affordable the escape to Egypt and safety there.

> When they had gone, an angel of the Lord appeared to Joseph in a dream. "Get up," he said, "take the child and his mother and escape to Egypt. Stay there until I tell you, for Herod is going to search for the child to kill him."
>
> So he got up, took the child and his mother during the night and left for Egypt, where he stayed until the death of Herod. And so was fulfilled what the Lord had said through the prophet: "Out of Egypt I called my son."
>
> When Herod realized that he had been outwitted by the Magi, he was furious, and he gave orders to kill all the boys in Bethlehem and its vicinity who were two years old and under, in accordance with the time he had learned from the Magi. Then what was said through the prophet Jeremiah was fulfilled: "A voice is heard in Ramah, weeping and great mourning, Rachel weeping for her children and refusing to be comforted, because they are no more."
>
> After Herod died, an angel of the Lord appeared in a dream to Joseph in Egypt and said, "Get up, take the child and his mother and go to the land of Israel, for those who were trying to take the child's life are dead."
>
> So he got up, took the child and his mother and went to the land of Israel. But when he heard that Archelaus was reigning in Judea in place of his father Herod, he was afraid to go there. Having been warned in a dream, he withdrew to the district of Galilee, and he went and lived in a town called Nazareth. So was fulfilled

what was said through the prophets: "He will be called a Nazarene." (Matthew 2:13-23)

> "Safely in Egypt, Mary, Joseph, and little Jesus had no fear of Herod's soldiers."

Safely in Egypt, Mary, Joseph, and little Jesus had no fear of Herod's soldiers. Those tools of a wicked tyrant marched into Bethlehem and other nearby villages. They forcibly entered the homes of Judean families whose only crime was that someone in their family had given birth to a male child near the time of Jesus' birth. One King came to bring life abundant, and the other king lent himself as an instrument to the one who comes to kill, steal, and destroy. The obedient Mary was safe, with her husband and Son, in Egypt.

Mary and Joseph Observed God's Son in His Father's House

Joseph and Mary went to the Passover celebration in Jerusalem each year. When Jesus was twelve years old, He went with them and a revealing incident took place. After the Passover, Joseph and Mary assumed that Jesus was among the other children walking with the families on their way back to Nazareth. But they could not find Jesus at the end of the day. They looked for Him for a day and concluded He must still be in Jerusalem. It took another day to get back to Jerusalem. This would explain why they searched for Him for three days before finding Him.

> After three days they found him in the temple courts, sitting among the teachers, listening to them and asking them questions. Everyone who heard him was amazed at his understanding and his answers. When his parents saw him, they were astonished. His mother said to him, "Son, why have you treated us like this: your father and I have been anxiously searching for you." (Luke 2:48)

Jesus' response was "Why were you searching for me? ... Didn't you know I had to be in my Father's house?" (Luke 2:49). Even though Joseph and Mary did not understand what Jesus was saying to them, Mary, the thinker, pondered it.

Then he went down to Nazareth with them and was obedient to

them. But his mother treasured all these things in her heart. And as Jesus grew up, he increased in wisdom and in favor with God and people. (Luke 2:51-52)

Years later, Mary's attitude and behavior indicate that as a result of her treasuring and pondering, she reached a solid conclusion regarding the supernatural role Jesus was to fulfill. She knew her conclusion was right. The time would eventually arrive for her to go public with her belief in the uniqueness of the Child she had borne.

Mary Refused to be Insulted and Gave Good Advice at Cana

Almost thirty years after the carpenter and his little family returned to Nazareth, Jesus began His public ministry. The young man attracted a lot of attention in the Galilean region.

> On the third day a wedding took place at Cana in Galilee. Jesus' mother was there, and Jesus and his disciples had also been invited to the wedding. When the wine was gone, Jesus' mother said to him, "They have no more wine."
>
> "Woman, why do you involve me?" Jesus replied. "My hour has not yet come."
>
> His mother said to the servants, "Do whatever he tells you." (John 2:1-5)

Why did Jesus seem to distance himself from her? Was it not rather rude for Him to call her "woman," not "mother"? Why did He question her about her involvement with Him? She was His mother, after all. Yet Mary refused to take Jesus' question as an insult.

> ❝Yet her kind advice to the servants at the wedding remains the best advice one can give: 'Do whatever he tells you.'❞

Evidently, Jesus preferred to develop independence from her. Yet her kind advice to the servants at the wedding — "Do whatever he tells you"

(John 2:5) — remains the best advice one can give to anyone within range of hearing the good words of instruction Jesus gives to willing servants.

John was careful to tell us that this miracle was Jesus' first. Up until then, He had done none. "What Jesus did here in Cana of Galilee was the first of the signs through which he revealed his glory; and his disciples put their faith in him" (John 2:11). Extra-biblical literature has a reference to Jesus making clay pigeons as a child and then making them fly. John puts all such nonsense to rest.

If there was no precedent to this miracle, what prompted Mary to think Jesus could or would do anything about the problem of depleted wine supply?

Perhaps Mary spoke far beyond her own understanding about the Messiah within her body at her cousin Elizabeth's house. But that song is consistent with her suggestion to the servants at the wedding at Cana to do whatever Jesus said to do. Mary completely believed that Jesus was the Messiah. She was happy to do whatever she could to promote Him. This godly Jewish mother could not forget her astonishment and reflections when she found her Son at age twelve debating with the scholars in the temple.

After the wedding, Jesus went to Capernaum for awhile. "After this he went down to Capernaum with his mother and brothers and his disciples. There they stayed for a few days" (John 2:12). We don't know what happened there. We only know that soon after that, He returned to Nazareth. He was unable to perform many miracles and had to escape an attempted slaying as the Nazarenes tried to throw Him over a rough, rocky, and steep cliff.

Mary Was Jesus' Mother Biologically and Spiritually

Jesus said that believers have a unique opportunity to be close and intimate with Him if they do the will of the Father. Mary had that same opportunity and took it. By bearing God's Son, Mary was Jesus' mother biologically. By doing the will of the Father, she became His "sister and mother."

> While Jesus was still talking to the crowd, his mother and brothers stood outside, wanting to speak to him. Someone told him, "Your mother and brothers are standing outside, wanting to speak to you."
>
> He replied to him, "Who is my mother, and who are my

brothers?" Pointing to his disciples, he said, "Here are my mother and my brothers. For whoever does the will of my Father in heaven is my brother and sister and mother." (Matthew 12:46-49)

Have you ever wished that you could have lived during the days of Jesus on earth? If you ever thought it would be nice to have heard Jesus teach or to have watched Him perform a miracle, think again. Jesus tells us that any of us can be as close to Him as though we were His brother, sister, or mother. We just need to do the will of the Father. In this sense, I want to be another Mary.

Jesus is willing to be more intimate with us than we might commonly suppose. The same woman who said, "May it be to me according to your word" (Luke 1:38), later advised the servants at Cana to "do whatever he tells you" (John 2:5), and she herself did the will of the Father. Surely she was spiritually close to Him as well.

Mary Also Bore Some of Jesus' Stigma

Nazareth is built on a mountain. For miles, as you travel from Mount Tabor toward the city across the flatlands that lie below the mountain, you can see on its east side an extremely steep and unusually craggy cliff. It is made up of rough and jagged rock, like the sharp points of pencils in a box.

One day, Char and I sat on the top of that cliff and read this story from Scripture:

> Jesus returned to Galilee in the power of the Spirit, and news about him spread through the whole countryside. He was teaching in their synagogues, and everyone praised him.
>
> He went to Nazareth, where he had been brought up, and on the Sabbath day he went into the synagogue, as was his custom. He stood up to read, and the scroll of the prophet Isaiah was handed to him. Unrolling it, he found the place where it is written: "The Spirit of the Lord is on me, because he has anointed me to proclaim good news to the poor. He has sent me to proclaim freedom for the prisoners and recovery of sight for the blind, to set the oppressed free, to proclaim the year of the Lord's favor."
>
> Then he rolled up the scroll, gave it back to the attendant and sat down. The eyes of everyone in the synagogue were fastened on

him. He began by saying to them, "Today this scripture is fulfilled in your hearing."

All spoke well of him and were amazed at the gracious words that came from his lips. "Isn't this Joseph's son?" they asked.

Jesus said to them, "Surely you will quote this proverb to me: 'Physician, heal yourself!' And you will tell me, 'Do here in your hometown what we have heard that you did in Capernaum.'"

"Truly I tell you," he continued, "prophets are not accepted in their hometowns. I assure you that there were many widows in Israel in Elijah's time, when the sky was shut for three and a half years and there was a severe famine throughout the land. Yet Elijah was not sent to any of them, but to a widow in Zarephath in the region of Sidon. And there were many in Israel with leprosy in the time of Elisha the prophet, yet not one of them was cleansed — only Naaman the Syrian."

All the people in the synagogue were furious when they heard this. They got up, drove him out of the town, and took him to the brow of the hill on which the town was built, in order to throw him off the cliff. But he walked right through the crowd and went on his way. (Luke 4:14–30)

> "In failing to recognize Him they removed themselves from the fountain of every blessing."

Was Jesus unnecessarily abrasive in his presentation in Nazareth? Did He know what His townsmen thought about him, so He told the blunt truth? Surely He had good reason for doing what He did and saying what He said. Even the Son of God was limited by their unbelief.

These people lost the opportunity for all the good Jesus could have done for them. In failing to recognize Him, they removed themselves from the fountain of every blessing. Those who reject Jesus harm themselves as they try in vain to shame Jesus.

Mary observed her townspeople reject her Son and, as Simeon of Jerusalem had prophesied, the sword began to pierce her contemplative soul.

Mary Is Visible Near the Cross

> When the centurion and those with him who were guarding Jesus saw the earthquake and all that had happened, they were terrified, and exclaimed, "Surely he was the Son of God!"
>
> Many women were there, watching from a distance. They had followed Jesus from Galilee to care for his needs. Among them were Mary Magdalene, Mary the mother of James and Joseph, and the mother of Zebedee's sons. (Matthew 27:56)

This part of Matthew's record does not say that the second Mary mentioned here was Jesus' mother. But the James and Joseph named in it were evidently half brothers of Jesus. If so, their mother was also Jesus' mother. This is an indirect indication that Jesus' mother was loyally and faithfully watching her Son through to the end.

Jesus' weak, bleeding, and dying body was exposed to public shame on a cruel Roman cross. While He hung painfully on the nails that pierced either His hands or wrists, He lovingly provided care for His mother. John adds to the story:

> Near the cross of Jesus stood his mother, his mother's sister, Mary the wife of Clopas, and Mary Magdalene. When Jesus saw his mother there, and the disciple whom he loved standing nearby, he said to her, "Woman, here is your son," and to the disciple, "Here is your mother." From that time on, this disciple took her into his home. (John 19:25-27)

Mary moved with the grieving crowd from the cross to the burial site at the base of the hill. "Joseph bought some linen cloth, took down the body, wrapped it in the linen, and placed it in a tomb cut out of rock. Then he rolled a stone against the entrance of the tomb. Mary Magdalene and Mary the mother of Joseph saw where he was laid" (Mark 15:46-47). "Mary Magdalene and the other Mary were sitting there opposite the tomb" (Matthew 27:61).

Mary had tenderly lain Jesus' newborn (and possibly bloody) body in cloths in a manger at Bethlehem. It was just six miles south of where

Jesus' friends laid His dead body on the cold, hard stone in the tomb belonging to Joseph of Arimathea. There lay the bloody, wounded, broken, and lifeless Lamb of God. It was not yet time for the Lion of the tribe of Judah to rise with a mighty triumph over death, hell, and the grave. Sorrow filled the air. The sword further pierced Mary's soul.

Mary Was Present on Resurrection Morning and Later in the Upper Room

"After the Sabbath, at dawn on the first day of the week, Mary Magdalene and the other Mary went to look at the tomb" (Matthew 28:1). "When the Sabbath was over, Mary Magdalene, Mary the mother of James, and Salome bought spices" (Mark 16:1). We do not know for certain that Jesus' mother was one of these Marys. But this is not our last image of Mary's involvement with her Son, the Savior of the world.

Our last scriptural picture of Mary suggests that she was numbered among those who celebrated the resurrection. She may have been with the crowd of five hundred who saw the resurrected Jesus (1 Corinthians 15:6). She is recorded as being together with those who waited for the coming of the Holy Spirit in the extended days of prayer in the upper room. It is likely she was among those who listened to the "many convincing proofs" (Acts 1:3), "They all joined together constantly in prayer, along with the women and Mary the mother of Jesus, and with his brothers" (Acts 1:14). This woman of tenacious faith and endurance was still active in the middle of those who were ready to look forward, not backward.

Mary and these fellow believers had felt, seen, known, loved, and touched Him physically and emotionally. Their relationship with Him was now being further perfected as they knew Him spiritually. If anyone had reason to believe Jesus was the Messiah — the Christ — it would be Mary. If anyone believed He was from heaven, it was Mary. And she did.

The sword had pierced her soul. She had known it would. But no longer.

Epilogue

Mary may have been the original source Luke used in his presentation of the life of Christ. With all these rich memories in the heart of this contemplative woman, can you imagine what it would have been like for her to be interviewed by Luke? Luke was a vigilant researcher who systematically conducted his study. He therefore "carefully investigated everything from the beginning" and determined to write "an orderly account." (See Luke 1:3.)

Luke's interview of Mary may well have provided the rich data for the two long and detailed chapters with which Luke begins his gospel. Furthermore, much of the data about Mary reviewed here came from those first two chapters of Luke. Try to envision how the thoughtful Mary would have responded to his queries. Imagine how she related the fine points only she would have known so well — insightful details that now appear for us in Luke's gospel.

> *Mary gave her first-hand report to somebody.*

Whether Luke received his information first-hand from her, or learned her story through secondary sources, is unknown and irrelevant. Mary gave her first-hand report to *somebody*. How vividly she would have given her accurate and personal report. With what conviction she would have relayed her insights into the nature of the human Son of God whom she had conceived and to whom she had given birth. The fact that Mary was a reflective thinking person has benefited all of us.

For Further Thought

- How does Mary's ability to see the bigger picture of God's overall plan encourage you to remain objective in the work of the Lord?
- God warned Mary of future personal suffering. Has He warned you of the same? Are you willing to endure as Mary did?
- Have you ever had an experience like Mary and Joseph in receiving God's miraculous provision even before the need was apparent?
- What are you doing so your children will be about their Father's business as Jesus was?
- Can you resist insults and encourage people to obey Jesus as Mary did at Cana?
- Can you obey God and become close to Jesus — as close as a relative?
- Are you willing to bear the stigma of Jesus as Mary did?
- Will you remain near Jesus even when He is on a cross — even when people are jeering and expressing hatred and ridicule?
- Will you persist in following Jesus through days of darkness and suspense to the resurrection and on to the upper room?
- After reflecting on Mary's deep insights, do you want to change anything in your life so that your answers to any of the above questions will also change?

CHAPTER 22
PETER

Many people do not realize that Peter described the double focus of ministry — prayer and the Word — more clearly than any other disciple. Did you know that Peter had a private lesson from Jesus about cooperation with civil authorities? Are you aware that Jesus gave Peter a message — in front of the other disciples — about humbly receiving ministry from Him?

Peter was Jesus' most outspoken follower. His spontaneous and impetuous statements could have earned the disdain of the other disciples and certainly the open rebuke of Jesus. But Peter was an original thinker. He mellowed over the years to become a gentle, pastoral, and insightful leader in the early church, as well as a thoughtful counselor through his wise letters.

The Peter we see in his epistles appears more refined, astute, and gracious than the Peter portrayed in the Gospels. So the comparison of Peter when Jesus was on earth and Peter's character as revealed in his letters reflects a learning process. What does Peter's life have to say to us today? What does his life say to you?

This chapter does not include a treatment of the story of Peter walking on the water found in Matthew 14. For the many lessons to be learned in that rich drama, I invite you to examine "How to Do the Impossible," Chapter 4 of my book *Rise to Seek Him: The Joy of Effective Prayer*. You may also read the message on the Leadership Empowerment Resources website (www.leresources.com). You can access it by selecting the Seminars tab and then clicking on the link that says "How to Do the Impossible." The book is available at the website also.

Peter Was Called to Follow Jesus and Fish for Men

Following Jesus and fishing for people were at the heart of Peter's original call. "As Jesus was walking beside the Sea of Galilee, he saw two brothers, Simon called Peter and his brother Andrew. They were casting a net into the lake, for they were fishermen. 'Come, follow me,' Jesus said, 'and I will send you out to fish for people'" (Matthew 4:18-19).

In the early years of the church, Peter summarized his apostolic assignment as prayer and ministry of the Word. "In those days when the number of disciples was increasing, the Hellenistic Jews among them complained against the Hebraic Jews because their widows were being overlooked in the daily distribution of food. So the Twelve gathered all the disciples together and said, 'It would not be right for us to neglect the ministry of the word of God in order to wait on tables. Brothers and sisters, choose seven men from among you who are known to be full of the Spirit and wisdom. We will turn this responsibility over to them and *we will give our attention to prayer and the ministry of the word*'" (Acts 6:1-4, emphasis mine).

> **Staying with the specific work God has given each of us benefits everyone.**

Peter later expressed his call as devoting himself to prayer and to the Word. The two parts of this call are:

- Representing people to God and following Jesus by seeking God
- Representing God to people and presenting His Word to them.

These two factors are still central to a call to ministry. It is easy to become distracted from ministry priorities by seemingly legitimate requests for help. Yet God can give us the wisdom to encourage others not to become dependent on us. Staying with the specific work God has given each of us benefits everyone.

Peter Learned from Jesus about Support for Civil Governments

> After Jesus and his disciples arrived in Capernaum, the collectors of the two-drachma temple tax came to Peter and asked, "Doesn't your teacher pay the temple tax?"

"Yes, he does," he replied.

When Peter came into the house, Jesus was the first to speak. "What do you think, Simon?" he asked. "From whom do the kings of the earth collect duty and taxes — from their own children or from others?"

"From others," Peter answered.

"Then the children are exempt," Jesus said to him. "But so that we may not cause offense, go to the lake and throw out your line. Take the first fish you catch; open its mouth and you will find a four-drachma coin. Take it and give it to them for my tax and yours." (Matthew 17:24-27)

Jesus instructed Peter to find a coin in a fish's mouth with which to pay the temple tax. Then He expanded the conversation to include civil taxes. Why did He not just stay with the subject raised by the collectors of the temple tax? It was because this was a learning experience for Peter. And because Matthew recorded it, it is also instruction for us.

God tells us to pay our taxes. "This is also why you pay taxes, for the authorities are God's servants, who give their full time to governing. Give to everyone what you owe: If you owe taxes, pay taxes; if revenue, then revenue; if respect, then respect; if honor, then honor" (Romans 13:6-7). Is it important for Christians to pay their taxes? Is God really concerned about civil government? Yes.

> *Everywhere around the globe Christians who obey the Bible are good citizens of their countries.*

When taxes were owed — even to the hated Romans — they were to be paid. Rome was not generous toward Christians when Paul wrote the book of Romans. But within several centuries, the Christians won the respect of the empire.

Think about how far-reaching and profound this policy is. Christianity can enjoy a good reputation in any nation of the world because of its supportive position toward human government and civil responsibility. Everywhere

Choose Your Character

around the globe, Christians who obey the Bible are good citizens of their countries. What other religion provides its faithful adherents with moral motives for paying taxes?

Peter Learned the Need for Daily Cleansing in the Process of Sanctification

Peter's conversation with Jesus the night He was betrayed gave Peter another opportunity for a private lesson from Jesus.

> He [Jesus] came to Simon Peter, who said to him, "Lord, are you going to wash my feet?"
>
> Jesus replied, "You do not realize now what I am doing, but later you will understand."
>
> "No," said Peter, "you shall never wash my feet."
>
> Jesus answered, "Unless I wash you, you have no part with me."
>
> "Then, Lord," Simon Peter replied, "not just my feet but my hands and my head as well!"
>
> Jesus answered, "Those who have had a bath need only to wash their feet; their whole body is clean. And you are clean, though not every one of you." For he knew who was going to betray him, and that was why he said not every one was clean. (John 13:6–11)

When Jesus tried to wash Peter's feet at the Last Supper, Peter declined the offer at first: "I won't let You wash my feet. I won't let You humble Yourself this way." But when Peter found out that he could not be a part of Jesus without allowing Jesus to wash his feet, Peter reversed his position, saying, "Wash all of me." Jesus insisted that everything need not be washed. This unique conversation is rich in symbolism.

> **"Salvation is efficacious; once is enough. Yet daily travel on earth gets dust on our feet."**

Salvation is efficacious; once is enough. Yet daily travel on earth gets dust on our feet. Every day, life may involve minor relapses or sins, and Jesus is there to wash those away. Another conversion is not necessary, but cleansing on a daily basis is. This is why it is important that we humble ourselves to receive cleansing day by day.

Peter Learned the Need for Quiet Submission

In the garden of Gethsemane, where Jesus prayed and His disciples slept, the leading disciple received more private tutelage.

> Jesus went out as usual to the Mount of Olives, and his disciples followed him. On reaching the place, he said to them, "Pray that you will not fall into temptation." He withdrew about a stone's throw beyond them, knelt down and prayed, "Father, if you are willing, take this cup from me; yet not my will, but yours be done." An angel from heaven appeared to him and strengthened him. And being in anguish, he prayed more earnestly, and his sweat was like drops of blood falling to the ground.
>
> When he rose from prayer and went back to the disciples, he found them asleep, exhausted from sorrow. "Why are you sleeping?" he asked them. "Get up and pray so that you will not fall into temptation." (Luke 22:39-46)

Jesus wrestled in prayer and yielded to the cup of suffering He had to drink. Peter observed this. The story continues:

> When Jesus' followers saw what was going to happen, they said, "Lord, should we strike with our swords?" And one of them struck the servant of the high priest, cutting off his right ear.
>
> But Jesus answered, "No more of this!" And he touched the man's ear and healed him. (Luke 22:49-51)

We then move from Luke's to Matthew's comments:

> With that, one of Jesus' companions reached for his sword, drew it out and struck the servant of the high priest, cutting off his ear. "Put your sword back in its place," Jesus said to him, "for all who draw the sword will die by the sword. Do you think I cannot call on my Father, and he will at once put at my disposal more than

twelve legions of angels? But how then would the Scriptures be fulfilled that say it must happen in this way?" (Matthew 26:51–54)

John also records this event:

> Then Simon Peter, who had a sword, drew it and struck the high priest's servant, cutting off his right ear. (The servant's name was Malchus.) Jesus commanded Peter, "Put your sword away! Shall I not drink the cup the Father has given me?" (John 18:10–11)

When Jesus told Peter to put his sword away and asked if He shouldn't drink the cup the Father required, impetuous Peter received some special insight. Jesus could have called for 120,000 angels to defend him. He didn't need Peter's sword. The Lion played the part of the Lamb. And we must too.

Many years later, a gentler, more gracious and mature Peter wrote:

> Finally, all of you, be likeminded, be sympathetic, love one another, be compassionate and humble. Do not repay evil with evil or insult with insult. On the contrary, repay evil with blessing, because to this you were called so that you may inherit a blessing. For, "Whoever among you would love life and see good days must keep your tongue from evil and your lips from deceitful speech. Turn from evil and do good; seek peace and pursue it. For the eyes of the Lord are on the righteous and his ears are attentive to their prayer, but the face of the Lord is against those who do evil."
>
> Who is going to harm you if you are eager to do good? But even if you should suffer for what is right, you are blessed. "Do not fear their threats; do not be frightened." But in your hearts revere Christ as Lord. Always be prepared to give an answer to everyone who asks you to give the reason for the hope that you have. But do this with gentleness and respect, keeping a clear conscience, so that those who speak maliciously against your good behavior in Christ may be ashamed of their slander. It is better, if it is God's will, to suffer for doing good than for doing evil. For Christ also suffered once for sins, the righteous for the

> **"The Lion played the part of the Lamb. And we must too."**

> unrighteous, to bring you to God. He was put to death in the body but made alive in the Spirit. (1 Peter 3:8–18)

Is the man who penned these words the same man who spontaneously whipped out his sword and cut Malchus' ear off his head? Yes and no. It is the same man, but he was greatly changed, refined, humbled, and made useful in the Master's hand.

We still see this process today. Young Christian leaders are sometimes like the earlier Peter. Older leaders mellow and become more gentle. How far along this road of progress are you? How many experiences of failed anger will it take to learn that a gentle shepherd does a better job of leading God's sheep, "not lording it over those entrusted to you, but being examples to the flock" (1 Peter 5:3)?

This verse, addressed to Christian leaders by Pastor Peter, is good for all of us. The profound wisdom of Proverbs 15:1 applies to Christian care for others: "A gentle answer turns away wrath, but a harsh word stirs up anger." Peter eventually learned to stop drawing swords and cutting off ears.

Peter Denied Jesus Three Times but Was Tactfully Restored by Jesus

When Jesus and John were in the courtyard, Peter was brought in to experience his own revealing adventure.

> Peter had to wait outside at the door. The other disciple, who was known to the high priest, came back, spoke to the servant girl on duty there and brought Peter in. "You aren't one of this man's disciples too, are you?" she asked Peter.
>
> He replied, "I am not."
>
> It was cold, and the servants and officials stood around a fire they had made to keep warm. Peter also was standing with them, warming himself. (John 18:16–18)

While the trial proceeded, the saga of Peter's denials continued outside.

> Meanwhile, Simon Peter was still standing there warming himself. So they asked him, "You aren't one of his disciples too, are you?"
>
> He denied it, saying, "I am not."

> One of the high priest's servants, a relative of the man whose ear Peter had cut off, challenged him, "Didn't I see you with him in the garden?"
>
> Again Peter denied it, and at that moment a rooster began to crow. (John 18:25-27)

Matthew tells us that after Peter was accused of being one of the disciples the third time, "he began to call down curses, and he swore to them, 'I don't know the man!'" Immediately a rooster crowed. Then Peter remembered the word Jesus had spoken: "Before the rooster crows, you will disown me three times." And he went outside and wept bitterly (see Matthew 26:74-75).

Peter was crushed. He had denied the Lord, just as predicted, in spite of his stated determination to even die with Jesus.

Denial is caused by human weakness. Betrayal is the result of deliberate and premeditated ill will. Deliberate sin is more serious than an unintended mistake made in a moment of weakness. Peter did not deliberately betray Jesus. Rather, in a time of weakness, he denied his relationship with Him. And what did Jesus do? He focused on restoration at a later time, not even referring to the denials.

Jesus dealt with the denial problem in a tactful, loving, yet firm way. In a conversation recorded in John 21:1-19, Jesus brought Peter through a three-step restoration process. Peter was allowed to confess his love for Jesus the same number of times he had earlier denied Him. And Jesus lovingly and graciously accepted Peter's confession of love for Him.

Jesus accepts and restores. Whenever you and I fail Jesus out of weakness, we need to let Him restore us in His own loving way. And we need to reaffirm our love to Him. In the same way, we must restore the weak and errant person with whom the Holy Spirit is dealing as He brings him or her closer to Himself. We must be like Jesus in order to represent Him.

Peter, the Missionary to Samaria (Peter's First Missionary Trip)

We will skip over Peter's experiences as a leader in the church of Jerusalem when he led the discussion of replacing Judas (Acts 1), his sermon at

Pentecost (Acts 2), the healing of the lame man (Acts 3), the trial before the Sanhedrin (Acts 4), and the deaths of Ananias and Sapphira (Acts 5). Instead, we'll move on to Peter's three missionary journeys, the first of which took him to Samaria.

> When the apostles in Jerusalem heard that Samaria had accepted the word of God, they sent Peter and John to Samaria. When they arrived, they prayed for the new believers there that they might receive the Holy Spirit, because the Holy Spirit had not yet come on any of them; they had simply been baptized into the name of the Lord Jesus. Then Peter and John placed their hands on them, and they received the Holy Spirit.
>
> When Simon saw that the Spirit was given at the laying on of the apostles' hands, he offered them money and said, "Give me also this ability so that everyone on whom I lay my hands may receive the Holy Spirit."
>
> Peter answered: "May your money perish with you, because you thought you could buy the gift of God with money! You have no part or share in this ministry, because your heart is not right before God. Repent of this wickedness and pray to the Lord in the hope that he may forgive you for having such a thought in your heart. For I see that you are full of bitterness and captive to sin."
>
> Then Simon answered, "Pray to the Lord for me so that nothing you have said may happen to me."
>
> After they had further proclaimed the word of the Lord and testified about Jesus, Peter and John returned to Jerusalem, preaching the gospel in many Samaritan villages. (Acts 8:14-25)

Philip started the revival in Samaria. The apostles in Jerusalem later sent Peter and John there. Peter showed himself to be a no-nonsense man. The above verses tell the story of his laying hands on the Samaritans and how they received the Holy Spirit.

Then Peter corrected Simon. Philip evidently did not discern Simon's spirit, but Peter did.

The spiritual gift of discerning of spirits is valuable if the purity of the church is to be preserved. If the enemy is allowed to work unhindered or unexposed within Christian ranks, how can the church be clean, healthy, and unified? And how can it grow? Peter's contributions to the revival in Samaria were to bring the message of the Holy Spirit baptism and the correction of Simon. Both of these ministries are still needed today.

Peter, the Missionary to Caesarea (Peter's Second Missionary Trip)

Peter had other experiences outside of Jerusalem. At Lydda, Aeneas was healed of palsy.

> "Aeneas," Peter said to him, "Jesus Christ heals you. Get up and roll up your mat." Immediately Aeneas got up. All those who lived in Lydda and Sharon saw him and turned to the Lord. (Acts 9:34-35)

At Joppa, Tabitha was raised from the dead.

> In Joppa there was a disciple named Tabitha (in Greek her name is Dorcas); she was always doing good and helping the poor. About that time she became sick and died, and her body was washed and placed in an upstairs room. Lydda was near Joppa; so when the disciples heard that Peter was in Lydda, they sent two men to him and urged him, "Please come at once!"
>
> Peter went with them, and when he arrived he was taken upstairs to the room. All the widows stood around him, crying and showing him the robes and other clothing that Dorcas had made while she was still with them.
>
> Peter sent them all out of the room; then he got down on his knees and prayed. Turning toward the dead woman, he said, "Tabitha, get up." She opened her eyes, and seeing Peter she sat up. He took her by the hand and helped her to her feet. Then he called for the believers, especially the widows, and presented her to them alive. (Acts 9:36-41)

Lydda and Joppa are both in Israel. This was not a cross-cultural missionary trip — not yet. While in Joppa, Peter saw a vision with extremely important missiological implications.

> About noon the following day as they were on their journey and approaching the city, Peter went up on the roof to pray. He

became hungry and wanted something to eat, and while the meal was being prepared, he fell into a trance. He saw heaven opened and something like a large sheet being let down to earth by its four corners. It contained all kinds of four-footed animals, as well as reptiles and birds. Then a voice told him, "Get up, Peter. Kill and eat."

"Surely not, Lord!" Peter replied. "I have never eaten anything impure or unclean."

The voice spoke to him a second time, "Do not call anything impure that God has made clean." This happened three times, and immediately the sheet was taken back to heaven. (Acts 10:9-16)

While attending a Chinese church in Beijing, China, I heard a liberal theologian speak. He was a visiting foreign Christian leader. He used the above text one Sunday morning to suggest that Christians should accept not only people of other faiths but also their faiths. The Chinese pastors of the church tactfully said nothing while the guest was there. The following Sunday, without drawing attention to the sermon of the week before, one of them correctly taught that Christians are to accept one another and all people, but not all religious beliefs. All roads do not lead to heaven. Jesus is the only way. I was glad I had learned the Chinese language and could enjoy this bit of subtle drama. I was even more glad that the Chinese pastor knew how to correctly teach the message of Peter's experience in Cornelius' home.

Peter, while still in Joppa, accepted an invitation to visit a God-fearing non-Jew in Caesarea. He then embarked on his second missionary trip. He went with the host delegation and met the Roman centurion Cornelius and a house full of guests who were waiting for his message. This event is recorded in Acts 10:23-48.

Later, under attack by his Jewish believer friends, Peter defended the ministry to the non-Jews in Caesarea by referring to the vision and the descent of the Holy Spirit as he spoke in Cornelius' home (see Acts 11:1-18). At the Jerusalem council recorded in Acts 15, Peter again defended the idea of ministry to non-Jews. He once more based his argument on the outpouring of the Holy Spirit God had given at Cornelius' home.

This missionary trip to Caesarea could be considered a great success. Yet the lesson about accepting non-Jewish believers as they were without Gentiles needing to conform to Jewish law (the lesson Peter learned in Caesarea and then explained in Jerusalem) was even more important. What happened at Cornelius' home was undoubtedly a blessing to Cornelius, but the lesson Peter learned was extremely valuable to the church.

> "The lesson Peter learned in Caesarea and then explained in Jerusalem was even more important."

That lesson had to be learned by the church again however. Even Peter had to relearn it through an embarrassing public incident. The outgrowth of that incident eventually positioned the Christian church with a philosophy and policy that was suitable in multiple cultural contexts the world over. It enabled it to become the world's leading religion. The repeat lesson occurred on Peter's third missionary journey.

The visions Peter experienced leading up to his dynamic experience at Cornelius' home played a crucial role. The lesson for Peter personally, or the Church generally, would not have been successful without them. The event at Cornelius' home and Peter's speech about it at the Jerusalem council combine to be a pivotal influence in the life, growth, and policy of the church.

Peter, the Missionary to Antioch (Peter's Third Missionary Trip)

Paul and Barnabas went to Antioch on a problem-solving mission.

> Certain individuals came down from Judea to Antioch and were teaching the believers: "Unless you are circumcised, according to the custom taught by Moses, you cannot be saved." This brought Paul and Barnabas into sharp dispute and debate with them. So Paul and Barnabas were appointed, along with some other believers, to go up to Jerusalem to see the apostles and elders about this question. The church sent them on their way, and as they traveled through Phoenicia and Samaria, they told how the Gentiles had been converted. This news made all the believers very glad. (Acts 15:1–3)

Paul reports about this incident in his letter to the Galatians. Evidently, Peter (Cephas) had also come to Antioch.

> When Cephas came to Antioch, I opposed him to his face, because he stood condemned. For before certain people came from James, he used to eat with the Gentiles. But when they arrived, he began to draw back and separate himself from the Gentiles because he was afraid of those who belonged to the circumcision group. The other Jews joined him in his hypocrisy, so that by their hypocrisy even Barnabas was led astray.
>
> When I saw that they were not acting in line with the truth of the gospel, I said to Cephas in front of them all, "You are a Jew, yet you live like a Gentile and not like a Jew. How is it, then, that you force Gentiles to follow Jewish customs?
>
> "We who are Jews by birth and not sinful Gentiles know that a person is not justified by observing the law, but by faith in Jesus Christ. So we, too, have put our faith in Christ Jesus that we may be justified by faith in Christ and not by observing the law, because by observing the law no one will be justified.
>
> "But if, in seeking to be justified in Christ, we Jews find ourselves also among the sinners, doesn't that mean that Christ promotes sin? Absolutely not! If I rebuild what I destroyed, then I really would be a lawbreaker.
>
> "For through the law I died to the law so that I might live for God. I have been crucified with Christ and I no longer live, but Christ lives in me. The life I now live in the body, I live by faith in the Son of God, who loved me and gave himself for me. I do not set aside the grace of God, for if righteousness could be gained through the law, Christ died for nothing!" (Galatians 2:11-21)

Acts does not say who was in Antioch or who came from Judea to Antioch. However, we know that Peter had been there fellowshipping with the non-Jewish converts. He was later led astray by Jewish persons from Judea who taught that Gentiles must learn and keep the Jewish law. Paul had to publicly speak against Peter's duplicity.

Peter had many successes as an apostle, church leader, healer, preacher, and missionary statesman. But Peter failed to stay true to the message of the threefold vision of the sheet from heaven and what his trip to Cornelius' home had taught him. He had defended the work of the Holy Spirit at Cornelius' home in Jerusalem, yet Peter had a serious cross-cultural missionary relapse in Antioch.

Four important lessons can be gleaned from this incident:

> "They acknowledged that the Christian message does not require people to change their culture to be Christians."

- Even a great and highly successful leader can be mistaken in a specific area (missiology, for example) that requires specialized training or understanding.
- Non-Jewish converts do not need to keep the Jewish laws. Similarly, today's converts do not need to keep either the Jewish law or the missionary's home cultural norms.
- At the Jerusalem council, Peter had the grace to refer to his earlier experience in Cornelius' home and admit before the council that Paul was right. This would have happened soon after being corrected by Paul at Antioch as recorded in Galatians 2:11-21.
- The Church did not have just one leader. Four persons spoke authoritatively.

> Peter spoke: "After much discussion, Peter got up and addressed them: 'Brothers, you know that some time ago God made a choice among you that the Gentiles might hear from my lips the message of the gospel and believe.'" (Acts 15:7)
>
> Barnabas and Paul spoke: "The whole assembly became silent as they listened to Barnabas and Paul telling about the signs and wonders God had done among the Gentiles through them." (Acts 15:12)
>
> James spoke: "When they finished, James spoke up. 'Brothers,' he said, 'listen to me.'" (Acts 15:13)

As recorded in Acts 15, the council led the Church in one of its most profound, insightful, foresightful, and far-reaching policy decisions. They acknowledged that the Christian message does not require people to change their culture to be Christians. After conversion, the Holy Spirit will lead individuals to change what He wants them to change. Peter actively participated in this decision, even though it meant he had to backtrack and admit he had made a mistake. To Peter, the work of the church and its growth were more important than his ego, reputation, or need to be right.

Peter, the Pro-Family Man

In all the New Testament — perhaps all of the Bible — Peter drew the clearest parallel between correct family life and receiving the blessings of God. In his instructions to wives, Peter describes behavior and attitude as being a more important factor in the beauty of women than physical appearance:

> Wives, in the same way submit yourselves to your own husbands so that, if any of them do not believe the word, they may be won over without words by the behavior of their wives, when they see the purity and reverence of your lives. Your beauty should not come from outward adornment, such as elaborate hairstyles and the wearing of gold jewelry and fine clothes. Rather, it should be that of your inner self, the unfading beauty of a gentle and quiet spirit, which is of great worth in God's sight. For this is the way the holy women of the past who put their hope in God used to adorn themselves. They submitted themselves to their own husbands, like Sarah, who obeyed Abraham and called him her lord. You are her daughters if you do what is right and do not give way to fear. (1 Peter 3: 1-6)

In the next verse, he tells husbands three ways to bless their wives so that their prayers will not be hindered. Peter taught, "Husbands, in the same way [1] be considerate as you live with your wives, and [2] treat them with respect as the weaker partner [3] and as heirs with you of the gracious gift of life, *so that nothing will hinder your prayers*" (1 Peter 3:7, emphasis mine).

In the Old Testament, Malachi drew a parallel between behavior in the family and the receiving of spiritual blessings. Weeping at the altar doesn't get answers or blessings; obedience does. He taught:

> Another thing you do: You flood the Lord's altar with tears. You weep and wail because he no longer looks with favor on your

offerings or accepts them with pleasure from your hands. You ask, "Why?" It is because the Lord is the witness between you and the wife of your youth. You have been unfaithful to her, though she is your partner, the wife of your marriage covenant. Has not the Lord made the two of you one? You belong to him in body and spirit. And why has he made you one? Because he was seeking godly offspring. So be on your guard, and do not be unfaithful to the wife of your youth. "I hate divorce," says the Lord God of Israel, "and I hate it when people clothe themselves with injustice," says the Lord Almighty. So be on your guard, and do not be unfaithful. (Malachi 2:13–16)

No Christian wants his prayers hindered. Peter tells husbands that if they want God's blessings and answers to prayer, they need to treat their wives considerately. They must regard them as the weaker, fragile, delicate, and fine vessels they are, and consider them equal partners in receiving the blessings of God. That is what 1 Peter 3:7 means when it says: "… be considerate as you live with your wives, and treat them with respect as the weaker partner and as heirs with you of the gracious gift of life."

> "God is my father-in-law. He likes it when I treat His daughter well."

God is my father-in-law. He likes it when I treat His daughter well. For the reader who is a husband, if you want God to bless you and answer your prayers, treat His daughter (your wife) well. The Bible teaches that there is a direct relationship between how we treat our wives and how many blessings and answers to prayer we receive. We can thank the strongly pro-family man Peter for these insights.

For Further Thought

- Have you ever had to counsel someone about the need for regular spiritual checkups and cleansings even though we are thoroughly cleansed when we are born again? How did you handle it? What might you do differently if a similar situation occurred again?
- How will you apply to your life what you learned about Peter becoming more submissive and cooperative later in life?
- Using the same tactic Jesus used in restoring Peter, what can you do for people who have erred or denied Jesus?
- What ways can you use your ministry gifts to help another person's ministry just as Peter did for Philip in Samaria?
- Peter learned an important lesson at Caesarea about overcoming personal bias against people of another ethnicity, tribe, or culture. How will you apply this lesson in your life?
- Peter showed a teachable attitude in receiving the correction that Paul gave him in front of a group of Christians. What can you do to demonstrate the same teachable attitude?
- What will you do when you have an opportunity to admit an error publicly?
- Were you surprised to learn that Peter made such strong pro-family statements? In what ways will you follow his instructions so that your prayers will not be hindered?

CHAPTER 23
PHILIP

Do you realize that Philip the deacon and evangelist has a more visible and apparently important role in Acts than Philip the apostle? Were you aware that God does not need us to be perfectly motivated in order to use us? Did you know that Philip received on-the-job training in Samaria?

The Philip we meet in the book of Acts was a deacon; he served others. He was not, at first, a full-time professional. He did the practical things involved in pastoral care, like waiting on tables. Yet God used this man in wonderful ways. Philip provides valuable and practical lessons about teamwork, communication of the gospel, and Christian family living that are useful to us today.

God Uses a Wide Variety of Motives

Years before the events recorded in Acts 8, Jesus told His disciples to communicate the gospel. In Acts 1, He instructed them to leave Jerusalem and go to Judea, Samaria, and the uttermost parts of the earth. Why didn't anyone move out of Jerusalem between that declaration of the Great Commission and the outbreak of persecution recorded in Acts 8 (approximately eight years later)? Not even to nearby Judah or Samaria? It was probably for the same reason that many people today don't leave their homeland and go somewhere else with the intention of doing gospel work. I do not mean to speak disparagingly of these people; I just want to draw a parallel between Philip's day and our day. It is our natural tendency to stay home. Philip and the other believers in Jerusalem remained in

Jerusalem until persecution broke out. It either forced or frightened them into doing what Jesus had told them to do years before.

> On that day a great persecution broke out against the church in Jerusalem, and all except the apostles were scattered throughout Judea and Samaria …
>
> Saul began to destroy the church. Going from house to house, he dragged off both men and women and put them in prison. Those who had been scattered preached the word wherever they went. Philip went down to a city in Samaria and proclaimed the Messiah there. (Acts 8:1, 3–5)

From the above Scripture, it is apparent that Philip left Jerusalem for Samaria to flee persecution. That is not the best reason to go to the mission field, but it is good enough. God is willing to accept less than ideal reasons for our going to the mission field. He can still use us in an imperfect yet developing condition.

Most of us have multiple reasons for doing what we do. Sometimes we give a publicly suitable reason even though we may have a private reason that is more important or motivational to us. We may have noble motives of obeying God and being concerned for the health of the church in a foreign country. But that motive could be partially clouded by an inferior motive, such as wanting to have an adventure abroad. However, that doesn't mean I should not go.

> "He can still use us in an imperfect yet developing condition."

The right reason for doing anything is obedience. But we should not refuse to go just because our motives may be less than pure. Ultimately, every one of us ought to do what we are doing because we believe it is what God wants us to do. Let's work to purify our motives so that we do everything for the best possible reason. At the same time, let us not allow wrong or inferior reasons to hinder us from doing what we are called to do.

Philip went to Samaria to escape persecution in Jerusalem, and look what happened. A revival broke out, and many were saved, healed, and delivered. A city in Samaria was changed by the Lord working through a man who fled persecution. How great is that?

Expect a Fight If You Are Successful in Ministry

A Christ-centered ministry with miracles and deliverance from evil spirits may produce revival and rapid numerical growth in God's church. On the other hand, don't get too elated or ego-inflated over early successes. Our enemy does not happily yield his "spoils." The evil spirits that shrieked as recorded in Acts 8:7 returned in an even more vicious and devious counterattack later in the story of Philip in Samaria.

> When the crowds heard Philip and saw the signs he performed, they all paid close attention to what he said. With shrieks, evil spirits came out of many, and many who were paralyzed or lame were healed. So there was great joy in that city. Now for some time a man named Simon had practiced sorcery in the city and amazed all the people of Samaria. He boasted that he was someone great. (Acts 8:6-9)

Simon the sorcerer had been a chief spiritual influence in that city of Samaria. Upon hearing Philip's message, he believed and was baptized. However, he did not want to give up his place of prominence. When Peter and John joined Philip, Simon the sorcerer was amazed at what Peter did. However, Peter rebuked him for his shallow belief and selfish motives.

> When Simon saw that the Spirit was given at the laying on of the apostles' hands, he offered them money and said, "Give me also this ability so that everyone on whom I lay my hands may receive the Holy Spirit."
>
> Peter answered: "May your money perish with you, because you thought you could buy the gift of God with money!" (Acts 8:18-20)

Prepare yourself emotionally and spiritually to deal with your "Simon the sorcerer." Consider what is happening spiritually. Love people.

> "Fight against the spirits that work through people, but not with the people through whom the spirits work."

Choose Your Character

Fight against the spirits that work through people, but not with the people through whom the spirits work.

The apparent issues of personal conflict in God's work may be money, power, authority, or ego. Look beyond, beneath, and behind the person to the spiritual forces that work through him or her. Wage war against the real enemy. Be prepared to fast, pray, intercede, and travail until spiritual victory is fully accomplished.

Remember, people are not our enemy; spiritual forces are. "For our struggle is not against flesh and blood, but against the rulers, against the authorities, against the powers of this dark world and against the spiritual forces of evil in the heavenly realms" (Ephesians 6:12). There is a real adversary today just as in Philip's experience.

Make Room for the Ministry of Others

But Philip did not become agitated, jealous, or disturbed when they arrived. Peter and John outranked Philip. The drama focused more on their gifts, discernment, power, and victory than on Philip. He was willing to step aside and let others participate in leadership even though their success reduced his own authority and prestige. It is possible that Philip himself had suggested that the apostles come because he saw the Holy Spirit had not yet baptized his new converts. He knew they needed Him.

> When the apostles in Jerusalem heard that Samaria had accepted the word of God, they sent Peter and John to Samaria. When they arrived, they prayed for the new believers there that they might receive the Holy Spirit, because the Holy Spirit had not yet come on any of them; they had simply been baptized into the name of the Lord Jesus. Then Peter and John placed their hands on them, and they received the Holy Spirit. (Acts 8:14–17)

"The revival was not Philip's; it was God's."

Philip could step aside because the position of leading revivalist was not important to him. Revival was. The move of God was. The good that was being done for the people was important to him. The revival was not Philip's; it was God's. Though waiting on more important tables now, Philip maintained the serving attitude he had as a deacon back in Jerusalem.

What will you do when another Christian appears who seems to have the gifts that are needed at the moment — gifts you do not have? Will you be a team player? If God wants to use a Peter and John in "your" revival, let Him. Merely tolerating the ministry of others is better than rejecting it, but genuinely and unselfishly welcoming it is better still. The work belongs to God, and He delights to see His workers deferring to, cooperating with, and supporting one another, allowing each diamond to shine in the way that is the most glorious.

I like to spell TEAM this way:

> Together
> Everyone
> Accomplishes
> More

Obedience Is Success

Success in God's work is measured by the degree to which we obey God.

> After they had further proclaimed the word of the Lord and testified about Jesus, Peter and John returned to Jerusalem, preaching the gospel in many Samaritan villages. Now an angel of the Lord said to Philip, "Go south to the road — the desert road — that goes down from Jerusalem to Gaza." So he started out, and on his way he met an Ethiopian eunuch, an important official in charge of all the treasury of the Kandake (which means queen of the Ethiopians). This man had gone to Jerusalem to worship. (Acts 8:25-27)

Philip obeyed the angel and went south to a desert road even before he knew whom he would meet.

Some of us need to change our definition of success. What God calls success is different from what the world considers it to be. People measure success using criteria of size, number, strength, results, and recognition. God's definition is obedience. This is better than sacrifice,

> "What God calls success is different from what the world considers it to be."

creativity, hard work, or any of the other things we usually admire. The ultimate criterion for reward — the standard for measuring worth in God's eyes — is never to be numbers, appearances, things, connections, or any of the issues with which many become preoccupied.

Once we have this paradigm shift, our whole perspective changes. We begin to serve an audience of One.

Wherever You Go, God Is at Work Before You Get There

Do not assume that God will begin to work in a place only after you arrive. God may have been working long before you got there.

The Ethiopian eunuch "had gone to Jerusalem to worship, and on his way home was sitting in his chariot reading the Book of Isaiah the prophet. The Spirit told Philip, 'Go to that chariot and stay near it'" (Acts 8:27–29).

This passage tells us what God was doing before Philip got there.

Whether God is leading you to go to a specific place or just to go somewhere, anywhere, to take the gospel message, assume He is there ahead of you. That is why He led you to go. Find out what He is doing and move with Him.

God has been at work preparing people to receive the gospel. Every culture has proverbs, histories, jokes, heroes, metaphors, dreams, legends, and folklore that have been passed down from previous generations. Some of these can be creatively used as illustrations of Christian truth. You can become familiar with them and use them to great advantage as a Christian communicator. In missiology, these are called "redemptive analogies." Crosscultural workers can use them as conceptual tools. They can effectively communicate our message of Jesus to the local people in countries we wish to evangelize. We will later observe how Paul did this at Athens.

Receptor-Oriented Communication Is Effective

When you go to a foreign country in response to a call from God, get acquainted with the local customs before you say anything about God.

> The Spirit told Philip, "Go to that chariot and stay near it."

Then Philip ran up to the chariot and heard the man reading Isaiah the prophet. "Do you understand what you are reading?" Philip asked.

"How can I," he said, "unless someone explains it to me?" So he invited Philip to come up and sit with him.

This is the passage of Scripture the eunuch was reading:

> He was led like a sheep to the slaughter, and as a lamb before its shearer is silent, so he did not open his mouth. In his humiliation he was deprived of justice. Who can speak of his descendants? For his life was taken from the earth.

The eunuch asked Philip, "Tell me, please, who is the prophet talking about, himself or someone else?" Then Philip began with that very passage of Scripture and told him the good news about Jesus. (Acts 8:29-35)

God told Philip to get close to his target audience and stay there awhile. What wise words! In our mission fields, in order to "stay close," we need to be socially connected with people where they live. It enables us to assess the situation.

In agriculture, farmers test the soil. These tests enable farmers to treat each type of soil correctly. The information also guides them to plant the crop that is most productive in a particular kind of environment. Do a "soil test" among your adopted people so you can do well at planting the gospel seed and harvesting many souls wherever God takes you. Learn the language, culture, history, jokes (also finding out why they are funny to the local people), proverbs, and contemporary issues, and read the local newspaper. Then speak.

"Philip ran up to the chariot and heard the man" (Acts 8:30). The crosscultural communicator should know the local culture. He or she must also take individual and personal differences between people into consideration. Philip went close to the chariot, and then he listened to the man in it. This principle adds the

> "When we know what a person is thinking, we can communicate more even if we say less."

uniqueness of individual personalities. We can determine what questions to ask and what to say when we listen to people. When we know what a person is thinking, we can communicate more even if we say less.

Show interest in the other party by asking questions. When Philip spoke, he began with a question. "Do you understand what you are reading?" (Acts 8:30). Questions are marvelous tools; they show interest, humility, and willingness to learn. They move us into the conceptual world of the other party. Questions give us the information we need to reach the other person's heart. It is more important to reach people's hearts than to impress them with our knowledge. This is why questions often serve our purpose better than statements.

Arriving physically and geographically is the easiest part of missionary work. Getting into the conceptual world of the other party requires some effort and professionalism.

What is the family situation of the person? What are his or her interests? How much does he or she know, if anything, about God? What offenses have other believers caused that we may be able to diffuse?

Start where the persons (in missiology, we call them "receptors") are. "Philip began with that very passage" (Acts 8:35). People are at different stages of development culturally, morally, intellectually, and spiritually. Accept them at their present stage, and begin with that. This is called "starting point and process" in missiology. God begins with people where they are, and so should we. Of course, God doesn't leave them there. He moves them forward, and so should we.

We have an important life- and eternity-changing message we want to share. That is why we go to the mission field. We must learn about the local culture and the living situation of the individual to whom we are presenting the gospel before beginning with our message. It allows us to speak more accurately into his or her life. Every person's needs are different. Whatever the situation, we have the answer. Jesus. But unless we ask some questions and listen to the answers, we will not know what aspect of Jesus' adequacy would best fit our listener's situation.

Receptor-oriented communication enables us to understand our hearers. We can communicate more effectively because we understand how to direct every word based on the receptor's unique circumstances.

Let God Open the Doors

On a road in a desert, the eunuch invited Philip into his chariot. "He invited Philip to come up and sit with him" (Acts 8:31).

God knows where the curious seekers are. He knows how to lead us to them. The only way Philip was able to enter this open door was to be where God wanted him to be.

To the natural eye, the road to Gaza did not seem like an important ministry opportunity. It was not even a place. It was a road going to a place. It was in the middle of a lonely desert. There were rarely any people there. The eunuch was simply traveling through. But Philip was in the right place at the right time because he obeyed God and went to that place.

> **If we are in wrong places, we are not available when the right doors could have opened.**

Sometimes our efforts to open wrong doors, or walk through distracting open doors, put us in incorrect places. If we are in wrong places, we are not available when the right doors could have opened.

Baptism and Post-Baptismal Care

There is nothing wrong with baptism soon after conversion.

> As they traveled along the road, they came to some water and the eunuch said, "Look, here is water. What can stand in the way of my being baptized?" And he gave orders to stop the chariot. Then both Philip and the eunuch went down into the water and Philip baptized him. When they came up out of the water, the Spirit of the Lord suddenly took Philip away, and the eunuch did not see him again, but went on his way rejoicing. (Acts 8:36-39)

The initiative for baptism came from the eunuch, not Philip.

Baptism, an initiation rite, provides a public confession. It is a rite of passage from one belief system to another. Opinions differ about how much time should pass between conversion and baptism. Cultural issues must be considered. However, the Bible places no emphasis on proving sincerity, learning doctrine, or passing numerous tests.

Some missionaries in history were overly concerned about the development of Christian character as a prerequisite to water baptism. It caused them to retard or even halt a movement of large groups of people to Christ. The Bible does not substantiate such a position. Church and missions history indicate that post-baptismal care and incorporation into fellowship with the family of God are more important than the amount of elapsed time, or even proof of change in a person's life.

> **The Bible reveals the pattern of the early church that baptism need not be delayed.**

How could Philip measure the depth of this man's conversion in the few minutes they spent together? Philip was miraculously transported to his next destination immediately after baptizing the eunuch. He was unable to provide any post-baptismal teachings. How could Paul at Philippi know the quality of the jailor's conversion? Both of these evangelists baptized their converts on the spot. The stories of Philip in the desert in Acts 8 and Paul at Philippi in Acts 16 illustrate that baptism was done right away. In both cases, the Bible reveals the pattern of the early church that baptism need not be delayed.

Quality post-baptismal care is the training that young Christians should receive after conversion. This guidance and assimilation into the fellowship of believers helps converts live up to their baptism.

Ministry in "Closed" Places

Christians need not fear ministry in "closed" countries, even in enemy territory.

> Philip, however, appeared at Azotus and traveled about, preaching the gospel in all the towns until he reached Caesarea. (Acts 8:40)

Azotus was in Philistine territory, where enemies of the Jews lived. Yet

Philip was there, traveling about, preaching in all the towns. He did not allow geopolitical considerations to influence his missionary strategy.

The matter of geopolitical issues must be considered in deciding where to go as missionaries, but it is not the most important criterion. Two good criteria to use are:

- Where the Spirit leads
- The responsiveness of the local people to the gospel.

Char and I lived and worked for five years in a "closed" country. Politically, it was inconvenient to live there. However, the hearts of the people were wide open. They still are. Open hearts is a more important consideration than the convenience of our living situation.

Philip was able to lay aside whatever his background had taught him about the descendants of the Philistines. He traveled throughout the territory of Israel's traditional enemies. He went from village to village until he reached Caesarea, a major city in northern Philistia.

Don't Forget Your Family

Keep your family in good order, and your ministry will continue into the next generation. You may ask where that idea is recorded in the story of Philip. Acts 8:40 says "He reached Caesarea."

As recorded in Acts 21, Paul and his companions traveled through Caesarea. Luke makes this observation: "Leaving the next day, we reached Caesarea and stayed at the house of Philip the evangelist, one of the Seven. He had four unmarried daughters who prophesied" (Acts 21:8-9).

Acts 21 records that years after Philip traveled from Gaza through the Philistine territory of Azotos, his four daughters were prophetesses in Caesarea. The Bible does not say whether they prophesied to Paul, but they could have.

> *Philip and his wife must have intentionally raised their daughters to serve God.*

Philip was a traveler, missionary, and cross-cultural worker — a busy man. Yet he had daughters who served the Lord in Caesarea. That did not "just happen." Philip and his wife must have intentionally raised their daughters to serve God. Raising the next generation to carry on where we leave off is good missionary strategy.

The desirability of Philip's character qualities are not limited to foreign missionaries. They are equally applicable in our home countries. Let's allow the Bible to influence our methodology as well as dictate our message. We should try to be the best missionaries possible wherever God places us.

For Further Thought

- Do you make room for others' ministries? How do you decide when to do that and when to not do that?
- Do you feel that "obedience is success" is a valid spiritual principle? How does this apply to your life and ministry?
- What difference will it make to you if you consider that God is already at work in your next place of ministry?
- Are you receptor-oriented? Do you ask questions and try to understand your audience?
- How do you intend to let God open doors for ministry?
- If converts revert to their old ways, do you tend to blame the convert or do you work harder at post-baptismal care?
- Have you ever ministered in a "closed" place? How did you sense God's presence there?
- What did you learn about attention to family matters from the fact that Philip had four daughters who prophesied?

CHAPTER 24
PAUL

You may be surprised to learn that Paul's life teaches us that how we end is more important than how we begin. Did you know that God gave advance notice to Paul that he would suffer much for the sake of the gospel? It is not well known, but Paul had practical multicultural experience. He perhaps even received cross-cultural communication lessons when he was a child, growing up in a home with both Roman and Jewish influences.

Paul is arguably the most prominent person in the Bible outside of Jesus Christ. His influence on centuries of European thought and Western civilization is profound. He wrote more of the New Testament than any other writer. His writings impacted world history and still affect all of Christendom.

In this chapter, we will examine both the life of Paul and his writings. His actions speak to us today, and his letters clarify his ministry-related lessons.

Paul Teaches Us That What We Finish Is More Important Than What We Begin

By human temperament, Paul was choleric. A person with a choleric personality is often a doer and a leader. Cholerics have ambition, energy, and passion; and they attempt to instill those qualities in others. They can dominate people of other temperaments. Many strong charismatic military and political figures were cholerics. The negative side of a choleric is that he or she can become easily angered or bad-tempered. Paul fits all of these characteristics.

Choose Your Character

Paul was passionately motivated. First, he strongly opposed the Church. After his dynamic conversion, he planted churches in a wide area. It's a good thing this strongly motivated high achiever and hard driver was on the right team. But that was not always so.

"Saul began to destroy the church. Going from house to house, he dragged off both men and women and put them in prison" (Acts 8:3). The good news is that he did not complete this project; he changed. Few of us are totally happy about how we began life, where we have traveled, or everything that has happened thus far with our lives. None of us had any control over where, when, or how we were born. If we focus our attention on our past, we become discouraged because we can do nothing about it.

> **We can set goals, redefine objectives, and determine where to go from here and how we will end.**

But all of us can do something about what we do from now on. We can set goals, redefine objectives, and determine where to go from here and how we will end. It is far better to develop constructive plans to finish well than to lament our mistaken beginnings. Later in life, Paul wisely said, "But one thing I do: forgetting what is behind and straining toward what is ahead" (Philippians 3:13).

Paul Knew the Difference between Opposition and a Closed Door

Is the fact that a door is open enough reason to walk through it? No. Some "opportunities" seem right because the door is open, but they are distractions from God's plan for our lives. In addition to the "open door," we need the witness and impulse of the Spirit to know if we should walk through it.

On the other hand, is the fact that a door is closed enough reason to not pray that it will be opened? No again. Some doors that seem to be closed need to be prayed open. Some barriers need to be overcome. The witness of the Spirit guiding us in our praying will enable us to persevere until the door opens. This enablement, in such a case, is a great gift.

So how do we interpret open doors and closed ones? Let's take a lesson from Paul's experience in Ephesus. Paul spoke of a great door of opportunity. Yet in the same sentence, he said there were many who opposed him. When opposition arises, some people are inclined to assume the door must be closed, even though they thought they had an opportunity for ministry. That is too bad.

Paul said he had an opportunity *and* there was opposition. He did not interpret opposition to mean the door was closed. "I will stay on at Ephesus until Pentecost, because a great door for effective work has opened to me, and there are many who oppose me" (1 Corinthians 16:8-9).

We now know that a great and strong church was eventually established at Ephesus. Look what happened in that place where Paul had many who opposed him:

> "He did not interpret opposition to mean the door was closed."

> A number who had practiced sorcery brought their scrolls together and burned them publicly. When they calculated the value of the scrolls, the total came to fifty thousand drachmas. In this way the word of the Lord spread widely and grew in power. (Acts 19:19-20)

The book of Ephesians (a letter written to the believers in Ephesus) is the only book Paul wrote that did not address local problems. Instead, Paul moved from grand subject to great theme. The maturity level of the believers in Ephesus — where at one time there were many who opposed him — is a testimony of the openness of what might have seemed like an impossible ministry situation.

Isaiah understood open and closed doors and that God was the door-opener and the door-closer. He wrote of His servant Eliakim, "I will place on his shoulder the key to the house of David; what he opens no one can shut, and what he shuts no one can open" (Isaiah 22:22).

John also understood open and closed doors. In Revelation, God told him, "To the angel of the church in Philadelphia write: These are the words of him who is holy and true, who holds the key of David. What he opens no one can shut, and what he shuts no one can open. I know your deeds. See, I have placed before you an open door that no one can shut" (Revelation 3:7-8).

When God opens a door, no one can hinder His purpose. Yet determining the will of God, discerning what is a truly open door and what is not, isn't simple. Discerning God's will is not as easy as not proceeding when a door is closed or walking through when the door is open. In addition to apparent circumstances in the natural realm, we must know spiritually that the open door is to be walked through or the closed door is to be accepted.

Some "open" doors are veiled distractions. If we go through the wrong doors, we will not be where God wants us. Some "closed" doors need to be pried open by strong intercession and spiritual warfare as Paul did in Ephesus. We should not walk glibly through every open door or stop at every closed one. We need to have the Spirit of God interpret to us whether the barrier is to be overcome or accepted, and whether the opportunity is to be followed or not.

Paul knew the difference between the two. Even though he faced opposition, he referred to Ephesus as an "open door." Let's take a lesson from Paul and learn to interpret opportunities and barriers based on more than just circumstances. We may miss some chances on the other side of what we first thought was an obstacle. Or we may carelessly proceed into what seemed like an open door only to find we should not have.

Paul Connected the Great Themes of Faith and Righteousness

Habakkuk connected these themes centuries before, but Paul understood them more perfectly and emphasized them more clearly. Habakkuk said, "See, he is puffed up; his desires are not upright — but the righteous will live by their faithfulness" (Habakkuk 2:4).

Based on Habakkuk, Paul taught, "For in the gospel the righteousness of God is revealed — a righteousness that is by faith from first to last, just as it is written: 'The righteous will live by faith'" (Romans 1:17).

Moses wrote, "Abram believed the Lord, and he credited it to him as righteousness" (Genesis 15:6). Centuries later, Paul referred to that, saying, "What does Scripture say? 'Abraham believed God, and it was credited to him as righteousness'" (Romans 4:3).

Paul further emphasized the need to trust God: "However, to anyone who does not work but trusts God who justifies the ungodly, their faith is credited as righteousness" (Romans 4:5).

Paul said, "David says the same thing when he speaks of the blessedness of those to whom God credits righteousness apart from works" (Romans 4:6). Here is what David had said: "Blessed are those whose transgressions are forgiven, whose sins are covered. Blessed are those whose sin the Lord does not count against them and in whose spirit is no deceit" (Psalm 32:1-2). Paul quoted it almost exactly as David wrote it.

Paul argued that righteousness by faith applies equally to non-Jewish people. "This righteousness is given through faith in Jesus Christ to all who believe. There is no difference between Jew and Gentile" (Romans 3:22). "Is this blessedness only for the circumcised, or also for the uncircumcised? We have been saying that Abraham's faith was credited to him as righteousness ... And he received circumcision as a sign, a seal of the righteousness that he had by faith *while he was still uncircumcised*. So then, he is the father of all who believe but have not been circumcised, in order that righteousness might be credited to them" (Romans 4:9, 11, emphasis mine).

We believers today are included in this promise. "It was not through the law that Abraham and his offspring received the promise that he would be heir of the world, but through the righteousness that comes by faith ... This is why 'it was credited to him as righteousness' ... but also for us, to whom God will credit righteousness — for us who believe in him who raised Jesus our Lord from the dead" (Romans 4:13, 22, 24).

If righteousness by faith is applied to Abraham, how much more does it apply to those who put their faith in Jesus? "For if, by the trespass of the one man, death reigned through that one man, how much more will those who receive God's abundant provision of grace and of the gift of righteousness reign in life through the one man, Jesus Christ! ... so that, just as sin reigned in death, so also grace might reign through righteousness to bring eternal life through Jesus Christ our Lord" (Romans 5:17, 21).

People labored under the yoke of attempting to earn their salvation through keeping the law for many centuries. We understand today that we could never earn our salvation that way. We gradually get that wonderful message deeper into our thankful hearts as we each grow in our understanding of God's ways. But in Paul's day, it was an important new truth that he wanted to pass on to his generation.

Old Testament scholar that he was, Paul quoted and referenced stories of Abraham written by Moses, statements by the poet David, and prophetic insight given by Habakkuk. Paul was no less a luminary in the history of the Church than Martin Luther. Luther tried desperately in vain for many years to please God. He joyfully experienced salvation when he found that righteousness comes by faith, not works. Luther is considered to be one of the first leaders of the Protestant Reformation five hundred years ago. That reformation led Christians of Europe away from a false doctrine of dead works into the light of salvation by grace through faith. Righteousness by faith is one of the grandest themes in the New Testament.

> "People labored under the yoke of attempting to earn their salvation through keeping the law for many centuries."

Paul Understood and Experienced Suffering

We understand the role of suffering in the Christian life better because of the teachings of Paul on the subject. We also understand it better because it was illustrated so dramatically in Paul's own life. Paul suffered more than any other apostle. He received more direct revelation from God than any other apostle. He understood the Old Testament better than any other New Testament writer. He also wrote more of the New Testament than any other, some of which he penned while in prison. God used Paul mightily, and his suffering evidently played a part in his development and his writings. Perhaps it was allowed so that Paul would not become puffed up.

Just what did Paul believe and teach about suffering? The following are the Pauline verses we observed in the chapter on Job. In that place, we reserved all comment. Here we make short observations that will help illustrate how useful to all Christians Paul's theology of suffering is. Both Job and Paul teach us that our suffering is neither aimless nor purposeless.

- We should not be ashamed of suffering, but rather look for the good it produces. "Not only so, but we also glory in our sufferings, because we know that suffering produces perseverance" (Romans 5:3).
- Suffering is one of the ways we share in the life of Jesus. It is somehow related to the way we will share in His glory. "If we are children, then we are heirs — heirs of God and co-heirs with Christ, if indeed we share in his sufferings in order that we may also share in his glory. I consider that our present sufferings are not worth comparing with the glory that will be revealed in us" (Romans 8:17-18). Evidently the eternal rewards of the faithful will be greater than their temporary sufferings.

> "Both Job and Paul teach us that our suffering is neither aimless nor purposeless."

- The process of suffering and receiving comfort qualifies us to pass comfort and endurance on to others. "For just as we share abundantly in the sufferings of Christ, so also our comfort abounds through Christ. If we are distressed, it is for your comfort and salvation; if we are comforted, it is for your comfort, which produces in you patient endurance of the same sufferings we suffer. And our hope for you is firm, because we know that just as you share in our sufferings, so also you share in our comfort" (2 Corinthians 1:5-7).
- We can find glory in suffering. It is no disgrace, but rather a sign of identifying closely with Christ. "I ask you, therefore, not to be discouraged because of my sufferings for you, which are your glory" (Ephesians 3:13).
- Suffering is one way we participate in following Jesus. "I want to know Christ — yes, to know the power of his resurrection and participation in his sufferings, becoming like him in his death" (Philippians 3:10).
- There is still great opposition to the gospel. Suffering is necessary where we are extending the kingdom of God and building His church. "Now I rejoice in what I am suffering for you, and I fill up in my flesh what is still lacking in regard to Christ's afflictions, for the sake of his body, which is the church" (Colossians 1:24).
- If our attitude toward suffering is correct, Christians can suffer joyfully

as the Holy Spirit assists us. "You became imitators of us and of the Lord, for you welcomed the message in the midst of severe suffering with the joy given by the Holy Spirit" (1 Thessalonians 1:6).

- Our suffering is one way we can be counted worthy of the kingdom. "All this is evidence that God's judgment is right, and as a result you will be counted worthy of the kingdom of God, for which you are suffering" (2 Thessalonians 1:5).
- Paul invited others to participate in suffering. "Do not be ashamed of the testimony about our Lord or of me his prisoner. But join with me in suffering for the gospel, by the power of God" (2 Timothy 1:8).
- Paul knew that the reason for his suffering was his appointment: "I was appointed as a herald and an apostle and a teacher. That is why I am suffering as I am. Yet this is no cause for shame, because I know whom I have believed, and am convinced that he is able to guard what I have entrusted to him until that day" (2 Timothy 1:11-12).
- Good soldiers suffer. "Join with me in suffering, like a good soldier of Christ Jesus" (2 Timothy 2:3).
- Paul suffered for the gospel. "This is my gospel, for which I am suffering even to the point of being chained like a criminal. But God's word is not chained" (2 Timothy 2:8-9).
- Every Christian will suffer and be delivered. "… persecutions, sufferings — what kinds of things happened to me in Antioch, Iconium and Lystra, the persecutions I endured. Yet the Lord rescued me from all of them. In fact, everyone who wants to live a godly life in Christ Jesus will be persecuted" (2 Timothy 3:11-12).

Paul's character and teachings in the New Testament combine to create a rich tapestry of human experience. It enables us to identify closely with the Lord Jesus Christ, whom we love and whose example we want to follow. "Son though he was, he learned obedience from what he suffered" (Hebrews 5:8). Suffering can be positive, personally beneficial, and God-glorifying. It serves an eternal purpose.

Paul Interpreted the Jewish Message to the Non-Jewish World

Jesus was the Jewish Messiah, and the first believers were Jewish. Today, people of many cultures all over the world believe in Jesus. Some of them

— Jewish Christians and some Arab believers, for example — are not called Christians. But being *called* a Christian is not a requirement of believers.

Most believers in the Jewish Messiah around the world are called Christians. But if our belief system had not grown beyond its Jewish roots, we could be just a segment of Judaism; our religion's name might be Messiahism, and we might be called Messiahists. But our religion's name is Christianity, and we follow Jesus the Christ, using the Greek words *Iesous* and *Christos* rather than the Hebrew words *Yeshua* and *Mashiach*. How did this happen?

Barnabus, a Jewish believer, went to Saul's hometown to bring him to Antioch to serve with him there. "Barnabas went to Tarsus to look for Saul, and when he found him, he brought him to Antioch. So for a whole year Barnabas and Saul met with the church and taught great numbers of people. The disciples were called Christians first at Antioch" (Acts 11:25–26). During the first year after he arrived, it may not be a coincidence that Paul was active in ministry in the very city where believers were first called "Christians."

This development may point out the effectiveness of Paul's ability to express faith in the Jewish Messiah in ways the Hellenistic (Greek-oriented) non-Jewish people could understand it. Paul was the apostle to the Gentiles. He contextualized Jewish theology in the Hellenistic culture. He was the most proactive Christian missionary of the early church. Other missionaries of that time seem to have traveled only secondarily. Philip fled persecution in Jerusalem; and Peter responded to invitations to places such as Caesarea. But Paul deliberately went out.

Paul tailored his message at Athens to the Athenian mind and context. He referred to the Athenians' own cultural matters. "For as I walked around and looked carefully at your objects of worship, I even found an altar with this inscription: TO AN UNKNOWN GOD. So you are ignorant of the very thing you worship — and this is what I am going to proclaim to you" (Acts 17:23).

Later, he quoted their own poet. "'For in him we live and move and have our being.' As some of your own poets have said, 'We are his offspring'" (Acts 17:28).

Paul's speech at Athens is a demonstration of his attempt to bridge the cultural gap between the Jewish and Hellenist worlds. The eventual success of these efforts in the growth of the church in Europe in the centuries that followed speaks for itself. Paul helped contextualize the message. In doing so, he taught thinking Christians all over the world that we must keep the core message of the gospel the same. However, just as important for the sake of communication and acceptance, it should be expressed in culturally sensitive and innovative ways. As we learned in the chapter on Philip, receptor-oriented communicators can help us become more effective cross-cultural workers.

> *Paul's speech at Athens is a demonstration of his attempt to bridge the cultural gap between the Jewish and Hellenist worlds.*

It is regrettable that Jewish people over the centuries lost the Jewishness of belief in "*Yeshua* the *Mashiach*" (the Hebrew name for Jesus the Messiah). In recent decades, thankfully, we have seen a resurgence of Messianic Jews and a wider acceptance of them by the Jewish community in the world.

Much to Paul's credit, the widespread belief in Jesus from his time forward was not limited to the Jewish people; it was shared in multiple cultural contexts throughout the entire world. This ability to adjust to different cultures is the principle way the gospel spread so rapidly. Paul, himself a Jew, was the leading personality by which the whole world was blessed through Abraham's offspring.

Paul Did Not Abandon His Jewish Roots

Having considered Paul's success as apostle to the Gentiles, let us briefly ponder Paul's Jewish side. How did Paul perceive himself? Even though he was the apostle to non-Jews, he never lost sight of his own Jewishness. He maintained his deep respect for his traditions and his people. Paul, son of a Roman citizen from Tarsus, was also the son of a Jewish mother. He had sat at the feet of the best Hebrew scholar in Jerusalem in his day: Gamaliel. Paul probably knew the Law and the Prophets (the Old Testament) better than any other follower of Jesus.

Four times in the early chapters of Romans, Paul refers to his own people as a priority:

> I am not ashamed of the gospel, because it is the power of God that brings salvation to everyone who believes: first to the Jew, then to the Gentile. (Romans 1:16)

> There will be trouble and distress for every human being who does evil: first for the Jew, then for the Gentile. (Romans 2:9)

> Glory, honor and peace for everyone who does good: first for the Jew, then for the Gentile. (Romans 2:10)

> First of all, the Jews have been entrusted with the very words of God. (Romans 3:2)

Successful apostle to the Gentiles though he was, as he traveled, Paul always went to Jewish synagogues first. In city after city, only after the Jewish people refused to receive his message did he turn to the Gentiles.

Paul wrote three masterly crafted chapters in Romans 9–11, showing that God was not finished with the Jews. Here are some samples of his expression of love for the Jewish people:

> Brothers and sisters, my heart's desire and prayer to God for the Israelites is that they may be saved. For I can testify about them that they are zealous for God, but their zeal is not based on knowledge. Since they did not know the righteousness of God and sought to establish their own, they did not submit to God's righteousness. (Romans 10:1-3)

> I ask then: Did God reject his people? By no means! I am an Israelite myself, a descendant of Abraham, from the tribe of Benjamin. God did not reject his people, whom he foreknew. (Romans 11:1-2)

> I do not want you to be ignorant of this mystery, brothers and sisters, so that you may not think you are superior: Israel has experienced a hardening in part until the full number of the Gentiles has come in, and in this way all Israel will be saved. As it is written: "The deliverer will come from Zion; he will turn godlessness away from Jacob. And this is my covenant with them when I take away their sins." (Romans 11:25-27)

No one knows who wrote the book of Hebrews. The author did not disclose his or her identity. It is possible that Apollos wrote it. It could even have been written by Pricilla, the knowledgeable female teacher who worked with Paul at Corinth in tent-making as well as gospel work. It is also possible (and even likely) that Paul wrote it. If so, the reason he kept his identity secret was probably to make the book acceptable to the Jewish people who misunderstood and hated him. He was more concerned that the message be received than he was about getting credit for writing the masterpiece.

Hebrews has a long, beautiful theological section showing Christ in the tabernacle, the sacrificial system, and Melchizedek's priesthood. That is followed by a practical section, just as in other books written by Paul. Hebrews refers to Timothy in much the same way Paul's books do. Paul was a brilliant Old Testament scholar. It is doubtful that anyone besides Paul in the Christian Church at that time had the knowledge and intellect to write such a work of genius as the book of Hebrews.

Paul Had a Radical Desire for His People to Know God

> I speak the truth in Christ — I am not lying, my conscience confirms it through the Holy Spirit — I have great sorrow and unceasing anguish in my heart. For I could wish that I myself were cursed and cut off from Christ for the sake of my people, those of my own race. (Romans 9:1-3)

Moses expressed a similar sentiment: "But now, please forgive their sin — but if not, then blot me out of the book you have written" (Exodus 32:32).

It is beyond human explanation how great men with fine minds like Moses and Paul could make such a radical statement. Why would they be willing to spend eternity away from God for the sake of others? Jesus, after He was crucified, went to hell in our place. He knew He was not going to remain there for eternity because He would be resurrected. The passion must have burned in the hearts of these giants of the faith for them to say what they did. It certainly communicates their noble heart's desire for all people to know God totally possessed these two godly men.

Paul's Church-Planting Mission Team Was Mobile and Autonomous

When the church at Antioch sent Barnabus and Saul, and later Paul and Silas, they released them to be led by the Holy Spirit. The team did not have to report back at every juncture and obtain permission to move as the Holy Spirit led them. This is illustrated throughout Paul's journeys, but nowhere more clearly than in the momentous transition from Troas to Macedonia. This story represents the movement of the gospel team from Asia into Europe. It was a change that has had profound effect on the history of Europe, North America, and Christian missions throughout the world.

> Paul and his companions traveled throughout the region of Phrygia and Galatia, having been kept by the Holy Spirit from preaching the word in the province of Asia. When they came to the border of Mysia, they tried to enter Bithynia, but the Spirit of Jesus would not allow them to. So they passed by Mysia and went down to Troas. During the night Paul had a vision of a man of Macedonia standing and begging him, "Come over to Macedonia and help us." After Paul had seen the vision, we got ready at once to leave for Macedonia, concluding that God had called us to preach the gospel to them. (Acts 16:6–10)

> "The Christian church should grant experienced missionaries on the field the liberty to follow the Paul model."

Paul's team had the autonomy and liberty they needed to respond obediently to the Holy Spirit. As a result, they did not preach the word in the province of Asia. They obeyed again when the Spirit stopped them from entering Bithynia. And they had the liberty to go on from Troas by sea to Macedonia in response to the vision of the Lord to move into Europe.

True enough, missionary administrators may need to provide some safety nets for missionaries who are young and inexperienced. Nevertheless, the Christian church should grant experienced missionaries on the field the liberty to follow the Paul model. They need the freedom to listen to and obey the leading of the Holy Spirit. If we don't trust certain missionary candidates, we should not send them. That would be better than giving them responsibilities without the authority to execute those responsibilities. Let's trust those we send.

Paul Knew Who He Was

> Once safely on shore, we found out that the island was called Malta. The islanders showed us unusual kindness. They built a fire and welcomed us all because it was raining and cold. Paul gathered a pile of brushwood and, as he put it on the fire, a viper, driven out by the heat, fastened itself on his hand. When the islanders saw the snake hanging from his hand, they said to each other, "This man must be a murderer, for though he escaped from the sea, Justice has not allowed him to live." But Paul shook the snake off into the fire and suffered no ill effects. The people expected him to swell up or suddenly fall dead, but after waiting a long time and seeing nothing unusual happen to him, they changed their minds and said he was a god. (Acts 28:1-6)

The islanders thought Paul was a murderer and said so. How do you think he reacted to this gross misunderstanding? He was not likely to think, *"Oh, no, my ministry is ruined. How will I ever be able to influence them to believe in Jesus? I will never be successful in Rome now. They think I am a murderer. My reputation is ruined!"*

It is doubtful that Paul internalized the critical opinion the islanders expressed or allowed their misjudgment to affect his peace of mind. Paul knew who he was. We know from his writings what Paul thought.

> I have been crucified with Christ and I no longer live, but Christ lives in me. The life I now live in the body, I live by faith in the Son of God, who loved me and gave himself for me. (Galatians 2:20)

> Christ Jesus came into the world to save sinners — of whom I am the worst. (1 Timothy 1:15)

> Therefore, there is now no condemnation for those who are in Christ Jesus. (Romans 8:1)

> I can do all this through him who gives me strength. (Philippians 4:13)

People can be very unkind, even to those appointed to be their spiritual leaders. "Our preacher can't preach. His sermons are boring. When he prays for the sick, they get worse and die. He has no faith. And when he sings, he can't stay on the right tune."

How do you react when people speak ill of you? Can you remember who you are in Christ and say the same things Paul did?

As the people of the island watched Paul, they noticed that he did not die or even get sick as a result of the snake bite. He was fine. "After waiting a long time and seeing nothing unusual happen to him, they changed their minds and said he was a god" (Acts 28:6). In the brief span of a few moments, the islanders' opinion of Paul shifted from believing he was a murderer to thinking he was a god.

How did Paul react now? Did he say to himself, "*Ah, at last! Now my day has come. People recognize what a gift I am to the human race. Now my success will really begin. They think I am a god. Just you wait until we get to Rome. I will be a great success there too?*"

No. Paul still believed the same things he did before:

> I have been crucified with Christ and I no longer live, but Christ lives in me. The life I now live in the body, I live by faith in the Son of God, who loved me and gave himself for me. (Galatians 2:20)

> Christ Jesus came into the world to save sinners — of whom I am the worst. (1 Timothy 1:15)

> Therefore, there is now no condemnation for those who are in Christ Jesus. (Romans 8:1)

> I can do all this through him who gives me strength. (Philippians 4:13)

What will you do when people say, "Our Christian friend has the voice of an angel. When he sings a song, it sounds like a choir of angels. When he speaks in public, his words are like the combined messages of a hundred prophets from the Bible. And when he prays, I feel like I am in heaven and Jesus is interceding for me before the Father's throne." What will you say? How will you think about yourself? Will you be able to stay on an even keel, hold steady, and say what Paul said?

How much do we allow people's opinions to affect our self-appraisal? How much should others' opinions be considered as we formulate our opinions of ourselves?

We are all thankful for mothers who unconditionally believe the best about us. Their belief in us encourages us enormously and bolsters our self-confidence. But we are also grateful for honest friends who tell us when we are wrong. Proverbs 27:6 says, "Wounds from a friend can be trusted." Most of us would rather develop in our character than stumble along through life ignorantly happy with the mediocre.

The issue raised by the islanders' repeated misunderstanding of Paul forces us to address the question of how we handle people's opinions, bad or good. How do we resist becoming discouraged by negative opinions? When others think more highly of us than we deserve, how do we resist pride?

The Bible tells us who we are in the Lord. We should be self-confident, but our self-confidence must come from the presence of Christ in us. Paul knew that, and we need to know that.

If we allow the Word of God to be our personal evaluation plumb line, we will not be swayed, discouraged, or ego-inflated by the opinions of others. "Anyone who listens to the word but does not do what it says is like a man who looks at his face in a mirror and, after looking at himself, goes away and immediately forgets what he looks like" (James 1:23). Paul allowed the Word of God, not people's opinions, to tell him who he was.

> "We are not as good as certain people say. And we are not as bad as some other people say."

God will allow people into our lives to keep us humbly trusting him, and He will use others to encourage us. That helps us keep humility and self-confidence balanced. We are able to do what we do through Christ who strengthens us, and this is possible only through Him. The Bible provides appropriate push and pull between dependence on Christ and awareness of His strength within us. We are not as good as certain people say. And we are not as bad as some other people say.

Human opinions are better used as an encourager than as a discourager. No weapon formed against God's children will prevail (Isaiah 54:17). If you lean toward being critical of other Christians, remember what God has promised them. Don't unwittingly become a weapon formed against any of God's children. If you want things to go well for you, be an encourager.

For Further Thought

- How will you harmonize what you've learned about God opening doors for Philip and the lesson from Paul about persevering through what might seem to be closed doors?
- Have you ever had an experience in which you rejoiced that your faith, not your works, provided your righteousness in God's eyes? If so, describe it.
- Can you follow Paul's example and make the Christian message relevant to the specific people to whom God has sent you?
- Can you remain comfortable in your own cultural background even while you minister to others in another cultural setting?
- What is your opinion of Paul's radical statement about being willing to be accursed for the sake of the salvation of the Jews?
- Do you give autonomy to those to whom you delegate a missionary responsibility? If you have not done so in the past, how will your views and actions change?
- What assistance to your own self-worth do you derive from knowing who you are? How do you avoid allowing the opinions of others to affect your self-image?

CHAPTER 25
PHOEBE

Many people have never heard of Phoebe. Did you know that she was an outstanding New Testament Christian leader? Were you aware that Paul himself claims to have benefited from her ministry? There are many "Phoebes" today who need to know about Phoebe and Paul's high opinion of her.

I grew up in a pastor's home. My mother and father were both ordained ministers in a reputable Protestant denomination, believed in the gospel message of the Bible, preached it in the church, and lived it in our home. They worked together in public, private, and personal aspects of ministry as a team. We who sat under their ministry did not refer to them as "co-pastors" of our church, but that is what they were.

They each preached every other Sunday morning and alternate Sunday evenings. So we in the congregation heard from each of them every Sunday. Both were equally devoted to the work they did and the God they served, but Mom seemed to study harder, prepare better, and have richer content than Dad.

Growing up in this environment in the 1950s, I thought that was the way all pastors and their spouses worked together. As I grew older and answered questions from my friends at school about my mother being a lady preacher, however, I realized that my parents were the exception. Nevertheless, I was totally comfortable with Mother having a successful public ministry as a teaching preacher.

You may have grown up believing that it was inappropriate for women to be preachers. If so, your view on this subject would be just as natural to you as my view was to me. As the years pass, the number of people who accept women in the ministry is increasing. This alone would not justify the belief, but it can indicate a trend.

My parents were not the norm, but they were not abnormal. Many other successful, endearing lady preachers serve in nations around the world. This is in spite of the fact that some churchmen misunderstand what Paul the apostle taught in Corinthians and Timothy regarding women in ministry. In one of the cases Paul addressed, he corrected a unique local problem; in neither case did he close the door to women ministers.

I am grateful to Joel David Hamilton for his permission to use some of the ideas from his excellent dissertation on the subject of women in ministry. This chapter is the only exception to the statement made in the introduction that this book was not a research project. I referred to Hamilton's scholarly work in writing parts of this chapter.

Phoebe Was an Actual Person

> I commend to you our sister Phoebe, a deacon of the church in Cenchreae. I ask you to receive her in the Lord in a way worthy of his people and to give her any help she may need from you, for she has been the benefactor of many people, including me. (Romans 16:1-2)

Paul *commended* Phoebe; in the Greek language, he *stood with* her. He endorsed her. Paul spoke against those who speak well of themselves: "For it is not those who commend themselves who are approved, but those whom the Lord commends" (2 Corinthians 10:18). Paul's acclaim would have been valuable and encouraging to Phoebe.

The believers in Rome were to "receive her." Paul used the same word in Philippians 2:25-30 to encourage the Philippians to receive Epaphroditus.

> I think it is necessary to send back to you Epaphroditus, my brother, co-worker and fellow soldier, who is also your messenger, whom you sent to take care of my needs. For he longs for all of you and is distressed because you heard he was ill. Indeed he was ill, and almost died. But God had mercy on him, and not on him only but also on me, to spare me sorrow upon sorrow. Therefore I am all the more eager to send him, so that

when you see him again you may be glad and I may have less anxiety. *Welcome* him in the Lord with great joy, and honor *people* like him, because he almost died for the work of Christ. He risked his life to make up for the help you yourselves could not give me. (emphasis mine)

The believers in Philippi were to *welcome* Epaphroditus, and the believers in Rome were to *receive* Phoebe. The Greek word Paul used was the same. Today's New International Version says that we are to honor *people* like that. Though some translations inaccurately read to honor *men* like that, Paul was not saying that men were to be honored and not women.

First Timothy 5:17 explains how churches are to receive God's servants. "The elders who direct the affairs of the church well are worthy of double honor, especially those whose work is preaching and teaching." Paul said the same thing to the church at Rome when he instructed them to honor Phoebe. "I ask you to receive her in the Lord in a way worthy of his people" (Romans 16:2).

> "Paul paid Phoebe a high compliment in using this word to describe her."

Paul also said the Romans were to "give her any help she may need" (Romans 16:2). Paul gave far more respect and attention in his good description and introduction of Phoebe than to any of the other individuals whom he said they were to greet in the subsequent verses.

Phoebe was the "benefactor" of many people. This is the only place in the Bible where this word is used. What did it mean to the original readers of Romans? In the culture of that day, this term usually referred to a particularly gracious, helpful, or beneficial captain, public officer, official, or ruler. Paul paid Phoebe a high compliment in using this word to describe her. Not only had others received help from Phoebe, but Paul had personally benefited from her ministry. Whether she ministered to him or ministered on his behalf — having been appointed by him — is not known.

Given the culture of the day, Paul would have been hard pressed to recommend her more strongly than he did. In essence he said, "I commend her. I stand with her; you stand with her. She is a benefactor, helping others. You help her. Give her whatever she needs."

Are there women you know for whom these words could make a world of difference? Has God placed you in a position to either release women to ministry or restrict their influence? How have you used that power in the past? How will you use that power in the future?

Phoebe Represents Thousands of Women Like Her

Phoebe is by no means an exception in Scripture. There are many New Testament references to women in service to the Lord in the church. This is equally true of the Old Testament, in which numerous women led God's people. Esther and Deborah come to mind as ready examples. Consistent with the place the entire Bible gives to women leaders, Peter quotes Joel, who predicted that God's Spirit would be placed on women as well as on men:

> This is what was spoken by the prophet Joel: "In the last days, God says, I will pour out my Spirit on all people. Your sons *and daughters* will prophesy, your young men will see visions, your old men will dream dreams. Even on my servants, both men *and women*, I will pour out my Spirit in those days, and they will prophesy." (Acts 2:16–18, emphasis mine).

Paul gave due recognition to several other women who served God in the church:

> Greet Tryphena and Tryphosa, those women who work hard in the Lord. Greet my dear friend Persis, another woman who has worked very hard in the Lord. (Romans 16:12)

> I plead with Euodia and I plead with Syntyche to be of the same mind in the Lord. Yes, and I ask you, my true companion, help these women since they have contended at my side in the cause of the gospel, along with Clement and the rest of my coworkers, whose names are in the book of life. (Philippians 4:2–3)

Paul gave instructions to Timothy to be respectful toward women:

> Treat younger men as brothers, older women as mothers, and younger women as sisters, with absolute purity. (1 Timothy 5:1–2)

> Teach the older women to be reverent in the way they live, not to be slanderers or addicted to much wine, but to teach what is

good. Then they can urge the younger women to love their husbands and children, to be self-controlled and pure, to be busy at home, to be kind, and to be subject to their husbands, so that no one will malign the word of God. (Titus 2:3-5)

These verses in Titus do not teach that women should teach only women. They instructed women to teach women certain things that would be particularly good for young women to know.

Chloe of Corinth may well have been a pastor. "My brothers and sisters, some from Chloe's household have informed me that there are quarrels among you" (1 Corinthians 1:11). In the English translation, the word *household* is also used twice in Romans 16:10-11 to refer to churches in Aristobulus' and Narcissis' homes. "Greet Apelles, whose fidelity to Christ has stood the test. Greet those who belong to the household of Aristobulus. Greet Herodion, my fellow Jew. Greet those in the household of Narcissus who are in the Lord" (Romans 16:10-11).

In Greek, the word *household* is not there in any of the three cases: Chloe, Aristobulus, or Narcissis. Bible scholars tend to believe "those" refers to households or perhaps families. Only in English is "households" equally present in all three. The Greek grammar uses just the phrase "those of Chloe" (1 Corinthians 1:11), "those of Aristobulus" (Romans 16:10), and "those of Narcissus" (Romans 16:11). What did it mean to be "of Chloe," "of Aristobulus," or "of Narcissus"? Since Paul wrote both Romans and Corinthians, shouldn't each of these three references all have the same translation, connotation, and interpretation? Could not the same phrase — "those of" — indicate that Chloe was also a pastor? Either that, or Aristobulus and Narcissus were *not* pastors.

> "Chloe of Corinth may well have been a pastor."

Bible scholars believe these three references are to churches in the homes of Aristobulus and Narcissus. So why would "those of Chloe" not also mean the church of which she was either the pastor or a pastor?

The New Testament also refers to what evidently was a leading *couple* in the early church. Many are the references to these two people (a man and his wife) who were tentmakers and partners in ministry with Paul. In every reference Luke and Paul make to Aquila, his wife, Priscilla, is mentioned too. In five of those seven references, Priscilla is named first. Could that be because she was more gifted than her husband?

> He met a Jew named Aquila, a native of Pontus, who had recently come from Italy with his wife Priscilla, because Claudius had ordered all the Jews to leave Rome. Paul went to see them. (Acts 18:2)
>
> Paul stayed on in Corinth for some time. Then he left the brothers and sailed for Syria, accompanied by Priscilla and Aquila. Before he sailed, he had his hair cut off at Cenchrea because of a vow he had taken. (Acts 18:18)
>
> They arrived at Ephesus, where Paul left Priscilla and Aquila. He himself went into the synagogue and reasoned with the Jews. (Acts 18:19)
>
> He [Apollos] began to speak boldly in the synagogue. When Priscilla and Aquila heard him, they invited him to their home and explained to him the way of God more adequately. (Acts 18:26)
>
> Greet Priscilla and Aquila, my fellow workers in Christ Jesus. (Romans 16:3)
>
> The churches in the province of Asia send you greetings. Aquila and Priscilla greet you warmly in the Lord, and so does the church that meets at their house. (1 Corinthians 16:19)
>
> Greet Priscilla and Aquila and the household of Onesiphorus. (2 Timothy 4:19)

It seems that these mature Christians were both teachers. Together they invited the esteemed church leader and evangelist, Apollos, to their home for private instruction. "*They* invited him [Apollos] to their home and explained to him the way of God more adequately" (Acts 18:26, emphasis mine).

The verses above suggest strong partnership between the husband and wife. They imply that Paul respected both. And that they each have distinct value in the work of the Lord.

Scripture gives us the picture of a man and his wife who were a ministry team — both gifted, tested, recognized, released, used, and fruitful in ministry. Apparently, in fulfillment of Joel's prophecy, God's Spirit was not only poured out on men. It also worked in wisdom, power, and love through this son and daughter of God and of Abraham.

Phoebe Was Instructed in Public Ministry

Paul wrote openly about gender issues in public ministry. In 1 Corinthians, he instructed both men and women about public ministry. The word *prophesy* here could also be translated as "preach," "teach," or "speak in public."

> I praise you for remembering me in everything and for holding to the traditions just as I passed them on to you. But I want you to realize that the head of every man is Christ, and the head of the woman is man [or "of the wife is her husband"], and the head of Christ is God. Every man who prays or prophesies with his head covered dishonors his head. But every woman who prays or prophesies with her head uncovered dishonors her head — it is the same as having her head shaved. For if a woman does not cover her head, she might as well have her hair cut off; but if it is a disgrace for a woman to have her hair cut off or her head shaved, then she should cover her head.
>
> A man ought not to cover his head, since he is the image and glory of God; but woman is the glory of man. For man did not come from woman, but woman from man; neither was man created for woman, but woman for man. It is for this reason that a woman ought to have authority over her own [or have the sign of authority on her] head, because of the angels. Nevertheless, in the Lord, woman is not independent of man, nor is man independent of woman. For as woman came from man, so also man is born of woman. But everything comes from God.

> "The word *prophesy* here could also be translated as 'preach,' 'teach,' or 'speak in public.'"

Choose Your Character

Judge for yourselves: Is it proper for a woman to pray to God with her head uncovered? Does not the very nature of things teach you that if a man has long hair, it is a disgrace to him, but that if a woman has long hair, it is her glory? For long hair is given to her as a covering. If anyone wants to be contentious about this, we have no other practice — nor do the churches of God. (1 Corinthians 11:2-16, bracketed material taken from the TNIV footnote)

Paul is providing instructions for those who minister in public. That men and women ministered in public was not his point. He assumed that. He is teaching members of both genders the ground rules for their conduct when speaking publicly. He did not say women were not to prophesy or pray publicly. He said they were not to do it with their heads uncovered.

Basically, he was saying, "Women, cover your head *when* you prophesy and when you pray in public, in keeping with the local custom." Even though Paul referred to women covering their heads in public as "the very nature of things," that was a local custom.

Paul was not saying that a woman had to have a covering on her head even when she was in private. How could she live with her head constantly covered in order to "pray without ceasing," as Paul also instructed?

> "He is teaching members of both genders the ground rules for their conduct when speaking publicly."

If Phoebe was a fellow worker with Paul, as Romans 16 says, she would have received from Paul the same instructions he wrote for the Corinthians. If Paul instructed the women in Corinth how to minister in public, we can assume that Phoebe (Paul's benefactor and coworker) also received those instructions. We can also assume she implemented them to minister either to, with, or for Paul.

Phoebe, the women of Corinth, and all women called by God to public ministry, from then until today, have the same teachings from Paul. They can all minister publicly with sensitivity to local custom.

The original readers were also to be sensitive to the Corinthian custom of women having long hair. Phoebe was under the same direction, even if the customs in Rome were different. Likewise, today's women ministers should maintain the proper cultural decorum.

Paul Addressed the Issue of Order and One Particular Disorderly Woman

It is very possible that one insubordinate woman in Corinth caused disorder, and to her Paul addressed specific restrictions. Here is what Paul said about order:

> What then shall we say, brothers and sisters? When you come together, each of you has a hymn, or a word of instruction, a revelation, a tongue or an interpretation. Everything must be done so that the church may be built up. If anyone speaks in a tongue, two — or at the most three — should speak, one at a time, and someone must interpret. If there is no interpreter, the speaker should keep quiet in the church; let them speak to themselves and to God.
>
> Two or three prophets should speak, and the others should weigh carefully what is said. And if a revelation comes to someone who is sitting down, the first speaker should stop. For you can all prophesy in turn so that everyone may be instructed and encouraged. The spirits of prophets are subject to the control of prophets. For God is not a God of disorder but of peace — as in all the congregations of the Lord's people.
>
> Women should remain silent in the churches. They are not allowed to speak, but must be in submission, as the law says. If they want to inquire about something, they should ask their own husbands at home; for it is disgraceful for a woman to speak in the church. Or did the word of God originate with you? Or are you the only people it has reached? If any think they are prophets or otherwise gifted by the Spirit, let them acknowledge that what I am writing to you is the Lord's command. Those who ignore this will themselves be ignored.
>
> Therefore, my brothers and sisters, be eager to prophesy, and do not forbid speaking in tongues. But everything should be done in a fitting and orderly way. (1 Corinthians 14:26-40)

If Paul instructed the women of Corinth how to minister in public, does it make sense that he would say, three chapters later, that they should not speak in public? Clearly Paul would not contradict himself in this way. He addresses both brothers and sisters in 1 Corinthians 14 when he says, "Each of you has a hymn, or a word of instruction, a revelation, a tongue or an interpretation." Later in the same passage, he says to both brothers and sisters that they should be eager to prophesy. Again, Paul would not contradict himself by saying how they should minister publicly and then forbid women to speak in public.

So what did Paul mean when he said, "Women should remain silent in the churches" and "They are not allowed to speak, but must be in submission, as the law says" (1 Corinthians 14:34)? Could it be that he was correcting the way *some* women in Corinth were ministering?

It is quite possible that the last part of 1 Corinthians 14:35 ("It is disgraceful for a woman to speak in the church") is a quotation — not Paul's thoughts, but a wrong idea that he is preparing to refute. In his letters, Paul often quotes someone's words or a common saying and then refutes it. Quotation marks are not included in the original Greek New Testament but are inserted in our English translations. Could it be that quotation marks should have been included here? If so, the verse would look like this: "If they want to inquire about something, they should ask their own husbands at home; for 'It is disgraceful for a woman to speak in the church'" (1 Corinthians 14:35).

> "Could it be that he was correcting the way *some* women in Corinth were ministering?"

The statement "It is disgraceful for a woman to speak in the church" is contrary to everything else Paul says about recognizing and releasing women to public ministry. Paul is talking about maintaining order in public worship; he is not concerned here about all women, just disorderly women.

The grammatical reason for interpreting this verse this way is based on a small word in the Greek New Testament. Forty-nine times in 1 Corinthians, Paul uses the one-letter Greek word η (pronounced "eh") — sometimes used as an expletive of disapproval, according to Greek scholars, that serves to identify a ridiculous idea. In these cases, it would be rather like "Huh?" or an exclamation emphasizing that what was just said is preposterous. It could have been used in sarcasm, or as obvious reverse psychology, or perhaps to indicate that a strong overstatement has just been made to gain the attention of the reader.

Here are three examples of the use of η (parenthetical translations mine):

> 1 Corinthians 1:13: "Is Christ divided? η (Of course not!) Were you baptized into the name of Paul? (Not so!)"

> "He is not concerned here about all women, just disorderly women."

> 1 Corinthians 9:7: "Who plants a vineyard and does not eat of its grapes? η (No one!) Who tends a flock and does not drink of the milk? (Nobody!)"

> 1 Corinthians 9:9-10: "Is it about oxen that God is concerned? η (Nonsense!) Surely he says this for us, doesn't he? (Of course!)"

Paul wrote a η after writing, "It is disgraceful for a woman to speak in the church."

> 1 Corinthians 14:35-36: "If they want to inquire about something, they should ask their own husbands at home, for 'It is disgraceful for a woman to speak in the church.' η (What?) Or did the word of God originate with you? η (Obviously not!) Or are you the only people it has reached? η (That's ridiculous!)"

In earlier verses, Paul addressed the problem of people speaking in tongues, telling them to speak "one at a time" or to keep quiet (1 Corinthians 14:27-28). Then he addressed prophecy, saying that "two or three" prophets should speak "in turn" (1 Corinthians 14:29-31). When he addressed the problem of women speaking in the church, he was not prohibiting participation. On the contrary, he welcomed participation. He only wanted orderly participation. Whether speaking in tongues, or prophesying, or women speaking, the problem was order. "Everything should be done in a fitting and orderly way" (1 Corinthians 14:40).

"Be silent" was a request to take turns rather than a request to stop participating. If Paul had to correct the way women were participating, doesn't that indicate that they were already participating?

The pagan background into which Paul spoke was chaotic and disorderly. Paul did not want that in the church. Yet he encouraged everyone's participation:

> What then shall we say, brothers and sisters? When you come together, *each of you* has a hymn, or a word of instruction, a revelation, a tongue or an interpretation. Everything must be done so that the church may be built up. (1 Corinthians 14:26–27, emphasis mine)

Rather than prohibiting women's participation, Paul was liberating, releasing, and encouraging, while instructing them how to do it. Women were not as well educated as men in those days. Some of them may have followed the chaotic pattern of contemporary religions, and some may simply have lacked self-control. For Paul to teach them how to minister would have been a huge step forward for women in the days of the dominating Greek and Roman cultures. Centuries later, the result of the seeds of freedom and opportunity Paul planted are bearing fruit. Phoebe and all others like her have Paul's instructions and the liberty to serve Christ's Church.

Phoebe Was Not Like the Women Paul Addressed in His Letter to Timothy

Other Pauline Scriptures have been misunderstood for centuries, including the instructions he gave to Timothy, pastor of the church of Ephesus, on the subject of men and women in ministry. Pricilla was one of the founding leaders of this church. After telling the church in Rome to receive Phoebe with honor, would he really contradict himself in his letter to Timothy? Let's look at what Paul said and try to determine what he meant.

In the verses quoted below, notice the shift from the use of the word *women* to *a woman* and then back to *women*. Let's consider the possibility that when speaking of *women*, Paul was making blanket statements about women in general, and when he mentioned *a woman,* he had a specific problematic female in mind. It was she, not all women, who needed to be curtailed in her activities.

First Timothy 2:8-10 is addressed to men and women:

> I want the men everywhere to pray, lifting up holy hands without anger or disputing. I also want the *women* to dress modestly, with decency and propriety, adorning themselves, not with elaborate hairstyles or gold or pearls or expensive clothes, but with good deeds, appropriate for *women* who profess to worship God" (emphasis mine).

> "Notice the shift from the use of the word *women* to *a woman* and then back to *women*."

First Timothy 2:11-14, the next verses, is addressed to a woman (singular):

> A *woman* should learn in quietness and full submission. I do not permit a *woman* [or "a wife"] to teach or to assume authority over a man [or "to teach a man in a domineering way or teach or to exercise (or have) authority over a man]; she must be quiet. For Adam was formed first, then Eve. And Adam was not the one deceived; it was the woman who was deceived and became a sinner" (emphasis mine, bracketed materials are TNIV footnotes).

First Timothy 2:15 is again addressed to women (plural):

> *Women* will be saved through childbearing — if they continue in faith, love and holiness with propriety.

First Paul speaks of women who "profess to worship God" (1 Timothy 2:10). The word translated *profess* conveys the meaning of proclamation and expertise. It would be difficult to profess, proclaim, or share one's expertise and remain silent. Paul asked women to dress appropriately because they publicly professed themselves to be God-worshippers. That is certainly understandable.

What is written next, about a specific woman, is written within the context of the fact that women were proclaiming — professing — their message. Paul wanted it to be the right message delivered with the right attitude.

Paul uses the singular when addressing the issue of being quiet, in full submission, and not having permission to teach or have authority over

Choose Your Character

men. There may be an important message in his use of the singular and the plural. This is not the only place in the New Testament in which Paul speaks boldly about silencing nameless as well as named individuals who were teaching falsehoods.

> Evildoers and impostors will go from bad to worse, deceiving and being deceived. (2 Timothy 3:13)

> As I urged you when I went into Macedonia, stay there in Ephesus so that you may command certain persons not to teach false doctrines any longer. (1 Timothy 1:3)

> Some have departed from these and have turned to meaningless talk. They want to be teachers of the law, but they do not know what they are talking about or what they so confidently affirm. (1 Timothy 1:6–7)

> Their teaching will spread like gangrene. Among them are Hymenaeus and Philetus. (1 Timothy 2:17)

No one would conclude that just because some men teach falsehoods, no men should be allowed to teach. Some women also taught falsehoods, but that does not mean that no woman is ever permitted to teach.

Paul instructed Timothy to pass his teachings on so they could in turn be passed on yet again. "The things you have heard me say in the presence of many witnesses entrust to reliable people *(anthropois)* who will also be qualified to teach others" (2 Timothy 2:2, emphasis mine). Today's New International Version translates the word that was formerly translated "men" as "people." Women are included in Paul's instructions. Paul used ανθρωποις *(anthropois),* the gender-inclusive word for mankind. We can assume Paul chose this word deliberately, for many times he used the word for "man" or "men." Women, therefore, are included in the Scripture in which Paul urges Timothy to pass his knowledge on to others who will, in turn, pass it on again.

> "No one would conclude that just because some men teach falsehoods, no men should be allowed to teach."

Paul defends women by referring indirectly to the promise given to Eve, fulfilled at least in part by Mary's Child. Adam, formed first, sinned fully aware of God's command, but Eve, formed second, was deceived. Paul may have been suggesting that this deceived woman in Timothy's church in Ephesus could be saved by believing in the Seed of woman who was promised when Adam and Eve sinned. She could be saved through believing in the Child Mary bore, just as all women who believe are saved. This did not mean that she or any other woman has to bear a child to be saved. She could be saved from the errors by which she was bound — the errors Paul was saying should not be allowed to be taught — by believing in the truth of Jesus, who came through the woman Mary.

In 1 Timothy 3:1-10, Paul spoke of qualifications for leaders of the church. He gave women equal opportunity in his instructions: "In the same way, the women are to be worthy of respect, not malicious talkers but temperate and trustworthy in everything" (1 Timothy 3:11).

Paul gave women controls for their own safety (and for the safety of their congregations) and freedom to minister. God calls and anoints His ministers of both genders, and mankind is to receive and welcome them.

How Do We Regard "Phoebes" Today?

Provide ministry opportunities for the Phoebes — the spiritually gifted women — around you. Your Phoebe may be your mother, daughter, sister, spouse, neighbor, or pastor. You will recognize her by her spiritual insights and her desire to share her understanding with others. Give her the support she needs. Listen to the perspective she has on the Word of God. If she is wrong, gently and lovingly instruct her privately. Don't criticize her in public — ever. Create opportunities for her to minister.

The Bible says that no weapon formed against us will prevail (see Isaiah 54:17). Don't be a weapon against one of God's servants. Things will not go well for you if you do. Even if your culture or tradition does not make room for women in leadership, recognize the teachings of the Word of God. God will look favorably on anyone who is kind and supportive to one of His daughters. When she is worthy of commendation, commend her.

If you are married to a Phoebe, consider it your special behind-the-scenes ministry to God and His people to be her supporter. She needs you to be her encourager, confidant, and counselor. She does not need you to be her critic — not in the negative sense of destructive criticism. If you have a mutually beneficial agreement with her that you each offer helpful criticisms for the development of the other, she can benefit from your comments. But if your criticisms are destructive, keep them to yourself. You will have many opportunities to serve the Lord in the home, at work, and at church. Let serving your spouse be one of those ways. Pray for her. Pray with her. Speak truth, love, and affirmation into her spirit. Build her up. Make her strong. God will bless you for it.

> **She needs you to be her encourager, confidant, and counselor.**

Are You a "Phoebe"?

If you are a modern-day Phoebe, serve with humility. The best contribution you can make toward making room for women in ministry is to be the best minister you can be without making an issue of women's entitlement to preach. If you staunchly defend your right to preach and focus on how women are misused and how tough it is for women to minister, you may need personal affirmation before you can minister encouragement to others.

Find your sufficiency in your time alone with God in prayer and Bible study. Out of that strength, minister comfort, affirmation, and encouragement to your listeners every time you stand before them. Some speakers, both men and women, need their listeners to say "amen" just for encouragement. This is a reversal of roles. You should have such rich, encouraging, and helpful information and content in your sermons that people want to listen to you. Your listeners need you to minister to *their* needs, not listen to you tell them or even hint to them about *your* needs.

Study hard, pray fervently, and present good, professional sermons. If you feel you're being ignored, don't increase your volume, become agitated, or use emotional language. Inspire and be anointed. Teach the Word. Have good content in your messages. Build people up. A shepherd does not beat the sheep; a shepherd leads them.

Cultivate the spirit of a benefactor. Don't be jealous of the men you benefit. If you complain that others receive while you give, you do not have the heart of a servant. It is God you serve, as well as the men and women in your circle of influence. Affirm, encourage, and minister in a positive way to all the people God places in your path. Listen to their needs and find ways to support and serve them. Don't compete with them. As you become a benefactor to men, they will benefit from your ministry. Then they will commend you as Paul commended Phoebe. Your gift will make room for you.

> Some speakers, both men and women, need their listeners to say 'amen' just for encouragement. This is a reversal of roles.

God's call and anointing for ministry falls on both men and women. How many more women might step forward if we understood that? What change in our attitude or policy needs to be made to make that possible?

For Further Thought

- How do you feel about Paul's high commendation of Phoebe — the best he gave to any of his fellow workers?
- How many "Phoebes" can you identify in your circle of influence?
- What would you need to do to give your Phoebes positive instructions for public ministry?
- If you see that Paul would have been inconsistent to give instructions for public ministry to men and women readers and then immediately say that women cannot minister in public, will you utilize opportunities to share that observation with others?
- How do you intend to combat the bias of men against women in ministry, a bias we now know that Paul never intended?
- What did you learn from the discussion of the η that appears so often in Paul's letters?
- Is there a woman in your circle of influence who, for a valid reason, should be denied the privilege to continue her ministry? How will you handle that situation?
- If you are a Phoebe, how will you benefit from this chapter?
- If you are married to a Phoebe, in what way will you adjust your attitude toward her?
- What can you do to release ministry by women more fully?

AFTERWORD

The people whose lives are recorded in the Bible are not fictitious storybook characters; they were real people. How they dealt with life issues in their time can help us today. I trust you have been able to grasp some of the rich lessons available from studying their lives.

I also hope this study has stimulated a desire in your heart to think carefully about other characters in the Bible not included in this volume. As you read of their adventures, imagine what they may have looked like or what clothes they might have worn. Maybe even give them a nickname. Try to think of what life lessons they have for you.

Another benefit of this book is to show the power of regular Bible reading. I highly recommend this beneficial habit. As I wrote this manuscript, I thought over the life messages of each of the persons I selected. If you become a regular reader of God's Word, you too will find understanding and insight into life issues that you will want to share with others.

Just as the Bible's personalities speak to us, our lives speak to those around us. What we say will have more meaning if it is supported by how we live. Our loudest voice is our actions. What if people a hundred years from now were to examine your life, how you lived, and what you did? What will they learn? What will they write about you to benefit their generation? What is your life saying? Do your good works glorify your Father in Heaven? Just as you've learned from analyzing the stories of people in the Bible, so may your actions illustrate life lessons from which others can learn.

ABOUT THE AUTHOR
Ron Meyers

Ron Meyers was born in 1944 and raised in a pioneer pastor's home. In July 1965, he began pastoral ministry as a student pastor in a rural community seventy miles from the Bible College he attended in mid-Ohio.

From 1996 until 2006, he served as the Professor of Missions and Coordinator of the Master of Arts in Missions program in the School of Theology and Missions of Oral Roberts University. During those years, Ron traveled to African, Asian, European, and Middle Eastern nations during his summer breaks from university responsibilities.

He, with his wife, Char, have served more years outside the United States as pastors in Canada and missionaries in Korea, China, and Africa than their years in the U.S. Since January 2007, Ron and Char have lived in Africa and traveled full-time to African nations Conducting Empower Africa Christian Leadership Conferences. Ron has a PhD in Intercultural Studies and Char has an EdD. The Meyers have two adult sons, one daughter-in-law, and eight grandchildren.

ONLINE TOOLS FOR LEADERS

Leadership Empowerment Resources Website

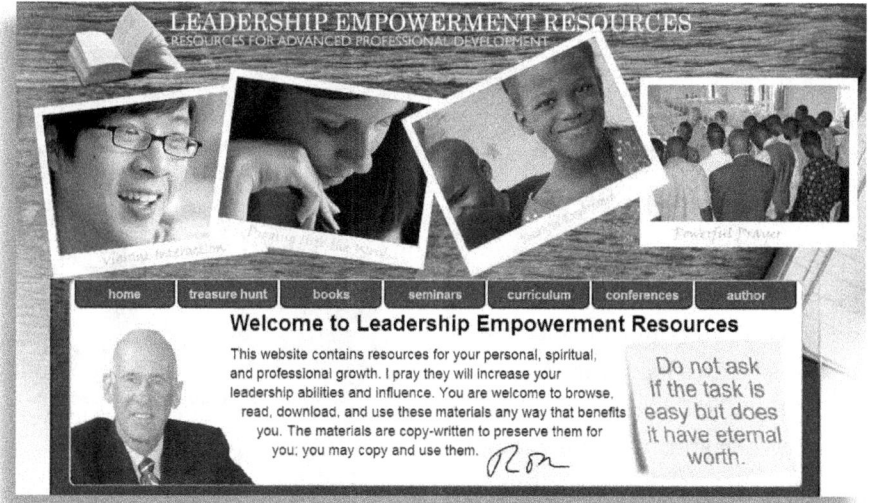

This website provides additional resources for Dr. Meyer's mission work abroad. It includes information on:

- **Books:** Resources written by Ron Meyers for expanding your wisdom and knowledge to use in any way that serves your purpose in helping to enrich the lives of Christians you know

- **Leadership Empowerment Conferences:** Ron and Char Meyers' Africa-based vehicle for strengthening His Church by training the leaders of churches

- **Treasure Hunt:** A Christian conversational game intended to be a catalyst for drawing out practical wisdom and understanding — treasures — from the hearts of Christians who enjoy wholesome conversational fun

Visit the Website

To read the code, download the QR Reader app for your cell phone and scan it.

OTHER BOOKS BY RON MEYERS

Habits of Highly Effective Christians Book and Study Guide

Habits of Highly Effective Christians Makes a Great Bible Study Program

When Ron Meyers followed his passion for international missions work forty years ago, he never imagined the rich educational curriculum God had in store for him. A lifetime of spiritual challenges groomed him for his role at the School of Theology and Missions at Oral Roberts University in Tulsa, Oklahoma. Then, after ten years educating Christian ministry candidates at ORU and serving as Coordinator of the Master of Arts in Missions program, he and his wife moved to Africa where they now train pastors and missionaries throughout the southern African nations.

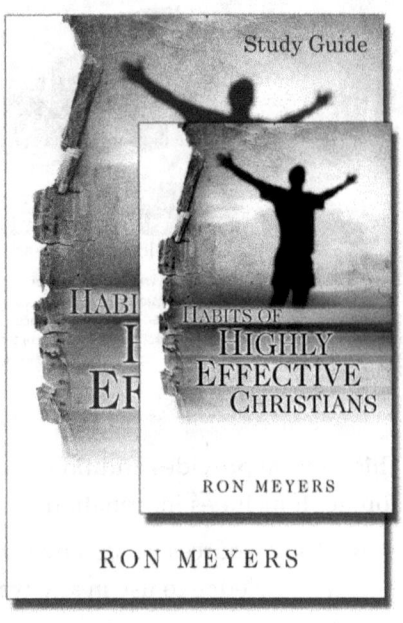

Meyers wrote his book with life application in mind. He weaves his stories into each habit by providing real-life, insightful, and applicable examples. *Habits of Highly Effective Christians* guides you through biblical resources for creating a rich tapestry with the fibers of your own life.

A Great Tool for Growth and Discussion

Proven to create rich discussions, *Habits of Highly Effective Christians* is perfect for small-group Bible studies or college classroom discussions. Meyers has also written the *Habits of Highly Effective Christians Study Guide*. Together, this study combo will etch biblical principles on every aspect of the lives you encounter.

OTHER BOOKS BY RON MEYERS

Rise to Seek Him: The Joy of Effective Prayer

Allow God to Do Immeasurably More in Your Life

Effective prayer is more about becoming useful tools in God's hands than imposing our plans and desires on Him. In *Rise to Seek Him*, we learn that we accomplish much more when God uses us through prayer than when we try to use God to accomplish our objectives.

This is not just another book on prayer. Ron Meyers invites you to experiment for yourself how God can accomplish "immeasurably more" than you could ever ask or imagine. This book reveals fresh insights about the meaning of prayer — insights that were in the Bible all the time.

Rise to Seek Him offers practical solutions to the questions we all ask:

- How do we discipline ourselves to pray?
- How can we know what to pray for?
- Why is it difficult to pray?
- What is the focus of prayer?
- Does prayer really "work?"

This book testifies to the expansion in influence, effectiveness, and success possible with increased personal prayer. As in *Habits of Highly Effective Christians*, Meyers again describes self-discipline as a fruit of the Spirit to increase personal spiritual growth and improvement in public ministry. God-fearing Christians of any vocation who are serious about serving God at maximum levels of effectiveness will benefit from this book.

Books and e-books by Ron Meyers are available at online bookstores.

Quantity discounts are available by contacting Soar with Eagles (www.soarhigher.com).

A Thoughtful Gift

Order *Choose Your Character*
as a gift for family members and friends.

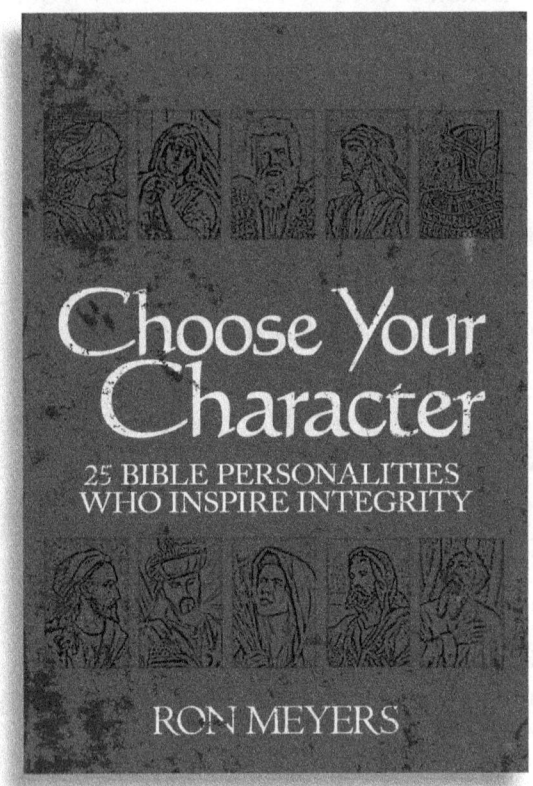

You can order additional copies at
online bookstores.

Quantity discounts are available by contacting
Soar with Eagles (www.soarhigher.com).

www.ingramcontent.com/pod-product-compliance
Lightning Source LLC
Chambersburg PA
CBHW070715160426
43192CB00009B/1199